ATLANTIC OCEAN

ATLANTIC OCEAN

THE ILLUSTRATED HISTORY OF THE OCEAN THAT CHANGED THE WORLD

Martin W. Sandler

Foreword by Dennis Reinhartz

STERLING

New York / London
www.sterlingpublishing.com

STERLING and the distinctive Sterling logo are registered trademarks of
Sterling Publishing Co., Inc.

Library of Congress Cataloging-in-Publication Data Available

10 9 8 7 6 5 4 3 2 1

Published by Sterling Publishing Co., Inc.
387 Park Avenue South, New York, NY 10016

© 2008 Sterling Publishing Co., Inc.
Text © 2008 by Martin W. Sandler
Foreword © 2008 by Dennis Reinhartz

Please see picture credits page for image credits.

Distributed in Canada by Sterling Publishing
c/o Canadian Manda Group, 165 Dufferin Street
Toronto, Ontario, Canada M6K 3H6
Distributed in the United Kingdom by GMC Distribution Services
Castle Place, 166 High Street, Lewes, East Sussex, England BN7 1XU
Distributed in Australia by Capricorn Link (Australia) Pty. Ltd.
P.O. Box 704, Windsor, NSW 2756, Australia

Book design and layout: Amy Henderson

Printed in China
All rights reserved

Sterling ISBN 978-1-4027-4724-3

For information about custom editions, special sales, premium and
corporate purchases, please contact Sterling Special Sales
Department at 800-805-5489 or specialsales@sterlingpublishing.com.

DEDICATION

*This book is dedicated to the scholars who have informed
us of the primacy of the Atlantic world in shaping our past, present,
and future, and the artists who have transported us into its reality.*

CONTENTS

FOREWORD

As Geography without History seemeth a carkasse without motion, so History without Geography wandereth as vagrant without certain habitation.

— Captain John Smith, *The General History of Virginia*, 1624

As demonstrated by this fine volume, *Atlantic Ocean: The Illustrated History of the Ocean that Changed the World*, the Atlantic world and its history are as vast and complex as the Ocean itself. The study of the Atlantic Ocean and its environs begins with the age of myth and flows inexorably into the more concrete present. Directly touching upon four continents, Atlantic history encompasses mystery and high adventure, expansion and modernization, victory and defeat, hardship, courage and realization, and so much more. And to be more fully appreciated, it must never be viewed absolutely in isolation from the yet more extensive global perspective. But in the end, and at the center of it all there is always the sea.

In its earliest history, the Atlantic world was not a real unity, but rather existed, partially cloaked in legends and by impenetrability, in two parts. Each was essentially ignorant of the other. First contact launched awareness and then understanding. Soon thereafter, Eurasia and Africa came to see their part as the "Old World" and the other as a "New World."

The documented transatlantic encounter was initiated by the seafaring Norse in their voyages from their homelands in Scandinavia across the North Atlantic to Iceland, Greenland, and, late in the tenth century, to Markland and Vinland in the New World. There for the first time Europeans met the local inhabitants, whom they called "Skraelings" and would much later come to be known as "Indians." But the time for sustained contact was not yet right and it ended with the Norse withdrawal from the New World early in the eleventh century to be lost for almost a half of a millennium in the obscurity of the sagas and folklore that recorded it.

Once the Iberians began to move out into the sea southward and westward for fortune, glory, and their faith in the fourteenth century, it did not take long to reforge contact between the two parts of the Atlantic world, a lasting and extraordinary contact. Over time, this reestablished encounter has yielded discovery, exploration, exploitation, exchange, comprehension, and accord. The commerce of commodities and peoples and their cultures and ideas that developed across the Atlantic before long streamed beyond it out to the rest of the world and changed it forever. At the same time, Atlantic world was opened up to the countersurge of global influences to be permanently affected by them as well. The oceans that had long divided humanity became connectors on the planet and in its history.

As alluded to in the quotation above by Captain John Smith, the Atlantic Ocean as such does not exist outside of history; it is rather a part of the waters that cover most of the earth. With the ending of the Cold War and the growth of globalism, in the past quarter century there has been a major resurgence of interest in Atlantic history, academically and popularly. A growing number of institutions of higher learning across the country and Europe are now offering courses, majors, and advanced degrees in the study of the Atlantic Basin and its hinterlands. For example, my own university, The University of Texas at Arlington, has a Ph.D. program in Transatlantic History that is flourishing in its second decade.

Atlantic history is regional within a global context and strongly geographical, interdisciplinary, and transnational. Beyond the allure of the traditional subject matter, Atlantic history is nature centered and embraces environmental history. It is readily compatible with the history of cartography and historical geography. And it also incorporates the histories of diverse commodities such as cod, sugar, spices, slaves, silver, and many more to offer an alternative to the race-class-gender academic paradigm in social, cultural, and economic history.

The *Atlantic Ocean* wonderfully exemplifies how Atlantic history should be done. This volume begins with myth and throughout its pages gives myth, myth-history, and other controversies their fitting evidential consideration as part of the Atlantic story; then onto first contact and reconnection and the audacious age of discovery and exploration. At this juncture and in what follows, the telling never strays too far from the sea (and its mastery) that is so central to and binds the Atlantic world. The Ocean is restored to Atlantic history, and

there is no shyness of nature here. The long ships, caravels, clippers, men-of-war, steamers, pleasure and racing yachts, and others are all there.

The diverse exchanges between the Old World and the New are next, and appropriately comprise the major part of this book and the history it recounts. From alien environments and encounters to commodities to colonization and empires to revolutionary and other ideas, all and sundry are taken into account. But most important is the narrative of the exchange of peoples in slavery, indenture, and more willing migrations and the consequential creolization of their traditions and technologies into yet newer transatlantic cultures in a momentous prelude to globalization. It concludes in the present in the midst of the rejuvenated ecological trepidation of the twenty-first century.

The *Atlantic Ocean* also tells the history as it happened, in color, with a very readable text overflowing with marvelous maps and other illustrations. In the end, Atlantic history is an expedition of the imagination. So, if you have not made this journey before, begin, learn, and enjoy now. And if you have, come along to savor and voyage on.

—*Dennis Reinhartz,*
The University of Texas at Arlington

INTRODUCTION

Exploration, discovery, conquest, and piracy; political, industrial, and technological upheavals; the greatest human migrations the world has ever known—it would be difficult to imagine a more compelling saga. Yet that is but part of the story of the making of the Atlantic World, a story dominated by human beings pitted against the sea, the natural desire for freedom, and humankind's determination to expand horizons no matter what the cost.

At the heart of the story is the Atlantic itself. Regarded for centuries as the "sea of darkness," it was the foreboding and storm-tossed Atlantic that became the main artery of the world, the tumultuous, often battle-scarred stage upon which many of history's greatest dramas were played. Most important, it was the Atlantic that connected and combined the histories of Europe, Africa, the Americas, and the Caribbean, resulting in what can only be described as one of history's greatest developments, the making of an Atlantic community.

Most of us have grown up with a false notion of the world. We were compelled to study the histories of the nations and regions touched by the Atlantic and its basins in isolation. Increasingly, however, we have come to realize that it is only through a knowledge of the way these areas have been connected and the impact they have had on each other that we can fully comprehend our own history and that of the world. In recent times, historians, scholars, and writers have expanded our understanding of almost every aspect of the making of the Atlantic world. They have, for example, provided us with new information and added their insights into the slave trade, transatlantic commerce, the impact of the Old World upon the New, and the ways in which two world wars brought about a full confirmation of the reality of an Atlantic community. They have even defined for us the surprising role played by such seemingly simple products as cod, sugar, and tobacco in this unprecedented drama.

The purpose of this book is to bring together in one cohesive story the imaginings, events, and developments that made the Atlantic world. Its purpose also is to present the first fully illustrated history of this adventure. From the ancient depictions of the sea monsters that kept even the bravest mariners

The Clipper ship *Three Brothers*; when this lithograph was created by Currier & Ives in 1875, they added a caption to the image touting the *Three Brothers* as the largest sailing ship in the world.

OPPOSITE This cartouche detail from a 1686 map of North America by French cartographer Jean Baptiste Louis Franquelin depicts the mapmaker's interpretation of Quebec's skyline and harbor.

from entering the Atlantic, to the exquisitely illustrated maps that disclosed the birth of an Atlantic community, through the more than five hundred years of paintings, drawings, etchings, book illustrations, and other visual representations created by the world's greatest artists, to the magical images captured by photographers, we have become the beneficiaries of an astonishing pictorial record of Atlantic history, presented here in unprecedented scope.

The existence of an Atlantic World, as historian Carlton J. H. Hayes reminds us in an article in *American Historical Review*, Volume 51 (1946), "is an outstanding fact and a prime mover of modern history." As historian Leonard Outhwaite expressed it in his book *The Atlantic: A History of an Ocean* (1957), "Even if we hang a satellite station in space or if we reach the moon, the Atlantic Ocean will still be the center of the human world." It still is.

—*Martin W. Sandler*

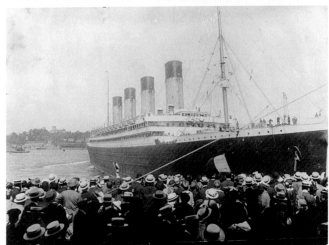

Crowds gather on the dock in New York City's harbor to welcome the ocean liner SS *Olympic*, ca. July 1914.

10764. - COAST VIEW KYNANCE

1

THE ATLANTIC

THE SEA OF DARKNESS

The mysterious Atlantic;
this photochrome print
ca. 1890 shows the Atlantic
coastline in Bude, North
Cornwall, England.

THE ATLANTIC

Father Zeus, at the ends of the earth, presented a dwelling place, apart from man and far from the deathless gods. In the Islands of the Blest, founded by deep-swirling ocean, they live untouched by toil or sorrow.

—Hesiod, *Works and Days*, eighth century BCE

Although they never entered the Atlantic, the ancient Egyptians, along with the Sumerians, were the first to put to sea for the purpose of exploration. This Egyptian tomb painting from 1450 BCE shows the chief officer at the stern signaling for the ship to slow down while other officers with cat-o'-nine-tails stand ready to prod the crew along.

An age will come after many years," wrote the Roman philosopher and dramatist Seneca the Younger in his circa 54 CE play *Medea*, "when the Ocean will loose the chain of things and a huge land lie revealed, when Tethys will disclose new worlds and Thule no longer be the Ultimate." The ocean to which Seneca referred was the Atlantic, named for the Greek god Atlas. His prediction of the "chain of things" that this mysterious body of water would "loose" was far more perceptive than he could ever have imagined.

Seneca made his prediction in the first century CE. More than four hundred years later, the European world still centered around the Mediterranean Sea. The Atlantic was still a frightening mystery. How far did it stretch? No one knew. Many were convinced that it went on forever. What even the bravest mariners comprehended was that there were no charts or maps and no adequate navigational instruments to guide them into this "sea of darkness." Most terrifying of all was the common belief that this endless ocean was filled with ferocious monsters and angry gods. No wonder no one had dared cross its horizon. No wonder, that as late as the sixteenth century, one guide to Atlantic travelers opened with the words, "First make thy will."

MYTHICAL ISLANDS

Not that these untraveled waters were without their lure. The same classical writers and sages who warned of ship-devouring sea monsters also described fantastic and mysterious lands that lay far out in the middle of these foreboding

Sea Monsters

he belief that the Atlantic was inhabited by terrifying creatures of all forms and sizes, monsters that devoured both ships and men, dated back to the most ancient times and was particularly prevalent as mariners began to contemplate what lay beyond the Atlantic's horizon. Long after the New World had been discovered, belief in sea monsters persisted. Drawings and tales of such creatures of the deep filled the world's maps and manuscripts until the beginnings of modern cartography.

ABOVE: A deity riding a fearsome-looking sea dragon carries the Portuguese coat of arms, in this detail from a 1562 Spanish map of the New World entitled *Americae sive quartae orbis partis nova et exactissima descriptio,* by royal Spanish cosmographer Diego Gutiérrez.

BELOW: The beliefs of early mariners in the terrors of the sea were well rooted in both mythology and ancient literature. In Homer's epic poem *The Odyssey,* the king of Ithaca must wander the sea for ten years before returning home. As seen in this 1891 painting by John William Waterhouse, Odysseus desperately tries to resist the sirens' lure.

ABOVE: **Sea monsters were not the only strange creatures believed to inhabit the waters of the Atlantic. This 1696 drawing by German illustrator and author Johann Zahn depicts the "Satyrus marinus"— a merman satyr who is part man, part goat, and part fish.**

seas. They wrote of idyllic islands with names such as Saint Brendan, the Fortunate Islands, or the Hesperides, Antilla, Brasil, and Salvagio. All of these places, they claimed, were inhabited by gods or demigods or by humans living in a perpetual state of happiness. There was even talk of the existence somewhere far out into the Atlantic of a land known as the Terrestrial Paradise, claimed to be the original Garden of Eden.

Most fabled of all was the island utopia called Atlantis, first mentioned and described by the classical Greek philosopher Plato in his dialogues *Timaeus* and *Critias*, written around 360 BCE. According to Plato, Atlantis, the kingdom of the god of the seas, Poseidon, was rich in advanced knowledge and commerce and was ruled by benevolent leaders. It was also a nation determined to expand its domain. "Now in this island of Atlantis," the philosopher wrote in *Timaeus*, "there was a great and wonderful empire which had rule over the whole island and several others, and over parts of the continent and furthermore, the men of Atlantis had subjected the parts of Libya within the columns

This illustration depicting the destruction of Atlantis is from the original 1869–70 edition of Jules Vernes's *20,000 Leagues Under the Sea*.

of Heracles as far as Egypt and of Europe as far as Tyrrhenia." Plato's legend, however did not have a happy ending. The people of Atlantis, he proclaimed, eventually became greedy; their leaders became arrogant; and as punishment, angry gods flooded and sank the island. Plato's account spawned generations of debate as to its veracity. Aristotle, Plato's student, rejected the story, although the Greek historian Plutarch (first century CE) espoused it in his writings. Perhaps the most vivid "confirmation" came from Proclus, one of the last of the major Greek philosophers, in the fifth century CE. In his commentary on Plato's *Timaeus*, Proclus wrote:

> That an island of such nature and size once existed is evident from what is said by certain authors who investigated the things around the outer sea. For according to them, there were seven islands in that sea in their time, sacred to Persephone, and also three others of enormous size, one of which was sacred to Pluto, another to Ammon, and another one between them to Poseidon,... and the inhabitants of it, they add, preserved the remembrance from their ancestors of the immeasurably large island of Atlantis and which had really existed there and which for many ages had reigned over all islands in the Atlantic sea and which itself had like-wise been sacred to Poseidon.

The sunken Atlantis became one of the world's great mysteries, inscribed on many early ocean maps, sought by explorers even in modern times.

VENTURING INTO THE GREEN SEA OF DARKNESS

In the end, it was not the search for utopia that motivated the first peoples to unlock the secrets of the Atlantic but rather two groups of Northern Europeans—each drawn by their own particular desires—who dared to venture into what the ninth-century Baghdadi geographer al-Mas'udi called the "green sea of darkness." One of these groups was the Irish, whose priests and monks first broke the shackles of the European world. They were followed by seafarers from the Scandinavian countries of Norway, Sweden, and Denmark known as the Vikings.

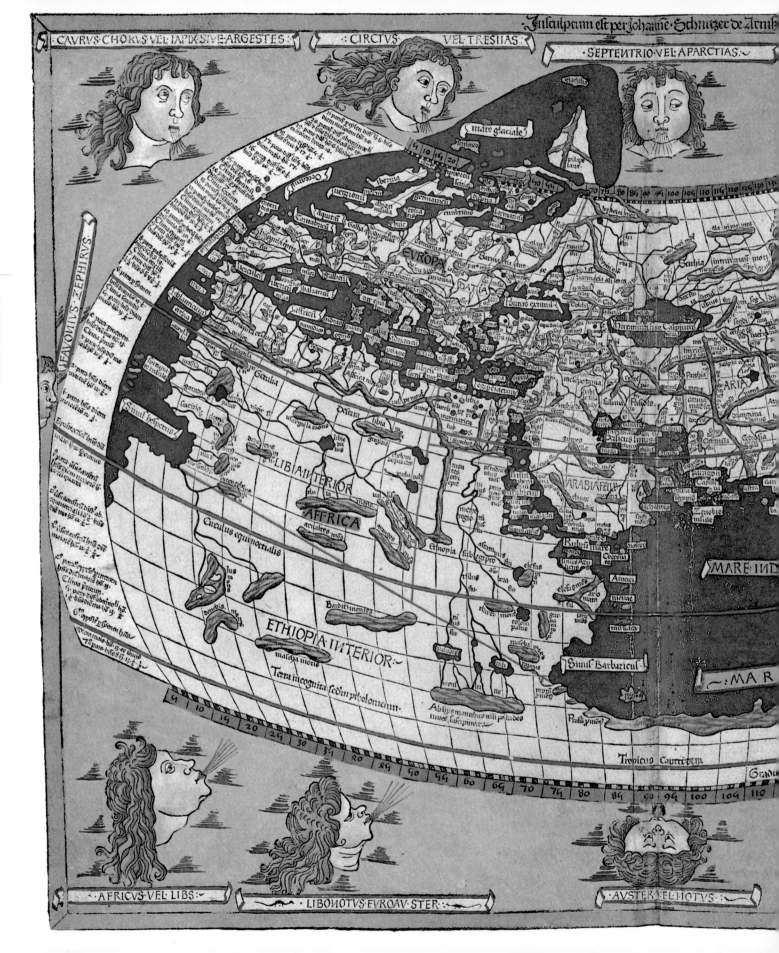

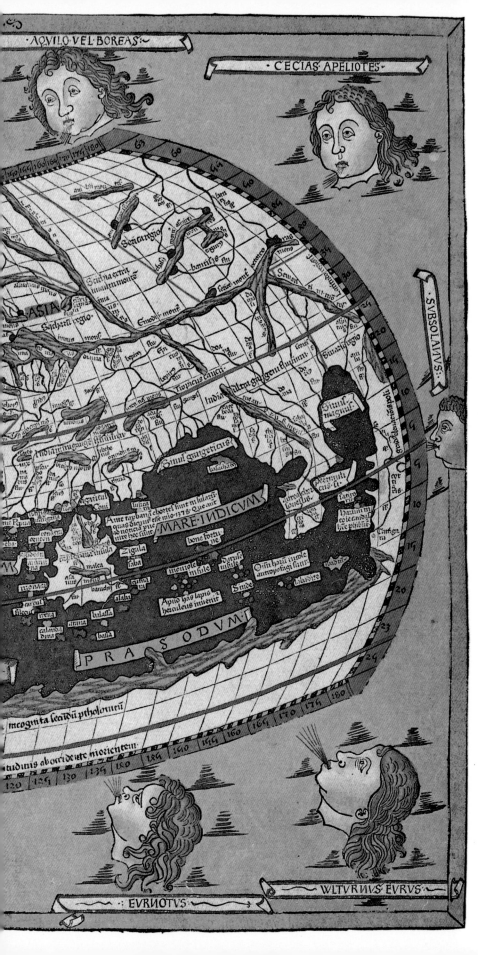

This map, drawn in 1482 by Johannes Schnitzer of Armsheim ("Johannes the blockcutter"), was based on the geographic writings of Claudius Ptolemaeus (known in English as Ptolemy), the greatest geographer of the ancient world. Historians differ as to whether Ptolemy, who was a mathematician, astronomer, and astrologer as well as a geographer, was Greek or Egyptian. What is known is that he lived from approximately 100 to 171 CE and that he resided in Roman Egypt. What is also true is that when this map was drawn, Ptolemy's book *Geographica* was still the chief source of reference for geographers. Some historians speculate that St. Brendan, believed to be among the first to venture forth into the Atlantic, was guided by a map drawn by Ptolemy. When Schnitzer drew this map, the size and nature of the Atlantic was still a mystery. Today we know that the ocean was formed some two hundred million years ago when the dramatic shifting of subterranean plates caused the super continent Pangaea to break apart into two continents: Laurasia (present-day North America, Europe, and Asia) and Gondwanaland (present-day Antarctica, Africa, Arabia, Madagascar, India, Australia, and South America). As a result, the Atlantic, which covers approximately twenty percent of the Earth's surface, became an immense S-shaped north-south channel extending from the Arctic Ocean in the north to the Antarctic continent in the south, flowing between the eastern coastlines of the Americas and the western coasts of Europe and Africa. Including its marginal seas—the Gulf of Mexico, the Caribbean Sea, the North, Baltic, Mediterranean, and Black seas—The total area of the Atlantic is approximately forty-one million square miles. The oldest known mention of the name Atlantic is contained in *The Histories*, written by Herodotus about 440 BCE.

Actually, the Irish and the Vikings were not the first to navigate Atlantic waters. As early as 800 BCE, seamen from Phoenicia—an ancient eastern Mediterranean country on the coasts of what is now Syria, Lebanon, and Israel—had defied the notion that the earth dropped off once one sailed through the Strait of Gibraltar (known then as the Pillars of Heracles or Hercules) and had made their way into the Atlantic. By the fourth century BCE, Phoenician mariners had reached the British Isles and had established trade with the coastal inhabitants. In about 325 BCE, a Greek explorer named Pytheas had sailed beyond Britain and, according to his accounts, had reached the Arctic. But none of these courageous mariners, including sailors from the Phoenician city of Carthage (in present-day Tunisia) who had sailed down the west coast of Africa, had ventured far out of the sight of land. It was the pious Irish, in their desire to convert nonbelievers wherever in the North Atlantic they could find them, and the marauding Vikings, intent on raiding whatever prosperous regions they could reach, who first crossed the Atlantic horizon.

IRISH MARINERS

For more than four hundred years, beginning in the 500s, Irish holy mariners sailed forth in their *currachs*, small fragile wooden boats covered with ox hide. Although these boats were frail, they were so light that they rode with the waves and were unlikely to sink.

The most famous of all these voyagers was the legendary Irish abbot Saint Brendan "the Navigator." It would have been impossible for him to have completed all of the journeys attributed to him, but there is enough historical evidence to suggest that, in the middle 500s, this earliest northern sailor known to us by name in all probability sailed to what are today the Faroe Islands and visited both the Shetlands and the Outer Hebrides. Records housed in monasteries confirm that, in his quest for converts, he reached Scotland, Wales, and Brittany. Other factual descriptions reveal that on one of his voyages he encountered icebergs off the eastern Greenland coast and reached the south shore of Iceland.

THE VIKINGS

Some two centuries after St. Brendan made his daring voyages, the bold and ruthless Vikings burst upon the scene. In the ancient Norse language the word *viking* defined a person whose home was near a fjord. It soon came to describe a person intent on raiding, pillaging, and destroying.

The Vikings—also called Norsemen or Northmen—were the most skilled and daring sailors of their day. And their ships

> " *From the fury of the Northmen, good Lord, deliver us!* "
>
> —Northern European prayer

were perfectly suited for their purposes. There were actually two main types of Viking vessels. The *knarr*, (also known as the *knorr*), was a square-rigged, single-masted ship used for trade and cargo. However, the vessel for which the Vikings became known (and feared) was called a *drakkar*, or longship. Because their prows featured ornate carvings of beasts and dragons (to ward off the sea monsters prevalent in Norse mythology), they were also called dragon ships. Forty-five to seventy-five feet long, the longships were extremely strong yet graceful vessels whose shallow draft allowed them to navigate in shallow

waters, which made them ideal for the Vikings' lightning-fast, hit-and-run attacks on European towns and monasteries. Built to carry a crew of from fifty to sixty men, longships were fitted with oars along almost their entire length. By the tenth century, most longships also featured a rectangular sail that provided relief to the oarsmen during long voyages.

For three centuries, the Vikings swept down upon the peoples of western Europe, burning and looting as they went. Traveling farther and farther afield, they carried out their raids throughout the Baltic and North Seas and made their way to northern England, Scotland, Ireland, the Isle of Man, the Orkneys, Shetlands, and Hebrides. Cities such as Paris,

This 1621 engraving illustrates St. Brendan giving mass on the back of a whale, one of the tales about his legendary voyage. Other parts of the journey are depicted as well, as the saint's *currach* is shown in various stages of the trip. The illustration appears in *Nova Typis Transacta Navigatio*, written by the Austrian Benedictine abbot Caspar Plautius.

This illustration from *The History of France from the Earliest Times to the Year 1789* (1883), by François Guizot, depicts the Viking Siege of Paris (885–6).

Hamburg, Utrecht, Bordeaux, Nantes, and Seville all came under their attacks. Wherever they landed, they struck terror into the inhabitants' hearts. "From the fury of the Northmen, good Lord, deliver us!" became a common prayer among the people of the coasts, rivers, islands, and peninsulas of northern Europe.

The Vikings were not only raiders, but explorers and colonizers as well. In about 874 CE, Norse chieftains established a settlement in Iceland. A century later, under the leadership of Norwegian-born Erik Thorvaldson, known as Erik the Red, they explored and colonized the southwestern part of Greenland.

What has truly earned the Vikings a place in history lay ahead. There are those who believe that it was a course of events that took place by accident. However, according to the Icelandic sagas—mythicized historical accounts written in the thirteenth and fourteenth centuries describing events that took place in the late tenth and early eleventh centuries—the Vikings' arrival in North America in the year 1000, some five hundred years before Columbus, did not come by chance. As described in the sagas, in 986 an Icelandic trader named Bjarni Herjulfsson, driven far off course by a fierce storm between Iceland and Greenland, sighted heavily forested land far out to the west. While he never set foot onshore, this sighting made Herjulfsson the first European to set eyes on

LEFT: This woven image of a *knarr*—the square-rigged, single-masted ship used by the Vikings for trade—is from the Överhogdal tapestry, a Swedish wall hanging ca. 1100 CE.

BELOW: An illumination from an eighteenth-century Icelandic manuscript illustrates the myth of the Norse gods Thor and Hymir fishing for Thor's mortal enemy, the Midgard Serpent, or Jörmungandr.

BELOW: The very real threat of Viking attack precipitated panic throughout Europe. The Vikings carried out their raids without warning and without mercy. "It is nearly 350 years since we and our fathers have inhabited this lovely land," the learned English scholar and theologian Alcuin wrote in a letter to King Æthelred I of Northumbria and his nobles, in 793, "and never before has such a terror appeared in Britain as we have now suffered from a pagan race, nor was it thought that such an inroad from the sea could be made." This detail from the *Bayeux Tapestry*, depicting a scene from the Norman invasion of England in 1066, is particularly revealing in that it shows the longboats used in the invasion, those vessels that enabled the Vikings to carry out their widespread explorations and conquests. The *Bayeux Tapestry*, annotated in Latin, is a 20-inch by 230-foot-long embroidered cloth that depicts the events leading up to the Norman invasion and conquest of England. While historians differ over the origin of the tapestry, many believe that it was created by Anglo-Saxon artists and that it was probably commissioned by Odo of Bayeux, a Norman bishop and English earl who was the half-brother of William the Conquerer.

North America. According to the sagas, Leif Eriksson, one of Erik the Red's sons, determined to confirm Herjulfsson's claim, bought Bjarni's ship, mounted an expedition, and set out to discover the new land. Sailing due west, Eriksson and his men first passed what is now Baffin Island, which they named Helluland or Flat-Stone Land. Moving southeast, they encountered present day Labrador, to which they gave the name Markland or Woodland. With harsh weather approaching, they sailed on and found a place that they felt would be a safe spot to spend the winter. Discovering "fields of self-sown wheat" and wild grapes out of which a robust wine could be made, they named it Vinland. The exact location of Vinland remains controversial. Some historians believe that a campsite unearthed in the 1960s at a place called *L'Anse aux Meadows*, on the northeastern tip of Newfoundland, could be the remains of the legendary Vinland settlement.

Vinland was a welcome relief to the Vikings, who were used to the sparse, bitter environment of the Far North. "There was no lack of salmon there in river or lake, and salmon bigger than they had seen before," reads the Saga of the Greenlanders (ca. 1300s). "The nature of the land was so choice, it seemed to them that none of the cattle would require fodder for the winter. No frost came during the winter, and the grass hardly withered. Day and night were more of an equal length there than in Greenland or Iceland. On the shortest day of winter the sun was visible in the idle of the afternoon as well as at breakfast time."

The following summer Leif Eriksson and his men returned to Greenland. His father had died, and Leif now felt it his duty to remain at home and care for his family. His brother Thorvald, however, was anxious to see for himself the land that Leif had so glowingly described. Borrowing

OPPOSITE: This wood engraving of Erik the Red's discovery of Greenland illustrated a story in *Harper's Weekly* in 1875.

LEFT: Erik the Red, the first European to explore Greenland, is portrayed here in a woodcut from the Icelandic scholar Arngrímur Jónsson's treatise *Gronlandia (Greenland)*, published in 1688.

Leif's ship, Thorvald and a party of thirty men set sail for Vinland. In yet another example of the Viking's navigational skills, they had little trouble finding the exact spot where Leif had established his camp. After spending the summer exploring the coast, they wintered down at a site they named Leifsbudir (Leif's hut). The following summer brought disaster in the form of a violent encounter with natives of the region, who the Vikings called Skraelings. In the ensuing battle, in which eight natives were killed, Thorvald received a fatal wound from an arrow, prompting all of his men to return to Greenland.

But the Vinland adventure was still not over. In 1010, Thorfinn Karlsefni, who had married Thorvald's widow, organized an expedition of three ships and some two hundred would-be settlers in an attempt to establish a permanent Vinland colony. After spending an uneventful autumn and summer in their new home, Karsefni's party, like Thorvald and his men before them, suddenly became rudely acquainted with the Skraelings. The unexpected attack by a horde of natives wielding battle staves and firing poisoned arrows was enough to convince Karlsefni and his settlers that Vinland was no place for them, and the entire party returned to Greenland.

The final chapter in the saga was played out by Leif Eriksson's courageous but deceitful sister Freydis who, in about 1013, in partnership with two Icelandic brothers and their party, led yet another expedition to Vinland. It was the most disastrous Vinland experience of all, one in which the relationship between the brothers and Freydis grew so heated that Freydis had the brothers and their party brutally murdered. Freydis then returned to Greenland where she claimed that the brothers and the men and women they had brought with them had decided to remain in Vinland.

The Viking's accomplishment in reaching what they called Vinland was a historic achievement. From authenticated relics that have been found, it seems certain that they also set foot on other parts of North America and even might have reached as far inland as present-day Kensington, Minnesota.

However, according to such respected historians as Daniel J. Boorstin, this does not mean that they "discovered" America. As Boorstin wrote in his 1983 book, *The*

The Vinland Map

The archeological findings at L'Anse aux Meadows in 1960 provided what many regard as indisputable proof that the Vikings were in North America some five hundred years before Columbus. In 1957, a different type of evidence emerged, one that has been subsequently regarded as either one of history's most exciting cartographic discoveries— or a fake.

In 1957, two antiquarian book dealers offered to sell to the British Museum what they claimed was a manuscript containing a fifteenth-century *mappa mundi* (map of the world) redrawn from a thirteenth-century original. In addition to showing Asia, Africa, and Europe, the map depicted a large island west of Greenland in the Atlantic labeled "Vinland." The British Museum declined, believing it was a fake. The map was then shown to a New Haven, Connecticut, book dealer, who bought the map for $3,500. He, in turn, offered to sell it to Yale University.

While Yale officials immediately realized the potential importance of what has come to be called the Vinland Map, they were unable to meet the dealer's asking price. The map curator contacted longtime Yale benefactor Paul Mellon, who agreed to purchase it for the university, but only if it could be authenticated. What followed was almost six years of the map's examination by two British Museum curators and a Yale librarian, a study that resulted in the pronouncement that the Vinland Map was genuine. In 1965 Yale published both the map and the research team's findings, and the controversy began.

From the time Yale revealed the map to the world, doubters expressed skepticism regarding the parchment on which the map was drawn. However, an intense 1995 analysis of the parchment conducted by scientists from the University of Arizona, Brookhaven National Laboratory, and the Smithsonian Institution, using carbon-dating technology, revealed that the Vinland Map parchment dated back to approximately 1434 CE, nearly sixty years before Columbus set foot in the West Indies.

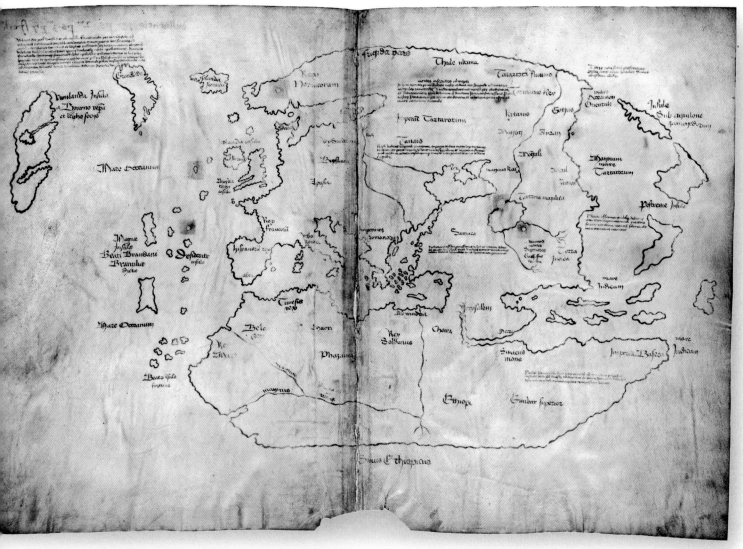

An even greater controversy regarding the genuineness of the map arose over the chemical composition of the ink used to draw it. A study conducted by a Chicago laboratory soon after the map was published concluded that since the ink was found to contain carbon, a modern-day ingredient of ink, the map had to be a forgery. More recent studies, however, have disclosed both that carbon can be found in medieval ink, and that it was not unusual for carbon to form naturally on ancient documents.

Controversy over the Vinland Map continues today. It is an important debate. In 2002, a team of scientists from the Smithsonian Institution, Brookhaven National Laboratory, and the University of Arizona researching the Vinland Map acknowledged that if in fact, the map is authentic, it would be the first known cartographic representation of North America—but if the map was found to be a forgery, it was a forgery of the utmost skill.

In this painting, Norwegian artist Christian Krohg depicted the historic moment when Leif Eriksson and his crew first came upon the coast of North America.

> "*What is remarkable is not that the Vikings actually reached America, but that they reached America and even settled there for a while without discovering America.*"
>
> —Daniel J. Boorstin, *The Discoverers: A History of Man's Search to Know His World and Himself*, 1983

Discoverers: A History of Man's Search to Know His World and Himself: "What they did in America did not change their own or anybody else's view of the world. Was there ever so long a voyage (L'Anse aux Meadows is a full forty-five hundred miles as the crow flies from Bergen!) that made so little difference? There was practically no feedback from the Vinland voyages. What is remarkable is not that the Vikings actually reached America, but that they reached America and even settled there for a while without *discovering* America."

That the Irish and then the Vikings were able to sail so far into unknown waters fraught with both real and imaginary dangers was truly remarkable. While it is true that their ships were perfectly designed for their purposes, they accomplished their voyages without the advantages of what could be regarded as even primitive navigational instruments or prior knowledge of the seas in which they sailed. Their journeys were made in cold weather and frigid waters, often against adverse winds. That both these groups of early penetrators of the Atlantic accomplished so much was testimony to both their courage and determination. It was these early wayfarers who shaped the true beginnings of an Atlantic world and who paved the way for those later fifteenth- and sixteenth-century explorers, sailing warm waters with favorable winds, from Portugal, Spain, the Netherlands, France, and England.

The creation of this world provides a profound example of the vital relationship between geography and history, for all of the societies that led the way in the exploration and discovery of the Americas bordered on the Atlantic. That the various currents in the North Atlantic move clockwise and that that ocean's prevailing winds are westerly was also instrumental in the accidental and then deliberate discovery of the American Indies and the continents that lay beyond. What resulted was far more than the discovery of a world that Europeans did not know existed or the eventual transfer of Europeans to the Americas. Rather, it was the integration of Europeans, Africans, and those who would call themselves Americans, one in which the interaction of diverse cultures, religions, and political and commercial systems from four continents and numerous ethnicities would challenge and change age-old assumptions about geography, history, theology, and human nature. In the process, traditional institutions would be dramatically altered, old rivalries would be intensified, and new ways of life would be introduced.

Almost fifty years ago, historian Frederick Tolles stated in his book *Quakers and the Atlantic Culture* that "I don't know whether the term 'Atlantic culture'... is yet an expression in common use or not. But if it is not, it should be. For it seems to me as useful and necessary a term as the indispensable

19

THE ATLANTIC

phrase 'Mediterranean culture' which we use to denominate the civilization of the ancient world."

Historian John Gillis has emphasized the way in which the Atlantic Ocean that had for so long divided continents came to unite them and how the artificially separated histories of Europe, Africa, North America, and the Caribbean came to be connected. The result, wrote Gillis in his book *Islands of the Mind: How the Human Imagination Created the Atlantic World* (2004), was that this new Atlantic world became not "an appendage of European civilization...but something with its own history and geography, forged as much offshore as onshore." Perhaps the most precise summation of this historic development was provided by historian D. W. Meinig in the first volume (1986) of his work *The Shaping of America: A Geographical Perspective on 500 Years of History*: "The [Atlantic] ocean [became] the inland sea of Western civilization,...with old seats of culture on the east, a great frontier for expansion on the west, and a long and integral African shore. Instead of a European discovery of a new world," Meinig wrote, "we might better consider it as a sudden and harsh encounter between two worlds that transformed both and integrated them into a single New World."

OPPOSITE: The Atlantic has a greater shoreline than the Pacific and Indian oceans combined. The continental areas drained by rivers emptying into the Atlantic are also twice as great as these other two oceans combined. It is not surprising that more major seaports and more great industrial centers developed throughout the Atlantic world than in any other place, and that the Atlantic became the major artery for commerce, travel, and the transfer of ideas and culture between Europe, Africa, and the Americas. One of the major features of the Atlantic is that powerful, warm, and extremely rapid current known as the Gulf Stream, a current encountered by many of the early explorers of the New World. It is believed that the first written reference to what became known as the Gulf Stream appeared in an April 22, 1513, entry in the log of Spanish conquistador Ponce de León's voyage in Atlantic waters, an entry that noted "A current such that, although they had great wind, they could not proceed forward, but backward and it seems that they were proceeding well; at the end it was known that the current was more powerful than the wind." Several early maps of the Gulf Stream exist; the first was printed in 1769–70 by Benjamin Franklin and Nantucket whaler Timothy Folger. An edition of Franklin's map, shown here, was engraved by James Poupard for the 1786 edition of the *Transactions of the American Philosophical Society*.

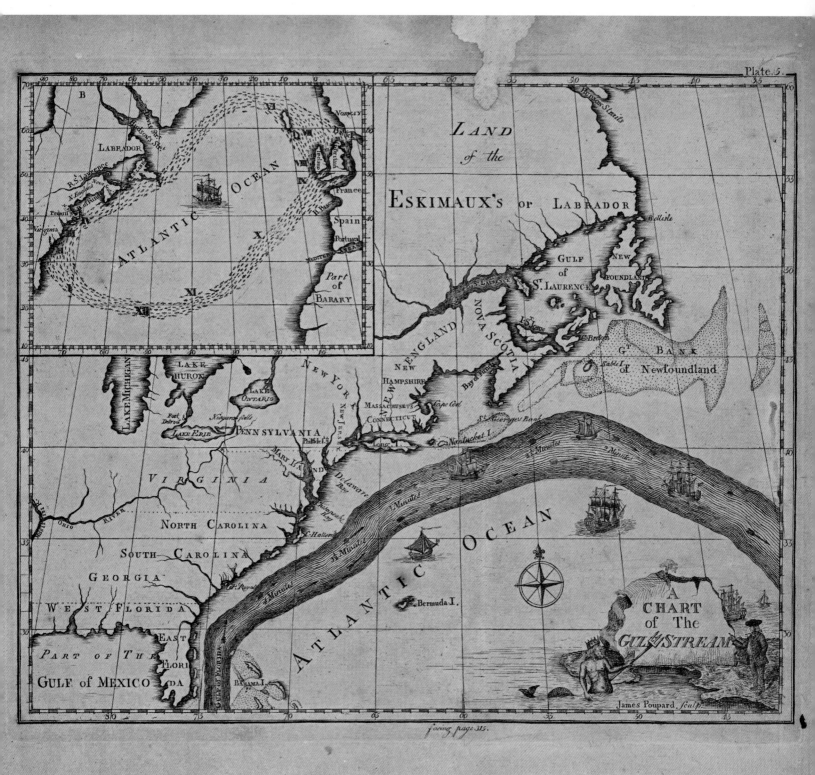

A
CHART
of The
GULF STREAM

James Poupard. sculp.

2

EXPLORATION AND DISCOVERY

EUROPEANS ENCOUNTER A NEW WORLD

The first landing of
Columbus on the shores
of the New World, as
portrayed by Currier &
Ives, ca. 1892.

EXPLORATION AND DISCOVERY

And if there had been more of the world, they would have reached it.

—LUÍS DE CAMÕES, *Os Lusíadas* (*The Lusiads*), VII, 14, 1572

At the beginning of the fifteenth century, the Atlantic Ocean remained a great mystery. No one yet knew how wide it was or to where it led. Ancient misconceptions still kept mariners in deadly fear of venturing out too far upon the ocean. No one more eloquently described the cause of these fears than the Portuguese chronicler Gomes Eanes de Zurara. Explaining why even the boldest seafarers had not dared sail beyond Africa's Cape Bojador, Zurara wrote in his 1453 treatise *Crónica dos Feitos da Guiné* (*The Chronicle of the Discovery and Conquest of Guinea*):

> For certainly it cannot be presumed that among so many noble men who did such great and lofty deeds for the glory of their memory, there had not been one to dare [sail beyond Cape Bojador]. But being satisfied of the peril and seeing no hope of honour or profit, they left off the attempt. For, said the mariners, this much is clear, that beyond this Cape there is no race of men nor place of inhabitants…the sea so shallow that a whole league from land it is only a fathom deep, while the currents are so terrible that no ship having once passed the Cape, will ever be able to return…those mariners of ours [were] threatened not only by fear but by its shadow.

The European world in which Zurara lived was one in which poverty, greed, and war were mingled with hope, idealism, and courage. Never was a new world more needed. The crossing of the Atlantic Ocean and the discovery of this new world were due to the determination and skill of a unique breed of men, bold adventurers, many navigating only by the stars in ships astonishingly small, men with the courage to disregard the warnings and follow their own path and dreams.

THE AMBITION OF
PRINCE HENRY THE NAVIGATOR

It began with Portugal, a nation anxious to expand for both religious and commercial reasons. Despite the "Holy Wars" (1095–1270) known as the Crusades, the crusaders never succeeded in driving the Muslims out of the eastern and southern shores of the Mediterranean. The frustration that came with this failure was heightened by the fact that during their campaigns the crusaders had seen such riches as tapestries, porcelain, and precious stones. Even more coveted were the treasured spices of the East; pepper, cloves, nutmeg, cinnamon, and other condiments that could enhance the European diet and preserve food, and, in some instances, had medicinal benefits.

FRANCISCI
DE VERULAMIO,
Summi Angliæ
CANCELARIJ
Instauratio
magna.

Multi pertransibunt & augebitur scientia.

Sim: Pass: sculp:

Anno

LONDINI
Apud Joannem Billium
Typographum
Regium.

1620.

From the days of antiquity until the late fifteenth century, the western entrance to the Straits of Gibraltar had been known as the Pillars of Heracles, where, according to firm medieval beliefs, the world ended—a conviction supported by the renowned mapmaker Ptolemy, the Bible, and the Popes. This engraving of the Pillars illustrated the frontispiece of English philosopher Francis Bacon's *Instauratio magna (Great Instauration)*. It was published in 1620, after the Atlantic had already been crossed and the colonization of North America was in its infancy.

The desire of European kings and explorers to find a water route to the East dated back to the late eleventh century, when the Byzantine Empire was threatened by a new, aggressive, and powerful enemy, the Muslim Seljuq Turks. When the Byzantines called upon the Christian European kingdoms for help, among them England, France, and the Holy Roman Empire, the result was a long series of military and religious campaigns supported by the popes that lasted almost two centuries. Called the Crusades, the backbone of these holy wars was the well-trained, combat-tested medieval knights. Joining them were tens of thousands of clerics, peasants, and men—as well as women—from every walk of life. This circa fourteenth-century illuminated manuscript portrays Godfrey de Bouillon—a French leader of the First Crusade who took part in the capture of Jerusalem from the Turks in 1099. The crusaders then returned to Europe with the first widespread accounts of the riches and other wonders of the East.

Around 1299 Marco Polo dictated a book of his travels. Known by a number of titles, the *Travels of Marco Polo, Le livre des merveilles (The Book of Wonders)*, or *Il milione (The Million)*, a title used to disparage his stories as exaggerations), motivated generations of explorers, including Christopher Columbus, whose possessions included a heavily marked-up copy of the volume. Even though Polo supposedly returned from at least one of his trips with his pockets filled with rubies and other jewels, there have always been those who have believed that his accounts were exaggerated. Asked on his deathbed if he had stretched the truth, the intrepid traveler replied, "I have not told half of what I saw." During his travels to the East, Polo became a favorite of the great Kublai Khan, Mongol emperor of China, and was employed by him for seventeen years. These illustrations from *Il Milione* depict Marco's father and uncle presenting the Khan with gifts from Pope Gregory X (BOTTOM RIGHT), and Khan's army attacking the king of Mien (now Burma) (TOP RIGHT).

The Portuguese appetite to attain these treasures had been whetted by tales of the fabled East, particularly those written by Marco Polo, the thirteenth-century Venetian trader and explorer. Polo's writing inspired centuries of search for a water route to the East. As one of the first Westerners to travel what was known as the Silk Road to China (which he called Cathay), Polo described "all kinds of spicery" he had encountered and wrote of Cathay's extraordinary walled cities and palaces "all painted in gold." Other early travelers to the East, most notably the early fourteenth-century Italian friar Odoric of Pordenone, also waxed poetic about a land that contained the world's most fabulous markets and about such cities as Canton: "as big as three Venices and all Italy has not the amount of craft this one city hath." Odoric had also described "the vast scale of shipping in these parts…And as for the women," he also observed, "they are the most beautiful in the world."

With Muslims still blocking overland trade routes to the treasures of the East, the Portuguese turned their attention to exploring the unknown waters of the west coast of Africa, hoping to find a passage to India and the East. And they had another agenda, the age-old lust for gold. During the Middle Ages, gold dust from the rivers and streams of the Sahara had been shipped to Spain and other European regions. Now Portugal was anxious to establish its own gold trade.

BELOW: The Italian friar Odoric of Pordenone preaches to a group of Chinese during his travels to the Far East.

Of all the European peoples, the Portuguese were in the best position to carry out their risky ambitions. Although geographically Portugal had never had direct access to the Mediterranean, it had lengthy navigable rivers and deep-water harbors that opened to the Atlantic. And, unlike its Iberian neighbor Spain, fifteenth-century Portugal was a united kingdom, free of civil strife. Ushering the world into a golden age of exploration was, without question, one of the great achievements in history. That it was the Portuguese who led the way was due to the vision and the efforts of one man.

He was born Infante Dom Henrique in 1394, one of the sons of King John I and Philippa of Lancaster, the sister of King Henry IV of England. He would go down in history as Prince Henry the Navigator. Zurara described him as "big and strong of limb, his hair... of a color naturally fair, but by which constant toil and exposure had become dark. His expression at first sight inspired fear in those who did not know him, and when wroth, though such times were rare, his countenance was harsh. Strength of heart and keenness of mind were in him to an excellent degree and beyond comparison, he was ambitious of achieving great and lofty deeds."

His life was also characterized by irony. Prince Henry never himself went out on an exploring expedition, yet he can legitimately be regarded as the father of modern exploration. He lived like a monk, yet he was a brilliant organizer whose achievements were due to his talent for bringing together the best minds and bodies for whatever endeavor he launched. Like many members of royalty of his day, he placed great faith in astrology and believed that his destiny had been predicted by court astrologers who, according to Zurara, had foreseen that the prince was "bound to engage in great and noble conquests, and above all was he bound to attempt the discovery of things which were hidden from other men, and secret."

The astrologers were right. For what most motivated Prince Henry was the unknown, particularly whatever lay in the Sea of Darkness to the west and southwest along the uncharted African coast. Before his days were over, his navigators would explore these waters and the seas beyond and, in the process, unlock many of the mysteries of the Atlantic itself.

It was also ironic that Prince Henry's career began not with an exploratory endeavor but with a military campaign. Even as a young man he shared his nation's desire to launch a new crusade against the Muslims. In 1413, he and his two brothers persuaded their father to launch an all-out attack on Ceuta, a Muslim trading center and stronghold in Morocco. Although he was only nineteen, Prince Henry helped plan the expedition and was assigned the important task of building a fleet.

It took two years for the ships to be made ready and for the necessary archers and other troops to be assembled. But

ATLANTIC OCEAN

on August 24, 1415, the Portuguese fleet attacked Ceuta and gained a quick one-sided victory. Within a day, Prince Henry had become a hero. To him it was more than a military triumph. For in Ceuta, he gained his first view of the treasures that lay locked within Africa—huge stores of gold, silver, jewels, and spices of every variety.

The overwhelming victory that had been achieved at Ceuta and the riches that Prince Henry had seen there whetted his appetite for further incursions against the infidels. After returning from Ceuta he organized an expedition to attack Gibraltar. His fleet was en route to the Muslim fortress when King John abruptly ordered its return. Rather than rejoin the court in Lisbon, the bitterly disappointed prince relocated to a village called Sagres on Portugal's Cape Saint Vincent at the southwestern tip of Europe.

Until modern times, it was commonly written that, at Sagres, Prince Henry established what became the world's first exploration laboratory by bringing together sea captains, pilots, mariners, instrument makers, and ship builders. Modern historians, however, have refuted this belief. While it now appears certain that no "school" of navigation ever existed at Sagres, what is true is that Prince Henry did employ cartographers to draw maps to guide the explorers he sent into the unknown. What also is certain is that it was from Sagres that Prince Henry employed that type of ship that,

Linschoten

Mocadaon

Baptista à Doe. fec

Naves celoces seu biremes, quibus Bello et transportandis
mercibus utuntur Lusitani, et corum hostes Malabares.

Fusten welcke die Portugeesen en haer vianden die Malabaren
gebruycken ter oorloch, en om coopmanschap te voeren

46 en 47

A hand-colored engraving of a fusta from *Itinerario: Voyage ofte schipvaert van Jan Huyghen van Linschoten naer Oost ofte Portugaels Indien, 1579–1592 (Travel Account of the Voyage of the Sailor Jan Huyghen van Linschoten to the Portuguese East India)*, published in 1596. *Fustas* were small fast ships, with sails and oars (here manned by slaves) that were initially used by the Portuguese for trading and eventually used by the corsairs for raids.

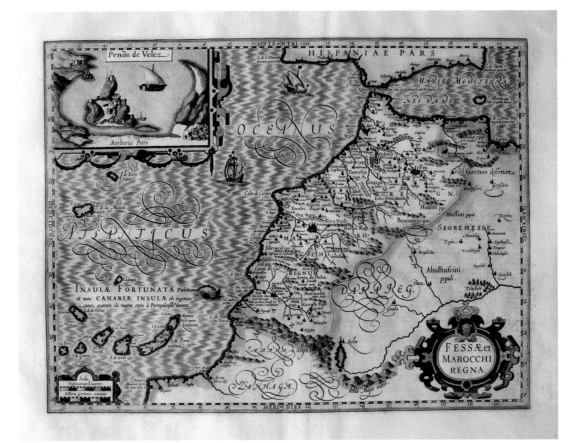

This map of Morocco and the northeast coast of Africa was drawn about 1628 by Jodocus Hondius, the founder of a noted seventeenth-century Dutch map publishing family. Cape Bojador can be seen on the lower left section of the map.

first with the Portuguese and then the Spanish, launched the world into what became known as the Great Age of Exploration.

Called a *caravel*, its origins are unknown, although a similar type of vessel was used by thirteenth-century Andalusian explorers. Unlike the heavy, square-rigged cargo-laden ships that had long plied the Mediterranean, it was designed for exploration. Because of its shallow draft, it could penetrate inshore waters and, unlike heavier vessels, could be beached for repairs with ease. Most important to Prince Henry's sailors, lateen sails, mounted on two or three masts (later types had four masts), made the vessel extremely fast, maneuverable in high winds, and able to tack in a considerably shorter time and distance than one-masted, square-rigged ships.

All of these innovations were designed to overcome Prince Henry's greatest challenge: diminishing his explorers' fear of navigating in untested seas—particularly the terrifying prospect of rounding Africa's Cape Bojador. Until that obstacle was overcome, he knew, the distant seas to which he planned to send his explorers would never be reached, let alone attempted.

Between 1424 and 1434, Prince Henry sent out fourteen expeditions seeking to round the foreboding barren but consequential cape. None succeeded. Then, in 1434, a year after he had made a failed attempt, Gil Eannes—a former squire—accomplished what had for so long been thought impossible. After rounding the cape, he landed on the African shore and found that he was not only still alive but that the waters beyond did not drop precipitously off; nor did they seem to be the gateway to unimagined terrors. "And as he proposed, he performed," Zurara wrote, "for in that voyage he doubled the Cape, despising all danger, and found the lands beyond quite contrary to what he, like others, had expected. And though the matter was a small one in itself, yet on account of its daring it was reckoned great."

Great indeed, for with his mariners' greatest fears allayed, Prince Henry was able to launch one expedition after another, each designed to explore farther than the last. By 1445, Dinis Dias had reached the most westerly part of Africa, and Portuguese trade with western Africa had begun, trade that involved not only African goods but slaves. Prince Henry justified this slave trade by claiming that his purpose was to convert the slaves to Christianity. But as Peter Russell, in his book *Prince Henry the Navigator* (2001), stated, "In Henryspeak, conversion and enslavement were interchangeable terms."

By 1457, Alvise Cadamosto—the first of the many Venetian mariners who eventually sailed for Portugal, Spain, and England—discovered the Cape Verde Islands and penetrated the Senegal and Gambia rivers some sixty miles into the African interior. When Prince Henry died in 1460, the exploration of the West African coast was far from completed, and the continent itself had not been rounded. But his accomplishments were extraordinary. By developing the first incremental system of exploration, he truly paved the way for the monumental discoveries that would be made before the fifteenth century had run its course.

Prince Henry's passing did not diminish the work that he had begun. In 1469, a new king, Prince Henry's nephew King Alfonso V, signed a unique contract with the merchant-explorer Fernão Gomes, in which Gomes committed himself to exploring at least three hundred miles farther down the African coast each year. Spurred on by the arrangement—which granted him a monopoly on the Guinea trade—Gomes succeeded in investigating most of the remainder of the coastline.

THE CAPE OF GOOD HOPE

In 1481, King Alfonso was succeeded by his son John II, ushering in what has been termed "the great age of Portuguese seafaring." By this time, many explorers were becoming impatient with the focus on Africa. It was time, they believed, to turn full attention to finding the coveted route to India. Arguably the most impatient of all was Bartolomeu Dias, a

OPPOSITE: A statue of Bartholomeu Dias adorns the South African High Commission building in Trafalgar Square, London. In 1500, Dias, while accompanying Pedro Álvarez Cabral on a voyage that resulted in the discovery of Brazil, was killed when his ship was wrecked off the same cape he had been the first to round.

ABOVE: The legend of Prester John, the priest-king who supposedly ruled over a vast Christian kingdom in the East or in the midst of Muslim territory, persisted throughout Europe from the twelfth through the seventeenth centuries. Though Prester John was never found, his possible existence as an ally against the foes of Christianity was a vital factor in helping fuel European exploration of Africa and India. In 1573, the prolific Flemish cartographer Abraham Ortelius—generally regarded as the creator of the first modern atlas—drew the first version of this map, which is commonly called the Prester John Map. Prester John's coat of arms is featured on the upper left corner, and the map is adorned with elephants and sea monsters.

Portuguese knight and royal fleet commander. In October 1486, Dias got his wish when King John named him to head an exploration whose mission it was to sail around Africa in hope of finding a trade route to the East. Another important goal, one that had been unsuccessfully pursued by Prince Henry, was to attempt to find the legendary African ruler known as Prester John, and to establish friendly relations with the man who was purported to have built a powerful Christian kingdom while surrounded by infidel neighbors.

With a fleet of three ships, Dias left Lisbon in 1487 and sailed first toward the Congo River. Then, as he sailed southward along the African coast, he was struck by a violent storm that lasted for thirteen days and drove him far to the south. When the storm abated, he headed east but sighted no land. Turning northward, he rounded the southern tip of Africa. Thanks to the unplanned storm, Bartolomeu Dias had accomplished what Prince Henry, some thirty years before, had fervently hoped one of his mariners would achieve.

Dias was determined to press on until he found the Indian Ocean, but his crew, exhausted and terrified by the journey through the vicious seas, demanded that he turn back. With a near mutiny on his hands and provisions running out, he had no choice. Reluctantly he realized that he would have to settle for having proven that it was indeed possible to sail around Africa. However, yet another discovery awaited. As Dias followed the coastline on his return voyage, he came to a mountainous shore and to a cape that he named Cape of Storms. When, after having been gone for almost seventeen months, he finally reached Lisbon and submitted his report to King John, the monarch renamed Dias's discovery the Cape of Good Hope.

Dias's accomplishments were considerable. In one voyage he added 1,260 miles to the known African coastline. He became the first European since ancient times to round the Cape of Good Hope. Not only had he solved the mystery of the African pathway to India, he had achieved something even more significant. He demonstrated that there was a way out of the Atlantic Ocean.

THE ADMIRAL OF THE OCEAN SEA

As Dias made his triumphant return to Lisbon harbor in 1488, a forty-year-old Genoese seafarer was also in Lisbon, at the court of King John, seeking funds for a most unlikely project. The man who would be known as Cristóvão Colombo to the Portuguese, Cristoforo Colombo to the Italians, Cristóbal Colón to the Spanish, and Christopher Columbus to the pages of English history, was a most imposing man. In an era when the height of the average male was five feet four inches, he stood almost six feet tall. Written accounts describe him as freckled and fair-skinned, and with prematurely white

Christopher Columbus pleads his case to the Spanish monarchs Ferdinand and Isabella, in a nineteenth-century French lithograph.

or gray hair that had once been flaming red. The fast-talking Columbus was apparently regarded by many who had met him as stubborn, obsessive, and filled with himself. He was also an unwavering romantic, deeply religious, intensely curious about everything geographic, and, above all else, driven by a sense of mission.

He had already led a most interesting life. The son of a weaver, most scholars believe that he was born in Genoa in 1451. Seeking to avoid being apprenticed to his father's trade, he became a sailor and went to sea, making his first long voyage in 1474 on a ship bound for the Mediterranean. In 1476, he sailed with a Genoese fleet that was escorting a cargo ship through the Strait of Gibraltar, when they were set upon by French privateers. The fleet was sunk, but fortunately the attack took place near the Portuguese port of Lagos, close to where Prince Henry the Navigator had launched his explorations. According to legend, the twenty-five-year-old Columbus latched on to a floating oar and managed to make his way to the safety of shore.

Undaunted, he made a series of other voyages, including several with the Portuguese merchant marines, which took him to ports in England, Ireland, and possibly Iceland. He sailed westward from the Aegean to the Azores and sailed along Africa's Gold Coast as a trader. Although Columbus never received a formal education, he taught himself to read and write and voraciously devoured every book and manuscript on geography, astronomy, and westward voyages that he could lay his hands on—becoming, in the process, a master mariner. His readings inspired him to devise a bold, unprecedented plan that he called his "Enterprise of the Indies." The riches of the East, he was convinced, could be reached not by sailing east around Africa, but by sailing west. Columbus first presented the plan to King John in 1484, and the royal advisers scoffed at the Genoan's idea: not because they thought the Earth was flat—most modern historians concur that medieval sailors and scholars knew that the world was round—but because they believed that Columbus had greatly underestimated the length of such a voyage. No ship of the day could possibly travel that far.

Columbus was not easily discouraged. His fortunes took a more tragic turn when he lost his wife to illness in 1485. Yet even this did not make him lose sight of his dream. Taking his five-year-old-son Diego with him, he moved to Spain where he hoped he could convince the Spanish monarchs Queen Isabella and King Ferdinand to embrace his project.

He began by trying to get influential members of the Spanish court to plead his case with the royal couple, without success. Then, in late 1486, he befriended a nobleman and several members of the clergy who helped him obtain an audience with the court. However, Spain was embroiled in a protracted and expensive war against the Moors in the Islamic stronghold of Granada, and its leaders were uninterested in Columbus's "Enterprise." Undeterred, he continued to lobby the court.

In the meantime, the Portuguese king was still reluctant to dismiss Columbus's proposal out of hand and agreed to meet with him again in 1488. Columbus was so determined; and he certainly believed that success could be achieved. And what, if by some miracle, he actually reached Cipango (Japan) or Cathay (China) or some other magic land by sailing west? The rewards would be enormous. Abruptly, however, all considerations ceased when Dias returned from the Cape of Good Hope. Dias had made his report, and, if it was accurate, an eastern sea route to the riches of the Orient now seemed possible. Why chance a decidedly risky venture in the other direction? King John rejected Columbus a second time. The Genoan returned to Spain and continued to petition Ferdinand and Isabella.

By 1491 even the indefatigable Columbus was becoming dispirited: "Everyone to whom I spoke of this enterprise," he was said to have complained, "thought it a mere jest." Those who refused to sponsor his project were undoubtedly put off by the extraordinary demands he made, should his plan be adopted. Along with the financing he sought, he required that he be given the title Admiral of the Ocean Sea. Ten percent of all the gold and other treasures he acquired along the way,

OPPOSITE: The three immortal ships of Columbus—the *Niña*, the *Pinta*, and the *Santa María*—are portrayed at sea in this undated engraving.

BELOW: Columbus's landing on the Bahamian island which he named San Salvador has been the subject of more artists' interpretations than any other event that took place during the Age of Exploration. In this nineteenth-century hand-colored lithograph, Columbus shows various simple European objects to the natives, which they had never seen before. Before the arrival of Christopher Columbus and the other Europeans who followed him, the Native Americans had never seen a ship or a white man. None had any way of knowing that their lives were about to change forever.

he stated, should be his. In addition, he demanded that the governorship of every new land he might discover had to pass through his eldest son to his heirs "for evermore."

Finally, in late 1491, he got his answer. Ferdinand and Isabella had said "no." Almost immediately, his fortunes turned. According to legend, the royal comptroller Luis de Santangel, an influential member of the Spanish court, stepped in, offered to put up some of his own money, and per-suaded the monarchs to reverse their decision. It was a reversal based in great measure on the fact that with the fall of Granada on January 2, 1492, Spain's seven-hundred-year-old civil war with the Moors had ended. What better way to celebrate that victory than to support an endeavor that might spread Christianity farther than ever before and might, at the same time, bring the riches of the East to Spain.

On August 3, 1492, with three ships, the *Niña*, the *Pinta*, and the *Santa María* manned by eighty-eight men, Columbus sailed from Spain into the unknown. His goal, unlike that of the Portuguese, was not to discover land but to avoid land until he reached China or Japan. He had no idea which country he might arrive at first. What he eventu-ally found was as much of a surprise to him as it

was to the rest of the world. "My intention in this navigation," he later admitted in a letter to the king of Spain, "was to reach Cathay and the extreme east of Asia, not expecting to find such an obstacle of new land as I found."

Rather than sail directly westward, Columbus deliberately stayed clear of the strong North Atlantic winds by proceeding south toward the Canaries. After reaching this destination in a week, he turned due west, hoping that the northeasterly trade winds would carry him to Cathay. Almost every suc-

OPPOSITE: Columbus's letter was reproduced in many editions and formats. This 1494 Basel version was the second part of a book that also included a play by one Carolus Verardus, about the victorious Spanish conquest of the Moors. Together, the two works were an early form of propaganda meant as a paean to the continued rule of the Catholic King of Spain.

cessful venture is blessed with its share of luck and Columbus's voyage was no exception. His journey was marked by smooth seas and benign weather. But even this good fortune did not calm the fears of his men. The captain might be convinced that the world was round and that there was no falling off (actually, from all he had read and studied, he believed it was shaped more like a pear), but many of his sailors were not convinced. To them, even the blessings of the voyage were cause for alarm. If there was no rain, would they run completely out of water? The benevolent wind was driving them ever forward. But if it never shifted, how would they ever get back home?

Four weeks out of the Canaries, the crews were more anxious than ever, despite the fact that birds, floating plants, and other harbingers of land were being spotted. Then, at two o'clock in the morning on October 12, the cry "Tierra, Tierra" rang out from Rodrigo de Triana, a lookout aboard the *Pinta*. Five weeks after leaving the Canaries, Columbus had reached the Americas, or more precisely the Bahamas. Of course he didn't know that. He firmly believed that he was in Asia. Nothing that he encountered after he and his men set foot on the islands convinced him otherwise. He continually mistook the plants he found to be those described by Marco Polo and others in their Asian travels. He was even convinced that the smell of the vegetation was Oriental.

From the Bahamas, the three ships sailed along the northern coast of eastern Cuba and Hispaniola, skirting the island of San Salvador. Ferdinand and Isabella had given Columbus a letter of introduction to Cathay's Great Kahn, and his one disappointment was in not having found him. On the other hand, he was truly fascinated with the natives he managed to encounter, as recounted in his letter to King Ferdinand:

"I did not find any towns and villages on the seacoast" he wrote, "save small hamlets with the people whereof I could not get speech, because they all fled away forthwith. The people of another island and of all others that I have found and seen, or not seen, all go naked…just as their mothers bring them forth… they all believe very firmly that I with these ships and crews, came from the sky…others went running from house to house and to the neighboring villages, with loud cries of 'Come! come to see the people from Heaven…This is a land to be desired, and once seen never to be relinquished."

As author/historian Marshall Davidson wrote in his 1951 book *Life in America*: "Had Columbus known that it was a barbarous wilderness half a world away from his true goal, the explorer would have died a bitterly frustrated man."

De Insulis nuper in mari Indico repertis

Insula hyspana

De Insulis nuper inuentis

Epistola Christoferi Colom (cui etas nostra mul=
tum debet: de Insulis in mari Indico nuper inuen=
tis: ad quas perquirendas octauo antea mense: au=
spiciis & ere inuictissimi Fernandi Hispaniarū Re=
gis missus fuerat) ad Magnificū dominū Raphae=
lem Sanxis: eiusdem serenissimi Regis Thesaurari
um missa : quam nobilis ac litteratus vir Aliander
de Cosco: ab Hispano ideomate: in latinum con=
uertit: tercio Kalendas Maii.M.cccc.xciij.Pontifi=
catus Alexandri Sexti Anno primo.

Q̃voniam susceptę prouinciæ rem perfectã
me consecutū fuisse: gratum tibi fore scio.
Has constitui exarare: quæ te vniuscuiusq̃
rei in hoc nostro itinere gestę inuetēq̃ admoneāt.
Tricesimotercio die postq̃ Gadibus discessi: in ma
re Indicū perueni: vbi plurimas Iusulas innumeris
habitatas hominibus reperi: quarū omnium p̃ foe=
licissimo Rege nostro: præconio celebrato / & vexil
lis extensis: cōtradicente nemine possessionē acce=
pi. primeq̃ earum: diui Saluatoris nomē imposui.
cuius fretus auxilio: tam ad hanc q̃ ad cęteras alias
puenimus. Eam vero Indi Guanahanyn vocant.
Aliæ etiam vnãquanq̃ nouo nomine nūcupaui.
Quippe aliam Insulam Sanctę Marię Conceptio=
nis. aliam Fernandinam. aliam Hysabellam. aliã

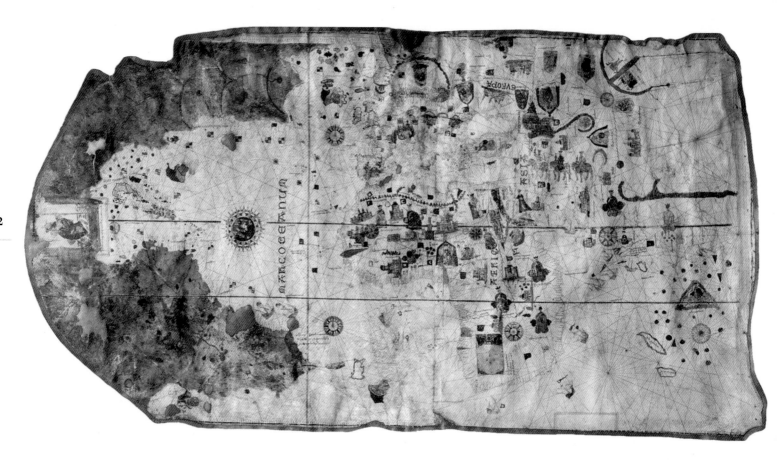

This is the earliest known map showing the lands discovered by Christopher Columbus, the *Mappa Mundi*. It was drawn in 1500 by Juan de la Cosa, who had sailed with Columbus on his first three voyages to the New World and was owner and master of Columbus's flagship the *Santa María* on the first journey. In the center and right of the map are the outlines of Europe, the Mediterranean Sea, and Africa, drawn to a smaller scale than the New World.

But he did not, (nor would he ever know) that he was not in Asia, and by mid-December he was ready to sail home with his glorious news. Two weeks later his exploration suffered its one disaster. On December 24 the *Santa María* ran aground on a reef off of Hispaniola and had to be abandoned. The situation was made worse by the fact that, a few days earlier, the *Pinta*'s captain Martin Pinzón had, on his own, taken his ship and crew on a jaunt to search for treasure and new land. Columbus took as many of the *Santa María*'s crew as he could safely fit aboard the *Niña* but was forced to leave the rest behind on Hispaniola in a hastily constructed fort built from the *Santa María*'s timbers. Soon after sailing away from this first New World settlement, which he named Navidad in honor of the time of its construction, Columbus joined up with Pinzón and the *Pinta*,

> *" This is a land to be desired, and once seen never to be relinquished "*
>
> —Christopher Columbus, from his letter to King Ferdinand, 1493

and together, on January 16, 1493, the two vessels headed back to Spain. But as they recrossed the Atlantic, the ships became separated in a wild storm. Later a second storm compelled Columbus to land not in Spain, but in Portugal. It was truly ironic. The Admiral of the Ocean Sea, the man who, in his mind, had succeeded in reaching the East by sailing west, was forced to reenter Europe by first setting foot in the very country that had rejected his "Enterprise."

News of what Columbus had discovered reached the public through an announcement written by the explorer himself. Published as a small pamphlet and translated into several languages, it was a surprisingly modest presentation of such remarkable news. Traditionally, historians believed that Columbus wrote three missives; two addressed to Spanish court officials and a different report addressed to Ferdinand and Isabella. It is thought today, however, that Columbus wrote only one long letter, which was then copied and dispersed. Columbus's intent, along with describing what had been found, was to secure even more funding for a second voyage. The explorer emphasized how the lands he had discovered would, as he had promised, secure both Spain's religious and commercial interests: "In all these islands," he wrote, "I saw no great diversity in the appearance of the people or in their manners or language. On the contrary, they all understand one another, which is a very

curious thing, on account of which I hope that their Highnesses will determine upon their conversion to our holy faith, towards which they are very inclined." Stating that he had established Navidad in a location where he was certain that gold could be mined, Columbus went on to promise the monarchs "as much gold as they may need, if their Highnesses will render me very slight assistance; moreover, I will give them spices and cotton, as much as their Highnesses shall command; and [gum] mastic, as much as they shall order shipped…I believe also that I have found rhubarb and cinnamon, and I shall find a thousand other things of value, which the people whom I have left there will have discovered, for I have not delayed at any point, so far as the wind allowed me to sail."

Columbus made three more voyages to the "East." His second took place only six months after he had returned from his first historic journey. This time there was no haggling over finances, ships, or provisions. His expedition consisted of a fleet of seventeen vessels carrying more than twelve hundred sailors. It was on this voyage in particular that the Admiral of the Ocean Sea demonstrated his remarkable and considerable navigational skills. Not only did he manage to keep all seventeen of his ships together throughout the entire Atlantic crossing, he landed at the exact spot that he had selected when planning the voyage,

The Face of Columbus

For one who achieved such abiding fame, not much is known about Columbus's early life. Because no portraits were made during his lifetime, what he really looked like is equally unclear. A sampling of but a few of the countless "likenesses" of the Admiral of the Ocean Sea that were drawn reveals how artists, deprived of having their subject sitting before them, brought their own interpretations to the face of the man who changed history.

CLOCKWISE FROM TOP:

Engraving by Theodor de Bry, from volume 5 of his *Grand Voyages*, 1595.

A lithograph by Currier & Ives, 1892.

Detail of Columbus in *Virgin of the Navigators*, by Alejo Fernández, 1531.

A mid-nineteenth-century engraving by John Sartain, after an original 1519 painting by Sebastiano del Piombo.

an island he named Marie Galante in honor of his previous ship, the *Santa María*. This second journey was marked by the extraordinary number of islands that he "discovered," many of which he named in honor of the saints he venerated. Among the lands he encountered were Dominica, Guadeloupe, Antigua, Nevis, Saint Kitts, Saint Eustatius, Saint Martin, Saint Croix, and Puerto Rico.

On his third voyage, launched on May 30, 1498, Columbus explored the American mainland. Sailing with six vessels, his first major discovery was an island he named Trinidad in honor of the Holy Trinity. From that point he sailed between Trinidad and the east coast of Venezuela, unknowingly stumbling into the Gulf of Paria. That body of water is now considered one of the best natural harbors on the Atlantic coast of the Americas. Yet it was not the gulf but the freshwater Orinoco River running into it that most amazed him. As he explored this great waterway and the idyllic terrain through which it flowed, he became convinced that he had found much more than yet another island. He was convinced that he had discovered a previously unknown continent, not part of a new world, but attached to China, which he believed he soon would reach. He believed that he had found nothing less than the Terrestrial Paradise that had existed in myth and legend for ages. Columbus wrote of his theory in a letter to the Spanish court:

I am convinced, ... that it is the spot of earthly paradise wither no one can go but by God's permission ... I do not suppose that the earthly paradise is in the form of a rugged mountain, as the descriptions of it have made it appear, but that it is on the summit of the spot which I have described ... I think also that the water I have described may proceed far from it, though it be far off, and that, stopping at the place which I have just left, it forms this lake. There are great indications of this being the terrestrial paradise, for its site coincides with the opinion of holy and wise theologians ... moreover, the other evidences agree with the supposition, for I have never either read or heard of fresh water coming in so large a quantity in close conjunction with the water of the sea; the idea is also corroborated by the blandness of the temperature; and if the water of which I speak does not proceed from the earthly paradise, it appears to be still more marvelous, for I do not believe that there is any river in the world so large or so deep.

After having made this momentous discovery, the explorer moved on, sighting and naming both the islands of Tobago and Grenada. He then sailed to Hispaniola in order to check on the condition of the men he had left there. He was shocked by what he found. Having not discovered any of the riches that Columbus had promised them when he had left them behind, the settlers accused him of having deliberately misled them. The situation became so contentious that, in 1500, Ferdinand and Isabella sent a royal administrator, Francisco de Bobadilla, to assess the situation. Immediately upon his arrival in Hispaniola, Bobadilla was barraged with complaints about the way Columbus had mismanaged the territory over which he had been granted governorship—difficult conditions had led to a breakdown in order.

As the result of testimonies that were given to Bobadilla, Columbus, and his two brothers—who had been in charge during Columbus's absence—were placed in chains and put into prison. In October 1500, the Admiral of the Ocean Sea, still in chains, was shipped back to Spain, where he composed a plaintive letter to one of his friends in court:

> It is now seventeen years since I came to serve these princes with the Enterprise of the Indies. They made me pass eight of them in discussion, and at the end rejected it as a thing of jest. Nevertheless, I persisted therein... Over there I have placed under their sovereignty more land than there is in Africa, Europe, and more than 1,700 islands... In seven years I, by the divine will, made that conquest. At a time when I was entitled to expect rewards and retirement, I was incontinently arrested and sent home loaded with chains.

The letter worked. Not only was Columbus set free, he was granted the resources for yet another journey. But not without a price. He was stripped of all the titles he had originally been granted.

Determined that this would be the trip in which he would find a passageway to Cathay, he named the expedition *El Alto Viaje*, the High Voyage. It was his least successful trip, a journey on which, for the first time, he encountered severe and dangerous weather. After exploring the coasts of Honduras, Nicaragua, and Costa Rica, he landed in Panama. Then resuming his search for the passage to either Japan or China, he sailed along the coast of Cuba where his ships were suddenly struck by a violent storm and so badly damaged that they were forced to put into St. Ann's Bay in Jamaica, where they were beached. Columbus and his men were then stranded on the island for more than a year while a message seeking help was sent to Hispaniola and repairs were finally made. It was the final chapter in history's most momentous series of voyages. The Admiral of the Ocean Sea returned to Spain in November 1504, having seen no evidence to disprove his belief that he had found the golden lands of the East—although, as historian Valerie Flint has written, the "most apparently fantastic of Columbus's ideas were precisely the ones which allowed him to make the most important of his real discoveries." And his misconceptions in no way

diminish his majestic achievements. He was not the first to believe that one could reach the East by traveling west. But it was Columbus whose courage, extraordinary seamanship, and unyielding sense of mission made the idea a reality.

At the same time, an appreciation of his accomplishments must be tempered by the reality of his brutal treatment of the natives and the fact that it was Columbus who set the pattern for slavery in the New World. Far more serious were the atrocities he carried out against those he named Indians. Many historians now believe that of the more than three hundred thousand inhabitants known as the Taínos, who lived in five kingdoms or territories on Hispaniola, Columbus and his men killed or exported one-third of them as slaves.

In his historic book *Atlantic: A History of an Ocean* (1957), one of the first studies of its kind, Leonard Outhwaite pointed out one of the least recognized of Columbus's contributions. "Columbus," Outhwaite wrote, "made eight crossings of the Atlantic Ocean. Each one of these goings and returnings followed a different band of latitude. He never sailed home along the same course that he had employed in the outward voyage and he never repeated a course. Such a diversity of passages can hardly have been achieved by mere accident. It seems natural to infer that this pattern represents a realistic and scientific attempt to investigate the Atlantic Ocean itself."

VASCO DA GAMA

What is certain is that Columbus's discoveries almost immediately intensified the Spanish and Portuguese rivalry over finding a passage to the East. A year before Columbus sailed for the third time, a new Portuguese king, Manuel I, determined to capitalize on what Bartolomeu Dias had accomplished, sent out one of his court favorites to at last confirm the eastern sea route to India. A skilled and courageous navigator, Vasco da Gama was also known for his violent temper and ruthless nature.

He sailed from Lisbon on July 8, 1497, in command of four vessels and 170 crewmen. By mid-December the fleet had passed the Great Fish River, a river running through what is now the South African province of Eastern Cape. Sailing on, da Gama entered waters totally unknown to the European world. As he progressed up the east coast of the Dark Continent, he made three stops, hoping to establish trading relations at the Arab-controlled ports of Mozambique and Mombassa. But he proved unsuccessful and in one instance was forced to flee for his life from a hostile Muslim crowd. Tradition holds that he had better luck at the port of Malindi, where he was also able to secure a pilot.

Now fully concentrating on reaching his country's long sought-after goal, da Gama, employing all of his navigational skills, led his fleet across the Arabian Sea and into the Indian Ocean. He arrived in Calicut, a major port on India's southwest coast on May 20, 1498. The Portuguese dream of reaching India by sea, begun some eighty years before by Prince Henry the Navigator, had been achieved.

After establishing what amounted to a shaky trading agreement with local rulers, da Gama sailed home to a hero's welcome. Made a count by the king, he was also given the title Admiral of the Indian Ocean. In 1502 he made the first of two more voyages to India, this time leading a fleet of twenty warships sent to enforce Portuguese trading rights. It was on this endeavor that da Gama's brutal nature came into full evidence. Spying a vessel carrying Muslim pilgrims on a return trip from Mecca, he ordered his crew to seize the ship and confiscate all the treasure aboard. As historian Daniel Boorstin writes in *The Discoverers* (1985), one of da Gama's crewmen later gave his account of what happened after the vessel's owners

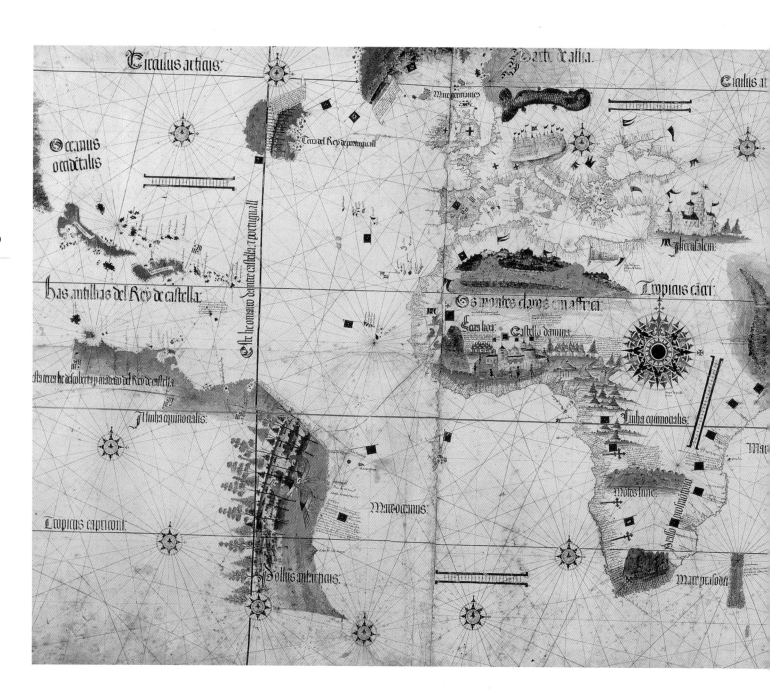

Circulus articus.

Parte dallia.

Oceanus occidentalis

Terra del Rey de portugall

Mare germanicus

Hierusalem

Las antilhas del Rey de castella.

Os montes claros em affrica

Tropicus cancri

Esta terra he descuberta p mandado del Rey de castella

Elte licomato ētre castella z portugall

Sara hoa

Castello damina

Linha equinocialis

Finha equinocialis

Montes lune

Mare oceanus

Tropicus capricorni.

Pollus antarticus.

Mare prasodi

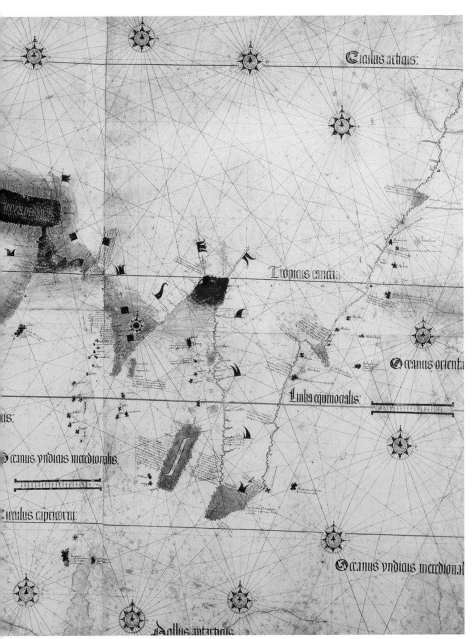

Tropicus cancri.

Oceanus orienta

Linea equinocialis.

Oceanus yndicus meridionalis.

Circulus capricorni.

Oceanus yndicus meridional

As historic as Christopher Columbus's achievements were, the claim could be made that, in several ways, da Gama's achievements were even greater. Columbus had vowed that he would find the great cities of China and Japan. He found none. He promised the Spanish monarchs that he would find gold mines, but again found none. Vasco da Gama, on the other hand, promised he would reach India and did so. Moreover, while Columbus made his epic discoveries while sailing with favorable winds and currents, da Gama had to battle opposing currents and winds all the way to the East. The Cantino World Map shown here, a navigational chart drawn in Portugal around 1500 by an anonymous cartographer, celebrates the achievements of da Gama and other great Portuguese navigators of the same period. A version of the map was smuggled out of the country in 1502 by Alberto Cantino, an agent for the Duke of Ferarra to Italy, hence its name.

balked at meeting da Gama's demands. "We took a Mecca ship on board of which were 380 men and many women and children, and we took from it fully 12,000 ducats, and goods worth at least another 10,000. And we burned the ship and the people on board with gunpowder."

In 1524 da Gama was once again sent to India, this time to serve as viceroy of the Portuguese colonies that his first voyage had spawned. But not long after arriving in Goa on India's west coast he contracted malaria and died in the city of Cochin on Christmas Eve, 1524.

AMERIGO VESPUCCI'S
NEW CONTINENTS

While the Portuguese were attempting to reap the fruits of their long, well-organized, step-by-step discovery of the eastern route to India, the Spanish were determined to follow the path blazed by Columbus. They chose Amerigo Vespucci, another Italian navigator sailing for Spain, to follow in Columbus's wake; a man who eventually gave his name to two "new" continents.

Born into a wealthy family in Florence in 1454, Amerigo Vespucci received an excellent technical and scientific education. He became a successful cartographer and respected astronomer. In 1493, when Columbus returned from his first

This illustration from a popular 1852 book chronicling the life and voyages of Amerigo Vespucci, imagines the moment when Vespucci first lands in the New World.

RIGHT: Amerigo Vespucci possessed geographic knowledge rare for his time. His early estimation of the size of the world's circumference proved to be accurate within fifty miles. In 1508, after his voyages to America were over, Vespucci was named to the post of pilot major (chief navigator) of Spain.

PRECEDING PAGES: **Martin Waldseemüller's historic 1507 map was entitled** *Universalis cosmographia secundum Ptholomaei traditionem et Americi Vespucii aliorum lustrationes*—**translated from Latin as "A Map of the World According to the Tradition of Ptolemy and the Voyages of Amerigo Vespucci." It was the first map to portray a separate Western Hemisphere, with the Pacific as a separate ocean.**

RIGHT: **In this sixteenth-century allegorical work, Amerigo Vespucci, holding a pennant and an astrolabe, encounters a native woman drawn to symbolize America. The image appeared in** *Nova reperta (New Discoveries)*, **a catalogue of engravings published in 1600 by the Flemish artist Jan Van der Straet.**

voyage, Vespucci was working as a mercantile representative of the Medici family and as an outfitter of ships. By this time he had become a voracious reader of nautical books and maps and was convinced that he could find the passageway to the Orient that had eluded Columbus. He got his chance when Alonso de Ojeda, a young mariner who had served as a lieutenant on Columbus's second voyage, asked him to join an exploratory expedition westward across the Atlantic. Vespucci quickly agreed on the condition that he would also be able to conduct explorations of his own.

In May 1499, the expedition sailed from Spain and made landfall on the coast of what is now Guyana. Here, Ojeda decided to sail northward in search of gold and other treasure. Vespucci, however, had a much different agenda. In command of two vessels, he sailed southeastward, searching for the passage that would lead him to the far greater riches of the East. As he proceeded southward he first encountered the mouth of the Amazon River and then the mouth of the Orinoco, the river that Columbus had believed flowed through the Terrestrial Paradise.

Unlike Columbus, Vespucci gave no holy attachment to the beatific region. He was convinced that what he had found was an eastern peninsula of Asia and that by continuing to sail southward he might find the coveted passage. But by this time sea worms had caused serious damage to both of his ships and his provisions were running low. He sailed back to Spain determined to continue his exploration on a second voyage.

Back in Spain, however, Vespucci received a rude shock. The Spanish court was not interested in launching a second expedition. Taking the reverse course that Columbus had followed—when his "Enterprise of the Indies" had been rejected by King John I—Vespucci traveled to Portugal where King Manuel I seized upon the opportunity of launching Portugal's first westward search for the East and agreed to finance him.

In 1501, Vespucci, this time carrying the flag of Portugal, sailed for the lands he had first explored. Making landfall in Brazil he pressed on, investigating more than six thousand miles of coastline. After a year of probing almost every bay and river at which he arrived and meeting with whatever natives he could find, he became convinced that the conclusions he had drawn on his first voyage were erroneous. There was no passage east. More important, this was no Asian peninsula, it was an entirely new continent. As he sailed for home and prepared his charts, he inscribed the words *Mundus Nevus* (New World) upon them.

His story was not over. Vespucci's published account of his voyages, which he also titled *Mundus Nevus*, was widely read. In 1507, the German cartographer Martin Waldseemüller produced both a world globe and a large map inscribing the name "America" upon his depictions of the new continents. And there they have remained, the subject of genuine controversy.

For years it was written that Vespucci deliberately named the continents for himself, which is not true. Generations of school children have been informed of the injustice attached to the fact that it was not Columbus but Vespucci who attained the honor of having the American continents named for him. But how much of an injustice was it? What cannot be denied is that Vespucci, not Columbus, was the first to realize that South America was a vast continent, very much apart from Asia. It was he who first realized that a New World had been discovered. Perhaps historian Daniel Boorstin put it best: "It was appropriate," he wrote, "that the name America

should be affixed on the New World in a manner casual and accidental, since the European encounter with this new world had been so unintended."

The news that two continents and a whole new world had been discovered inspired Portuguese and Spanish exploration as never before. The imposing presence of the continents erased all hope of a quick and easy western passage to India. But now there was a new agenda, an unprecedented opportunity to claim new lands for God and country. Actually, this agenda had begun some nine years before Martin Waldseemüller inscribed the name "America" on his map and his globe. In 1498, two Portuguese explorers, João Fernandes Lavrador and Pêro de Barcelos, became the first to sight the coast of present-day Labrador. Lavrador, who, in 1446 and 1447, had accompanied expeditions to West Africa in service to Prince Henry the Navigator, charted the North American coastline he and Barcelos had come upon, receiving in return the honor of having Labrador named for him.

In April 1500, another Portuguese navigator and explorer, Pedro Álvares Cabral, sailing with a fleet of thirteen ships and fifteen hundred men reached the coast of Brazil. Was he the first to discover that land? Historians are in disagreement. Many believe that a year earlier, in 1499, Vincente Pinzón, the *Pinta*'s captain on Columbus's first voyage, sailed to the South American coast and landed at Cape St. Roque on Brazil's east

BELOW: **This detail of *Victoria*, Magellan's flagship, is from the *Maris Pacifici* (Pacific Ocean) map by Abraham Ortelius, printed in 1589 in Antwerp.**

OPPOSITE: **This map of the Americas was created by German cosmographer Sebastian Münster, ca. 1540. The first map devoted entirely to the New World, it includes Magellan's flagship, the *Victoria*, on the left and a leg hanging from a stand of trees marked *canibali* (cannibals) in eastern South America on the right.**

coast, making the discovery of Brazil a Spanish rather than a Portuguese achievement.

In the first quarter of the sixteenth century voyages across the once impenetrable Atlantic, particularly on the part of Spain, followed hard on the heels of one another. By 1518, Spanish explorer Juan Díaz de Solís explored the South American coast as far south as Rio de La Plata. Francisco Hernández de Córdoba discovered the Yucatan and provided the Spanish court with the first account of the huge and opulent Mayan cities. And, first Juan de Grijalva and then Alonso Álvarez de Pineda accomplished the exploration of the Gulf of Mexico for Spain.

VOYAGE AROUND THE WORLD

A greater accomplishment lay ahead. Columbus had shown that the Atlantic could be penetrated. Vespucci had revealed that there were unknown continents in a whole new world. And in 1519, in "the bravest single voyage in the history of exploration," Ferdinand Magellan, a Portuguese mariner in the service of Spain, led a voyage that resulted in the first successful attempt to sail around the Earth.

Seeking to find a passageway through South America to the rich Maluku Islands (also known as the Spice Islands),

Prima ego velivolis ambivi cursibus Orbem,
Magellane novo te duce ducta freto.
Ambivi, meritoȝ vocor VICTORIA: sunt mi
Vela, alæ; precium, gloria; pugna, mare.

Magellan sailed from Spain with a five-ship fleet. Within three months he had reached present-day Rio de Janeiro. At that location, after putting into harbor for the winter, he was forced to suppress a potential mutiny led by one of his officers. He suffered a second setback when, after resuming his voyage, one of his ships was destroyed in a sudden storm.

His fortunes then took a dramatic turn when the fleet came upon what seemed to be the passageway west he was seeking. Undeterred by the fact that the captain of the ship he had sent ahead to see if the passage was open suddenly abandoned the expedition and headed his vessel back to Spain, and ignoring the reality of his rapidly diminishing

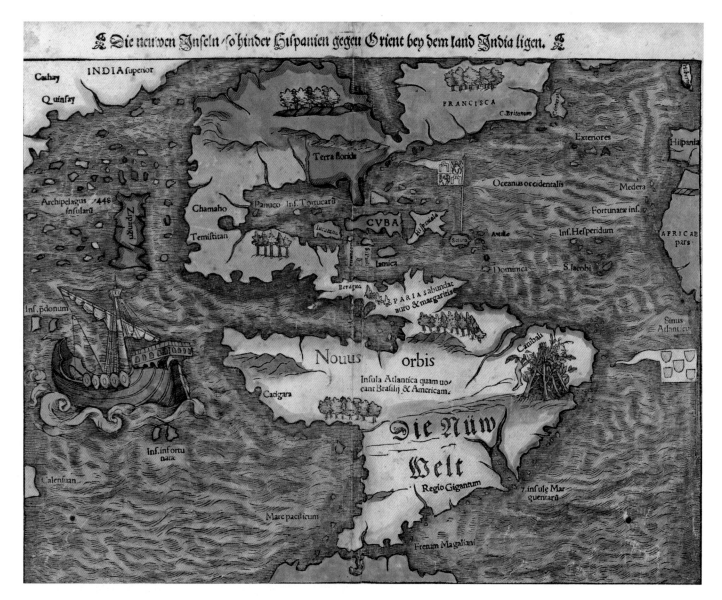

provisions, Magellan doggedly pressed on through what he now realized was a previously undiscovered strait. Thirty-eight days later, with his men forced to chew on leather to sustain themselves, he entered into what was clearly another vast ocean. Magellan had become the first to sail from the Atlantic into the Pacific.

But his problems were far from over. Just as Columbus had grossly underestimated the size of the Atlantic, Magellan could not fathom the enormity of the Pacific. By March 1521,

when he had crossed the equator and reached the Philippines, 120 of his original crew of 270 had died from scurvy.

For Magellan, the worst was yet to come. On April 27, 1521, after becoming entangled in a clash between Philippine natives, he and twenty of his men were killed. A fleet commander, Juan Sebastián Elcano, took charge, heading the expedition back to Spain, but not before scuttling one of the vessels in order to adequately man the two remaining ships. On the return voyage the vessels managed

ABOVE: Although he was killed before he could complete his expedition's circumnavigation of the globe, Ferdinand Magellan—shown above in an 1841 print—was one of the first explorers to cross all the Earth's meridians and the first to sail through the straits that bear his name.

RIGHT: Magellan's journey was mapped out in pure silver by Venetian cartographer Battista Agnese in 1544. Also charted—in gold—was the route from Spain to Peru. The clouds in the margins are cherubs, or wind heads, symbolizing the classical twelve-point winds from which modern compass directions developed.

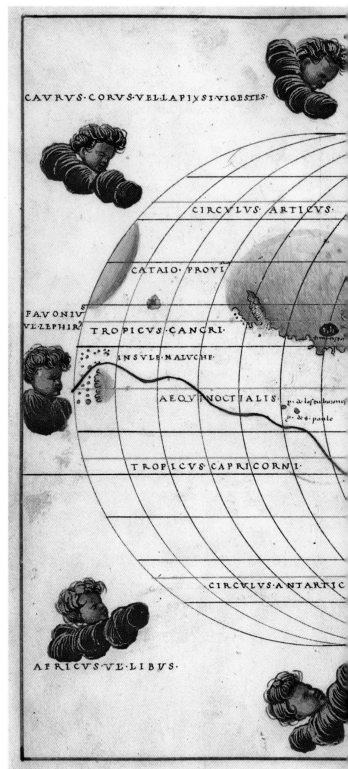

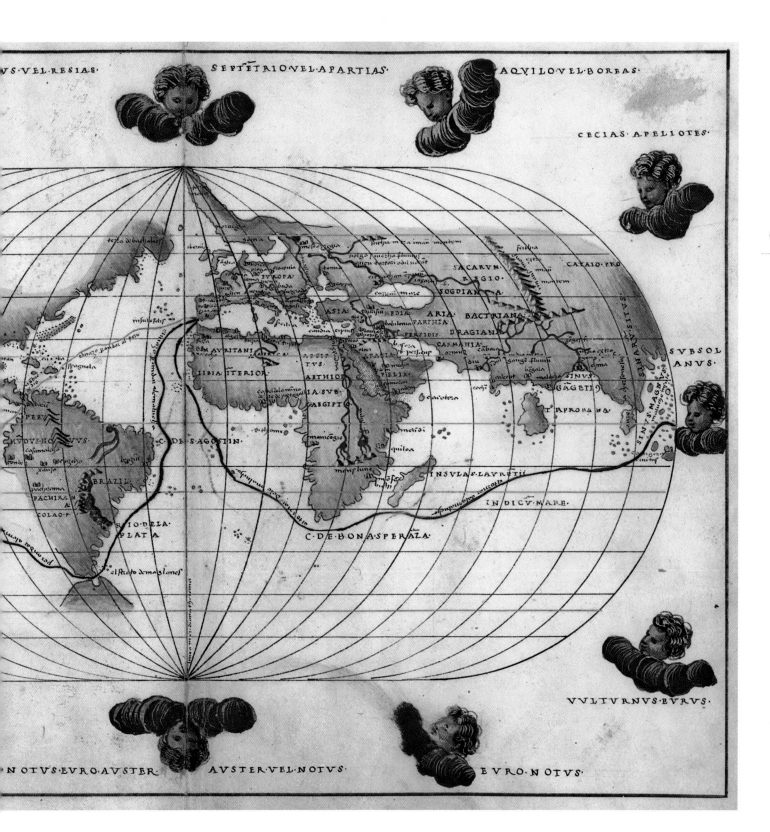

England's Henry the VII was the founder and first patriarch of the Tudor dynasty. In making John and Sebastian Cabot's voyage to America possible, the monarch launched Great Britain into the race for control of the New World. This painting was done in 1500 by Estonian-born Flemish painter Michael Sittow, known for his portraits of royalty.

to fulfill Magellan's original goal by putting into the Malucas where they loaded on the coveted spices.

After leaving the islands, however, one of the ships took on so much water that it had to be abandoned. On September 6, 1522, Elcano finally reached Spain on the expedition's one remaining vessel, Magellan's flagship *Victoria*. Less than one hundred crewmen were still alive. It had been a voyage filled with disaster. But due to Ferdinand Magellan's determination and navigational skills the globe had been circumnavigated, and the relationship between the Atlantic and the world's other oceans had been revealed.

From the time that Prince Henry the Navigator had set Portugal on its path of exploration through Columbus's historic ventures and the other Spanish discoveries they had spawned, the two Iberian nations had almost completely dominated the European presence in the still-mysterious New World. The Old World's two leading powers, England and France, had barely made their presence felt.

EARLY BRITISH
AND FRENCH EXPEDITIONS

Ironically, another Genoese explorer, this time sailing for Britain, made one of the first New World journeys soon after

Columbus. His name was Giovanni Caboto, a Venetian who, in 1485 had moved to England hoping to gain support for a voyage in search of a northwest passage to the East. It took Caboto, who became known to the English as John Cabot, more than ten years to get the backing he sought from King Henry VII, but in 1497 he sailed from Bristol in a single ship, the *Matthew*, accompanied by an eighteen-man crew that

Cod

hroughout history there have been products, such as gunpowder, tobacco, and salt, that have changed the course of history. Cod was such a product. Long before America's colonial days, Europeans were drawn to the waters of the Grand Banks off Newfoundland and off the cape that bore the fish's name. The codfish sustained those who settled in the American northeast and eventually formed the basis for their trade.

LEFT: In Massachusetts, the codfish became a proud symbol of trade and prosperity. The cod's strong identification with the state was lampooned in this political cartoon from 1812, by William Charles. It depicts Josiah Quincy III, representative from Massachusetts and opponent to the War of 1812, wearing two cods on his coat. The caption reads: "I Josiah the first do by this my Royal Proclamation announce myself King of New England, Novia Scotia and Passamaquoddy,—Grand Master of the noble order of the Two Cod Fishes."

TOP: The codfish became so vital to the life and economy of New England that it would be referred to as the "sacred cod." This exquisite drawing of a cod was done by artist H. L.Todd, for the U.S. Commission of Fish and Fisheries, in the 1880s.

ABOVE: For more than three centuries after the discovery of the New World, codfish continued to lure both fishermen and merchants. Currier & Ives printed this lithograph *Cod Fishing off Newfoundland* in 1872.

He was looking for a northwest passage to the East, but by setting foot in Newfoundland instead, John Cabot provided England with its claim to North American territory. This engraving of Cabot and his son discovering America appeared in *Ballou's Pictorial* in 1855.

included his son Sebastian. Thirty-three days later he landed on the coast of Newfoundland, not far from where the Vikings had set foot some four hundred years earlier. Details of this first English incursion into the New World are sketchy, but it is believed that Cabot explored enough of the coastline to suspect that perhaps this was a continent rather than an island.

A year later, intent on carrying out a larger exploration, he set sail again, this time with a five-vessel fleet and a crew of some three hundred. Except for one ship, the expedition was never heard from again. Cabot and four of his ships and their men had disappeared at sea. More than one hundred years passed before the British returned to North America.

The French did not wait that long. French fishermen had actually been dragging their nets off Newfoundland's Grand Banks since the early sixteenth century. But long,

costly wars with Spain and other European rivals had deterred France from making a serious New World effort. In 1515, however, a new and ambitious French monarch ascended to the throne.

Young Francis I refused to accept the validity of the Line of Demarcation, the imaginary longitude drawn by Pope Alexander VI, dividing the New World lands between Spain and Portugal. Nor was he willing to sit idly by while his two Iberian rivals increased their power and prestige. He also had another agenda—Francis needed a source of riches to pay for the wars in which his nation was still engaged. The answer, he believed, might well come in the discovery of that long sought-after northwest water route to the wealth of the East.

In 1524, the king sent a Genoese sailor in French employ named Giovanni da Verrazzano in the hope of finding the passage. Verrazzano crossed the Atlantic, reached the edge of

Florida and then began sailing up the North American coast searching for a passage. He had no luck finding one, but his journey took him all the way to Newfoundland. In the process he explored the mouth of the Hudson River, sailed between what is today Block Island and Martha's Vineyard, and entered Narragansett Bay at the site of present-day Newport. His voyage had two important results. It confirmed that—although there seemed to be no passage through it—North America was a long, unbroken continent. And it set the stage for the next French explorer of the American North.

His name was Jacques Cartier, and like his king, he was determined to find a northwest passage to the Indies. In 1534, he made his first transatlantic voyage, but, like Verrazzano, found no northwest passage. He did, however, discover a great river that he named the St. Lawrence and explored the mainland of what would become Canada all the way to what is now Montreal.

But he also encountered something else that excited him even more. As he conducted his explorations, Cartier met an Iroquois chief named Donnacona. The chieftain filled Cartier's head with tales of an inland kingdom called Saguenay, where there were mines that yielded enormous amounts of gold, silver, and other treasure. The kingdom, Donnacona stated, also contained enormous fields of spices and was inhabited by men bedecked in rubies. The more the chief waxed on, the more Cartier believed him. So much so that when the explorer returned to France, he took the chief with him so that he could repeat his tale to the king.

If anything, Francis I was even more excited about the Iroquois leader's story than Cartier, and within a year he sent the explorer and the chief back to find and exploit the extraordinary kingdom. Cartier spent months trying to find the treasure trove, always being assured by Donnacona that it lay just beyond the next mountain.

He never found it, but to his dying day Cartier believed in Saguenay's existence. To keep his king's interest in its treasures alive he actually filled his vessel with iron pyrite (fool's gold) before sailing back to France. What is most important is that neither Cartier's failure to discover a northwest passage nor his futile attempts to find a kingdom of gold diminish his impact on New World exploration. His discovery of the St. Lawrence and his extensive inland probing formed the basis for France's claim to an enormous portion of North America.

ABOVE: Jacques Cartier's obsession with finding the mythical kingdom of Saguenay does not diminish his achievements in making the most significant early French discoveries in what would become New France. In 1850 an artist depicted Cartier's first meeting with Native Americans in Hochelaga, a St. Lawrence Iroquoian village near present-day Montreal.

RIGHT: Jacques Cartier relates the story of his discoveries—and of mythical Saguenay— to Francis I, in this painting by Frank Craig, for a volume entitled *The King's Book of Quebec*, published in Ottawa in 1911.

3

IMPACT OF THE NEW WORLD

EUROPEAN AND NATIVE AMERICAN CULTURES COLLIDE

The New World and Old World collide in this monumental map entitled *Nova et accuratissima totius terrarum orbis tabula* (*New and Completely Accurate Map of the Whole World*), created ca. 1664 by Dutch cartographer Joan Blaeu.

IMPACT OF THE NEW WORLD

These new regions which we found and explored with the fleet…
we may rightly call a New World…a continent more densely peopled and
abounding in animals than our Europe or Asia or Africa.

—*Mundus Novus*, 1503, AN ANONYMOUS ADAPTATION OF AMERIGO VESPUCCI'S LETTER
TO LORENZO DE' MEDICI

The explorers who had begun to unlock the mysteries of the Atlantic were not searching for something new. They were seeking new routes to old lands. Christopher Columbus was not the only early European explorer who went to his grave convinced that he had discovered the western approach to the riches of the East. But something startlingly new *had* been found—whole new continents. It took several generations before information about these unexpected lands truly penetrated Europe, and once it did, the people of the Old World became increasingly curious and fascinated with what lay so many thousands of miles beyond. Through explorers' printed reports, dramatically illustrated maps, pamphlets, books, and artists' depictions, Europeans began to learn about places and people they had never imagined. And nothing fascinated them more than descriptions of those who had lived there long before the first white men appeared on the horizon.

LES SINGVLARITEZ

THE NATIVE AMERICANS

The existence of Native Americans was almost as much of a shock to Europeans as was the discovery of the Americas itself. This surprise was intensified by some of the earliest reports, accounts often both exaggerated and contradictory. One of the earliest was Amerigo Vespucci's description of the inhabitants of Brazil, sent to his patron Lorenzo de' Medici in 1501. "They go naked, both men and women," Vespucci reported. "They have well-shaped bodies, and in color nearly red; they have holes in their cheeks, lips, noses and ears, and stuff these holes with blue stones, crystals, marble and alabaster…They have no personal property but all things are in common. They all live together without a king and without a government, and every one is his own master…They eat one another…In the houses salted human flesh is hung up to dry. They live to be a hundred and fifty years old, and are seldom sick."

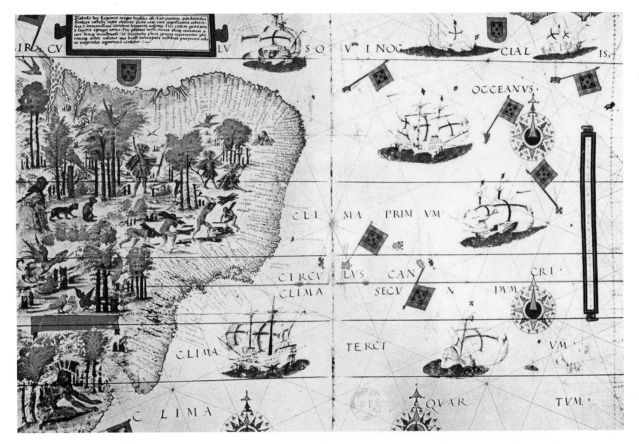

ABOVE: This map of Brazil is from as the *Atlas Miller* (named after its former owner), created in 1519 by master Portuguese mapmakers Lopo Homem and Pedro and Jorge Reinel and illustrated with exotic New World animals and natives at work by Flemish-born miniaturist António de Holanda. The atlas reflects the incredible wealth of anthropological and geographical knowledge gained by the Portuguese as they voyaged across the Atlantic and other seas.

LEFT: This depiction of Brazilian natives gathering cashews appeared in André Thévet's 1557 *Les Singularitez*.

RIGHT: Painter Albert Eckhout came to Brazil around 1637–44 as part of a Dutch scientific and artistic mission to document northeast Brazil's fauna, flora, and natives. He created hundreds of drawings and paintings, including this dynamic image called *Dance of the Tapuias*, depicting fearsome-looking warriors stamping their feet in a war dance while two women who look on whisper to each other about the performance.

A title page from a 1494–95 work by Italian poet Giuliani Dati, *Il secondo cantare dell'india* (*The Songs of the Indies*); the cyclops, pygmy, bigfoot, and other creatures included in the illustration sparked rumors of fantastical beasts in the New World.

The chief of the Floridian Outina (Utina) tribe defeats the Pontanou (Potano) with the aid of the French, 1564.

Illustrations for a New World

Published New World expedition accounts were typically illustrated with dramatic drawings and engravings that truly gave Europeans a glimpse into Native American culture. The two most important and influential New World illustrators were the Frenchman Jacques Le Moyne and the early English colonizer John White.

Jacques Le Moyne

Le Moyne accompanied the French explorer René Goulaine de Laudonnière on his mid-1560s attempt to found a colony in Florida that might serve as an asylum for the French Huguenots. Le Moyne's responsibility was to paint whatever he encountered. The renderings that he produced depicted the expedition's arrival on the Florida coast and its exploration of the area's rivers and islands. Most important, his illustrations depicted almost every aspect of the daily life of the native inhabitants, the Timucua, both in peace and at war. Many were scenes of the natives cooking their food and conducting religious ceremonies. One can only imagine the reaction of Europeans, however, as they viewed Le Moyne's drawings of the natives as they marched off to battle, scalped and disemboweled their victims, raucously rejoiced in their victories, and sacrificed their first born to their chiefs.

Timucua men cultivate a field while the women plant maize or beans.

Florida Native Americans attack and kill alligators.

Timucua women weep at the feet of the chieftain over the deaths of their husbands in battle.

Native men craft dugouts by burning the cores of a log and scraping the charred wood out with seashells.

John White

John White sailed to the New World with Richard Grenville in 1585. While arguably a more talented artist than Le Moyne, he was less an impartial portrayer than the Frenchman. Perhaps because he was intrinsically involved in his country's attempt to establish a colony in Virginia (he became governor of the colony of Roanoke in 1587), his depictions of Native Americans show nothing of their more warlike or brutal nature. Instead, he focused on such peaceful scenes as well-organized villages, fields of corn, and natives fishing, chopping timber, dancing, engaging in rituals, cooking, and eating. Most dramatic of all were White's portrayals of the Native Americans themselves—men, women,

children, conjurers, some tattooed or decorated with body paint, most adorned with their distinctive dress and jewelry. Both White's

and Le Moyne's drawings were later reproduced for publication by master Flemish engraver Theodor de Bry in the early 1590s.

Men and women fish in a canoe, while others in the shallows spear fish from the river.

Men and women gather around a campfire shaking rattles, for a religious ceremony.

Tribesmen roast fish on a wooden frame over a fire.

Another early account, by French explorer and Franciscan priest André Thévet, described the utopian habits of Brazilian natives in the French equatorial colony of France Antarctique. In his book, *Les Singularitez de la France Antarctique, autrement nommee Amerique* (*The Peculiarities of France Antarctique, also called America*), published in Paris in 1557, Thévet wrote:

> The natives desire nothing but is what necessary to their natural needs, so that they are not gourmets and do not go seek [exotic foods]; and their nourishment is healthy with the result that they do not know what it is to be sick. Rather, they live in continual health and peace and have no occasion to be envious of one another because of their property or patrimony—for they are all almost equal in possessions and are all rich in natural contentment and degree of poverty. They also have no place designated for administering justice because they do not wrong each other. They have no laws…other than that of nature.

ABOVE LEFT: **A regal 1776 portrait of the Mohawk chieftain Joseph Brant (Thayendanegea), a shrewd military leader and respected ally of the British during the American Revolution.**

ABOVE RIGHT: **The myth of the seductive Indian maiden was perpetuated through commercial packaging such as this illustration on a pouch of Pocahontas Chewing Tobacco, 1868.**

This burlesque poster from 1899 touted the promise of seeing "beautiful Indian maidens."

r WORTHY ALLIES

they'll in a dreadful Fright,
Refuge to the Woods in Flight;
ers then will quickly shake,
ngs shall restitution make.

W.ᵐ Charles del. et Sculp.

LEFT: **The epitome of the savage Native American— political cartoonist William Charles created this drawing to protest the brutal practice of scalping Americans during the War of 1812, which was endorsed by the British.**

79

IMPACT OF THE NEW WORLD

The written descriptions and artists' depictions of Native Americans had a greater impact on Europeans than simply providing them with their first views of a people far different from any they had ever known. These portrayals did nothing less than challenge traditional Old World beliefs about the origins and nature of humans, forcing Europeans to reconsider such notions as "savage" and "civilized"—although these extreme stereotypes would continue to persist for centuries. In the nineteenth century, Native Americans were portrayed as both savage hunters and brave warriors in James Fenimore Cooper's Leatherstocking tales, while François-René de Chateaubriand's 1801 popular novel *Atala* told the story of a chaste and virtuous Christian Indian maiden. In the first half of the twentieth century, Native Americas were typically depicted as bloodthirsty scalp-hunters. Even so, as historian Roger Schlesinger has stated in his book *In the Wake of Columbus* (1996): "The European encounter with Native Americans inevitably sharpened Europeans' awareness of the great diversity of human customs and practices throughout the world and, as a result, forced them to reexamine their own values and beliefs."

New World Flora and Fauna

Old World Europeans were also enthralled with descriptions and depictions of the animal life that inhabited the new lands. They were particularly taken with images of such exotic creatures as the brilliantly colored parrots and toucans that early explorers had encountered in Brazil, and with the strange-looking llama that Antonio Pigafetta, who had circled the world with Magellan, had written about. By the end of the first quarter of the 1500s, cartographers began adorning their maps with representations of these animals and with another creature that several mapmakers soon represented as the symbol of North American animal life. Various species of turkeys were known both in Europe and Asia, but none were quite like those pictured in the images produced in early America.

As intrigued as the Europeans were with the images of these and other New World animals, they were even more taken with the flora that had been discovered in the New World. It was so enduring a fascination that well into the nineteenth century the nations of Europe imported more exotic plants from the Americas than from any other region. Among the most popular of the plants that increasingly

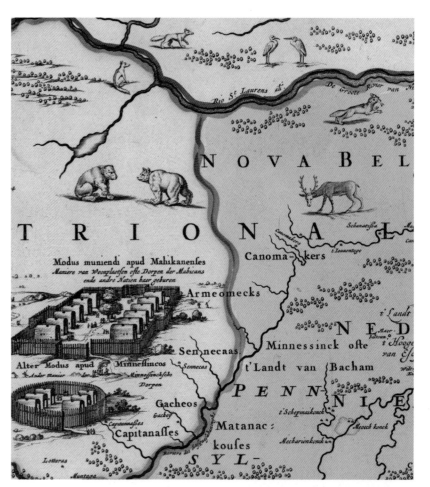

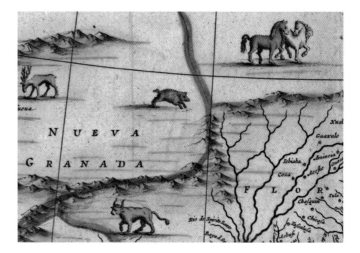

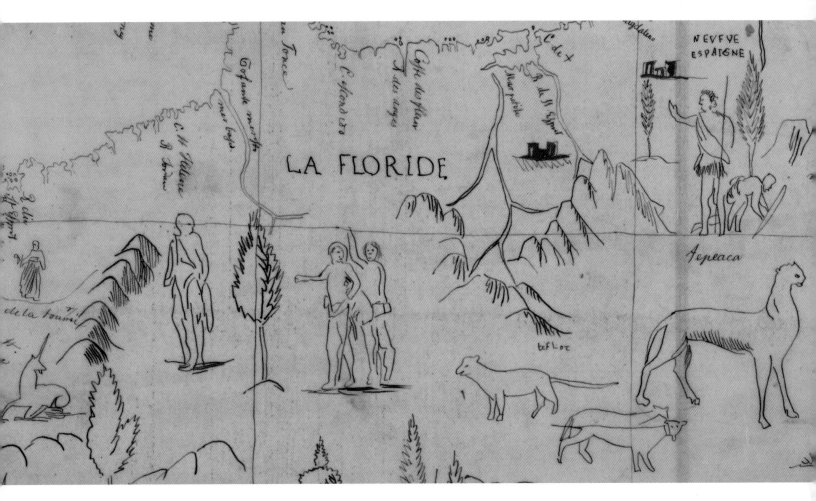

Text visible on the map: NEVVE ESPAIGNE, LA FLORIDE, Aepeaca

OPPOSITE TOP:
This detail from a map by Nicolaes Visscher of the Dutch colony of New Netherlands entitled *Novi Belgii Novaeque Angeliae* (ca. 1685) depicts several Mohican villages and bearlike creatures.

OPPOSITE BOTTOM:
A detail from a map of North and Central America by Dutch cartographer Johannes Janssonius, engraved by Henricus Hondius in 1658, depicts North American animals such as elk, boar, wild horses, and bison.

ABOVE:
Europeans were astounded when the first images of creatures they had never seen were published. To mapmakers and artists, the extraordinary colors and shapes of these unfamiliar animals represented both the beauty and the exotic nature of our Americas. "So many species could not have entered Noah's ark," wrote Amerigo Vespucci, as recorded in *Mundus novus* (1503) of the animals he encountered in the New World. And none of the depictions of these animals more captivated Europeans than did those of the llamas and alpacas of Central and South America. This detail of a French map of North America and the Caribbean, originally created for Henry II of France in 1542, includes alpacas (although they were native to South America) and even a unicorn among the Native American figures. The figures and text were drawn upside down on the map.

FOLLOWING PAGES:
Italian cartographer Paolo de Forlani created this world map in 1565. Strange and new creatures roam the North American plains, including an alligator and a half-goat/half-bird beast.

CIRCVLO ARTICO

Taila

TERRA INCOCNITA

Lago

NVEVA FRANZA   Golfo Labuelta   C d

LARCADIA

C de Mul

Quinnera   Montagnar

Tonton   Isleo

teanch   Modano

Cyuit   s.

Zangay   Tiguas   C d S Maria

Ara   Gra

Coco   Quimechas   Ipedra

R de S Giouani

Lacrus

Labermuda

Cazones   Tamaca   Cagnaueral

Madaleua   Collaoitot

LE SETE   OCEANO OCCIDENTALE

CITA   TROPERA

PRO   P Lana   PA   LA

Cimpaga   Tabursa   Ancones   FLO

B Canoa   Vicicla Loaton   RI   Babania   Lucaio

ONZA S Alad   Cipola   S Michiel   DA   Guanaban

B dS Chiamatlam

s.pablo   Loacam   Imaquia   TROPICO DE CANCRO

Balci-   Villa   CVBA   Maraguano

nas Xalico ricca   Cayacos

Tunstitam

Acapuleo   Lucatam   Iamuca   Spagnola Anatana

Virgines

Tutatipea C ds ani   Foua   S Ioan   Elangilo

Higneras   uico Lacerana   Labardada

Guatuleo   Cariaz   Planigoa

Guatima Lalaguna   Aidea Beragua   Desrada

sla   Beragua   Matinino

Lucia

Rabago

Latruuia

Arabi Erzeni   C S Romano   Bocca d'drago

Elzeni Cuela   Chenela   Gaira

L SVR   Cuela   Zuola C S Romano C dpanya Calua

P hermosso CAS   Bruczuola   Machina C Canoas

S Michiel TIGLIA   Paria

Pipiua   Paria

Cilos Queque   DE LORO Tierra ma lana

P Lerno

R des Nic

EOVINOTIALE   Barias   Aucha Iumbu   R Sal-

125 120 115 110 105 100 95 90   85 80   70 70 65 60 50 40 75 70

P Lana Piura   Quito QVITO Alber

P prieto Ribamba   Quaragui Tierra delos

S Tiago   humos

Y delos tubarones   C blanco   PERV   Humos

S Michiel   Garuca   Maraguon rio

C d'neus   Vacas   Rd

Y de S Pablo   C stamaria Chilasinga   B della

Tumbez   PRO   Buza

R dfrac

Vaza

S Gero

BRASIL   R del cos

S Helena Curcho CANAS   PRO   M Pasa

Arichipa   Mosso   Geneto   Ostia

B Pa

B

S Michel   Sal

Cazamalea Tarajaca   P de san   Sierra

ATACAMA   Sebastiano Luca

Pachirama

Charcas   Lacauane P d S Bastiano

Mepertas R d In

Barca

Ormigo   PLATA P delos

Nicatur Patos Y dd repa

The cardinal held a particular fascination for those in the Old World. Not long after the first cardinals were brought across the Atlantic, they became the most popular cage bird in Europe. This beautiful engraving was by Alexander Lawson, after Alexander Wilson, and appeared in the latter's *American Ornithology*, 1810.

1. Cardinal Grosbeak. 2. Female & egg. 3. Red Tanager. 4. Female & egg.

Of all the New World creatures, it was the indigenous wild turkey that most captivated artists and mapmakers, many of who presented the animal as symbolizing the New World. It was no wonder that some two centuries later, Benjamin Franklin would campaign for the designation of the wild turkey as America's national bird. This engraving of a wild turkey is from John James Audubon's *Birds of America, 1827–38.*

BELOW: Tobacco (*Nicotiana tabacum*) was a deceptively beautiful plant, as seen here in this German botanical illustration from 1885. England's King James I (1566–1625) spoke for many of his countrymen when he complained in his book *A Counterblaste to Tobacco* (1604) that smoking was "a custome loathsome to the eye, hatefull to the nose, harmfull to the braine, dangerous to the lungs, and in the blacke stinking fume thereof, neerest resembling the horrible Stigian smoke of the pit that is bottomelesse." Although the book was anonymously published, its authorship was an open secret.

OPPOSITE: This illustration shows the Dutch physician Dr. Giles Everard, happily smoking a pipe in his library. The image was the frontispiece to his book *Panacea; or the Universal Medicine, Being a Discovery of the Wonderfull Vertues of Tobacco*, which was published in Antwerp in 1587 and in London in 1659. Ironically, Everard ruminated in his book on the possibility that tobacco might eliminate the need for doctors in the future: "It is no great friend to physicians, though it be a physical plant; for the very smoke of it is held to be a great antidote against all venome and pestilential diseases."

appeared in gardens throughout the Old World were sunflowers, magnolias, dahlias, and dogwood.

Much of this was due to one man and one book. His name was Nicolás Monardes, a Spanish naturalist and physician who had first experimented with new world tobacco plants in Seville. His 1565 book *Historia medicinal de las cosas que se traen de nuestras Indias Occidentales* (*Medical Study of the Products Imported from our West Indian Possessions*, published in English as *Joyfull Newes out of the Newe Founde Worlde*), became, for more than a century, the most influential medical book in the world. "And as there are discovered new regions, new kingdoms, and new provinces by our Spaniards," Monardes wrote, "they have brought us new medicines and new remedies wherewith they cure and make whole many infirmities, which if we lack them, were incurable, and without any remedy."

The most important new "remedy," he felt, was tobacco, and in his book, Monardes made the bold, unequivocal claim that the plant could cure every type of headache, as well as stomachache, rheumatism, colic, and, in fact, any pain in any part of the body. Tobacco, claimed Monardes, also cured a wide range of other conditions, such as tumors, poisonous bites, burns, and obstructions in the intestines or chest. Depending on the illness, the plant was to be rubbed on the body as a hot poultice, mixed into sugar syrup and drunk, or

OPPOSITE: Tobacco became so important as a New World export that in many artistic depictions it was included as yet another symbol of America. In the early nineteenth century, several ornamental versions of the Declaration of Independence were published. This one, designed by Thomas Binns in 1818, includes tobacco plants (visible at bottom above the seal of Georgia).

BELOW: One of the most humorous illustrations dealing with tobacco was this one from the 1904 edition of D. H. Montgomery's *The Beginner's American History* (originally published in Boston in 1893). The picture depicts the apocryphal incident that supposedly took place when Sir Walter Raleigh's servant, after encountering his master enjoying his first bowl of tobacco, thought he was on fire and doused him with a pitcher of water in order to "save" him.

dried and smoked. Other authors, perhaps wishing to capitalize on the success of Monardes's book, also published medical tracts repeating the Spanish physician's claims and often adding new ailments that, they asserted, could be cured by tobacco.

At the same time, other accounts, including those from the New World, presented a very different view of tobacco's effects. Among them was an observation written by the Italian traveler Girolamo Benzoni in his *La Historia del mondo nuovo* (*History of the New World…Shewing His Travels in America, from AD 1541 to 1556*). Benzoni described the natives' experiences with tobacco: "The smoke goes in the mouth, the throat, the head, and they retain it as long as they can, for they find a pleasure in it and so much do they fill themselves with this cruel smoke, that they lose their reason. And there are some that take so much of it that they fall down as if they were dead, and remain the greater part of the day or night stupefied. Some men are found who are content with imbibing only enough of this smoke to make them giddy, and no more. See what a pestiferous and wicked poison from this devil this must be."

Despite such warnings, by the early 1600s the smoking of tobacco—not for medicinal purposes but for the sheer

Botanical Treasures

The discovery of the Americas coincided with the emergence of botany as a scholarly discipline. The relation of a vast new array of extraordinary trees, flowers, and other flora revolutionized the new science. Botanists throughout the Old World eagerly awaited the arrival of imported specimens and studied artists' drawings intently. And, since Europe shared the same high altitudes with the Americas, most New World plants could be successfully grown there. Eventually the plants of the New World would transform the appearance of Europe.

Among the New World delicacies that most captivated Europeans was the pineapple, which they found both exotic and delicious. Like the turkey, it was often depicted by artists and mapmakers as a symbol of the new lands. Here, the pineapple is exquisitely rendered in a nineteenth-century Spanish engraving.

Flos Solis maior.

ABOVE: German pharmacist Basilius Besler was asked by the bishop of Eichstätt to create a botanical garden at Willibaldsburg Castle in 1597. Besler's famous plant atlas, *Hortus eystettensis*, published in 1613, describes and illustrates the hundreds of plants in this garden, including the sunflower. Long cultivated by the Native Americans as a source for food, oil, building material, and for use in religious ceremonies, the sunflower was introduced into Europe within the first decade of Columbus's arrival in the New World.

RIGHT: Once known as the "Laurel Tree of Carolina," the magnolia astounded early explorers with its beauty. It elicited an equal reaction in Europe where it became the first New World tree planted in London's Kew Gardens. This engraving is from English naturalist Mark Catesby's *The Natural History of Carolina, Florida and the Bahama Islands*, 1731.

> " *And as there are discovered new regions… they have brought us new medicines and new remedies where with they cure and make the whole many infirmities.* "
>
> —Nicholás Monardes, *Historia medicinal …*, 1565

pleasure of it—spread first through the upper strata of European society and then throughout the lower classes as well. It was a development that not only affected Old World society but also would have vital ramifications for those American colonies that would come to depend upon the ever-increasing popularity of tobacco for their very survival.

Tobacco was far from the only New World plant claimed by sixteenth-century explorers, naturalists, and scientists to have healing effects. And many, such as bloodroot, cocoa, copal, sassafras, and sarsaparilla, to name a few, eventually proved to have genuine medicinal value. But another category of American plants had an even greater impact upon the people of Europe—food plants.

FOOD OF THE GODS

Before Columbus, the diet of Europeans had remained basically unchanged for tens of thousands of years, based mainly on oats, barley, and wheat. Within a quarter century of his first voyage, the European diet became richer, more varied, and more nutritious. As Roger Schlesinger wrote in his book, *In the Wake of Columbus*: "As far as dietary habits are concerned, no other series of events in all world history brought as much significant change as did [the discovery of the Americas]." The list of foods that made their way into Europe is extensive and includes maize (corn), squash, pumpkin, avocado, papaya, cassava, vanilla, tomatoes, potatoes, sweet potatoes (yams), strawberries, and beans of almost every variety.

The potato was one of the first American foods to be transported to Europe. Valued by the conquistadores, they made it a key item in the diet of their sailors. The potato then spread to England and Scotland, and to Ireland where it became the staple of the Irish diet.

It was also the Spanish who discovered the tomato, first distributing it throughout their Caribbean possessions and then bringing it to Europe. In both Italy and Great Britain, the tomato was first thought to be poisonous, and it was not until the 1700s that the fruit became widely eaten. As was the case with sweet potatoes, which were regarded by some Europeans as having aphrodisiac-like qualities, the tomato was also viewed in some circles as having medicinal value, particularly in the treatment of diarrhea, diphtheria, and even cholera. Actually, some of these claims may not have been as farfetched as they seem since many Old World ailments were caused by the lack of fresh fruits and vegetables.

Those Europeans first in the Americas also encountered two other important food-producing plants. Called *yuca* in Spanish and *macaxeira* in Portuguese, cassava was a basic food of Native Americans long before Columbus stumbled

Chap. 61. Of Turkie Corne.

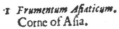
1 *Frumentum Asiaticum.*
Corne of Asia.

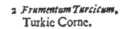
2 *Frumentum Turcicum.*
Turkie Corne.

¶ *The kindes.*

OF Turkie cornes there be diuers sorts, notwithstanding of one stocke or kindred, consisting of sundry coloured graines, wherein the difference is easie to be discerned, and for the better explanation of the same, I haue set forth to your view certaine eares of different colours, in their full and perfect ripenesse, and such as they shew themselues to be when their skinne or filme doth open it selfe in the time of gathering.

The forme of the eares of Turky Wheat.

3 *Frumenti Indici spica.*
Turkie wheat in the huske, as also naked or bare.

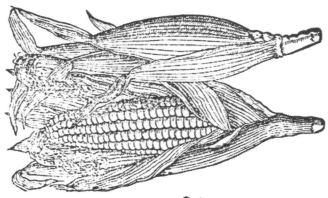

G 3

RIGHT: The tomato was called *pomme d'amour* (apple of love) by the French, likely because of a mistranslation. French botanist Joseph Pitton de Tournefort included the tomato in this 1719 edition of his *Elémens de botanique* (1694).

BELOW: Among the first images of the New World that Europeans encountered were those with which cartographers adorned their maps. This map detail from *Carte géographique de la Nouvelle France*, featuring representations of Native Americans and New World flora and fauna, was drawn in 1612 by Samuel de Champlain—widely regarded as the father of French settlement in the New World.

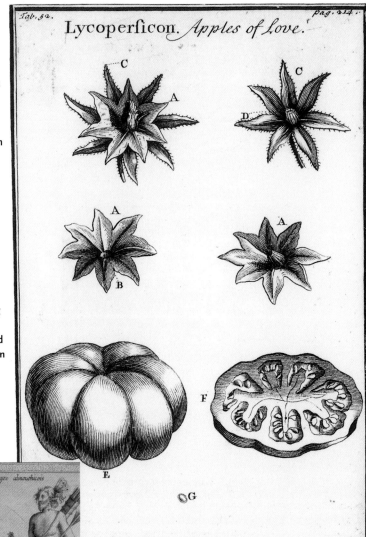

OPPOSITE: Every one of the plants in this print—an 1804 engraving after a drawing by eighteenth-century Swiss botanist Johann Gessner—was cultivated by Native American farmers, and none were known to Europeans before the arrival of Columbus. In the end, the food-bearing plants of the New World proved far more valuable to those across the Atlantic than the gold that so many of the explorers had vainly sought.

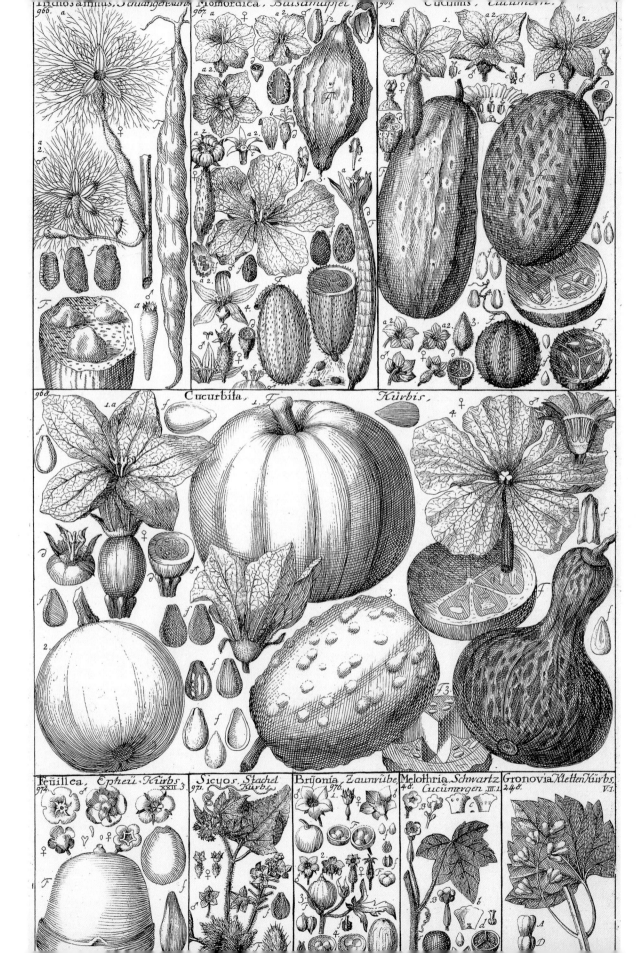

Trichosanthes, Schlangenkürbis. 966.

Momordica, Balsamapfel. 967.

Cucumis, Cucumern. 969.

Cucurbita, Kürbis. 968.

Feüillea, Epheü-Kürbs. XXII.3. 974.

Sicyos, Stachel Kürbs. 971.

Bryonia, Zaunrübe. 976.

Melothria, Schwartz Cucumergen. III.1.248.

Gronovia Ketten Kürbs. VI.1.

OPPOSITE: **African slaves work a sugar plantation in Hispaniola, in this 1595 engraving from part five of Theodor De Bry's *Descriptiones Americae*.**

upon the Indies. The early explorers found that once peeled, the plant could be grated into flour and turned into bread. By the mid 1600s, many Europeans regarded bread made from cassava preferable to the bread made from wheat, which, for centuries, had been among the most basic of Old World foods.

Tapioca, also made from cassava root, eventually became a European delicacy, as did a drink made from the cocoa plant. By the time that Hernán Cortés (see Chapter 4) and his men witnessed Aztecs drinking *chocolatl*, South and Central American natives had been consuming the beverage for hundreds of years. Cortés also learned that the natives regarded the drink as having properties that were instrumental in fighting fatigue. It was a belief that was shared by many Spaniards, and also eventually by members of the French court, when what became known as chocolate was carried across the Atlantic.

As diet transforming as all these newly introduced foods became, sugar, perhaps, had the greatest impact of all. As ever-increasing amounts of sugar were transported from New World plantations to Europe, the types of foods that were eaten, and just as significantly, the ways in which they were cooked, were changed forever. Before the early 1500s, sugar was sold in European apothecary shops where, because of its scarcity, only the rich could afford it. But as

Aztecs are shown roasting and grinding cacao beans to make chocolate, in Scottish author John Ogilby's *America*, 1671, which he translated from Dutch historian Arnoldus Montanus's work *Die nieuwe en onbekende weereld* (*The New and Unknown World*), published the same year in Amsterdam. In addition to using cacao beans to make *chocolatl*, the Aztecs also traded them as currency.

"What in times past was scarcely found but in Arabia ... or India, ... today the confectioner knows well how to apply to our use."

—André Thévet, *Les Singularitez*, 1557

sugar-laden ships arrived in Old World ports, prices tumbled and sugar became an important foodstuff for the masses. At the time, honey was both expensive and in short supply, but even if that had not been the case, most people found sugar to be a much more desirable sweetener. As a result, tea and coffee drinking gained a popularity that would never diminish.

Even more important, the availability of sugar led to the proliferation of confections and jams that soon graced tables

BELOW: **Vasco de Quiroga, first bishop of Michoacán, Mexico, and an admirer of sixteenth-century statesman Sir Thomas More, wrote in a 1535 letter to Spanish king Charles V: "Not, in vain but with much cause and reason is this called the New World, not because it is newly found, but because... almost everything as was** **the first and golden age." More based his 1516 book** *Utopia* **on stories that had been related by Amerigo Vespucci. It was a theme also expressed in allegorical representations such as this one, a cartouche from a 1782 edition of a seventeenth-century Dutch New World map titled** *America, the Land of Plenty.*

German artist Georg Flegel painted this scene of confections adorning a European table around 1600, an array of delicacies that would not have been possible without the importation of sugar from the New World.

throughout Europe. "What in times past was scarcely found but in Arabia…or India," wrote André Thévet, "and [which] the Ancients used only in medicines, today the confectioner knows well how to apply to our use." Nowhere was this more in evidence than in the Portuguese capital of Lisbon where, as historian Stuart Schwartz has documented in his book *Tropical Babylons: Sugar and the Making of the Atlantic World, 1450–1680* (2004), some thirty confectionary shops were kept busy making sugared pastries.

The making of jams and preserves not only provided even the lower classes with an important new and nutritious type of food, but it afforded European women a whole new pastime. Writing of the way in which women, particularly merchant's wives, found satisfaction in jam-making, late sixteenth-century French agronomist Olivier des Serres stated: "Thus it will be [in the preparation of jams] whence the honorable lady will find pleasure, continuing the proof of the subtlety of her spirit. So she can secure pleasure and honor when, on the unexpected arrival of her relatives and friends, she will cover the table for them with diverse jams carefully prepared."

Sugar's impact on the European diet went beyond jams and confections and the sweetening of tea, coffee, and other beverages. Such leftover foods as rice and bread could now be given new life and a whole new taste when sprinkled with sugar and reheated. Fruits and vegetables could be inexpensively preserved when immersed in a sugary syrup. Sugar's popularity also led to the introduction of a host of new cooking utensils and accoutrements, including new types of saucepans, pie plates, cookie molds, sugar pots, sugar spoons, and tongs.

Nothing better demonstrated the exalted role that sugar had gained in European society than what became known as the sugar banquet. In the palace of England's Henry VIII, cooks not only adorned the royal table with every type of pastry, marmalade, jam, and sugar-coated spices but also added figures of saints, soldiers, even St. Paul's Cathedral—all made out of sugar. The greatest sugar banquet of all took place in the royal palace in Brussels in November 1565 during the festivities accompanying the marriage of Alexander Farnese, the future Duke of Parma, to Princess Maria of Portugal. One of the highlights of the extravagant celebration was a panorama of the princess's journey to Brussels, set on a long table. The panorama included squadrons of ships, whales, dolphins, sea monsters, even a ship in flames with passengers throwing themselves overboard. Included were depictions of the princess's arrival in the city, her carriage ride to the palace, people cheering her appearance, and views of Brussels including houses, churches, theaters, and an animal park with lions and a herd

There was so much new about the New World that for several generations Europeans had difficulty making sense of all that had been discovered. For many, what had been discovered placed the Americas in the realm of nothing less that a new Eden, a land which, although inhabited by strange creatures and strange people, presented unprecedented opportunities for a fresh start in life. John White captured this attitude in his image of Adam and Eve in Virginia, shown here in a 1590 engraving by Theodor de Bry for *A Briefe and True Report of the New Found Land of Virginia*, by British scholar Thomas Hariot.

of elephants ridden by Indian keepers. All told, there were more than three thousand pieces—every one carved entirely out of sugar.

By the 1570s, the explorers' and travelers' accounts and the artist's depictions combined with the artifacts and products brought back to Europe created an image of the New World that, in many cases, bordered on the utopian. It was a notion bolstered in no small measure by the allegorical representations of the Americas that increasingly appeared. Many of these often elaborate allegories contained symbols of New World grandeur—lush vegetation, exotic animals, and natives planting crops or holding gold-mining tools. In many of the representations, America was depicted as a bold, attractive woman attired in feathered headdress, carrying a bow and a sheath of arrows.

The allegorical representations were, of course, based on their creators' imaginations. But exaggerated or not, what many Europeans, surrounded by continental warfare and unrelenting poverty, saw in the illustrations was a whole new promise, an opportunity, if one was willing to hazard the voyage across the still-perilous Atlantic, to transfer one's hopes to a whole New World.

4

COLONIZATION

SETTLING A NEW WORLD

The Embarkation of the Pilgrims, commissioned for the U.S. Capitol Rotunda in 1837, was painted by Robert W. Weir and depicts the Pilgrims gathered in prayer on the deck of the ship *Speedwell*.

COLONIZATION

There is but one entrance by sea into this Country, and that is at the mouth of a very goodly bay … Within is a country that may have the prerogative over the most pleasant places known … Heaven and earth never agreed better to frame a place for man's habitation.

—CAPTAIN JOHN SMITH, *A Map of Virginia: With a Description of the Countrey, the Commodities, People, Government and Religion*, 1612

Although it did not take place immediately, the westward transatlantic movement of people, spawned by the discovery of the New World and news of what had been found, was, as historian Bernard Bailyn has put it in *Atlantic History: Concepts and Contours* (2005), "one of the greatest events in recorded history. It's magnitude and consequences are beyond measure. It forms the foundation of American history and is basic…to the history of Europe, Africa, and even, to a lesser extent of Asia."

THE INDIES: PRIZED POSSESSIONS

The first genuine beginnings of the settlement of the Americas was due to the efforts of a man who, in great measure, has been lost to history. A commander in the Spanish chivalric order of Alcántara, Nicolás de Ovando, a favorite of Queen Isabella, was sent by the Crown to assume the governorship of Hispaniola. Sailing with thirty ships (the largest fleet that had ever crossed the Atlantic to the New World), Ovando left Spain in February 1502. The twenty-five-hundred people he brought with him included colonists, soldiers, and priests. Among the colonists was thirty-one-year-old Francisco Pizarro, destined to make his own infamous mark in the New World. Also aboard one of Ovando's ships was Bartholomé de las Casas, a Dominican priest who even-

tually became a champion of the rights of the natives of the Americas and who, in his book, *A Short Account of the Destruction of the Indies* (1552), documented the atrocities committed against the indigenous peoples by Pizarro and his fellow Spaniards.

Ovando's arrival in Hispaniola was greeted by a native revolt. In a harbinger of the Spanish presence in the New World, he carried out a series of campaigns in which thousands of natives were killed. On the positive side, Ovando established several cities in Hispaniola, developed a successful mining industry, and introduced the cultivation of sugarcane, the island's first major commodity.

Within a decade, the Spanish population in Hispaniola rose to some ten thousand; sugar products, as well as gold, copper, and other metals from the mines, were shipped back to Spain in increasingly greater amounts. Such an enterprise required many workers and, as early as 1496, both in the Canaries and on Hispaniola, enslaved natives had constituted the backbone of the labor force. But by the time Ovando arrived in Hispaniola, the native population had been severely depleted by the conditions of enslavement and the ravages of diseases transmitted by the Spaniards.

Ovando, however, had carried with him authorization from Queen Isabella to import Spanish-born slaves of African origin that had been born "in the power of Christians."

The great supply of labor required to grow, harvest, and ship the various crops of the islands led to the importation of forced labor. It was on the islands that slavery was introduced into the New World. This engraving depicts African slaves working on an indigo plantation in the Caribbean; the overseer stands to the right of center. It first appeared in the *Histoire générale des Antilles habitées par les Francois* (*General History of the Antilles Inhabited by the French*), 1667–71, by French botanist and missionary Jean Baptiste Du Tertre.

Ovando responded by importing the first slaves of African origin ever brought into the Americas: *negros ladinos* (Christianized, Spanish-speaking blacks, often born in Spain) and *bozales* (blacks brought directly from Africa). It was however, a short-lived endeavor. As documented by Cuban historian José Antonio Saco in his *Historia de la esclavitud de la raza african en el Nuevo Mundo* (*History of Slavery of the African Race in the New World*, 1876), Ovando soon reversed course. In 1503 he petitioned Queen Isabella that no more *ladinos* or *bozales* be sent to Hispaniola, stating as his reason the fact that, once in Hispaniola, many of the Iberian Negroes ran away and those who did not escape "demoralized the natives." Isabella acceded to Ovando's wishes, but the precedence of the importation of black slaves into the Americas had been set.

That so many of these beginnings took place on New World islands rather than on the mainland was not accidental. Throughout the first two centuries of American colonization, islands such as Jamaica, Puerto Rico, Cuba, Barbados, Hispaniola, Guadeloupe, St. Martin, St. Croix, and dozens of others were more highly prized than the continents. And although the sixteenth-century Spanish historian Francisco López de Gómara was obviously carried away when he proclaimed that "the greatest event since the creation of the world (excluding the incarnation and death of him who created it) is the discovery of the Indies," what was true was that, until the American continents were adequately explored and the natural resources contained there were discovered, it was the Atlantic and Caribbean Islands—with their climate and soil ideal for the cultivation of sugar and other treasured crops—that were the prized possessions. It was no accident

The islands were the first places where trade between the New World and the Old was established. This ca. 1639 watercolor of Havana, Cuba, is attributed to Dutch mapmaker Joan Vinckeboons (Johannes Vingboons in Dutch), cartographer to the Prince of Nassau.

that the first trade between the Americas, Europe, and Africa was begun from the islands and no wonder that the European powers fought so bitterly over them and that so many of them changed hands so often.

The Continent
and the Conquistadores

When Europeans finally did begin to settle the mainland, they entered a world much different from the primitive wilderness that generations of historians led their readers to believe. As Charles C. Mann wrote in his groundbreaking book *1491: New Revelations of the Americas before Columbus* (2005), scientific evidence has revealed that long before Columbus first set sail, there were probably more

ABOVE: **This map, drawn by Dutch- or German-born Herman Moll (1654–1732)— one of England's premier mapmakers in the Age of Discovery—shows the vast array of New World islands that not only launched Europe into its New World endeavors but also provided the springboard for the settlement of the American mainland. The map appeared in Moll's seminal atlas *The World Described* (1715–54).**

OPPOSITE: **Spanish historian Antonio de Herrera y Tordesillas illustrated the mysterious gods of the Aztecs, along with a portrait of conquistador Diego Velázquez de Cuéllar, on the title page of a *Descripción de las Indias Ocidentales (Description of the West Indies)*, a supplement to his masterwork *Historia general de los hechos de los Castellanos en las islas y tierra firme del Mar Océano (General History of the Deeds of the Castilians on the Islands and Mainland of the Ocean Sea)* (1601–15).**

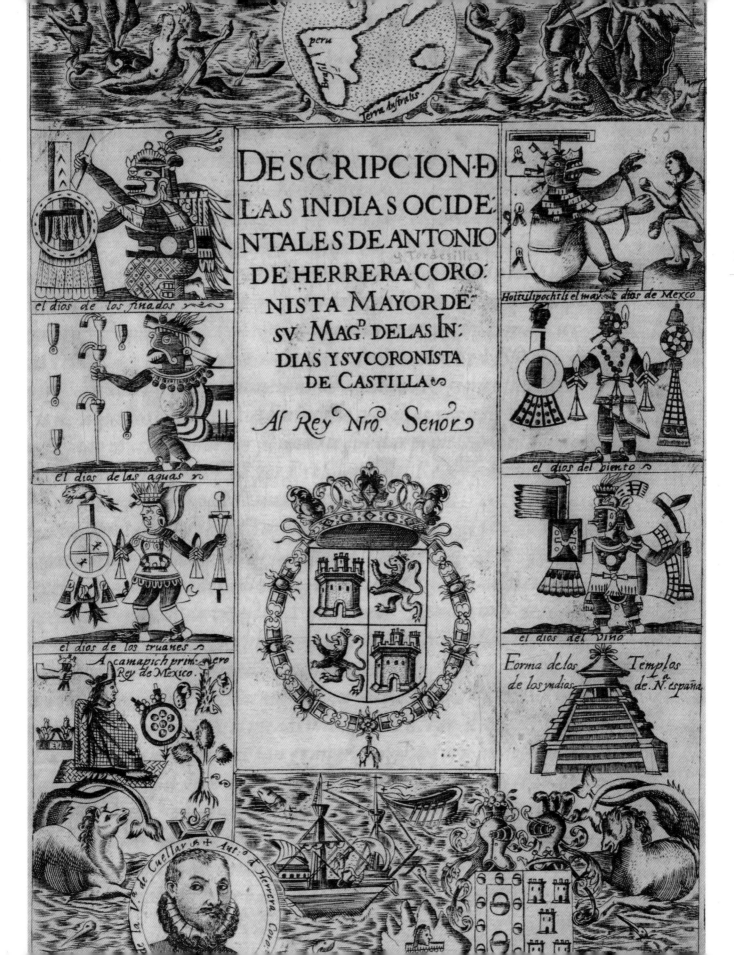

DESCRIPCION Đ
LAS INDIAS OCIDE
NTALES DE ANTONIO
DE HERRERA CORO:
NISTA MAYOR DE
SV MAGᴰ DE LAS IN:
DIAS Y SV CORONISTA
DE CASTILLA

Al Rey Nrō. Senor

el dios de los finados

Holtuilipochtli el mayᵒᵣ dios de Mexco

el dios de las aguas

el dios del biento

el dios de los truanes

A camapich prim̄ ero Rey de Mexico.

el dios del vino

Forma de los Templos de los yndias La de N. españa

> *"We came to serve God and his Majesty, to give light to those who were in darkness, and to grow rich, as all men desire to do."*
>
> —Bernal Díaz del Castillo

people making their home in what became Central and South America than in all of Europe. Some of the New World cities, built before the Egyptian pyramids, had populations well over 100,000, with as many as 250,000 living on their outskirts. Several of these cities featured wide, clean streets, beautiful gardens, and an efficient system of running water. Some of the native groups had developed highly sophisticated agricultural methods, including the cross-breeding of corn, which *Science* magazine characterized in a 2003 article as "man's first, and perhaps the greatest, feat of genetic engineering."

The first Europeans to enter the American mainland in great numbers, the Spanish, of course knew nothing of these sophisticated societies. The men who came to be known as *conquistadores* (conquerors) entered the New World looking for wealth in the form of gold and silver, and they were prepared to use any means to obtain it. They had also been charged with bringing the Spanish gospel as well as Spanish law to whatever peoples they conquered; but it was riches that were foremost in their minds. As conquistador Bernal Díaz del Castillo stated in his book *Historia verdadera de la conquista de la Nueva España* (*The True History of the Conquest of New Spain*), published posthumously in 1632: "We came to serve God and his Majesty, to give light to those who were in darkness, and to grow rich, as all men desire to do."

Mayan codices, folding books written in Mayan hieroglyphic script on bark paper, were sophisticated records of ancient Mayan civilization, religion, astronomy, and astrology. The Dresden Codex, a detail of which is shown here, was created in the Yucatán Peninsula by the Maya around 1200–50 CE. It was discovered in Dresden, Germany, in 1739.

Indicative of the advanced culture of the people who inhabited the Americas long before the first European explorers arrived was the Aztec sun stone. Unearthed in Mexico City (site of the Aztec capital Tenochtitlan) in 1790, the enormous stone weighs about twenty-four tons and measures twelve feet across. The enigmatic stone functioned as a ritual calendar with pictographs and hieroglyphs symbolizing days and months (the Aztec calendar was based on the interrelation of a sacred year of 260 days with the natural year of 365 days) as well as a symbolic representation of Aztec cosmology. This replica of the stone, located in El Paso, was cast from the original at the Museo Nacional de Antropología in Mexico City.

The first conquistador to set foot on what is now United States soil was Juan Ponce de León, a former governor of Puerto Rico and a member of Christopher Columbus's second expedition. Authorized by the king to establish a mainland colony in a place called Bimini (a mythical island believed to contain the Fountain of Youth), Ponce de León instead landed on the mainland, on the northeast coast of present-day Florida, on April 2, 1513. Ponce de León named the land Florida (the Spanish word for "flowery") either because he arrived during *Pasqua Florida* (Spanish for "Flowery Passover" or Easter season) or because he was so taken with the vibrant vegetation he encountered. According to long-standing legend, Ponce de León came to the mainland seeking not only slaves for the Spanish sugar plantations and untold riches but also the Fountain of Youth, a spring whose restorative waters had been written about long before the European Age of Exploration. While he may have heard of the supposed Fountain of Youth, there is no hard evidence that Ponce de León was either motivated by or indeed searched for the fabled spring. It was only after his death in July 1521, particularly in Gonzalo Fernández de Oviedo's *Historia general y natural de las Indias* (1535) (*General and Natural History of the Indies*), that such a story arose.

After landing in Florida, Ponce de León explored its southern coast, charting the rivers he encountered before returning first to Puerto Rico and then to Spain. He returned to Florida in 1521, this time to establish a settlement. His two ships and colonizing party of about two hundred men, which included farmers, craftsmen, and priests, landed on Florida's southwest coast. Soon, however, they were attacked by natives, and in the ensuing battle, Ponce de León was struck

An undated engraving portrait of Ponce de León, explorer of the land he named Florida. He wrote to his king on February 10, 1521 of his goal to settle Florida "that the name of Christ may be praised there, and Your Majesty served with the fruit that land produces."

The Fountain of Youth was
a subject of fascination for
countless medieval artists,
such as this fanciful
interpretation by German
artist Lucas Cranach the
Elder, 1546.

by a poisoned arrow. The would-be colonists then took to the ships and fled to Cuba where Ponce de León died of his wound.

In 1519, six years after Ponce de León claimed Florida for Spain, a much more ambitious and daring conquistador, Hernán Cortés, set out on what has been termed "history's greatest march of conquest." Since the time the Spanish had been exploring and settling the Caribbean islands, they had heard rumors of an opulent Indian empire located on the mainland. Actually, it was the land of the Aztecs, whose magnificent city Tenochtitlan stood on the site of present-day Mexico City. On April 22, 1519, Cortés landed near what is today the city of Veracruz. Although estimates vary, it is safe to say that he had with him between four hundred and six hundred men.

As he made his way inland, Cortés was forced to fight continual battles with the Tlaxcala, a union of four native kingdoms that had managed to keep its independence despite periodic attempts to defeat it by the greatest native force in Mexico, the Triple Alliance. Comprised of three Aztec city-states—Tenochtitlan, Texcoco, and Tlacapon—the Triple Alliance had ruled the entire region of the Valley of Mexico since 1428.

Cortés launched his invasion with three weapons that would prove decisive in the Spanish conquest of the Americas:

horses, cannon, and steel swords. Because of these weapons, along with body armor, none of which the Indians had ever encountered, Cortés and his men, although greatly outnumbered, won every battle with the Tlaxcala. But with each victory came a reduction of the Spanish forces, so serious an attrition that Cortés found himself on the brink of defeat.

But then unexpectedly, the four Tlaxcala kings presented Cortés with a proposal. They would stop attacking him if he would join them in a combined attack on Tenochtitlan, the most powerful of the Triple Alliance city-states. It was an offer that Cortés could not refuse.

In November 1519, Cortés and his men and some twenty-thousand Tlaxcalans entered Tenochtitlan, led by a number of the Spanish mounted on horses (the astounded Aztecs believed they were one terrifying creature made of animal and armor-plated man). No one was more astounded by the invading force, however, than Montezuma, the ruler of the Aztec Empire. For generations, many histories carried the story that when Montezuma first became aware of Cortés's presence, he thought he was the Toltec war god Quetzalcoatl, who had gone into exile some five hundred years earlier and was now returning to destroy the Aztec Empire. Modern historians, however, have refuted this story, basing their findings on the fact that nowhere in all the conquistadores' writings, including the many lengthy detailed letters that Cortés wrote

ATLANTIC OCEAN

to his Spanish king, Charles V, is there mention of this belief on Montezuma's part.

What has been documented is the fact that Tenochtitlan, with its wide streets, its bustling marketplaces, its beautifully carved buildings, and its long aqueducts that carried water into the city from far-off mountains, amazed the Spaniards. But Cortés knew that there was no time to spend admiring this city that was larger than any in all of Europe. Aware of the size of the army that Montezuma had at his command, he captured the Aztec ruler, held him prisoner in his own palace, and then had him killed.

The events so shocked the Aztecs that it took them some seven months before they retaliated. Then, led by their new ruler Cuitahuac, they mounted a fierce assault on the invaders, forcing them into the city's narrow alleys where their horses were of little use. It was an overwhelming Aztec victory in which the Spanish and their allies were forced to flee the city, but not before thousands of them were killed.

Cortés, aware that he was fortunate to still be alive, decided to flee with his remaining forces to Tlaxcala. He reached it, but not before being attacked on the plains of Otumba by an army made up of Aztecs and other Indian

FERDINAN DO CORTES
CAVATO DA VN ORIGINALE FATTO INAZI
CHE SI PORTASSI ALLA CONQVISTA DEL MESSICO

allies. The ensuing July 1520 battle was one in which, unlike the events at Tenochtitlan, the Spanish were able to strike terror into the hearts of their attackers through the use of mounted assaults. After the Aztecs and their allies fled in panic at the sight of "half men, half creatures," Cortés and his troops were able to make their way to Tlaxcala.

Arguably, the most determined of all the conquistadores, Cortés refused to give up his goal of conquering the Aztecs and plundering their extraordinary riches. Once in Tlaxcala, he persuaded tens of thousands of members of other Indian states opposed to the Triple Alliance to join his men and the Tlaxcalans in another attack on Tenochtitlan. Assembling a force estimated by some historians to have been as large as two hundred thousand men, he had thirteen ships built to help carry out his new plan to attack the Aztec stronghold by sea.

In 1521, with his new army fortified by reinforcements sent from Cuba, Cortés launched his second attack on Tenochtitlan. He began by laying siege to the city, a tactic that

CONQVISTA DE MEXICO POR CORTES. N.7

The dramatic painting *Conquest of Tenochtitlan*, shown here, is part of a series of eight large murals known as *The Conquest of Mexico*, painted by unknown artists in Mexico in the mid to late seventeenth century. The wealth of Tenochtitlan astounded Hernán Cortés, who wrote in a 1520 letter to Charles V his impressions about the city and the wealth of Montezuma:

"Can there be anything more magnificent than that this barbarian lord should have all the things to be found under the heavens in his domain, fashioned in gold and silver and jewels and feathers; and so realistic in gold and silver that no smith in the world could have done better, and in jewels so fine that it is impossible to imagine with what instruments they were cut so perfectly?... in Spain there is nothing to compare with it." This excerpt is from Cortés's so-called Second Letter to the king. Gathered together with four other letters, they were published from 1519–26 as the *Cartas de relación*, and were widely distributed. The letters were a masterful blend of fact and embellishment meant to impress the king and put a positive spin on Cortés's role in Mexico.

This portrait of Francisco Pizarro appeared in *The New World Heroes of Discovery and Conquest*, by D. M. Kelsey (ca. 1891). The people Pizarro had been sent to conquer were numerous beyond his imagination. The Inca Empire alone was larger than the Ming Dynasty of China, bigger than Ivan the Terrible's Russia, larger than the Ottoman Empire or the largest kingdom in Africa. It was, in fact, the largest empire in the world.

resulted in the death by starvation of many of its inhabitants. But even this result and the large army he had amassed might never have brought him victory had it not been for the fact that while Cortés had been assembling his forces in Tlaxcala, Tenochtitlan had been stricken with a deadly outbreak of smallpox, killing at least a third of its residents.

Cortés's victory and the enormous rewards it reaped bolstered the confidence and resolve of other conquistadores anxious to capture similar treasures. Most notable among them was Francisco Pizarro, who had first come to the New World with Nicolás de Ovando in 1502. In 1513, Pizarro took part in the expedition to Panama led by Vasco Núñez de Balboa in which the Pacific Ocean was discovered. He remained in Panama as a colonizer and from 1519 to 1523 served as the mayor and magistrate of Panama City.

But Pizarro, like Cortés before him, lusted after the riches that the New World had to offer. In 1532, he invaded Peru, climbed the highlands of the majestic Andes, and conquered the Inca Empire—which had also been decimated by smallpox—taking control of its great silver mines. Operating with the same deceitful and brutal manner that came to characterize many of the conquistadores, Pizarro captured the Inca emperor Atahualpa and promised that he would be released upon payment of the contents of an enormous room filled with gold. As soon as the payment was made, Pizarro

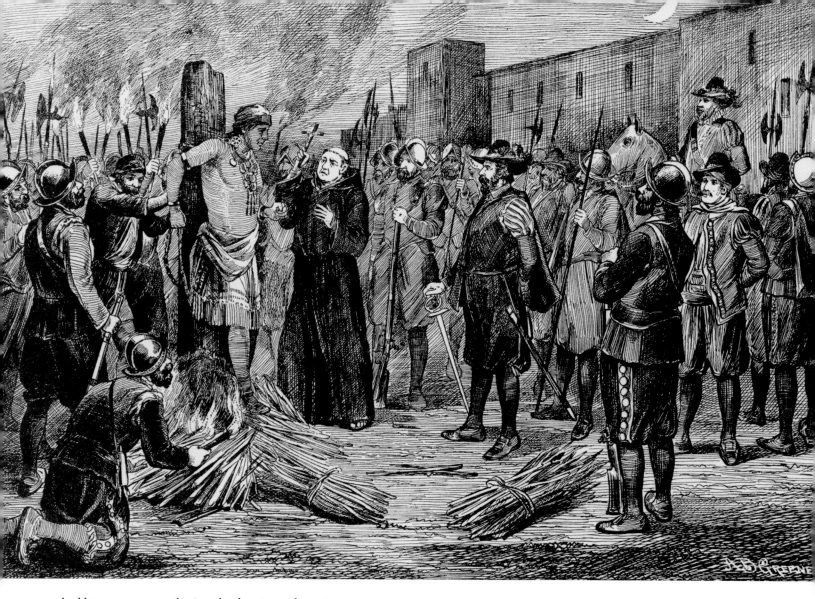

had his men execute the Inca leader. A year later, Pizarro successfully invaded Cuzco, the historic capital of the Inca Empire. In January 1535, convinced that this city was too high up in the mountains and too far removed from the sea, he founded the city of Lima and established it as the Spanish capital of Peru. With his achievements, Pizarro acquired for Spain not only most of Peru but the northern half of Chile and part of Bolivia, more territory than all the rest of South America combined, territory that would remain in Spanish control for the next three centuries. For Pizarro personally, however there was no happy ending. In 1537, his former

Francisco Pizarro oversees the execution of the Inca emperor Atahualpa, one of the thousands of deceits and atrocities inflicted upon the American natives by their Spanish conquerors. This engraving is also from the ca. 1891 Kelsey book.

Hernando de Soto discovers the Mississippi. In this 1847 painting by William H. Powell, which hangs in the U.S. Capitol Rotunda, Native Americans look on as their chief (far right) holds out a peace pipe. The soldiers and weapons included in the foreground indicate the attack upon the Indians that had taken place earlier.

BELOW: Francisco Coronado's extraordinary trek was made even more difficult by the fact that most of his horsemen and foot soldiers wore heavy armor most of the way and rarely found streams or lakes to bathe in or to supply them with drinking water. This nineteenth-century drawing depicting the march is after an original work by Frederic Remington.

121

COLONIZATION

partner Diego de Almagro, incensed by what he felt was Pizarro's failure to share with him both the plundered native treasure and jurisdiction over former Incan territory, rose up against him. Pizarro then captured and killed Almagro. But four years later, on June 26, 1541, followers of Almagro broke into Pizarro's Lima palace and executed him.

While Cortés's and Pizarro's conquests were the most notable of the Spanish conquerors, other conquistadores, suspecting that the New World mainland ran far to the north of Mexico, began seeking treasure there. In 1528, Pánfilo de Narváez led an expedition by boat north from Florida and then west along the Gulf Coast. Off the coast of what is now Texas, the party was struck by a violent storm and most of the expedition, including Narváez, was killed. The survivors managed to reach the mainland where they were captured by Native Americans and enslaved for several years. One of the Spaniards, Álvar Núñez Cabeza de Vaca, managed to escape and became a nomad during which time he not only established friendly relations with some of the natives but served as a medicine man. While living among the Indians he learned that three of his compatriots, now also free, were located nearby. In 1534, Cabeza de Vaca and the three men made their way to Mexico. Cabeza

de Vaca then wrote a tract, based on what he claimed were stories he had heard from his captors, in which he described seven cities constructed of gold, called Cíbola.

Cabeza de Vaca's story of the incredibly rich "seven cities of Cíbola" fanned the flames of conquistador ambition, and none more so than Hernando de Soto. In 1539, the man who had marched with Pizarro and had then served as governor of Cuba, received the Spanish king's permission to explore what is today the southeastern part of the United States. Leading a party of some six hundred, Soto landed at Tampa Bay and marched inland, torturing and killing the natives he encountered along the way. Reaching the Mississippi, he pressed on, entering

This map shows the range of the Spanish territory in the sixteenth century. It was published in 1601 as part of *Descripción de las indias occidentales (Description of the West Indies)*, a volume in Antonio de Herrera y Tordesillas' *Historia general de los hechos de los Castellanos en las islas y tierra firme del Mar Océano (General History of the Deeds of the Castilians on the Islands and Mainland of the Ocean Sea)*.

present-day Oklahoma. When it became clear that he would find no Cíbola, he turned back but was fatally stricken with fever. Because Soto had told the native population that he was an immortal, his men did not arrange an elaborate funeral but buried him in the Mississippi, the great river he had discovered.

The tale of the "seven cities of Cíbola" also aroused the interest of Francisco Vázquez de Coronado, a conquistador who was serving as governor of Nueva Galicia, a western province of Mexico. In 1540, Coronado set out to find the treasure. Thus would begin one of the longest treks in the American experience, a journey that took Coronado and his 250 horsemen, 70 foot soldiers, 1,000 friendly Indians, and a host of priests, well up the mainland coast of the Gulf of California, across Arizona, into New Mexico and Texas, and then across northern Kansas to the Nebraska border. Coronado and his party were the first Europeans to view the Grand Canyon. They also heard stories of yet another El Dorado, a place called Quivira, where inhabitants ate out of golden bowls and drank from golden jugs. But

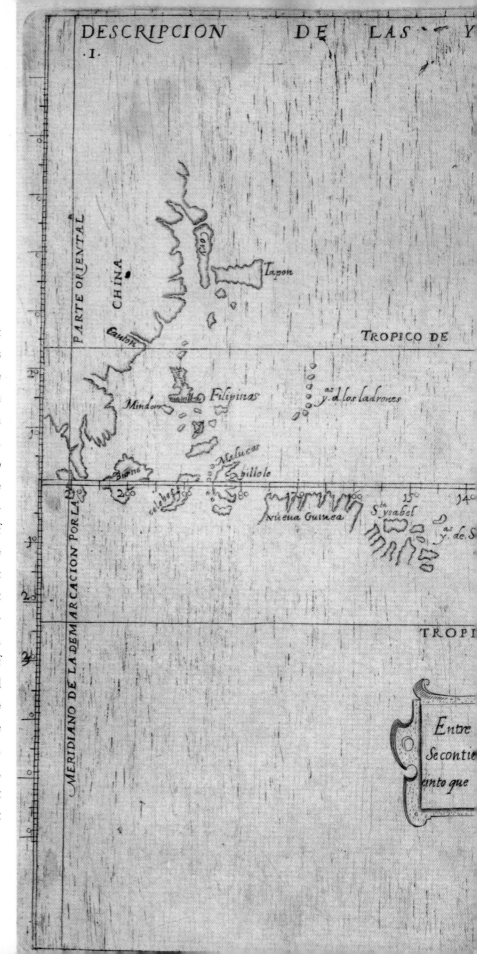

C. de fortun

California

y. de cedros

Roca partida

NVEVA ESPA
NA

Natividad
Mexico
Hapulco

Florida

Cuba

Honduras Jamaica

de
y. cocos

Panama

Bacallaos

la bermuda

CANCER

Domingo P. rico

Dominica

Trinidad

tierra firme

Canarias

Lisboa

R. de loro
C. Blanco

C verde

MAR DEL NORTE

33 I NO   32 CI AL 11°

MAR DEL SVR

DE CAPRICORNO

ar   y. de galapagos

P. viejo

R. de las amazonas

C. Patao

PERV

Callao

Arica

P. de chile

P. de baldivia

Prouincia de estrecho

R. de plata

C de las virgines

Estrecho de Magallanes

BRASIL

C de. S. Agustin

C. Frio.

S. Vicente

C de. S Maria

C. Blanco

MERIDIANO DE LA DE MARCACION POR LA PARTE OSCIDENTAL

The dedicated and courageous missionaries who accompanied the Spanish into the Americas not only established the first schools in New Spain but also introduced food crops never previously grown in the New World, including wheat, barley, rye, chickpeas, and lentils, as well as a variety of fruits, including apples, cherries, and apricots. This ca. 1524 illustrated catechism was drawn by Saint Pedro de Gante, who founded the first school in Mexico. The missions founded throughout New Spain by the Jesuits, and later run by the Franciscans, were built on the precept of protecting and helping Native Americans by Christianizing and civilizing them, but in the end, the rigid structure of mission life and exposure to European diseases proved devastating.

> " *The New World, conquered by you, has conquered you in its turn.* "
>
> —Justus Lipsius to Spanish friend, 1603

they found no golden cities. Instead they encountered seemingly endless plains, life-threatening heat, and one small primitive village after another. There were no seven cities of Cíbola. There was no golden Quivira. But de Soto's and Coronado's quests made the Spanish aware of the extraordinary vastness of the land that awaited settlement. By 1565, the Spanish had established a settlement at St. Augustine, which became the longest continually occupied European community in the continental United States. By 1607, the town of Santa Fe had been founded.

By 1580, Spain had become the richest and most powerful nation in the world. The empire of its King Phillip II, who had also become the ruler of Portugal and all its possessions, stretched from Manila in the Philippines (named for him) around the world to Mexico and to most of what is now the southwestern United States and Florida. More than a quarter million Spaniards, mostly from the poorest agricultural regions of Spain, had migrated to the Spanish New World. In the following half century, at least that many more would arrive.

Meantime, tons of gold and silver were being shipped from Mexico and Peru every year, not only increasing Spanish wealth but also having a profound impact on all of Europe. For as Spanish merchants traded the precious metals for all types of manufactured goods from France, Germany, Italy, Flanders, and England, and as these goods were transported into Spain's American possessions, the beginnings of an Atlantic, rather than a national, economic system took place.

All of it, of course, at the expense of the original owners of the wealth, the natives. The toll exacted on the Indians through exploitation was enormous. The death they suffered from such European diseases as smallpox, measles, diphtheria, typhoid, and whooping cough, to which they were not immune, was even more horrific, greater even than the Black Death that had swept through Europe in the mid 1300s. In less than fifty years, central Mexico's population was reduced from about 7 million to approximately 2.5 million. Peru's population declined from 9 million to 1.3 million. The natives on Hispaniola and the rest of the Caribbean islands were virtually exterminated. As one Spanish sergeant, recalling what he had witnessed during his tour of duty in the Americas, proclaimed, "There were more riches than health."

In the end, the Spanish would pay their own price for their lust for wealth. They had claimed and settled far too much land for them to govern effectively. The gulf between the Spanish noblemen who owned the land and the impoverished Spaniards who settled it created uncontrollable tensions. They were the first in the Americas, but they would not be able to make it their own. As Flemish humanist and classical scholar Justus Lipsius wrote to a Spanish friend in 1603, "The New World, conquered by you, has conquered you in its turn."

This 1591 Theodore de Bry engraving called *They Reach Port Royal* recreates a watercolor made by Jacques Le Moyne, who traveled to Florida and South Carolina with the French Huguenot explorers Jean Ribault and René Goulaine de Laudonnière. Ribault's 1562 French expedition, which established a short-lived colony at Port Royal, South Carolina, was an early challenge to Spanish control of the New World. The image includes depictions of the area's habitat, wild life, and native encampments.

Another de Bry engraving after Le Moyne depicts René Laudonnière, commander of the second French expedition to Florida, standing by a column erected by Jean Ribault during the first French first expedition. The native Floridians are shown worshipping the column and placing offerings before it.

THE FRENCH ATTEMPT COLONIZATION

The Spanish had come to the New World seeking treasure, and for the better part of a century, they succeeded. The French eventually found another type of treasure, but not before initial disastrous attempts at directly challenging both the Spanish and the Portuguese.

In 1555 the French, under naval officer Nicolas Durand de Villegaignon, attempted to colonize an island off the coast of Portuguese-held Brazil. It was not only a bold but also a unique endeavor, since it was the first European New World settlement to include both Protestants and Catholics—French Huguenots and Swiss Calvinists. From the beginning, however, the two groups clashed with each other, and Durand left the colony in frustration. In 1560, Portuguese soldiers captured the settlement, and those who survived the attack were forced to flee to the mainland, where they were rescued by friendly natives.

In 1562 another effort was made when French soldier and adventurer Jean Ribault, hoping to initiate a Protestant (Huguenot) New World presence, tried to found a colony named Charlesfort in the very heart of Spanish-held territory on Parris Island in Port Royal Sound, Florida (near present-day Beaufort, South Carolina). Due to a shortage of food, however, this colony also failed. In 1564, yet a third

ABOVE LEFT: A sixteenth-century French engraving depicts the Portuguese attack on Fort Coligny, at the French colony called France Antarctique, in Guanabara Bay (site of present-day Rio de Janeiro).

ABOVE RIGHT: Samuel de Champlain's third voyage to the New World brought him to the vicinity of the settlement he founded and named Quebec. Champlain's explorations took him as far south as present-day Chatham on Cape Cod. Here, the fabled discoverer is shown exploring the Canadian wilderness, in a ca. 1893 print.

RIGHT: By the mid eighteenth century, the settlement of Quebec was a flourishing city. Like many other renderings of New World communities drawn by Old World artists, this ca. 1770 hand-colored etching by German engraver Franz Xaver Habermann presents an idealized view of Quebec City as a typical European metropolis.

colonization endeavor was made when René de Laudonnière and some three hundred soldiers and colonists tried to settle at Fort Caroline near present-day Jacksonville, Florida. The Spanish responded quickly. In 1565 they sent a small army under the command of Pedro Menéndez de Avilés to destroy the Huguenots. In what turned into a massacre, Menéndez not only slaughtered all of the French settlers but also ordered that their bodies be butchered and dumped into a nearby river. It was a bloody maneuver, designed to discourage further attempts at encroachment upon Spanish territory, and it was effective. The French would not have a presence in what is now the southern United States until 1718 when they built New Orleans at the mouth of the Mississippi River.

These early failed attempts at challenging Spain's New World domination led to a concentration on what would truly represent France's interest in North America—the establishment of a prosperous trade in furs to satisfy the enormous demand created by gentlemen throughout Europe wishing to adorn themselves in fur hats and fur-trimmed coats.

In 1608, Samuel de Champlain established a small settlement in the region known by the natives as Quebec, which would be the beginnings of Quebec City. (Some seventy years earlier Jacques Cartier had established a short-lived settlement at nearby Cap Rouge.) During the summer of 1611, Champlain traveled to the area upon which present-day

Montreal would be built. But the French presence in the Canadian territories was almost totally characterized by a vastly scattered string of settlements, most of which were a combination of fur-trading stations and forts where soldiers were stationed to protect the traders. Most of these stations were located close to rivers or bays for easy transportation of furs and eventually stretched all the way to New Orleans.

As the fur trade grew, it came to depend on two types of Frenchmen—the *coureur des bois* ("runner of the woods"), renegade, unlicensed traders who hunted and traded in the forest, and the *voyageur*, those who searched for furs beyond the woods and out onto the vast Canadian plains, typically traveling by canoe. In direct contrast to the Spanish experience, the French fur hunting and trading operations were also characterized by a close relationship with many Native American tribes, made necessary by the need for Indian hunters and trappers. Many French trappers and traders not only lived among the Native Americans but married Indian women as well.

In the end, the French were not able to maintain possession of the northern American territory that they had named New France. Their failure was due in great measure to their intense concentration on furs rather than on the establishment of permanent settlements and economic diversification. But there were other reasons as well. In endeavoring to establish colonies in the northern wilderness, French authorities attempted to perpetuate the aristocratic French social system in the New World. This attempt at feudalism in America was seen most clearly in the effort made by France's Cardinal Richelieu to consolidate New World French possessions into a powerful empire. Establishing what he named the

OPPOSITE TOP: Voyageurs, employed by the Hudson Bay Company, travel by freight canoe through the wilderness of New France in this 1869 painting by Frances Anne Hopkins. The voyageurs were invaluable to the French not only for their hunting skills but also for their ability to carry supplies to the far-flung fur-trading stations.

OPPOSITE BOTTOM: The busiest places in all of New France were the first trading stations where furs were sold and traded and where *coureur des bois*, ("runners of the woods") and the Native Americans employed by the French were housed. Fur was a luxury item in Europe, and by the seventeenth century, beaver felt was used extensively for men's hats. This stylish nobleman, ca. 1630, is resplendent in a fur-trimmed coat and hat.

BELOW: Drawn in 1702 by Nicolas de Fer and published in his *L'Atlas curieux*, this map reveals the enormous amount of North American territory claimed by France. Note how *Canada, ou Nouvelle France* ("Canada, or New France") abuts the territory of Florida.

RIGHT: Armand-Jean du Plessis (Cardinal Richelieu) attained lofty positions in both church and state. He was ordained a cardinal in 1622 and was made King Louis XIII's chief minister in 1624, a position he held until his death in 1642. Flemish-born artist Philippe de Champaigne painted this portrait of the cardinal ca. 1642; it was sent to Rome as a model for the making of a bust by sculptor Francesco Mochi.

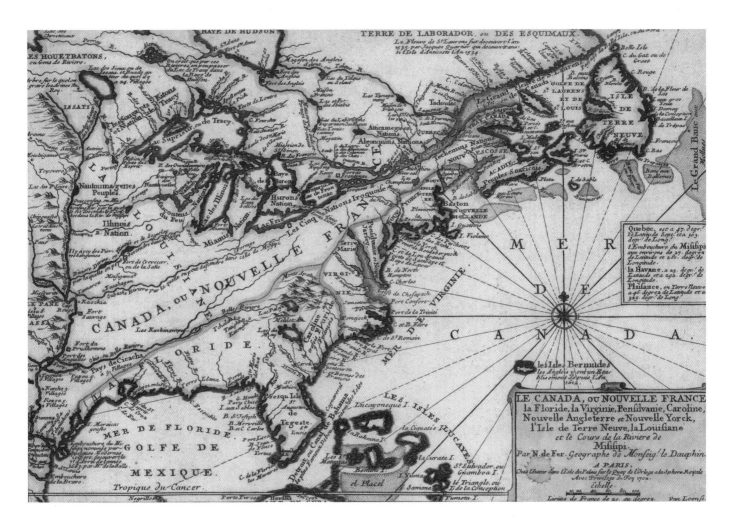

Company of New France, Richelieu created a society of noblemen called *seigneurs*, who were given huge land grants along lakes and rivers. The seigneurs were then charged with the task of bringing settlers, called *habitants*, to farm their land. Yet, once they settled in New France, the habitants were much more interested in furs than in clearing the land and tilling the soil. And in a colony located in so vast a territory—where habitants could easily steal off into the woods and to hunt and trade for furs on their own—Richelieu's plan simply could not be enforced.

Additionally, many of those who left France for the New World chose to settle on the balmier Caribbean islands. By the 1660s, for example, Haiti had a population of some fifteen thousand French settlers, a number five times greater than all of New France's population at the time. Ultimately, it was the French possessions in the West Indies, with their flourishing sugar and tobacco crops, that represented France's greatest New World success.

ENGLAND RULES THE NORTH

The Spanish and the Portuguese were the first to colonize the Americas. The French were the first to challenge the Spanish New World presence. Yet, in the end it was England, the last of the great European powers to seriously enter the quest

for possession of North America, which succeeded in ruling the continent.

It did not start auspiciously. In 1583, British navigator Sir Humphrey Gilbert, hoping to establish England's first presence in North America, received a charter from Queen Elizabeth I and, with a small fleet, sailed for Newfoundland. He stayed only about a month before setting out for home to pick up more supplies. Fortune, however, was not with Humphrey Gilbert. As he made his way back across the Atlantic, his ship the *Squirrel* suddenly vanished and he was never heard from again.

While saddened by Gilbert's disaster, his half-brother Walter Raleigh saw opportunity in Sir Humphrey's failure. Tall, handsome, and extremely eloquent, Raleigh was a personal favorite of Elizabeth I. And he had an all-consuming goal. "I shall," he told his friends, "but live to see America an English nation." He was also clear about what kind of colony he wanted to establish. Whereas Gilbert had, from the beginning, regarded his endeavor to bring settlers to Newfoundland as a social experiment, Raleigh's proclaimed

OPPOSITE: Known as the Virgin Queen because she never married, Queen Elizabeth I sponsored Sir Humphrey Gilbert's attempt to establish England's first American colony. Elizabeth, who lent her name to what became known as the Elizabethan Era, ruled Great Britain for forty-five years, a period marked by significant advances in England's worldwide power and influence. The *Armada Portrait* was painted by George Gower around 1588 to commemorate the defeat of the Spanish Armada (depicted through the window in the background). The queen's global power is reflected by her hand resting over the globe.

BELOW: Sir Walter Raleigh was a man of many talents and accomplishments. A skilled poet as well as a warrior, Raleigh, before attempting to establish an English colony in Virginia, was instrumental in suppressing an Irish rebellion and succeeded in destroying the lairs of Spanish and Italian pirates off the Irish coast. He is credited with popularizing the use of tobacco and, according to unproved legend, with bringing the potato to Ireland. This 1585 portrait miniature of Raleigh was painted by English artist Nicholas Hillard.

goal was to found "a genuine, self-perpetuating colony, not a mere trading post or garrison."

In early 1584, Raleigh initiated his quest by sending out two small ships, commanded by Philip Amadas and Arthur Barlowe, to find a suitable location for planting a colony. In July they reached the outer banks of what is now North Carolina and, after spending time exploring the area and observing the natives—particularly those on Roanoke Island—came to the conclusion that it was not only a suitable spot to establish a settlement but also an advantageous location from which to raid Spanish settlements to the south. The voyagers then returned to England, carrying back with them samples of the region's flora and fauna, two natives, and a detailed report of the area and its inhabitants. Arthur Barlowe, one of Raleigh's protégés, wrote a report entitled *The First Voyage to Roanoke. 1584...*, which was first published in 1589 in Richard Hakluyt's *The Principall Navigations, Voiages, and Discoveries of the English Nation.* Barlow speaks glowingly of the Native Americans he encountered:

We were entertained with all love, and kindness, and with as much bountie, after their manner, as they could possibly devise. We found the people most gentle, loving, and faithful, void of all guile and treason, and such as lived under the manner of the golden age...their meate is very well [stewed with corn and beans] and they make broth very sweete, and savorie. Their vessels are earthen pots...their dishes are wooden platters of sweete timber; within the place where they feede was their lodging, and within that their Idoll, which they worship, of whome they speake incredible things.

Encouraged by his explorers' reports, Raleigh wasted no time and within a year dispatched seven ships under the command of his cousin, Sir Richard Grenville, to establish "the first colony of Virginia." But after Grenville's party landed on the northern end of Roanoke Island, they almost immediately experienced a number of troubling incidents with the natives. Convinced, however, that with enough settlers all problems

This German version of a map drawn by John White and engraved by de Bry in 1590 shows the arrival of British ships (and a sea monster) off the coast of Virginia. The territories of two Native American tribes, the Weapemeoc and Secotan, are identified, along with the colony of Roanoke located on the island in the mouth of the river.

could be overcome, Grenville decided to leave a hundred men at Roanoke under the command of Ralph Lane, promising to return in no more than twelve months. He then sailed back to England to gather more colonists and supplies.

More than a year passed, then a second and a third. Still there was no Grenville. Finally, to the great joy of the colonists, now desperately short of food and in constant danger from various groups of Indians, sails were spotted. But it was not Grenville. It was Sir Francis Drake, on his way home from yet another of his successful raids on Spanish Caribbean possessions. Fearing for the settlers' survival, Drake convinced them that they should return to England with him. Ironically, a short time later, Grenville, having been long delayed by yet another lengthy series of British-Spanish conflicts, arrived with his relief expedition. Alarmed at finding the colony deserted, he made the immediate decision to turn back home, but not before leaving fifteen brave souls behind to maintain an English New World presence and to perpetuate Raleigh's claim.

Raleigh remained undaunted. In 1587 he sent out another group of colonists—ninety-one men, seventeen women, and nine children—all led by Raleigh's artist friend John White (see "Illustrations for a New World" in Chapter 3). The party landed at Roanoke on July 22, 1587, and was dismayed to discover that of the fifteen men who had been left behind, only the bones of one could be found. Encountering a group of Croatoans, who claimed to be the only tribe in the area still friendly to the whites, White and his party were told that the fifteen men had been attacked by members of other native tribes and that nine survivors of the assault had taken to a boat and had sailed up the coast.

As determined as Raleigh to make North America a British possession, White convinced the new colonists, including his daughter, who had given birth to the first English child born in America, to remain and build a permanent settlement. For more than a year, he led them in their struggle to survive. But with supplies running out and aware that more bodies were needed to provide additional protection against the threat of Indian attack, he finally decided that he needed to return to England to replenish the colony.

When, after two years, White finally made his way back to Roanoke he had no new settlers with him. Unable to find

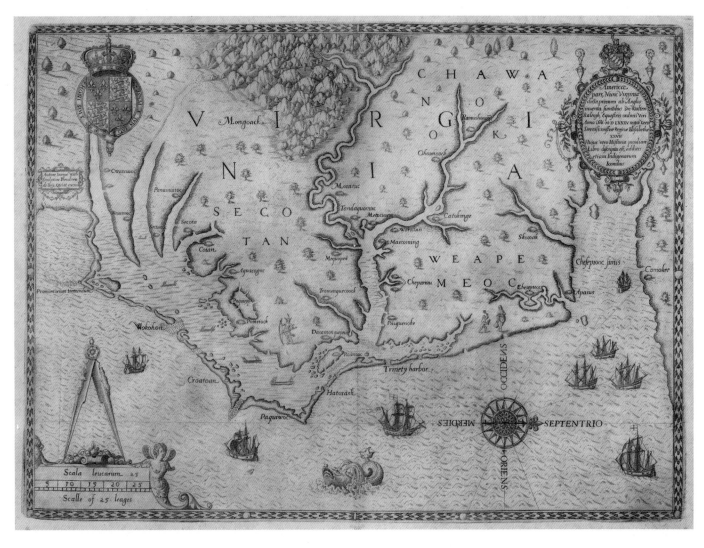

ships because almost every British vessel had been commandeered to fight back the attack by the Spanish Armada, the best he was able to do was to gain passage on a privateering expedition that promised to drop him off at Roanoke on their way back from their Caribbean raids. When White and the privateers finally arrived at Roanoke there was not a soul to be found. The only clue was the word "Croatoan" carved into a post and the word "Cro" etched into a nearly tree. Nothing else of the colony was ever found—a mystery that, to this day, historians struggle to explain.

The British attempt at establishing their first colony at Roanoke ended in both disaster and mystery. Much of what we *do* know about the failed attempt is due to the paintings created by John White before he left the island. While in Roanoke, White also drew this map of Virginia Colony, showing the North Carolina coast from Cape Lookout to the mouth of the Chesapeake Bay, which was engraved by de Bry and published in 1590. Roanoke Island, near Trinity Harbor, is shown in the center toward the bottom as "Roanoac."

Sir Francis Drake

Sir Francis Drake's exploits as a privateer earned him such fame throughout Great Britain that portraits of him, such as this one by an unknown artist ca. 1580, became extremely popular.

Of all the individuals who played their role in the drama of New World settlement, none was more daring or more feared than Sir Francis Drake. Among his many exploits was his accomplishment in becoming the first Englishman to circumnavigate the globe (1577–80). Drake was also second-in-command of the British fleet that, in 1587–88 in one of Great Britain's most heralded naval victories, defeated a Spanish squadron of more than 120 vessels. Known as the Spanish Armada, the Spanish fleet had been sent to the waters off Great Britain by King Phillip II in an attempt to halt England's raids on Spain's New World possessions and its Atlantic treasure ships. Drake later established himself as the most effective of all the British "sea dogs" who successfully raided Spanish treasure.

LEFT: From 1585 to 1604, England and Spain fought a series of battles. Never formally declared, the Anglo-Spanish War was a struggle over economic, political, and religious control. In 1587, Elizabeth sent Drake to boldly attack the Spanish port of Cadíz, completely surprising the Spanish. In this painting by Francisco de Zurbarán, *Defense of Cádiz against the English* (1634), Spanish leaders are shown against the backdrop of the battle, trying to plan what would be a futile defense.

BELOW: This pictorial diagram is part of a series of maps on the battle of 1588 created by artist Robert Adams and engraver Augustine Ryther for Petruccio Ubaldini's *A discourse concerning the Spanishe fleete invadinge Englande in the yeare 1588*, published in London in 1590. The image depicts the culmination of the battle, as the English fleet and Spanish fleet meet head on (upper right) just north of the Strait of Dover.

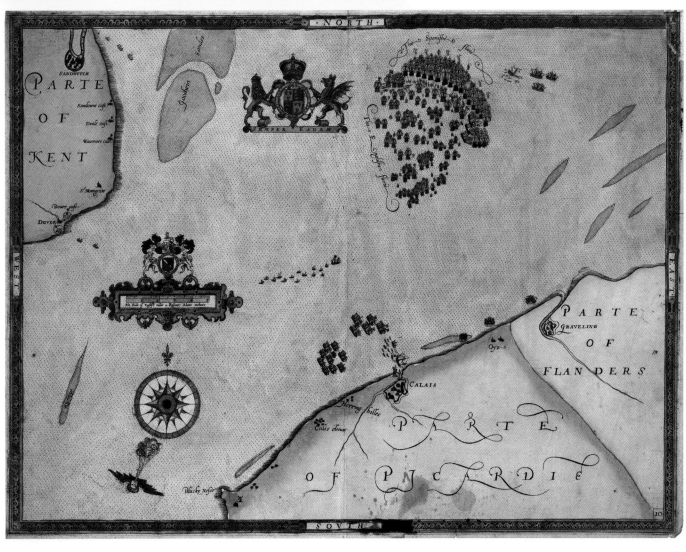

In addition to his scores of successful attacks on Spanish treasure ships, Drake also carried out effective raids on Spanish settlements in the Caribbean. This 1589 map painting by John White shows Drake's 1586 raid on St. Augustine and is one of the earliest printed depictions of any European town within what is now the United States.

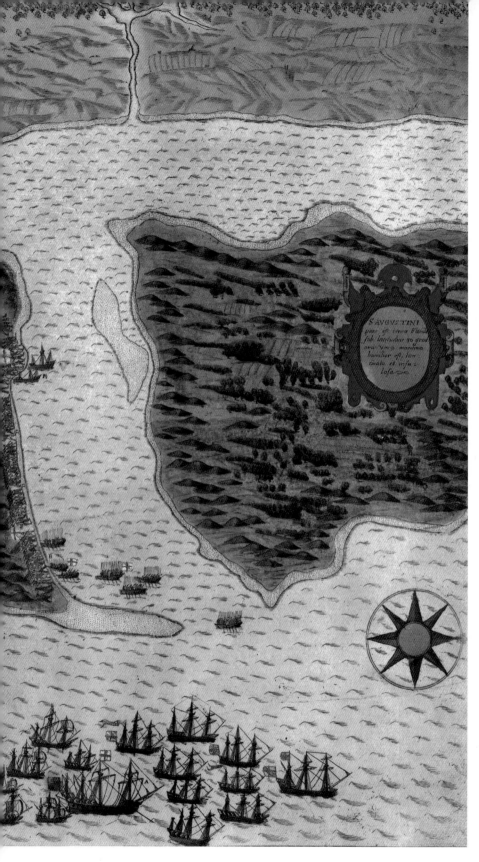

ABOVE: By raiding other ships and seizing their cargo, Sir Francis Drake was following a tradition of piracy that began as far back as classical antiquity, when the Etruscans and the Thracians earned notorious reputations as pirates, and reached a zenith with the Barbary pirates, privateers working for the Ottomans and the Barbary states (Algiers, Morocco, Tripoli, and Tunis). From early in the sixteenth century until the nineteenth, the Barbary pirates preyed on shipping along Africa's Barbary Coast and well into the Mediterranean. Whether they were called pirates, privateers, buccaneers, *kapers* (Dutch), freebooters (English), or *filibustiers* (French), those who raised havoc on the seas became a well-known part of popular culture, and the names of the most notorious of them, such as Sir Henry Morgan, Captain William Kidd, Jean Lafitte, and Edward "Blackbeard" Teach, became household words. The title page of *The Buccaneers of America*, written in 1678 by Alexander Exquemelin, believed to be a French surgeon who enlisted with the buccaneers for a time, illustrates the exploits of the English, French, and Dutch buccaneers who plied the waters among the Caribbean islands and along the coasts of Central and South America.

Soldier, sailor, author, mapmaker, and inveterate adventurer—John Smith was all of these. His greatest contribution, however, was as "founder" of New England, which he explored, named, mapped, and described. This engraving, which appeared in Smith's 1630 book *The* *True Travels, Adventures, and Observations of Captaine John Smith*, shows him proudly clad in armor, with his left hand resting on his sword handle.

The next British attempt at colonizing North America seemed destined for the same tragic ending. In May 14, 1607, three ships—the *Susan Constant*, the *Godspeed*, and the *Discovery*, sailed into the James River in Virginia and landed 104 would-be settlers at a site they named Jamestown. It had been a disaster-plagued voyage. Thirty-nine of the voyagers had died from scurvy on the journey across the Atlantic. Many of the remaining members seemed unlikely candidates to carve out a colony in the wilderness. They were not farmers or artisans but members of the gentry who had come to the New World seeking gold.

They had named their new home Jamestown, but a far more proper designation would have been Smithtown. For as events unfolded, the fact that the colony became the first English settlement to survive was due almost solely to the efforts and abilities of one man. He was only twenty-seven years old, but John Smith had already journeyed through much of Europe as a soldier of fortune. An eloquent and prolific writer whose tracts eventually launched what became known as the Great New World Migration, Smith was also a superb organizer and motivator. At Jamestown, he continually mediated disputes between rival factions that developed among the settlers. Most important, he managed to persuade the gold-seeking members of the colony to abandon their fruitless quest and to engage in the farming and other physical labor necessary to keep the settlers alive.

Spurred on by Smith's cheerful goading and direction, wells were dug, the manufacture of soap was begun, nets and traps for fishing were fabricated, and the first crops were planted. Eventually enough trees were felled so that cargoes of timber could be shipped back to England and exchanged for a steady flow of supplies. The establishment of this vital transatlantic trade was the beginning of the lifeline between the British colonies and the mother country throughout the entire Colonial Era.

In 1609, Smith was seriously burned in a freak gunpowder accident and was forced to return to England. But he left behind a settlement that, through his will, became the first

A DESCRIPTION of New England:

OR

THE OBSERVATIONS, AND discoueries, of Captain *Iohn Smith* (Admirall of that Country) in the North of *America*, in the year of our Lord 1614: with the *succeſſe* of *fixe Ships,* that went the next yeare 1615; and the accidents befell him among the *French men of warre:*

With the proofe of the prefent benefit this Countrey affoords: whither this prefent yeare, 1616, *eight voluntary Ships are gone to make further tryall.*

At *LONDON*
Printed by *Humfrey Lownes,* for *Robert Clerke*; and are to be fould at his houfe called the Lodge, in Chancery lane, ouer againft Lincolnes Inne. 1616.

Title page from John Smith's *A Description of New England* (1616), which was one of the most influential books written during the settlement of the New World; its "proofe of the present benefit this country affords" was instrumental in motivating Pilgrims to seek religious and political freedom in America.

English-speaking colony north of Spanish-held Florida. And his role as Great Britain's most important early American colonizer was far from over.

In 1614, Smith was once again back in the New World, but not as a settler. He had been hired by two London merchants, who sent him across the Atlantic to hunt whales. Cruising the waters off the coast of present-day Maine, he discovered no whales. But his voyage had far more important results. Continuing on down the coast as far south as Cape Cod, Smith mapped every bay and inlet he encountered, endowing various sites with such English place names as Plymouth, Cambridge, and Dartmouth. When he returned to England he described his discoveries in a book whose title, *A Description of New England*, endowed the land that had been known as Northern Virginia with a brand new name.

From that time on Smith, who, more than any of his contemporaries understood the extraordinary potential of America, devoted most of his energies to championing English colonization of the New World. If an Englishman "have but the taste of virtue and magnanimity," he wrote, "what to such a mind can be more pleasant than plating and building a foundation for his posterity." Commenting on his own personal experience he added "of all the four parts of the world I have yet seen not inhabited, could I have but means to transport a colony, I would rather live here than anywhere else."

BELOW: Pocahontas's life is filled with many legends. What is certain is that she eventually married British colonial leader John Rolfe and was baptized. This print, ca. 1870, illustrates the dramatic moment when Pocahontas is said to have saved John Smith.

RIGHT : This map, the first accurate description of the Chesapeake region, was drawn by John Smith in ca. 1606–8 and was based both on his own explorations of the area and descriptions of the territory he obtained from Native Americans. When it was first published in 1612, the engraver William Hole added the insert depicting Indian leader Powhatan's court. Smith recounted in numerous writings a romantic and unverifiable tale of how he had been captured in December 1607 and taken north of Jamestown to meet the chief of the Powhatans. According to a letter he wrote to Queen Anne in 1616, Smith claimed that just as he was about to be executed, the chief's daughter, Pocahontas, threw herself across his body "at the minute of my execution, she hazarded the beating out of her own brains to save mine; and not only that, but so prevailed with her father, that I was safely conducted to Jamestown."

VIRGINIA

Maſſaw-omecks

Maſſawomeck

MANN AHOACKS

HONI SOIT QVI MAL Y PENSE

Slegara
Shackaconia
Tauxſnitania
Huſutuga

Mahaſkahod
Sparkes
content
Democrites tree

N

Burſins Mount

Stegora

Tſaunack
Vtcuſtank
Accoqueck
Secobeck
Marteoughquaunk
Anaſkenoans
Muttuumſſinſack
Maſſaweteck
Sckobeck
Qunough
Checopiſſou
Waſaconias
Nandtanghtacum
Aſſuweſka
Aurenopeuah
Payſcone
Mattacunt
Kerahocak
Pamacocack
Piſſaſeck
Ottawomen
Nawacaten
Menaſcouſt
Niſſamek
Matalunkkquamend
Tanxcenent
Weuppom
Matchepick
Nuſhemouck
Pamacoack
Namaſſinaahent
Piſſacoack
Petapaco
Cinquocteck
Vttamuſſamacoma
Meyons
Aſſaomeck
Namorughquend
Pawatuxunt
Tſſamatuck
Weſamcus
Cecomocomoco
Monaſcunt
Nucetchtanck
Onawmanient
Wighcocomoco
Paweuxunt
Quactatamen
Opanient
Rickards cliftes
Tacuernes roade

T
A
N
A

S A Q V E
S A H A N
O V G H

Attaock
Teſinigh
Quadroque
The Saſqueſahanougs
are a Gyant like people &
Vtchowig thus a tyred

CHESAPEACK BAY
SASA:
Powels Iles
Winſtons Iles
Hamperler poynt
Raggedeſmock flu
Nauſe
Brookes Forest
Bornes poynt
Ozinies
Poynt Peſmec
Nantaquack
Kuſkarawack
Teckweah flu
Gunters Harbour.
Smyths fales
Saſqueſahanough
Salapaſabonough flu
Willoughbi flu

TOCK
WOGHS

Peregryns mount

ATOV

Aquanachuke

ANAC

Kuſkara
Reales poynt
Bolus flu

KVSKARA WA
OKS

HVKES

and halfe

Scale of Lea gues
Leagues

Chickahokin
Macocks

1   5   10   15

A

Diſcouered and Diſcribed by Captayn John Smith
1606

BELOW: Describing their landing on the bleak wintry shore of Cape Cod, Pilgrim leader William Bradford wrote in the *History of Plymouth Plantation* (ca. 1650), that they "fell upon their knees and blessed the God of Heaven who had brought them over the vast and furious ocean, and delivered them from all the perils and miseries thereof, again to set their feet on the firm and stable earth, their proper element." This lithograph from ca. 1846 recreates the landing scene.

Less than five years later, his proselytizing would have results. In Holland a religious group that had moved to the Netherlands to remove themselves from the dictates of the Church of England read Smith's *Description of New England* with growing interest. Alarmed that their children were beginning to become more Dutch than English and anxious to start life anew in a place where they could practice their religious views without interference, they made a bold decision. They would brave the dangerous Atlantic voyage and establish their own community in that new land that Smith had so glowingly described.

In July 20, 1620, the people who would forever be known as the Pilgrims sailed from Holland in two ships, the *Speedwell* and the *Mayflower*. They were not far out when the *Speedwell* proved unseaworthy and both ships were diverted to a port in England. There, as many of the *Speedwell*'s passengers as could be accommodated were transferred to the *Mayflower*. By the time that this was done, and the 102 men, women, and children aboard the *Mayflower* were ready to sail, it was mid September and the voyagers were forced to make the crossing with winter fast approaching.

Battered by winds and storms, the Pilgrims, on more than one occasion, considered turning back. But on November 10, 1620, land was spotted. They had reached Cape Cod, the area first described by John Smith. Smith, in fact, had offered his services to the Pilgrims before they had left Holland, but they had turned him down. Citing what he believed was the reason why they had declined his offer, Smith wrote in his book *The True Travels, Adventures and Observations of Captain John Smith* (1630): "My books and maps were much better cheape to teach them, than myselfe."

The Cape Cod the Pilgrims encountered was a barren, windswept place dominated by dunes and scrub oak, hardly an ideal place for settlement, so they attempted to sail around it toward the Hudson River; but, after immediately encountering shoals and dangerous currents, they turned around and, on November 11, anchored in what is today

Pilgrims, alone in a wilderness and escorted by armed members of their community, make their way to church, in a ca. 1893 print. "They had now no friends to welcome them nor inns to entertain them or refresh their weather-beaten bodies," Bradford wrote of the Pilgrim's arrival in *History of Plymouth Plantation*, "no houses or much less towns to repair to, to seek for succor."

Provincetown Harbor. It was while anchored there that they wrote and signed the now-famous Mayflower Compact, by which the settlers agreed to follow the rules and regulations set down in the compact and the Pilgrims' leaders agreed that they would formally recognize that the government that was about to be formed derived its powers from the consent of the governed. Over the next six weeks the Pilgrims searched for a more suitable site, until finally in late December they sailed into Plymouth harbor and decided to make that area their New World home.

Terrible times followed and despite the fact that the industrious settlers built houses, occasionally found buried Indian corn, and caught fish when they could, half of the colonists died during the first winter. There would be other devastating winters as well, but with each ensuing spring new crops blossomed and the colony survived. Its very survival became an inspiration to thousands of others back in England anxious to exchange the Old World for the New.

The Puritans were the first group of colonists to follow the Pilgrims. Also dissenters against the Church of England, the Puritans were even more radical than the Pilgrims. They were determined to escape the dictates of the Church (and many also, of the Crown) and live according to their own rigid dictates. The Pilgrims crossed the Atlantic in a trickle; the Puritans came in a torrent. The first seven hundred arrived in Massachusetts Bay in March 1630. By 1640, more than sixteen thousand followed, establishing villages all along the seventy-five-mile-long coast of Massachusetts. What was apparent from the beginning was that the pattern of life in this ever-growing number of settlements would be dictated by natural conditions. Given the harsh climate, the forests, and the rocky soil, farming would never be carried out in a grand scale. As legend has it, an anonymous early settler is said to have exclaimed, "The air of the country is sharp, the rocks many, [and] the trees innumerable." It was to the Atlantic that New Englanders looked for their prosperity.

OPPOSITE: This engraving published in 1821 by English printmaker Richard Holmes Laurie shows slaves at work on a tobacco plantation. The print is notable for its inclusion of the scallop shell, cask, and anchor at its center— symbolic of the ties between the plantations and merchant shipping.

The Puritans were a stern lot as evidenced in this portrait of Reverend John Cotton, a major figure in the early history of the Massachusetts Bay Colony. While even more religiously conservative than the Pilgrims, the Puritans, however, did not let piety stand in the way of their search for profits in mercantile activities. This painting was created by illustrator Howard E. Smith in 1930.

"The ocean," historian Marshall Davidson wrote in his book *Life in America* (1951) "was their plantation and their hunting ground; the cod and its scaly cousins was their staple crop." This pattern remained the same as New England colonies spread from Massachusetts to Rhode Island, Connecticut, Maine, and New Hampshire.

A very different pattern, again based on natural conditions, emerged in the British colonies that were established in the American South. In total contrast to the changeable New England climate with its harsh winters, the southern climate was mild and the soil rich and fertile. It was ideal for the growing of tobacco, destined to become the single most important crop in early colonial America (see "New World Flora and Fauna" in Chapter 3). Because the growing of tobacco almost immediately became so profitable, the crop not only dominated the southern colonies' economy, it dictated the area's physical and societal makeup as well. The vast region became a land not of industrial population centers as in New England but of enormous plantations, larger even than those that had first been developed in the islands. And, as on the islands, the southern plantations were owned by relatively few planters, all of whom relied on the labor of slaves for their prosperity. As early as 1653, one planter, Captain Adam Thoroughgood, boasted that his plantation encompassed 5,350 acres. Less than one hundred years later, Robert

Tobacco

Plantation

BELOW: The use of indigo as a blue dyestuff dates back to ancient times, when the wearing of indigo-dyed clothing was regarded as a sign of wealth. As in South Carolina, indigo was a major New World crop on the island of Jamaica. This engraving of an indigo plantation appeared in the London publication of *A New and Complete System of Geography* (1778–79), by C. T. Middleton.

RIGHT: The bustling skyline and harbor of Charleston can be seen in this panorama, published in *London Magazine* in 1762.

Engraved for Middleton's Complete System of Geography.

THE INDIGO MANUFACTORY

1 Vat. 2 Pounding Tub 3 Receiver. 4 The Water filtrating from the Indigo 5 Indigo Plants. 6 Indians carrying it in Sacks 7 Drying Cases 8 Indians carrying Indigo to the drying Cases

"King" Carter's plantation holdings in Virginia totaled more than three hundred thousand.

It was a system that endowed the wealthy planters with a lifestyle akin to the most privileged gentry back in England. "Such a country life as they had," wrote Andrew Burnaby, an English traveler, in his *Travels in the Middle Settlements in North America* (1759–60), "in the midst of a profusion of rural sports and diversions, with little to do themselves, and in a climate that seems to create rather than check pleasure, must almost naturally have a strong effect in bringing them to be just planters as foxhunters in England make farmers." According to English-born Virginia minister and scholar Hugh Jones's *The Present State of Virginia* (1724), in Williamsburg, the one major urban community to develop in colonial Virginia, the people, "behave themselves exactly as

the gentry in London, most families of note having a coach, chariot, berlin [a four-wheeled covered carriage], or chaise."

Tobacco culture gradually spread throughout the South although, unlike Virginia, the other southern colonies did not rely solely on this one crop. In North Carolina, pine and naval stores, products particularly suited to the demands of England's mercantile well-being, became essential to the colony's success. In South Carolina, rice, as well as indigo used in making dyes, were paramount to that colony's economy. "Your lordships' Country hath made more rice ye last crop than we have ships to transport," the colony's governor, Colonel James Moore, reported in a March 1700 letter to the English Lords Commissioners for Trade and Plantations. By 1750, South Carolina had become a sparkling gem in the British Crown: "It much be apparent at first sight,"

wrote the author of *American Husbandry* (published anonymously in London in 1775), that "no husbandry in Europe can equal this of Carolina: . . . plenty of good land free from taxes, cheapness of labour, and dearness of product sold . . . are, united sufficient to explain the causes of a Carolina planter having such vastly superior opportunities of making a fortune than a British farmer can possibly enjoy . . . liberty reigns in perfection; taxes are too inconsiderable to be mentioned; no military service; no oppressions to enslave the planter and rob him of the fruits of his industry. When all these great and manifest advantages are considered, I think it must appear surprising that more emigrants from different parts of Europe are not constantly moving from thence to America."

Along with its products, South Carolina also produced another jewel. Even before its rice trade had been developed,

Charleston had become a leading port for shipping timber and furs brought down from Canada. Gradually it grew into a social, cultural, and business center and one of the most attractive and cosmopolitan communities in all of America. Bostonian lawyer and patriot Josiah Quincy Jr. wrote in a March 1, 1773 letter to his wife (published in *Memoir of the Life of Josiah Quincy...*, 1875) that in "grandeur, splendour of buildings, decorations, equipages, numbers, commerce, shipping, and indeed in almost everything" there was nothing in America that could rival Charleston.

THE DUTCH EAST INDIA COMPANY

Of all the colonies that were established in British America, it was those referred to as the Middle Colonies in which the best-balanced economies were formed. While the Maryland landscape was dotted with tobacco plantations, its excellent harbor at Baltimore made it a thriving commercial and shipping center, particularly for the transportation of milling wheat and flour to the West Indies. New York, which was particularly prized by the British government because its location provided a bulwark against the French and Indian menace to the north and west, also had a magnificent harbor, one that gave indication of the colony's future prominence and prosperity.

Baltimore was not founded until 1729 and, in its earliest years, contained only twenty-five houses and some two hundred people. Its location beside a spacious harbor, however, led to rapid growth, and by 1754, Maryland's royal governor Horatio Sharpe stated in a report to Frederick, Lord Baltimore (governor of the entire province of Maryland), that the city had now attained "the appearance of the most increasing town in the Province." This aquatint shows a view of Baltimore and its harbor from Federal Hill, by American artist William James Bennett, ca. 1831.

The seamen who sailed for the Dutch East India Company were among the finest mariners in the world. The company itself was the first multinational corporation in the world and the first to issue stock. It maintained an important trading presence for almost two centuries. A painting from 1622 by Hendrik Cornelisz Vroom depicts a few of the company's many ships in the harbor of Hoorn, the Netherlands. One of the most powerful companies the world has ever seen, and one of the first thought to trade shares, by 1669, the Dutch company had approximately 40 warships, 150 merchant ships, 10,000 soldiers, and thousands of employees in ports across Europe and Asia.

LEFT: The Dutch East India Company (known as the *Vereenigde Oostindische Compagnie*, or *VOC*, in Dutch) provided Henry Hudson with his ship, the *Half Moon*, depicted here at anchor in the Hudson River. Note the Native American canoes approaching the ship. This print was created ca. 1895, after a painting by American artist Warren Sheppard.

New York did not start out as a British possession. In 1602, the Estates-General of the Netherlands established the Dutch East India Company, granting it a twenty-one-year monopoly to carry out colonial activities in Asia. Like Spain, France, and England, the Dutch were also anxious to find a water route to the East, and in 1609, the Dutch East India Company hired a veteran English explorer, Henry Hudson, who had already sought such a route through the frozen North, to carry out their quest.

In 1609, in his small Dutch ship, the *Half Moon*, Hudson reached North America, sailed along the Atlantic coast, and discovered the major river that bears his name. Based on his report of what he had found, the Dutch claimed all the land along the Hudson River. By 1614, they had built trading establishments on Manhattan Island and, by 1625, had sent settlers to the region and had established both the town and the colony they named New Amsterdam.

By the beginning of the 1660s, the town of New Amsterdam was a thriving port boasting some twenty-five-hundred people. From the start, there had been bitter tensions between the Dutch and the British over the Dutch

The Dutch claim to an American empire was both brief and modest. In his treatise *Korte historiael ende journaels aenteyckeninge (Short Historical Notes and Journal Notes of Various Voyages*, 1655), Dutch merchant captain David Pietersen de Vries complained of how the directors of the Dutch West India Company were far more interested in extracting heavy booty from Spanish shipping in the Atlantic: "The directors bestowed not a thought upon their best trading post. whether people were making farms there or not...[but] would rather see booty arrive than to speak of their colonies."

Peter Stuyvesant is shown arguing with residents of New Amsterdam, who plead with him not to open fire on the British. The painting is by Jean Leon Gerome Ferris, who in the early twentieth century created a series of commemorative interpretations of early American development called *The Pageant of a Nation*.

New Amsterdam in 1664, the year in which the Dutch colony was taken over by the English. This picture was made in 1644 for the Dutch West India Company (a smaller company than the VOC, also based in Holland) by Joan Vinckeboons.

NIEUW AMSTERDAM OFTE NUE NIEUW IORX OPT TEYLANT MAN

presence in the midst of the other English colonies. The situation was made worse when, during the English Civil War (1642–49), Dutch trading ships took advantage of Britain's preoccupation with the turmoil and began entering British ports, where they offered goods for sale at reduced prices. Added to it all was the fact that, beginning in 1647, New Netherlands was governed by the arrogant, heavy-handed Peter Stuyvesant, a man truly despised by the Dutch colonists.

In 1664, the inevitable showdown between the English and the Dutch took place when Britain sent four frigates to New Amsterdam and ordered the colony's surrender. Although his colony was practically unarmed, Stuyvesant was determined to resist the British demand but was unable to muster any support from the colonists whom he had so often offended. After the governor was forced to surrender without a single shot being fired, the English renamed the colony New York in honor of the Duke of York, whose brother King Charles II granted him proprietorship of the former Dutch possession.

PEACEABLE KINGDOM

Under British control, New York eventually became one of England's most valued holdings, but throughout the colonial period, it was not that possession but Pennsylvania that shone as the most economically diverse and successful of all the Middle Colonies. Pennsylvania was founded by the devout Quaker William Penn who, in 1681, received a land charter from King Charles II. (Legend has it that the grant was given to settle a monetary debt that the king owed to Penn's recently deceased father.) Penn's grant encompassed all of present-day Pennsylvania and all of what is now Delaware, one of the largest land grants in history ever awarded to an individual.

Folk artist Edward Hicks was a native of Pennsylvania and a devout Quaker. Among Hicks's most famous creations were his various versions of his painting *The Peaceable Kingdom*, many of which included scenes of William Penn's treaty with the Native Americans—such as this one (TOP LEFT) from ca. 1834. Years after Pennsylvania had been founded, French Enlightenment writer and philosopher François-Marie Arouet de Voltaire, in his *Lettres philosophiques* (*Philosophical Letters*, 1734) observed that Penn's treaty with the Indians "was the only treaty between these peoples and the Christians that was never sworn to and which has not been broken."

> *"In a short time this province will want very little from England, its mother country."*
>
> —Peter Kalm, writing about Pennsylvania in *Travels into North America* (1748)

Hicks also painted numerous idyllic scenes of Pennsylvania farms—farms that contributed so significantly to the colony's success. (TOP RIGHT) *The Residence of David Twining*, 1845–47, was created from memory of the farm Hicks lived on as a boy.

It was not only the size of Penn's grant that endowed him with good fortune. Because of its late founding, Pennsylvania was not plagued by the hunger, disease, and Indian hostility that had plagued the earliest attempts at New World colonization. However, the greatest difference was Penn himself. Many of the others who attempted to found colonies were driven by selfish interests or the desire to escape conformity. As the absolute proprietor of a staggering twenty-eight-million acres, Penn could have set himself up as a feudal lord. Instead, motivated by his Quaker's faith that goodness could be achieved in the temporal world, he crossed the Atlantic intent on establishing an ideal state, one in which the hallmarks would be religious freedom, fair treatment of the natives, and the establishment of a government based on people's needs and wishes.

Penn arrived in his new lands in 1682, accompanied by a group of one hundred fellow Quakers. Earlier, with his blessing, other Quakers had preceded him. It was the beginning of a colony that became a model of success in more diverse ways than any other in America. By 1760, the rich earth drained by the Delaware, Schuylkill, and Susquehanna rivers made Pennsylvania the breadbasket of the colonies.

BELOW: **By 1790, less than a century after its settlement, Philadelphia boasted a population of more than 42,000 people. The home of many distinguished scientists and men of letters, it attracted legions** of foreign visitors, some of whom referred to it as the **"London of America." German artist Balthasar Friedrich Leizelt engraved this colorful view of Philadelphia's waterfront in the 1770s.**

158

Visiting Englishman Alexander Mackraby wrote in a 1768 letter to Sir Philip Francis in London: "It is almost a proverb in this neighborhood that 'Every great fortune made hence within these fifty years has been by land'" At the same time, manufacturing grew to such an extent that Swedish traveler and diarist, Peter Kalm, wrote in *Travels into North America* (1748) that Pennsylvanians "make almost everything in such quantity and perfection, that in a short time this province will want very little from England, its mother country."

But for many Pennsylvanians, and for most that visited it, Philadelphia was the colony's crowning glory. By the mid 1700s, the city had blossomed into the most admired urban center in America. Carefully designed and laid out, the wide symmetry of its paved and curbed streets, its brick and flagstone sidewalks, its beautifully spaced trees, and the innovative architecture of its buildings combined to make it what D. W. Meinig in his book *The Shaping of America: Volume 1, Atlantic America, 1492–1800* (1986) characterized as "the first important example in America of the order so desired by the merchant and trader."

By 1775, the lure of the colonies had become so great that America's Atlantic seaboard was the home of the fastest growing population anywhere in the world. There were already more than two million people living there—twenty thousand in Boston, thirty thousand in New York, and forty thousand in Philadelphia alone—and the makeup of the population was unlike anything that had ever taken place. Anglicans, Quakers, Huguenots, Swiss, Germans, Creoles, French, Irish—all these and dozens of others were represented in a uniquely American mosaic. "It has not been necessary to force people to come and settle here," wrote Peter Kalm, "On the contrary, foreigners of different languages have left their country, houses, property and relations and ventured over wide and stormy seas in order to come hither."

He could well have added that, despite the many nations from which they had come, the polyglot of languages they spoke, and the wide diversity of their backgrounds, the colonization of the Atlantic seaboard was a unifying force. No matter what their differences, every one of the colonists had shared the often-terrifying experience of crossing the Atlantic. Once in America they shared the many challenges of starting life anew in a world that not that long ago had been totally unknown. They had all settled in colonies that faced the Atlantic. And it was the Atlantic that would determine their destinies.

From the very beginning, all of the colonies knew that, in order to survive, they had to trade. And well before the seventeenth century was over, small ships from every colony were moving in and out of eastern seaports. Massachusetts, Pennsylvania, and Rhode Island competed with each other to supply the foodstuffs and other goods that the southern colonies, concentrating on their staple crops, needed so badly. New York flour was exchanged in Charleston for rice. Charleston vessels carried freight to Savannah. The result was not only a needed exchange of goods but also a vital exchange of interests and ideas, another major force in unifying the disparate colonies.

BELOW: Along with becoming a vital part of the inter-colonial trade, schooners were also widely used in offshore fishing and became popular as pilot vessels, particularly in America and northern Europe. The schooner shown here was used for halibut fishing; the drawing was done by one Captain J. W. Collins as part of an 1881 report to the U.S. Fish Commission.

This map cartouche depicts tobacco traders conducting business at an American port, while slaves move cargo. It is an enlarged detail from a well-known map by surveyors and British landholders Joshua Fry and Peter Jefferson, called *A Map of the Most Inhabited Part of Virginia...*, published in 1755.

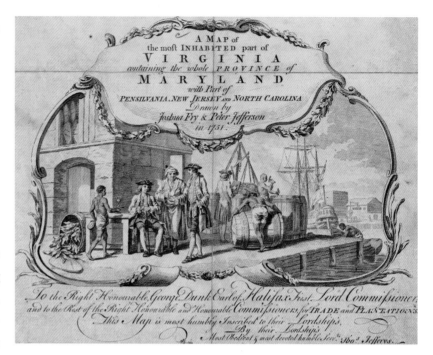

All of this ever-growing intercolonial maritime trade led to an early American shipbuilding industry, one in which colonial nautical designers, artisans, sail makers, and riggers proved themselves as skilled as any of their counterparts throughout the world, and in many cases even more innovative. In 1714, Captain Andrew Robinson of Massachusetts's Cape Ann created a sleek, two-masted vessel with a fore and aft rig and a forward jib that glided so gracefully over the water that upon observing her in action, according to legend one onlooker exclaimed, "See how she scoons." The name stuck, and the schooner, particularly adept at short-tack sailing and manageable even with the smallest crew, became the workhorse of intercolonial trade and shipping. Soon nations throughout Europe turned to the schooner for coastal commerce.

THE COMMERCIAL REVOLUTION

It was, however, not in intercolonial maritime activity but in international trade that the next important development in the making of the Atlantic world took place. Called the Commercial Revolution, it would change the commerce and economies of nations on both sides of the Atlantic and bring people from all those nations into closer contact than ever before. It had actually begun as far back as Jamestown when, under John Smith's leadership, the early settlers of that first colony began trading New World timber with England for life-sustaining supplies. It had continued with the Pilgrims during the earliest days of their Plymouth settlement, when they had sent a vessel back home loaded with clapboard superior to any that could be found in the mother country. And by 1617 Virginia was shipping ten tons of tobacco to England a year.

By the 1640s, the Commercial Revolution was well under way, brought on by an increasing desire by those in the colonies to obtain products not available in the New World. "All foreign commodities grew scarce," the Massachusetts Bay Colony's governor John Winthrop wrote. "These straits set our people to work to provide fish, clapboards, plank, etc., and to look to the West Indies for trade."

They also looked to Europe, drawing on the natural treasure that had lured so many of them to the New World in the first place. All along the Massachusetts coast, towns such

as Salem, Gloucester, Marblehead, and others developed into bustling fishing ports. In 1641 alone, more than three hundred thousand codfish were shipped across the Atlantic to Europe. By 1670, Massachusetts Bay was the home of 430 ships, some of them as large as 250 tons. It was the birth of the Yankee skippers, bold new seamen who instituted a triangular trade, bringing lumber, grain, and meat to the West Indies, dried cod and barrel staves to France and Spain, and wine, salt, and oranges that they had picked up in their ports of call to England. At the same time, trade between the southern colonies and Europe accelerated with the exchange of tar, resin, pitch, rice, and indigo for woolen goods, axes, cooking utensils, and other products so much in demand in the New World.

With the continual exchange of goods between Europe and the Americas, the Atlantic became the scene of the busiest commercial activity in the world. By 1750, more than 1,000 English ships were involved in the transatlantic commerce, some 450 engaged in the sugar trade with the Caribbean islands alone. In 1773, more than 1,360 French

ABOVE: Balthasar Friedrich Leizelt engraved this image of the port of Salem, Massachusetts, in the 1770s. By the eve of the American Revolution, colonial shipping had increased spectacularly, and colonial vessels were carrying goods throughout the world. "It is the great care of the [colonial] merchants to keep their ships in constant employ, which makes them try all ports to force a trade," British royal agent Edward Randolph wrote to his king in 1676. Remarking on the fact that there were so many colonial ships plying the Caribbean waters, Randolph added that "There is little left for all the merchants in England to import into any of the plantations."

This scene of Charleston's sail-filled harbor was representative of the maritime activity that had transformed the once struggling colonies into a major factor in the making of the Atlantic world. The print, ca. 1838, is by William James Bennett after a painting by George Cooke.

vessels crossed the Atlantic to pick up goods produced in the colonies. A staggering 3,500 ships from England, the Netherlands, France, Spain, Portugal, and Denmark were involved in the Atlantic wine trade, delivering the valued spirits they picked up in the Azores and the Canaries to ports throughout Europe, Africa, and North and South America.

The ramifications of the Commercial Revolution were many, not the least of which was a vital transformation in both Europe and New World society. As transatlantic trade became both increasingly vital and commonplace, the traders and merchants on both sides of the ocean gained a new and exalted status. In Europe, the merchants replaced the feudal landowners as the most powerful of all classes, eventually even controlling the politics and the government of many Old World nations. In America, the merchants not only took on a new status, but assumed roles that went well beyond the trafficking of goods. Before the Colonial period was over, many became the retailers and wholesalers of the goods they brought in; investors in grain mills, sawmills, foundries, wharfs, and shipyards; and even established themselves as the leading employers and moneylenders in the colonies.

It had been a remarkable two and a half centuries. The Atlantic, for so long feared and unknown, had been continuously transformed—first as the waterway to exploration and discovery; then to the avenue for the greatest migration the world had even known; and finally as the pathway to the world.

5

SLAVERY

INHUMAN BONDAGE

A Cotton Plantation on the Mississippi, by Currier & Ives (1884), presents an idealized view of the slave-driven cotton industry.

SLAVERY

When the anonymous author of *American Husbandry* wrote his 1775 tract (see "England Rules the North" in Chapter 4), in which he urged planters to leave England and move to the American southern colonies, one of the advantages he had listed was that there were "no oppressions to enslave the planter and rob him of the fruits of his industry." He was right. The planters would indeed not be enslaved. But that was hardly true of millions of others. And it was on the backs of the slaves, brought to the colonies in chains from Africa, that the planters in the southern colonies, as well as those in the islands, made their fortunes.

Slavery, of course, did not begin in the Americas—the practice can be traced back to civilization's earliest annals. In the Code of Hammurabi, the Babylonian code of law written around 1760 BCE, there are over twenty-five decrees regarding slaves, which at the time was already a well-established institution. Slavery occurred in every ancient civilization, including the Akkadian Empire, Assyria, Rome and parts of the Roman Empire, and in Arabia and Greece, where it was a key element in the development of the ancient Greek city-states. Early records also reveal that slavery as an institution included a mixture of debt-slavery, slavery as a punishment for crime, and, most commonly, the enslavement of prisoners of war or conquest. Almost nowhere was this slavery based on race, nor, cruel and degrading as it was, did it result in the mortality that the transatlantic slave trade would bring about.

A detail of *The Slave Market* (1888), by Gustave Boulanger; as illustrated here, Greek slaves represented a multitude of nationalities from across the Greek Empire. Aristotle espoused the view of Greeks on slavery in his *Politics*, 350 BCE: "And so, in the arrangement of the family, a slave is a living possession . . . For that some should rule and others be ruled is a thing not only necessary, but expedient; from the hour of their birth, some are marked out for subjection, others for rule."

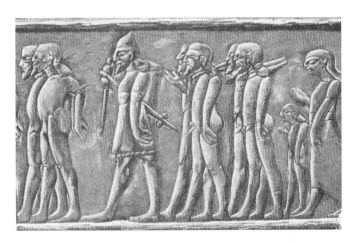

This image of a convoy of bound slaves in Assyria was drawn by French artist Faucher-Gudin, after a bas-relief from the gates of Balawat. The third from left figure is the slave master. The gates adorned a former palace in the ancient Assyrian city of Imgur-Enlil (in present-day Balawat, Iraq). The image appeared in volume VI of Gaston Maspero's *History of Egypt, Chaldea, Syria, Babylonia, and Assyria* (1903–6).

SLAVERY IN THE ATLANTIC WORLD

There had been slavery on the African continent from the beginning of recorded times. But, as historian Herbert Klein has pointed out in his essay "The Atlantic Slave Trade to 1650" in *Tropical Babylons: Sugar and the Making of the Atlantic World, 1450–1680* (2004), it was a domestic institution, confined to Africa's most developed societies. Caravan slave routes across the Sahara to the Mediterranean had also existed from pre-Roman times, but it was not until the ninth century CE, when the Arab Empire spread into India and the eastern Mediterranean, that a steady international slave trade took place. As historian Paul E. Lovejoy documented in his book *Transformations in Slavery: A History of Slavery in Africa* (1983), between the ninth and fifteenth centuries from five thousand to ten thousand slaves a year were transported along at least six interlocking caravan routes from Africa to the Mediterranean. According to Lovejoy, anywhere from 3.5 million to 10 million slaves, most of them women and children, were taken out of their homelands during this period.

Slaves wait to be sold at a slave market in Cairo, in a drawing by Scots artist David Roberts, ca. 1838, published as part of a collection of drawings in *Egypt and Nubia* (1842–49). The drawing was done from life by Roberts during his journeys in the region. Practiced since ancient times, slavery remained prevalent in Egypt throughout the nineteenth century; in the 1800s the majority of slaves were women, forced into domestic work.

The transportation of slaves across the great ocean to the Americas entailed the largest movement of slaves ever undertaken and had a profound and lasting impact on the Atlantic world. It began with the Portuguese, who, under the leadership of Prince Henry, were the first Europeans to reach Guinea (see "The Ambition of Prince Henry the Navigator" in Chapter 2). Henry at first actually tried to forbid slave traffic, but once early Portuguese settlers found that sugar could be profitably grown on islands off the African coast, they turned to African slaves for labor—and Henry, to whom profitability was always a god, reversed his course. Portuguese trading in slaves intensified when its explorers and colonists discovered and settled soil-rich Brazil. It was also the Portuguese who first became aware of the African practice of enslaving prisoners of war and who first began trading guns, liquor, and other European goods with black slave owners for slaves. By 1650, other European nations, particularly the Dutch, English, and the French, had responded to the ever-increasing New World demands for slaves and had begun trading with slaveholders from various West African nations.

The demand was brought about by the very nature of the New World economies. By the 1570s, the Portuguese had begun establishing sugar plantations in Brazil, and as discussed in the previous chapter, as the European desire for sugar grew, other nations began developing New World plan-

tations, particularly in the West Indies. These locales had everything required for the establishment of a successful plantation system—huge open land, fertile soil, good harbors, warm winds, and a climate particularly conducive to growing not only sugar, but tobacco, rice, and indigo—everything except the huge labor force needed to grow, process, and ship the crops. It couldn't be supplied by the Native American population, who were dying from the diseases the earliest Europeans had brought with them across the Atlantic. The Africans, however, were largely resistant to these diseases. Moreover, they were accustomed to agricultural labor and were used to a tropical climate, and thus could be worked as hard as their demanding owners required. No wonder that, in 1670, King Louis XIV of France reportedly proclaimed that

ABOVE: This depiction of sugar-making in the West Indies shows a white overseer directing slaves as they carry out various functions of the sugar-making process. The illustration appeared in the London publication *Universal Magazine of Knowledge and Pleasure*, in 1749.

RIGHT: Scenes of slaves at work in the far-distant islands were common artistic subjects for Old World illustrators. This nineteenth-century engraving of a sugar plantation is by Paolo Fumagalli.

In testament to the glory of Timbuktu, a West African Islamic proverb stated, "Salt comes from the north, gold from the south, and silver from the country of the white men, but the word of God and the treasures of wisdom are only to be found in Timbuktu." This engraving of the city as envisioned by J. Clark appeared in the 1830 book by August René Caillié, *Travels to Timbuctoo*. In the Middle Ages, Timbuktu was legendary to Europeans as a metropolis of unimagined treasure, an oasis in the Sahara. Over subsequent centuries, many Western explorers who dreamt of finding the city died before reaching their goal, whether succumbing to the brutal heat of the Sahara or being murdered by desert nomads. In 1824, the Société de Géographie of Paris offered 10,000 francs to the first European to reach the city—and return alive to tell about it. That man was French wine merchant August René Caillié, who discovered that Timbuktu was no longer an important intellectual and spiritual center of the Islamic world, but a small impoverished village on the edge of the desert.

"there is nothing which contributes more to the development of the colonies and the cultivation of their soil than the laborious toil of the Negroes."

Beginning in the 1600s, the number of slaves brought into Brazil, into Spanish-American territory, and into Dutch-held New World possessions increased dramatically. Before 1600 there had been fewer than 1 million slaves in the New World. By the end of the century, the number had grown to about 2.75 million. By the middle of the 1700s, due greatly to slaves transported to English southern colonies on the North American mainland to work the tobacco and cotton plantations, the number, according to conservative estimates, had increased to more than 7 million.

A CIVILIZATION THREATENED

Whatever the numbers, for the Africans in bondage, slavery was a catastrophic and dehumanizing experience, made even worse, if possible, by the fact that these were people who came from rich cultures that had flourished for thousands of years; cultures that were facing destruction. Long before the first Europeans arrived, sophisticated civilizations had thrived all along the coast of West Africa. The people there lived under highly developed political and social systems in kingdoms headed by well-established rulers.

Like Timbuktu, the city of Loango—part of a kingdom of the same name—was a highly advanced community. Established around the fifteenth century, at its height in the 1700s, the Loango Kingdom stretched from Mayombe in the north to the mouth of the Congo River and was an important trading center for ivory, copper, tin, and slaves. This panoramic depiction of the city was published in John Ogilby's *Africa; being an accurate description of the regions of Aegypt . . . (1670).*

172

Representative of the sophisticated communities in which many Africans lived was the ancient city of Timbuktu, located in present-day Mali. Established by the nomadic Tuareg around 1100 CE, Timbuktu grew into a city of enormous wealth through its key role in the trans-Saharan trade in gold, ivory, salt, and other precious commodities, goods brought to the city from the Islamic north and then transferred to boats on the River Niger. In the fourteenth and fifteenth centuries, the city became the jewel of several successive empires including the Ghana Empire, the Mali Empire, and the Sanghi Empire.

Stories of Timbuktu's great wealth helped prompt European exploration of Africa's west coast, tales such as that written by the sixteenth-century Moroccan traveler Leo Africanus, who wrote in his manuscript *The History and Description of Africa and of the Notable Things Therein Contained* (1550): "The rich king of Tombuto (Timbuktu) hath many plates and scepters of gold, some whereof weigh 1,300 pounds . . . He hath always 3,000 horsemen . . . [and] a great store of doctors, judges, priests, and other learned men, that are bountifully maintained at the king's expense."

Africanus's reference to "learned men" was particularly telling. For Timbuktu's lasting contribution to world civilization would not be its wealth but its scholarship. By the fourteenth century, scores of important books were written in the city, establishing Timbuktu as the center of a vital written tradition in Africa.

Africa was also a land whose artistic and material culture was characterized by both diversity and innovation. Their artistic creations not only combined form and function but, as the curators of the University of Virginia's Bayly Art Museum have stated, were "intended not only to please the eye but to uphold moral values." Everyday items such as bowls, knives, stools, hair combs, and drums were adorned with human, animal, and supernatural representations all with particular cultural and social meaning. African art also placed great emphasis on the three-dimensional, leading to sculptural works in stone, bronze, and terracotta that have rarely been surpassed.

Unarmed and taken unawares, most slaves fell easy prey to their captors. The least resistance was met with sheer brutality. African men and women, lashed together by rope, are led from their Mali homes to a ship waiting to take them across the Atlantic. The slave trader to the far left is identified in the original source as a Mande-speaking African. The illustration first appeared in 1885 in *Mission d'exploration du Haut-Niger 1879–1881* (*Exploratory Mission of the Upper Niger, 1879–1881*), by French colonial administrator Joseph Simon Gallieni.

This map, entitled *Africae Nova Descriptio*, was created by Willem Janszoon Blaeu in 1589. In addition to outlining the countries and cities of the African continent (and native animals such as elephants and monkeys) in the sixteenth century, in its left and right border the map featured illustrations of peoples from numerous African countries, and their various forms of dress. Ships and sea monsters ply the waters. Depictions such as this fired the ambitions of European rulers and adventurers eager to obtain the riches that lay within Africa.

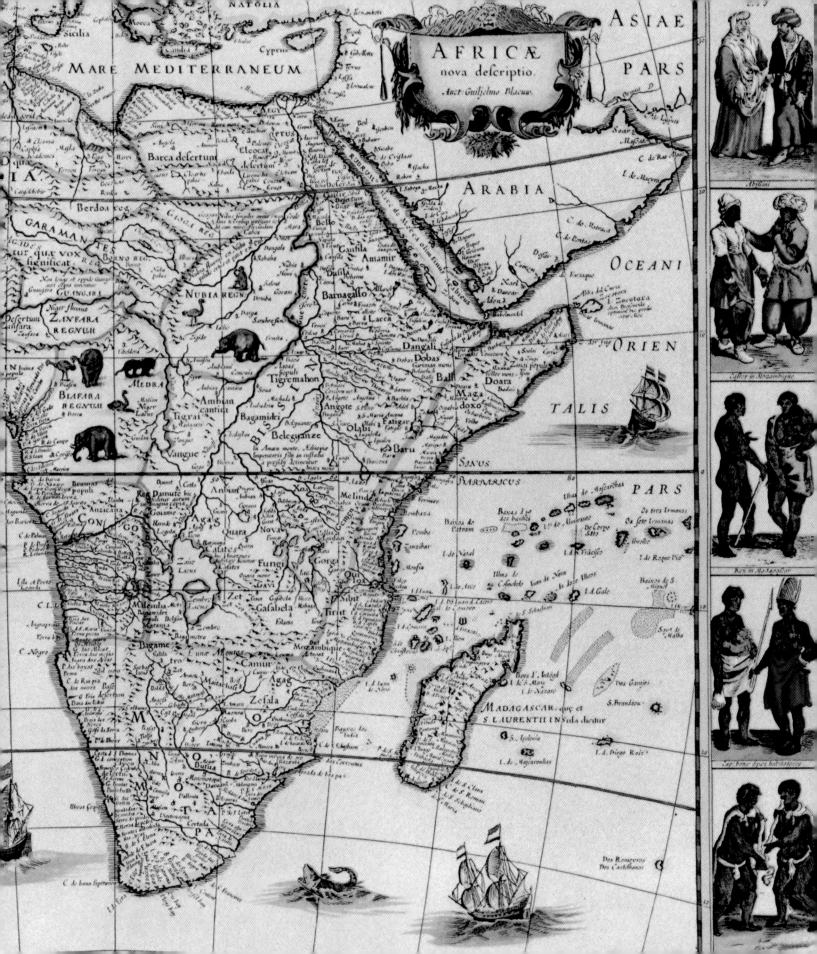

AFRICÆ
nova descriptio.
Auct: Guiljelmo Blaeuw.

NATOLIA

ASIAE PARS

MARE MEDITERRANEUM

Sicilia

Candia

Cyprus

AEGY

ARABIA

OCEANI

ORIEN

Barca desertum

GARAMANTES

Berdoa reg.

BORNO REG.

GUINGARA

NUBIA REGN.

Amamir

GIORG REG.

Barnagasso

Lacca

Dangali

Dobas

TALIS

TIS

Doara

Maga

doxo

Baru

BIAFARA REGNUM

MEDRA

Ambian cantin

Tigremahon

BISSIN

Tigrai

Bagamidri

Angote

Olabi

Fatigar

Beleguanze

Vangue

SINUS

BARBARICUS

PARS

Melinde

Anzicana

CONGO

Agas

Quara

Damute

Goiame

NOVA

Fungi

Mombaza

Pemba

Zanzibar

Zaire Lacus

Gavi

Zet

Sibit

Tirit

Casabela

Milemba

Bagame

Luna Montes

Camur

Agag

Zefala

MOTA

PA

Mozambique

MADAGASCAR, quæ et
S. LAURENTII INSula dicitur

C. de bona Speranza

Early African Art

The result of a continent inhabited by a multitude of societies and civilizations, the rich and diverse nature of early African art was dominated by the depiction of deities, spirits of ancestors, mythological beings, good and/or evil, the dead, animal spirits, and other beings believed to have power over humans. Perhaps the most shining examples of the way in which African art combined beauty with purpose were the costumes, textiles, and particularly the masks created to be worn during dances, ceremonies, and rituals. Dating back to beyond Paleolithic times, and each representing a particular spirit, African masks are today regarded as among the finest creations in the world of art.

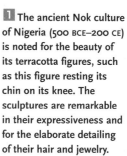

1 The ancient Nok culture of Nigeria (500 BCE–200 CE) is noted for the beauty of its terracotta figures, such as this figure resting its chin on its knee. The sculptures are remarkable in their expressiveness and for the elaborate detailing of their hair and jewelry.

2 A nineteenth-century Ci Wara headdress of the Bamana people of Mali. The Ci Wara ("farming beast") is a mythical animal, part antelope, part anteater, sacred to farmers; the wood and metal headdress is affixed to a cap and worn during paired ritual dances to bring strength and success to the farmer.

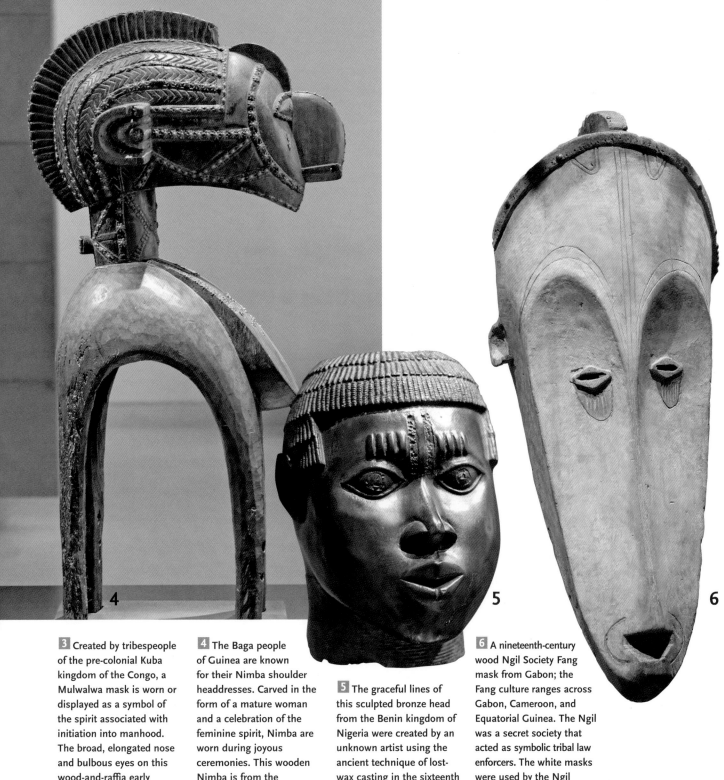

4

5

6

3 Created by tribespeople of the pre-colonial Kuba kingdom of the Congo, a Mulwalwa mask is worn or displayed as a symbol of the spirit associated with initiation into manhood. The broad, elongated nose and bulbous eyes on this wood-and-raffia early twentieth-century Mulwalwa are characteristic of the style.

4 The Baga people of Guinea are known for their Nimba shoulder headdresses. Carved in the form of a mature woman and a celebration of the feminine spirit, Nimba are worn during joyous ceremonies. This wooden Nimba is from the nineteenth century.

5 The graceful lines of this sculpted bronze head from the Benin kingdom of Nigeria were created by an unknown artist using the ancient technique of lost-wax casting in the sixteenth century.

6 A nineteenth-century wood Ngil Society Fang mask from Gabon; the Fang culture ranges across Gabon, Cameroon, and Equatorial Guinea. The Ngil was a secret society that acted as symbolic tribal law enforcers. The white masks were used by the Ngil Society in their rituals. The masks' bold abstractness and elongated lines inspiried modern Western artists such as Picasso.

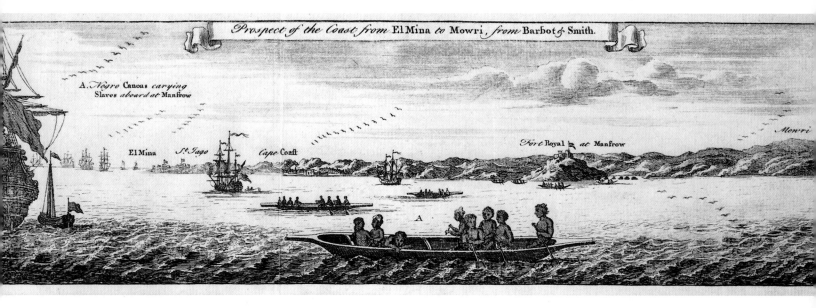

N. Parr Sculp.

Vol. 2. plate 61. p. 588

This illustration was created for volume two of a series of books by Thomas Astley entitled *A New Collection of Voyages and Travels* (1745–47), stories and essays from various European travelers to Africa, compiled and translated into four volumes. The top drawing, *Prospect of the Coast from El Mina to Mowri* (towns of the Gold Coast, Elmina is in present-day Ghana), shows slaves being rowed to a ship at left. The bottom image, *Prospect of St. George's Castle at El Mina*, shows the forbidding-looking fort at Elmina that functioned as a major Portuguese slave trading depot.

It is no wonder that for the heirs of such a rich culture their sudden transfer into the hands of the slave traders was such an incomprehensible experience. Most came from tribes that had been captured in tribal warfare. Many historians, in fact, now believe that, as the demands for slaves increased and became more profitable, many tribal wars were started for the sole purpose of acquiring captives that could be sold to the traders. Also taken as slaves were those who had been convicted of crimes. As historian Winthrop D. Jordan wrote in his book *The Americans* (1988), "As slavery became a growing business, African chiefs began to create more slaves. New crimes were invented so more criminals could be sold into slavery." As Jordan also pointed out, not all the victims of the slave trade were those sold by African rulers. Some had been captured directly by members of European slave ships. And a significant number of the captives had been sold to the slave traders by Arab slave merchants whose predecessors had been the first to deal in African slavery.

Whatever the source of their captivity, none of the slaves had any notion of what lay ahead. What they did know, at least by the time they were forced aboard the slave vessels, was that they were now no longer in the hands of their original captors, but under the control of men about whom they knew absolutely nothing.

TRIANGLE OF TRADE AND SUFFERING

These white men were engaged in a trading system that was at the heart of the slave traffic. At the center of this traffic was a product that—like the cod that had lured so many settlers to the New World and the economically important tobacco crop—played a pivotal role in shaping the early history of the Atlantic world. That product was rum, an extraordinarily popular beverage whose origins dated back to ancient China and India. Historians believe that the word "rum" derives from the Latin word *saccharum*, meaning "sugar," which is appropriate since it was from sugar that rum was produced. More accurately, it was from molasses, a by-product of the sugar-making, that rum was manufactured.

During the sugar-refining process that took place throughout the New World islands, an acre of sugar cane yielded enough molasses to produce about two hundred gallons of rum. But turning molasses into rum required further distilling, a process that plantation owners felt distracted from the main goal of producing the "white gold" that sugar had become, since this further distillation required so much labor and wood. By the time that England's mainland colonies had been established, however, plantation owners had found a solution to making rum profitable without disturbing their sugar-making operations.

O my great massa in heaven,
Pity me, and bless my Children!

Since early Colonial days, the manufacture of rum had been New England's largest and most prosperous industry. Throughout the sugar islands, planters began sending their molasses to New England, where it was turned into rum. The result was what became known as the "triangular trade." Molasses was shipped to the British mainland colonies and turned into rum. The rum, along with other products, including sugar and tobacco, was carried across the Atlantic to Africa where it was traded for slaves. The slaves, in what became known as the infamous Middle Passage, were taken to the sugar islands to raise more sugar and molasses—and the vicious cycle would begin again.

Of all the horrific experiences that the slaves would endure, from their capture to their labors on the plantations, it was the Middle Passage that was the most deadly. Often in bad shape both mentally and physically by the time they were led from the interior to the ships, the captives were stripped naked, examined thoroughly, and then forced below decks into the hold. As South Carolinian slave trader Joseph Hawkins observed in his memoir *A History of a Voyage to the Coast of Africa, and Travels to the Interior of that Country* (1797), the sight of slaves being put in irons and hoarded on to the ship was "one of the most affecting scenes that I ever witnessed . . . their wailings were torturing beyond what words can express."

Some of the captains of the slave ships were what were called "loose packers," believing that by packing fewer slaves in their holds than most of their counterparts they would

OPPOSITE: An American antislave illustration, ca. 1830s; depictions such as this one, created by artists for abolitionist publications as expressions of outrage against the slave trade, appeared on both sides of the Atlantic. But the desire for profits far outweighed humanitarian concerns, and from the sixteenth through the first half of the nineteenth century, the number of Africans placed in bondage increased dramatically.

BELOW: Slave ship owners and captains became masters of packing their vessels with as many captives as could possibly be placed onto their ships. This diagram of an inhumanely crowded ship from the Atlantic slave trade is from an *Abstract of Evidence*, which antislave activists compiled for their presentation to a select committee of the British House of Commons in 1790.

181

SLAVERY

reduce the mortality rate of the Middle Passage. But the vast majority of captains loaded as many of their human cargo as could possibly fit, convinced that the largest possible load would make up for whatever fatalities occurred. But whatever the predilection of the captain, the Middle Passage was, for the slaves, more brutal than can be adequately described. And it was not only the physical abuse they suffered. For most, still in shock from what had happened to them, the psychological damage was equally destructive. Many had never seen a white man, a ship, or the ocean. The emotional damage they suffered as they realized that they were being torn from home, family, native land, indeed everything they cherished, was, for many, as devastating as the suffocating conditions, the corporal punishment, and the lack of adequate food and sanitation, all of which resulted in a horrendous death rate on almost every voyage. It is estimated that as much as eighteen percent of all the millions of slaves forced to make the Middle Passage died somewhere on the Atlantic from some type of disease, lack of nourishment, or physical cruelty. A significant number, unable to endure the conditions and an unknown and terrifying future, took their own lives: "Two of my wearied countrymen who were chained together, preferring death to such a life of misery, somehow made through the nettings and jumped into the sea" wrote Olaudah Equiano, one of the most articulate of all

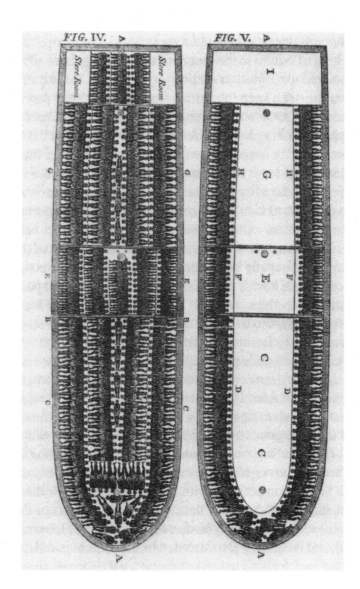

ABOVE: The number of slaves who died in the Atlantic crossing was staggering. Historian Patrick Manning, in his *Slavery and African Life: Occidental, Oriental, and African Slave Trades* (1990), has estimated that in order to deliver nine million slaves to the Americas in the period between 1700 and 1850, some twenty-one million people were captured. This harrowing ca. 1930 lithograph by American artist Bernarda Bryson Shahn depicts emaciated African captives on the deck of a slave ship.

OPPOSITE: Captioned "Stowing the Cargo on a Slaver at Night," this engraving was published in Connecticut historian Henry Howe's *Life and Death on the Ocean*, ca. 1855. The picture depicts seamen forcibly moving a group of slaves—who had been taken up during the day for air—back down to the airless, dark, and cramped hull of the ship, where disease was rampant. The slavers also succumbed to the unsanitary conditions aboard ship; it is estimated that ships lost an average of fifteen percent of their crew to disease during Atlantic crossings.

the Africans taken into captivity, in his book *The Interesting Narrative of the Life of Olaudah Equiano, or Gustavus Vassa, the African* (1789).

For those who managed to survive the voyage, the first hours in the Americas were equally traumatic. Once the ship docked, the slaves were sold either to planters or to wholesalers of slaves. Most were sold several times before reaching the far-off plantations where they would spend their lives in backbreaking labor. In the process, many suffered what for them was the ultimate misery, as families were broken apart forever. It was a misery that had begun with the very first separations initiated by the earliest Portuguese slave traders. "Mothers clasped their other children in their arms…receiving blows with little pity for their own flesh, if only they might not be torn from them," Portuguese chronicler Gomes Eanes de Zurara wrote in *Crónica dos feitos da Guiné* (*The Chronicle of the Discovery and Conquest of Guinea*)(1453). It continued on the auction blocks in the islands and later in the mainland colonies.

Until 1619, all the slaves transported to the New World were delivered to the various Caribbean islands. But in that year, a Dutch vessel brought twenty black captives to the American mainland at Jamestown. A torrent would follow. By the early 1700s, some 145,000 slaves worked the Virginia and

This lithograph after an 1851 painting by American artist Junius Brutus Stearns depicts President George Washington talking to the overseer at his Mt. Vernon farm, as slaves work his fields. The painting, created ten years before the Civil War broke out, depicts an unrealistic scene of idyllic contentment among the slaves. Although Washington owned many slaves (both inherited and bought), his attitude toward slavery changed as he grew older. As president he did not publicly oppose slavery because he feared it would divide the new nation. However, in his will he left instructions for all of his slaves to be freed after his wife's death.

The ABOLITION of the SLAVE TRADE.
Or the Inhumanity of Dealers in human flesh exemplified in Capt. Kimber's treatment of a Young Negro Girl of 15 for her Virji Modesty

To many of those who benefited most from the transatlantic slave trade—stock companies, merchants, insurers, bankers—the trade in humans was simply the global distribution of products. The publication of disturbing scenes such as this one left them unaffected. The caption in this hand-colored etching by popular English artist Isaac Cruikshank reads "The abolition of the slave trade. Or the inhumanity of dealers in human flesh exemplified in Capt'n Kimber's treatment of a young Negro girl of 15 for her virjen modesty." Cruikshank created this image for London print publisher S. W. Fores in April 1792, one week after British politician William Wilberforce publicly protested in the House of Commons against the brutality of slavery as epitomized by the murder of a young African girl. The girl was strung up and beaten by one Captain John Kimber, after she refused to dance for him on deck, and died several days later. Kimber was tried by the Admiralty Court in June 1792, but in the end was honorably acquitted.

BELOW: Maria Graham (later
Lady Maria Callcott), an
English writer and illustrator,
drew this image of a slave
market in Rio de Janeiro. It
was reproduced in her 1824
book *Journal of a Voyage to
Brazil, and Residence There,
During Part of the Years
1821, 1822, 1823.*

Maryland tobacco plantations alone. Tens of thousands of others toiled in the South Carolina and Georgia coastal rice belt. Slavery even flourished in some regions of the North, particularly in the farming areas of New York, New Jersey, and Rhode Island, where many Southern planters maintained summer residences with large slave estates.

By 1775, thirty-six percent of all the slaves had been brought to British America. Thirty-two percent labored in Portuguese territory, particularly in the fields and the mines of Brazil. Another thirteen percent labored on plantations in French New World territory, while nine percent toiled in Spanish America. The impact of the labor performed by those in bondage, represented by the tens of millions of dollars worth of commodities they produced and the trade it stimulated, led to nothing less than the emergence of the Americas into the international economy. As historian Barbara L. Solow has written in *Slavery and the Rise of the Atlantic System* (1991): "[It was slavery] that made the empty lands of the western hemisphere valuable producers of commodities and valuable markets for Europe and North America: what moved in the Atlantic in these centuries was predominantly slaves, the output of slaves, the inputs of slave societies, and goods and services purchased with the earnings of slave products…Slavery thus affected not only the countries of the slaves' origins and destinations but, equally, those countries that invested in, supplied, or consumed the products of the slave economies.

Recd of Judge S Williams six hundred
Dollars in full payment for Jane a
negro woman 18 years old and henry her
child about one year old together with her
future increase if any which negroes
I warrant to be sound in body and mind and
Slaves for life witness my hand and seal
this 20th Day of Decr 1849 –

The conditions of the above instrument are
such that if the undersigned shall pay or caus
to be paid to Judge S William by the 1st Jan
1851 the sum of six hundred Dollars good and
lawful money the property as above describ
to revert to the undersigned and the ob Instru
ment to be void, otherwise to remain in full
force and virtue this Day and Date above written
signed sealed and delivered in presence of –

Test J. M. Lamply   John Williams

The within Negroes sold under execution
sundry against the within John Williams
and bid of by the within S S Williams at
nine hundred Dollars

OPPOSITE: This receipt from December 20, 1849, records that a Judge S. Williams of Eufaula, Alabama, paid six hundred dollars for the purchase of an eighteen-year-old African woman named Jane, her one-year-old son, Henry, and all of her future children, dated December 20, 1849.

RIGHT: A family is separated at a slave auction, and the caption—"Buy us too"—expresses the mother's anguish. Many slave-owners, particularly in the American South, actually defended the institution by claiming that their slaves were content with their lot. This image is part of a series of twelve cards by Henry Louis Stephens, engraved by James Fuller Queen, which illustrated the journey of a slave from a plantation to his struggle for liberty as a Union soldier during the Civil War. Published as a set called *The Slave in 1863*, they were produced as part of William A. Stephen's *Album Varieties*, a series of collectible cards produced during the Civil War.

THE PARTING "Buy us too."

RIGHT: Artist William L. Sheppard drew this image, captioned "The First Cotton Gin" for the December 18, 1869 issue of *Harper's Weekly*. The incongruous scene envisions black slaves happily operating the gin while white landowners discuss the new invention.

By the 1800s, cotton grown in the American South had become one of the world's most valuable commodities. With this development, even the slightest chance of slavery being abolished there became nonexistent. This ca. 1850 lithograph by Bernhard J. Dondorf depicts the bustling harbor of New Orleans as viewed from the Levee Steam Cotton Press Company, which housed an enormous steam power plant that compressed cotton bales for shipping.

6

THE AMERICAN REVOLUTION

CUTTING TIES ACROSS THE ATLANTIC

This hand-colored, ca. 1781 French print depicts the surrender of British commander Charles Cornwallis to the Americans and French at Yorktown, Virginia. The French fleet is shown at right in the York River.

THE AMERICAN REVOLUTION

The sun never shined on a cause of greater worth. 'Tis not the affair of a city, a country, a province, or a kingdom; but a continent— of at least one eighth part the habitable Globe.

—THOMAS PAINE, *Common Sense*, 1776

By the third decade of the 1700s, England's trade with its American colonies had become a cornerstone of the British economy. Twenty percent of all the shipping that entered England's home ports came from the colonies. Industrial towns throughout Great Britain were busily occupied producing clothing, tools, cutlery, and a myriad of other goods for the American market.

Most of His Majesty's American subjects were equally sanguine about their condition, and their feelings were based not only on trade. The American colonies were both prospering and growing. Beyond the thriving seaport communities, more than two million people were already living in farms, villages, and towns. Colonial industry was expanding and a distinct culture had arisen. It was not an American culture, but a British-American culture. On all levels, colonial politics and government were based on British models. Throughout the colonies, the prevailing social values were also English. On the eve of events that were to profoundly change both the New World and the Old, the proudest boast of most of Great Britain's American subjects was that they were Englishmen.

THE BREACH BEGINS

It was not that England had refrained from trying to place controls on the colonies. As early as 1651, the British

In the middle of the 1700s, Boston was both the hub of New England and a principal trading port in America. Most of its citizens, like those in its sister colonies, were confident that nothing but increased peace and prosperity lay ahead. German engraver Franz Xaver Habermann made this print of Boston Harbor around 1770.

ABOVE: This 1736 view of the Britain's Fort George (originally Fort Amsterdam), on the southern tip of Manhattan, shows the skyline as it looked at the time. The image is by London engraver John Carwitham.

Parliament had passed the first of what would be a series of Navigation Acts designed to impose severe restrictions on colonial trade with any nation but England. However, the acts had never been enforced, and the colonists had happily ignored them. As Thomas Bredon, a New England royalist, had written in a letter in 1660: "[The colonists] look upon themselves as a free state,…there being many against the King, or having any dependence on England."

Alarms probably should have gone off when the Massachusetts legislature (called the General Court) openly proclaimed to the attorney general in October 1678, that "the laws of England are bounded by within the four seas, and do not reach America. The subjects of his majesty hence not being represented in Parliament, so we have not looked at ourselves to be impeded in our trade by them." As noted in a later book by Scottish writer George Chalmers, *Political Annals of the Present United States* (1680), the colonial agents had prophetically noted that unless these types of complaints were dealt with, "There can be nothing expected but a breach."

That the breach would come, was in many ways, preordained. As the colonies became more prosperous and as the colonists steadily developed ways of life and thinking that were more American than English, it became inevitable that an island nation three thousand miles away would find it impossible to control so vast a continent as America. Thomas

The title page of Thomas Paine's *Common Sense*, printed in Philadelphia in 1776. It includes as an epigraph a quote from Scottish poet James Thomson's *Liberty* (1734): "Man knows no Master save creating Heaven, Or those whom Choice and common Good ordain."

> " *Even the distance at which the Almighty hath placed England and America, is a strong and natural proof, that the authority of the one, over the other, was never the design of Heaven.* "
>
> —Thomas Paine, *Common Sense*, 1776

Paine, author of the pro-independence manifesto *Common Sense* (1776), spoke for millions of his countrymen when he declared that if God had meant for the colonists to be forever the subjects of Great Britain he would not have placed an ocean between them. The British statesman and political theorist Edmund Burke echoed the sentiment, stating that the only way that England would be able to forever hold on to her American colonies would be if the Atlantic were drained. The American patriot John Adams said it best. In an 1818 letter to Hezekiah Niles, the editor of the American publication *The Register*, Adams stated: "The Revolution was effected before the War commenced. The Revolution was in the minds and hearts of the people…this radical change in the principles, sentiments, and affections of the people, was the real American Revolution."

THE FRENCH AND INDIAN WAR

As late as 1763, however, when the British succeeded in driving the French out of North America, the thought of an American Revolution was hardly imaginable. Few could have foreseen that this English triumph, so celebrated in Great Britain at the time, would, in the end, be a vital catalyst in the colonies' movement toward independence. The events that led to the British victory were part of a long series of hostilities involving the key European powers of the mid-eighteenth century. Known in Europe as the Seven Years' War, it was fought around the globe and was later described by Winston Churchill in his book *The Second World War, volume I: The Gathering Storm* (1948), as the first world war. In America, where Britain and France battled over their claims on the colonial territory west of the Appalachians known as Ohio country, it was called the French and Indian War (1754–63)— a conflict that engulfed the American colonies and a number of Native American tribes, who allied with either the British or the French.

By 1717, the French had constructed forts on the Chicago and Illinois Rivers and had established a military post within striking distance of the Carolinas. When the British responded by erecting their own forts in the western hinterlands of their colonies, it became clear that a showdown was inevitable. The surveyor general of New York (and former mayor of New York City) Caleb Heathcote, stated in a 1715 letter to New York governor Robert Hunter: "It is impossible that we and the French can both inhabit the Continent in peace, but that one nation must at last give way to the other." As Marshall B. Davidson recorded in his two-volume history *Life in America* (1951), in 1716, a French settler declared that "it is not difficult to guess that [the British] purpose is to drive us entirely out…of North America."

In 1745, the prelude to the French and Indian War occurred when New England troops under the command of William Pepperell boldly attacked the heavily armed French fort at Louisbourg on Cape Breton Island, a fortress that guarded the approaches to the St. Lawrence River, the gateway to New France. To almost everyone's surprise, the assault succeeded. Three years later, however, in the Treaty of Aix-la-Chapelle, Britain gave Louisbourg back to France, a development that caused great resentment in the colonies.

Meantime, both sides intensified their preparations for what they knew was sure to come. Along with refortifying Louisbourg, the French erected a chain of forts from Lake Erie to the fork of the Allegheny and Monongahela rivers. In 1749, The British moved to increase their presence in the region, when a group of wealthy Virginia planters, supported by royal lieutenant governor Robert Dinwiddie and armed with a grant of over two hundred thousand acres, formed the Ohio Company for the purpose of settling the very area in which the French had built their forts.

The inevitable clash of interests began in October 1753. Dinwiddie, determined not to lose the Ohio country to the French, sent a twenty-two-year-old major in the Virginia militia named George Washington to deliver a message to the commander of the French forces in the Ohio country, Jacques Legardeur de Saint-Pierre, asking him to withdraw from the

This hand-colored print, published by English printer Carington Bowles around 1769, depicts the landing of William Pepperell and his New England troops at Louisbourg—a fortress thought to be so impregnable that it was referred to as the "Gibraltar of the New World." Pepperell's improbable victory was accomplished through a forty-day siege of the fort.

...nding the New England Forces in ye Expedition against CAPE BRETON, 1745,
...l Fortress of LOUISBOURG and the important Territories thereto belonging, were recover'd to the British Empire,
...rade Knight of the Bath, & Vice Admiral of ye White commanded the British Squadron in this glorious Expedition, The Hon.ble Will.m Pepperell Esq.r
...f the New England Men, who bravely offer'd their service and went as private Soldiers, in the hazardous, but very glorious Enterprize.

ATLANTIC OCEAN

In 1755, a year into the
French and Indian War,
English cartographers
William Herbert and Robert
Sayer threw down a
gauntlet to the French by
publishing a propaganda
map with a very
provocative title: *A New
and Accurate Map of the
English Empire in North
America; Representing
Their Rightful Claim as
Confirmed by Charters and
the Formal Surrender of
their Indian Friends;
Likewise the Encroachments
of the French, with the
Several Forts They Have
Unjustly Erected Therein.* It
was signed "A Society of
Anti-Gallicans." The box on
the lower right goes on to
announce that "The French
claim all the country within
the Hudson's Bay
Company's Southern Limits
and the Brown Line. The
Purple Line represents the
Western Boundary of the
hereditary & Conquer'd
Country of our Indian
Friends & Allies, which has
been ceded and confirm'd
to us by several Treaties
and Deeds of Sale."

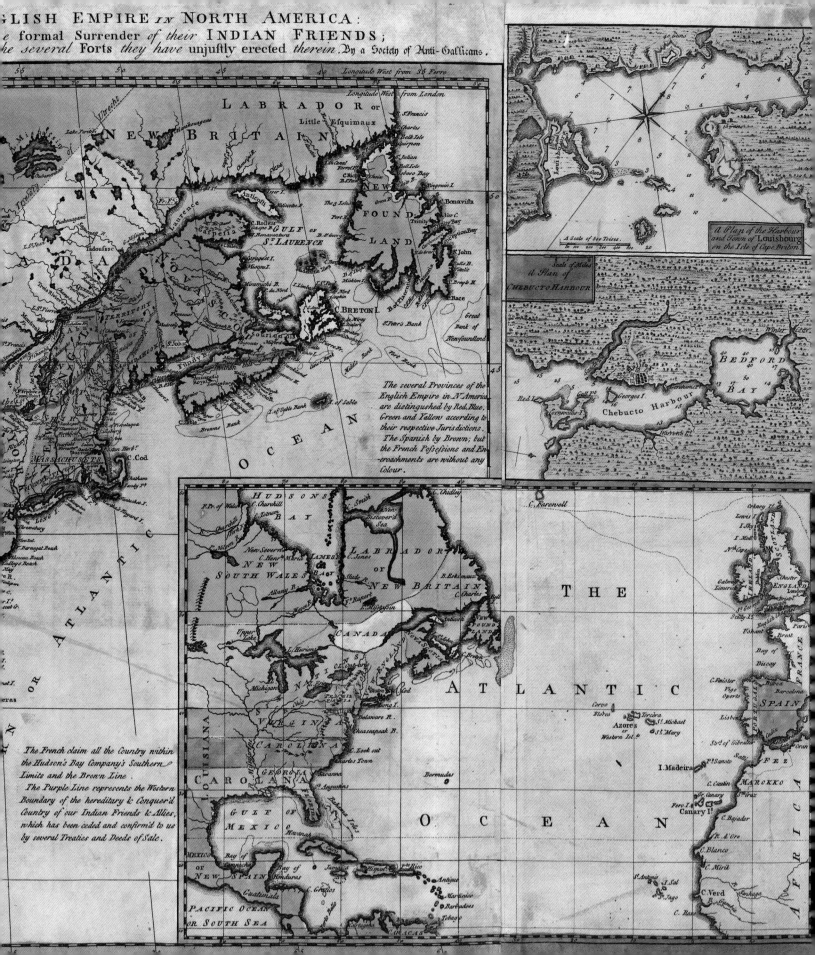

GLISH EMPIRE in NORTH AMERICA:
e formal Surrender of their INDIAN FRIENDS;
he several Forts they have unjustly erected therein. By a Society of Anti-Gallicans.

A Plan of the Harbour and Town of Louisbourg on the Isle of Cape-Breton

A Scale of 800 Toises

A Plan of CHEBUCTO HARBOUR

BEDFORD BAY

Chebucto Harbour

LABRADOR or NEW BRITAIN

NEW FOUND LAND

GULF or RIVER of St. LAURENCE

C. BRETON I.

Great Bank of Newfoundland

The several Provinces of the
English Empire in N. America
are distinguished by Red, Blue,
Green and Yellow according to
their respective Jurisdictions.
The Spanish by Brown; but
the French Possessions and Encroachments are without any
Colour.

ATLANTIC OCEAN

HUDSONS BAY

LABRADOR or NEW BRITAIN

NEW SOUTH WALES

CANADA

NEW FOUND LAND

The French claim all the Country within
the Hudson's Bay Company's Southern
Limits and the Brown Line.
The Purple Line represents the Western
Boundary of the hereditary & Conquer'd
Country of our Indian Friends & Allies,
which has been ceded and confirm'd to us
by several Treaties and Deeds of Sale.

VIRGINIA

CAROLINA

LOUISIANA

GEORGIA

GULF OF MEXICO

MEXICO or NEW SPAIN

PACIFIC OCEAN or SOUTH SEA

Bermudas

THE ATLANTIC OCEAN

Azores or Western Isl.

I. Madeira

Canary Is.

SCOTLAND

ENGLAND

IRELAND

FRANCE

SPAIN

PORTUGAL

Bay of Biscay

AFRICA

MAROKKO

C. Verd

Native American allies of the French—including Algonquin, Huron, Ottawa, and Shawnee tribes—close in on Braddock's army in the bloody, chaotic Battle of Monongahela. This illustration appeared in *Ballou's Pictorial* in 1855.

area immediately. Washington and his small entourage reached Fort LeBouef on December 12, 1753 where, over a cordial dinner with Saint-Pierre, he presented Dinwiddie's letter. The French commander's response was polite but to the point. "As to the Summons you sent me to retire," he replied in a return message, "I do not think myself obliged to obey it."

Washington carried the message back. The news of the French refusal to vacate the Ohio country brought about an immediate reaction from Dinwiddie and other influential Virginians, who ordered that a fort be built at the place where the Allegheny and Monongahela rivers converge to form the Ohio River. In April 1754, however, before the fort was completed, French forces drove the Virginians out of it, finished rebuilding it, and named it Fort Duquesne (the site of present-day Pittsburgh).

In May 1754, unaware that the fort had been lost to the French, Dinwiddie sent George Washington out with a small force to protect it. On their way, they were attacked by a French scouting party and forced to retreat. Sensing that the main French force was in the vicinity, Washington then ordered the construction of a stockade that he named Fort Necessity. On July 3, 1754, in what was to become the first battle of the French and Indian War, the French attacked and Washington, outnumbered almost two to one, was forced to surrender. Because war had not been officially declared, the colonel and his men were allowed to return to Virginia, bringing with them the news that the Ohio country was solidly in the hands of the French.

Alarmed at the defeat of Washington and his militiamen, Dinwiddie and other colonial governors pleaded with their superiors in England for help, and in April 1755, fourteen hundred British regulars under the command of General Edward Braddock arrived in the colonies. Considered to be one of England's most accomplished military leaders, Braddock wasted little time in launching an expedition aimed at driving the French out of the Ohio country by attacking their forts one by one—the first being Fort Duquesne.

It proved to be a disaster. Fortified by one thousand colonial militia, including Washington, who was assigned to

Braddock's staff, the expedition made the long trek through western Maryland and then into Pennsylvania toward Fort Duquesne. Braddock, in dogged allegiance to the European manner of proceeding, wasted both an inordinate amount of time and his troops' energy by insisting that a straight line of march be maintained, requiring that trees be felled and heavy logs placed over swampy terrain. Time and energy was also lost by having to widen the road that Washington had previously blazed to Fort Necessity to accommodate the British wagons and artillery.

Worse yet, although he had been repeatedly warned by Washington of the possibility of ambush, Braddock, never having encountered this type of frontier fighting, had no idea of how deadly it could be. He paid the price when, on July 9, his advance guard of approximately 1,460 men was ambushed at the Monongahela River by a French, Indian, and Canadian force of a little over half their size. The British soldiers, totally unaccustomed to frontier fighting, tried to form ranks and shoot in a line-of-fire formation; they were both shocked and terrified by the deadly French and Indian fire that came

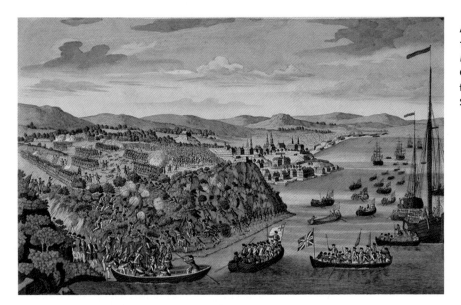

An engraving from the June 1760 issue of *London Magazine* illustrates British General James Wolfe's forces capturing Quebec in September 1759.

from men hidden behind trees and bushes. Panicked and in a state of disorganization, they fled, particularly after seeing Braddock, who had tried valiantly to keep them in line, severely wounded. To their credit, Washington and the Virginians tried desperately to cover the retreat but to no avail. By the time that the British regulars made their way back to camp, almost one thousand of them had been killed or wounded. Braddock died of his wounds four days later. It was a stunning defeat, and it was something more. The sight of one of England's top generals and his supposedly crack troops being unable to cope militarily in territory unfamiliar to them was something that the colonial militiamen, particularly George Washington, would not forget.

News of Braddock's disaster dismayed and angered England's King George II. In an effort to turn the tide, he appointed William Pitt to be his prime minister. It was an inspired choice. An extremely arrogant man, Pitt had, before assuming his new position, supposedly declared to the Duke of Devonshire: "I am sure that I can save this country and that no one else can." Fortunately for England, he backed up his claim. Almost immediately he sent military support to Britain's ally against France on the European continent,

Frederick of Prussia, which forced the French to commit more troops to the European theater—troops that might otherwise have been sent to battle the British in America. Then Pitt went over the heads of the English military establishment by placing British forces in America under the command not of senior officers, but under the control of two young and able generals—Jeffrey Amherst and James Wolfe.

His policies paid off, after some brutal setbacks. In August 1757, after the French captured Fort William Henry, their Native American allies attacked hundreds of men, women, and children leaving the fort. On July 8, 1758, the French took the strategic Fort Ticonderoga from the British. In late July 1758, the British rallied when a large British force under Amherst's command recaptured Louisbourg. In November, British troops recaptured Fort Duquesne, the largest of all the French fortifications in the American interior.

By 1759, the tide began to turn for the British. Their greatest and most decisive victory of all came in September when thirty-two-year-old James Wolfe, under the cover of darkness, led his army up the steep cliffs leading to Quebec, the capital of New France, and on to the Plains of Abraham. There, in a brief but violent battle in which both Wolfe and

General Wolfe wrote in a July 1755 letter to his mother that "his utmost desire and ambition is to look steadily upon danger." His death on the Plains of Abraham—shown here in a 1770 painting by American artist Benjamin West—was deeply mourned throughout Great Britain where he became regarded as one of England's greatest military heroes.

This map of the British possessions in North America was drawn in 1763 by English cartographer Thomas Kitchin, soon after the Treaty of Paris of 1763 that officially ended the French and Indian War. The map—entitled *A New and Accurate Map of the British Dominions in America*—indicates the enormous territory that, as a result of the conflict, had passed from the French into British hands.

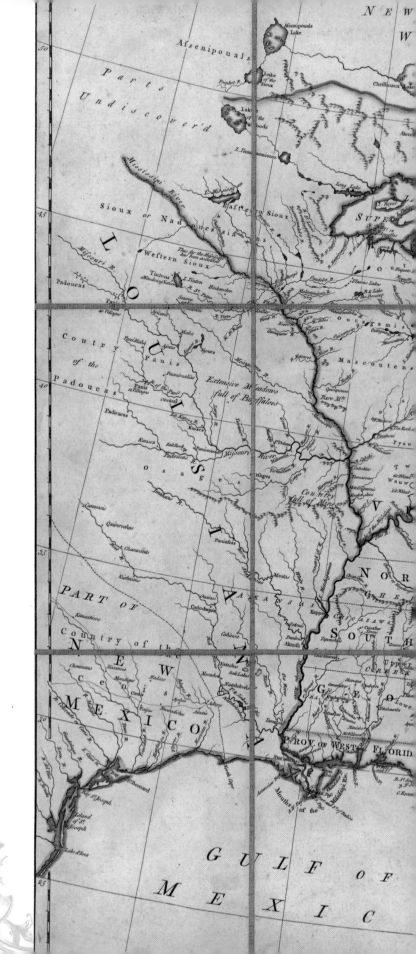

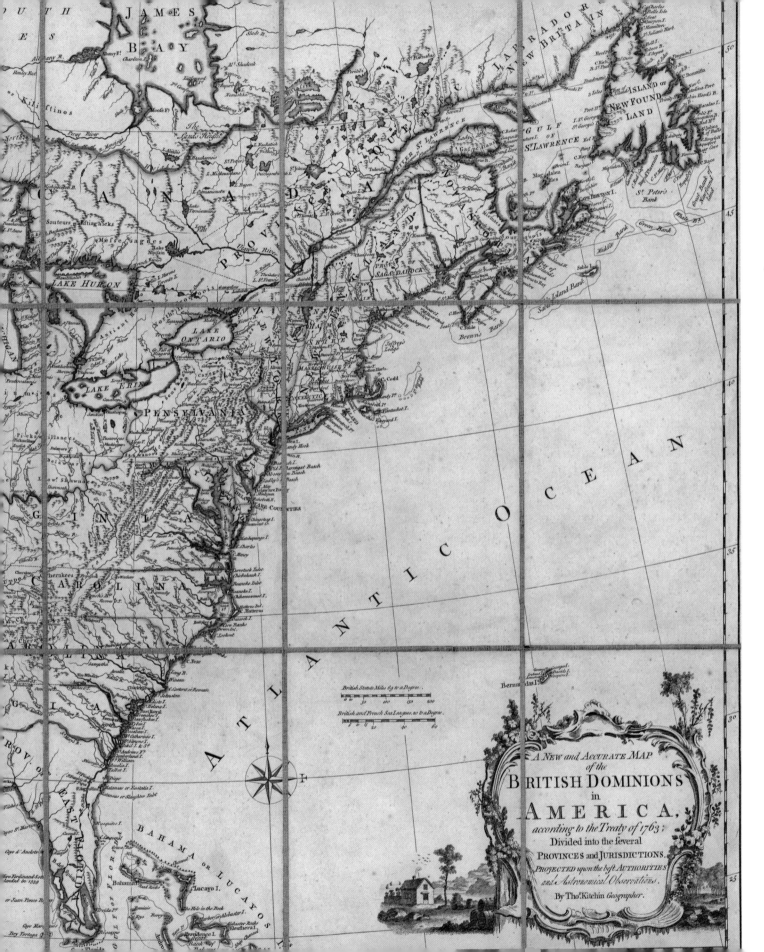

A New and Accurate MAP
of the
BRITISH DOMINIONS
in
AMERICA,
according to the Treaty of 1763;
Divided into the several
PROVINCES and JURISDICTIONS.
PROJECTED upon the best AUTHORITIES
and Astronomical Observations.
By Thoˢ. Kitchin Geographer.

> *" Now the king can sleep. "*
>
> —Madame de Pompadour

his French counterpart General Louis Joseph, Marquis de Montcalm were killed, the British won a resounding victory. The triumph was made even more complete when, at the same time, an English fleet commanded by Admiral Edward Boscawen, routed a French fleet attempting to bring reinforcements to Quebec. A year later, British troops, led by Amherst, captured Montreal. The bitter North American struggle between England and France was over. New France was now officially Canada, a British possession.

Interestingly, while all of Britain rejoiced at what had taken place, reaction on the part of many French thinkers and statesmen was not what might have been expected. According to *The Tercentenary History of Canada*, by Frank Basil Tracy, (1908), the renowned philosopher Voltaire actually expressed his gratitude for France's delivery from a vast stretch of frozen country. And King Louis XV's mistress Madame de Pompadour, aware of how France's long and costly endeavor in North America had resulted in so relatively little settlement, legendarily stated, "Now the king can sleep."

But it was a monumental development, one that affected the future of millions who had transferred their lives and their prospects to the New World. As historian Lawrence Henry Gipson wrote in his book *The Coming of the Revolution, 1763–1775* (1954): "[The French and Indian War] was destined to have the most momentous conse-quences to the American people of any war in which they have been engaged down to our own day—consequences therefore even more momentous than those that flowed from the victorious Revolutionary War or from the Civil War. For it was to determine for centuries to come, if not for all time, what civilization—what governmental institution, what social and economic patterns—would be paramount in North America."

DEBT, TAXES, AND REBELLION

For the American colonists, the removal of the French threat to their safety and their future brought with it a huge additional benefit. With the French threat gone, so too was the dependency upon the mother country for protection from their enemy to the north. The English, however, viewed it differently. The enormous cost of the long conflict with France had resulted in a British national debt of more than 130 million pounds. It was time, the British government believed, for the colonists to share the financial burden of their protection.

It was at this pivotal moment that a new British monarch ascended the throne. George III was an extremely insecure man who abhorred the responsibilities that had been placed upon him. But he was determined to be a strong ruler and,

King George III has not been treated kindly by history. His great misfortune was in being required to handle the immense burden of colonial unrest while he was so young (only twenty-two when crowned) and inexperienced. In the end, his unwavering belief in the absolute authority of Crown and Parliament proved his undoing. This mezzotint portrait of the youthful king was engraved by William Pether after Thomas Frye, and published in 1762.

to him, that meant ending the years of "benign neglect" that had previously characterized the British government's handling of its American possessions. As far as George III was concerned, any challenge to the authority of Crown and Parliament was treason.

The king and his ministers began this new approach by attempting to enforce the Navigation Acts for the first time since they had been passed, particularly those stipulating that the colonists must ship products designated as "enumerated articles" (including sugar, tobacco, cotton, and indigo), only to England or to other British colonies. To make matters worse, as far as the Americans were concerned, a five percent tax was placed on all these designated products. Also onerous to the colonials was the stipulation that imports from countries other than England had to sail first to Great Britain where duties were imposed on the goods. And, in what many colonial leaders regarded as the most unacceptable actions of all, the king ordered British privateers to attack and capture any colonial ships that attempted to trade with the French or the Dutch; he also authorized British customs officials to issue search warrants or "writs of assistance" to local authorities, allowing them to search the colonials' private homes and warehouses for smuggled goods.

More measures designed to force the colonists to pay a share of the cost of the French and Indian conflict soon

The Patriots

The events leading to the American Revolution produced a unique and diverse set of characters, each driven by his own dedication to cause, each playing a vital role in an unprecedented situation.

Samuel Adams

In 1743, while at Harvard, Samuel Adams titled his master's dissertation "Whether it be lawful to resist the supreme magistrate if the commonwealth cannot otherwise be preserved." It was a most prophetic subject for the man who would become the chief Massachusetts leader of the patriot cause and the protests leading to open rebellion. The portrait of Adams is by John Singleton Copley (1772).

James Otis

The British policy of issuing "writs of assistance" prompted Boston lawyer James Otis to resign as advocate general for the Admiralty Court, where he prosecuted customs violations for the Crown, and become the legal defense for a group of Boston merchants opposed to the writs. In a speech of February 24, 1761, during the trial, Otis uttered what would become the rallying cry of the revolution: "Taxation without representation is tyranny." Otis, a close associate of Samuel Adams, went on to become a leader of the colonial assembly and head of the Massachusetts committee of correspondence, but was disabled by mental illness in the late 1760s and retired from public life. This illustration appeared on the cover of *Bickerstaff's Boston Alamanack* in 1770.

Paul Revere

He is best known for his midnight ride, but Paul Revere's most important role in the American Revolution was as chief organizer of an intelligence system that kept close watch on British military movements. He was also one of America's most accomplished silversmiths. Later, as a large-scale manufacturer of metals, his company cast over a hundred huge bells, including the first to be produced in Boston in 1792. This portrait is also by Copley (1768).

Thomas Paine

Born in England, Thomas Paine migrated to the American colonies in 1774, just in time to become a key figure in the revolution. Pamphleteer and radical intellectual, his widely read pamphlet *Common Sense*, openly advocating independence from England, was, arguably, the most important publication of its kind during the tumultuous era. Also an important figure in the French Revolution, Paine's *Rights of Man* articulated the ideals of the Enlightenment. This painting is by Auguste Millière (1880), after an original portrait by George Romney (1792).

Benjamin Franklin

Involved in the writing of the American Declaration of Independence and the U.S. Constitution, Benjamin Franklin was renowned for his diversity of interests. As an Enlightenment philosopher, political writer, and activist, he was a vital figure in the birth of the American nation. As the country's earliest leading diplomat, he gained the respect of scientists and intellectuals throughout Europe who regarded him as the "First American." Joseph-Siffrède Duplessis, chief court painter of France, created this portrait of Franklin in 1785.

John Paul Jones

Perhaps the greatest naval hero in American history, Scottish-born John Paul Jones is considered the father of the American navy. In his twenties, Jones served as a British merchant marine, but an incident involving mutinous sailors that resulted in the death of several crewmen forced him to flee to America in 1775. Jones soon volunteered to serve in America's infant navy and became renowned for his daring raids along the British coastline and his famous victory of the *Bonhomme Richard* over HMS *Serapis*. This 1781 engraving is by French artist Jean Michel Moreau.

John Hancock

John Hancock, although one of the wealthiest merchants in New England, was one of the most prominent leaders of the revolutionary movement—and with his flamboyant signature, the most famous signer of the Declaration of Independence. Hancock's mezzotint portrait here was published by C. Shepherd in 1775, the year Hancock was elected president of the Continental Congress.

Thomas Jefferson

Horticulturist, architect, archaeologist, paleontologist, author, inventor, founder of the University of Virginia, principal writer of the Declaration of Independence—Thomas Jefferson was all these and more. His greatest contribution, however, may well have been his promotion of the ideals that resulted in the establishment of the world's first republican form of government. Henry Robinson created and printed this lithograph of Jefferson ca. 1840–51.

RIGHT TOP: Entitled *The Great Financier, or British Economy for the Years 1763, 1764, 1765*, this political cartoon, published in London in 1765, satirizes the taxation acts imposed by King George and George Grenville. Grenville—British first lord of the treasury and prime minister—holds a balance with scales that read "Debts" and "Savings" (the debt scale is overloaded and fallen to the ground. Commoners line up to pay taxes, along with a kneeling Native American woman representing America, who wears a yoke labeled "Taxed without representation."

RIGHT BOTTOM: The Stamp Act spawned so many protests and threats from the colonials, particularly the merchants, that it was eventually repealed. This October 31, 1765, issue of *The Pennsylvania Journal and Weekly Advertiser* featured a skull-and-crossbones parody of an official tax stamp on the upper right corner, a note on the upper left that read "The TIMES are Dreadful, Dismal, Doleful, Dolorous, and DOLLAR-LESS," and a front-page announcement from the publisher of the paper, William Bradford, stating "I am sorry to be obliged to acquaint my Readers, that as the STAMP Act, is fear'd to be obligatory upon us after the First of November ensuing... the Publisher of this Paper unable to bear the Burthen [burden], has thought it expedient to STOP awhile..."

The Great Financier, or British Œconomy for the Years 1763, 1764, 1765.

> *" I know not why we should blush to confess that molasses was an essential ingredient in American independence. "*
>
> —John Adams, in a 1818 letter to William Tudor

followed. In 1764, Parliament passed a new tax on molasses, a product important to the colonials in the making of rum and vital in the production of gunpowder as well. The Sugar Act actually reduced the tax of sixpence per gallon on molasses imposed by the Sugar and Molasses Act of 1733 to three pence per gallon. But the act also placed duties on other imports not previously taxed, including wine, sugar, indigo, and naval stores. Most important, unlike the Sugar and Molasses Act, the Sugar Act provided for the enforcement of all these duties. The act also contained another stipulation that would lead to vehement colonial opposition to the measure. According to the new act, violators of its provisos would be tried, not in local courts with their sympathetic judges and juries, but in Admiralty Courts, presided over by unfriendly judges sent over from England.

Outraged at the colonists' belligerent reaction to the Sugar Act, Parliament, a year later, passed an even more punishing measure. By requiring that a stamp be purchased and affixed to such common articles as newspapers, legal documents, almanacs, pamphlets, and playing cards, the Stamp Act affected almost all the colonists. Even greater protests than those that had accompanied the passage of the Sugar Act arose. In Boston, New York, and Philadelphia, secret societies known as the Sons of Liberty instigated mob violence that resulted in physical attacks on British stamp collectors, the burning of the houses of British colonial officials, and the widespread destruction of the detested stamps. In what was the most effective protest of all, colonial ship owners began withdrawing their vessels from service to England.

The resulting drop in trade hit British merchants, who had benefited from the enforcement of the Navigation Acts, squarely in their pocketbooks. So much so, that after a series of petitions from the most influential among them, Parliament was forced to repeal the act in 1766, but not before vehemently declaring its legal authority over the colonies. The colonists, having lived so long under a system in which they were relatively untaxed, opposed these new levies with a vengeance so pronounced that in 1818 John Adams stated in a letter to leading Boston citizen William Tudor, "I know not why we should blush to confess that molasses was an essential ingredient in American independence." To Adams and his fellow colonial leaders, the new taxes went beyond the monetary burden they placed on the colonists. How could Crown and Parliament, they demanded, lay such taxes on a people who had absolutely no voice in the government that imposed them? The phrase "no taxation without representation" became a rallying cry, not only in the colonies, but in England itself, where multitudes of British citizens had no Parliamentary representation. South

OPPOSITE: The landing of British troops in Boston in 1768, engraved by Patriot Paul Revere in 1770; for the already openly rebellious Bostonians, the presence of British troops in their midst and the edict that they must be housed in citizens' private homes and buildings was not only an outrage but an invitation to disaster.

A postcard created around 1903 re-creates the scene of an angry mob burning books of tax stamps in the street.

Carolina's Christopher Gadsden echoed the colonies' brewing discontent: "There ought to be no more New England men, no New Yorkers" he wrote in a 1765 letter to South Carolina agent Charles Garth, "but all of us Americans!"

The repeal of the Stamp Act engendered relief not only in America but also with sympathetic Englishmen such as Prime Minister William Pitt, who stated in a March 1766 meeting of Parliament that he "never had greater satisfaction than in the repeal of this Act." But the damage had been done. From that moment on, the events leading to the fight for independence moved at a rapid rate. When Parliament, urged on by Charles Townshend, the brash chancellor of the exchequer, passed the Townshend Acts in 1767—imposing taxes on such common items as glass, paint, lead, paper, and tea—colonists once again organized boycotts of these British imports. When British officials in Boston responded in 1768 by seizing colonial leader John Hancock's ship *Liberty*, a vessel suspected of smuggling in the newly taxed goods, mob violence became so pronounced that the customs officials sent a hasty message to London declaring that Boston was now in a state of rebellion.

Responding to the situation in Boston, four thousand British troops were dispatched to restore order. Regarding the soldiers as nothing less than an army of occupation, Bostonians refused to house the troops as the British had

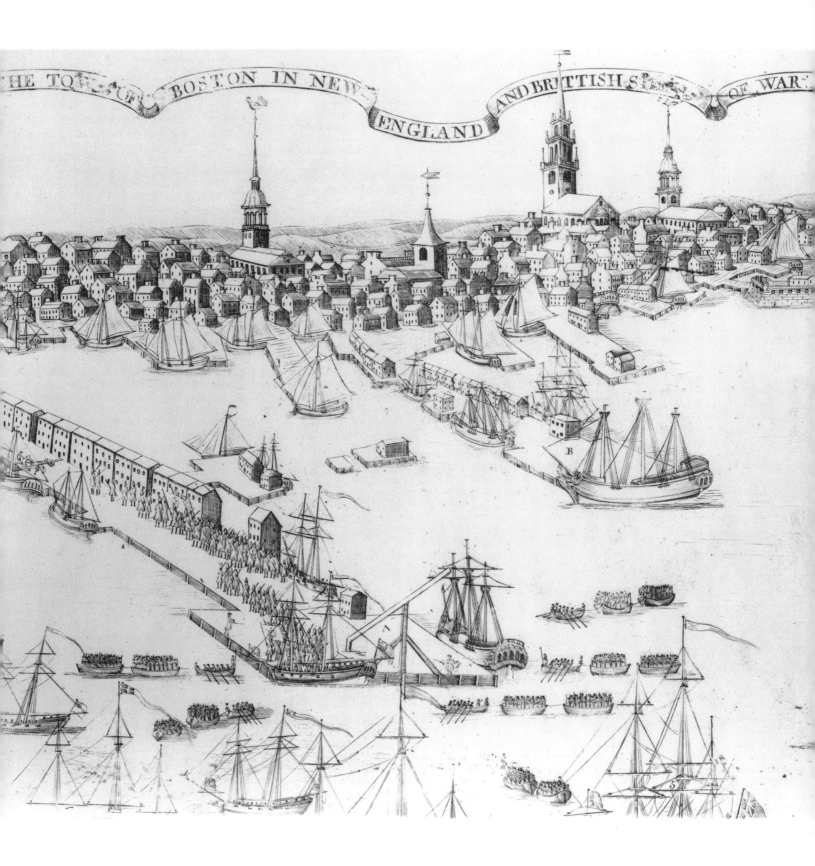

The BLOODY MASSACRE perpetrated in King—— Street Boston on March 5th 1770 by a party of the 29th REGT.

BUTCHER'S HALL

Engrav'd Printed & Sold by PAUL REVERE BOSTON

Unhappy BOSTON! see thy Sons deplore,
Thy hallow'd Walks besmear'd with guiltless Gore:
While faithless P——n and his savage Bands,
With murd'rous Rancour stretch their bloody Hands;
Like fierce Barbarians grinning o'er their Prey,
Approve the Carnage, and enjoy the Day.

If scalding drops from Rage from Anguish Wrung
If speechless Sorrows lab'ring for a Tongue
Or if a weeping World can ought appease
The plaintive Ghosts of Victims such as these:
The Patriot's copious Tears for each are shed,
A glorious Tribute which embalms the Dead.

But know, FATE summons to that awful Goal,
Where JUSTICE strips the Murd'rer of his Soul:
Should venal C——ts the scandal of the Land,
Snatch the relentless Villain from her Hand,
Keen Execrations on this Plate inscrib'd,
Shall reach a JUDGE who never can be brib'd.

The unhappy Sufferers were Messrs SamL GRAY, SamL MAVERICK, JamS CALDWELL, CRISPUS ATTUCKS & PatK CARR
Killed. Six wounded; two of them (CHRISTR MONK & JOHN CLARK) Mortally
Published in 1770 by Paul Revere

The British soldiers accused of killing five civilians in the Boston Massacre were legally defended at trial by John Adams, who believed that their actions had been provoked by an angry colonial mob. In his diary, however, Adams wrote on the third anniversary of the massacre that "This, however, is no reason why the Town should call the Action of that Night a Massacre, nor is it any Argument in favour of the Governor or Minister who caused them to be sent here. But it is the strongest Proofs of the Danger of Standing Armies." Paul Revere engraved and printed this now-famous image of the event, *The Bloody Massacre Perpetrated in King Street...by a Party of the 29th Regt.* in 1770. He copied the image almost exactly from a print by artist Henry Pelham, done weeks after the event.

ordered. English military officers then commandeered public and private dwellings as lodgings for their men. Tensions were now at a boiling point and when, on March 5, 1770, soldiers of the 29th British Regiment of Foot fired into an angry mob killing five, the first bloodshed of what became a full-blown revolt was spilled.

The consternation on both sides of the Atlantic engendered by this first bloodshed might well have caused a meaningful delay in the final rift. Affected by the furor caused by what became known as the Boston Massacre, Parliament repealed the Townshend duties a month later. But in doing so, it left the tax on tea in place—arguing for the tea tax, the king's frustrated new prime minister Frederick North exclaimed at a March 1770 meeting of Parliament, "But tea is not a manufacture of Great Britain. Of all the commodities it is the properest for taxation...Upon my word, if we are to run after America in search of reconciliation, I do not know of a single act of parliament that will remain."

The two-year period following the repeal of the Townshend duties was one of relative calm, but, in June 1772, another incident took place that once again fired the flames of colonial opposition to the mother country. For months, the British customs vessel *Gaspee* had been boarding colonial ships in Rhode Island's Narragansett Bay, checking to see if these ships were bringing in smuggled goods. The *Gaspee's*

sailors had further infuriated the people in the area by periodically coming ashore and stealing livestock from their farms.

On June 9, 1772, the *Gaspee* ran aground while chasing a local vessel. That night eight boatloads of Rhode Islanders rowed out to the stranded British ship, boarded her, wounded her captain, and removed her crew. They then burned the *Gaspee* down. Upon hearing what had taken place, King George named a special commission to hunt down those who had taken part in the incident and bring them back to England for trial. Although the British officials were unable to uncover the identity of the culprits, the fact that the English government was now prepared to bring American colonials to England to stand trial caused widespread alarm throughout the colonies, particularly in Massachusetts and Virginia, whose assemblies established committees of correspondence to communicate with all the other colonies on matters perceived to be threatening to colonial freedom.

By the end of 1773, most of the American colonies had formed committees of correspondence, not only to communicate with one another, but to coordinate resistance to the new British policies. As a result, throughout the colonies, committees of correspondence were formed to coordinate resistance to the new taxes. Mob protests arose, protests that led to the boycott of British goods. Even more significant, the widespread alarm occasioned by the new British policies led to a development that few could have foreseen only a short time earlier. From Georgia and the Carolinas to Massachusetts and Maine, the colonies had displayed marked differences in attitudes, ways of life, and approaches to government. Now the perceived threat to their liberty was bringing them together. "An attack made on one of our sister Colonies to compel submission to arbitrary taxes," read a May 1774 declaration signed by 89 members of the dissolved Virginia House of Burgess "is an attack on all British America."

Colonial resistance to the British policies culminated in the now-famous December 1773 "Boston Tea Party" in which 150 thinly disguised Boston citizens dumped 342 chests of tea into their harbor. There was no turning back.

There would be no reconciliation. The final stages of a drama that, by now, was being monitored with intense interest by all of the nations of the Atlantic world, was initiated in March 1774 when a still-defiant Parliament, in response to the Boston Tea Party, passed a series of measures variously called the Intolerable Acts, the Punitive Acts, or the Coercive Acts by the colonists. At the heart of these measures was the closing of the port of Boston until restitution was made for the tea that had been destroyed. Another portion of the acts did away with all elections for councilors, assistants, judges, and other officers in Massachusetts Bay, making all such positions subject to the appointment of the king and his officers.

Although not as well known as the Boston Tea Party or the Boston Massacre, the burning of the armed British schooner HMS *Gaspee*, which had run aground in Narragansett Harbor while chasing a vessel involved in smuggling, was another major event in the colonists' often violent protest of English acts and policies. *Harper's New Monthly Magazine* reproduced this depiction of the scene in their August 1883 issue.

Bostonians, some dressed as Indians, pour a cargo of tea into Boston Harbor. Nothing outraged the colonials more than the tax on the product that was both a staple American beverage and a major source of revenue. Nothing outraged the British more than the dumping of the tea. Nathaniel Currier printed this lithograph, *Destruction of Tea at Boston Harbor*, in 1846.

As far as the colonists were concerned, it was the final straw. As D. W. Meining wrote in *The Shaping of America: Volume 1, Atlantic America, 1492–1800* (1986): "The British people of the Atlantic World had become two peoples, separated by much more than an ocean." In the fall of 1774, delegates chosen from the various colonies met in Philadelphia "to concert a general and uniform plan for the defense and preservation of our common rights." It resulted in a declaration of independence and an eight-year armed conflict.

The events in the colonies had a dramatic effect not only in America but also on those champions of liberty in England who had become increasingly alarmed at the situation across the Atlantic and disenchanted with what they regarded as the tyranny of George III. In his typically eloquent style, Irish Whig Edmund Burke used the British press to present not only a defense of the colonists' cause but also an unprecedented attack on an English monarch in a 1775 speech to Parliament:

The people of the colonies are descendants of Englishmen. England, Sir, is a nation which still I hope respects, and formerly adored, her freedom. The colonists emigrated from you when this part of your character was most predominant, and they took this bias and direction from the moment they parted from your hands. They are therefore not only devoted to liberty, but liberty according to English ideas, and on English principles … The temper and character which prevail in our colonies are, I am afraid, unalterable by any human act. We cannot, I fear, falsify the pedigree of this fierce people, and persuade them that they are not sprung from a nation in whose veins the blood of freedom circulates.

Loyalists

Not all colonists were sympathetic to the patriot cause. Somewhere between fifteen and twenty-five percent remained loyal to the Crown. Called loyalists (or Tories or king's men), they were typically older, had ties to the Anglican Church, or were merchants with connections across the Atlantic. After the war, the vast majority of loyalists remained in America and resumed normal lives. Between fifty and seventy-five thousand, however, moved to Canada, Great Britain, or the British West Indies.

THE ALTERNATIVE OF WILLIAMS-BURG.

In August 1774, Virginia's elected representatives created an association to restrict trade with Britain. A month later Virginians pled for a full boycott at a Continental Congress in Philadelphia. A moratorium on imports was declared, and local committees of safety were created to enforce the boycott. Merchants who refused to cooperate were intimidated with searches, audits, and even tarring and feathering. This 1775 London print published by Robert Sayer and John Bennett, The Alternative of Williams-Burg, satirizes the American rebels as savages for their acts against loyalist merchants. It depicts Virginia merchants forced to sign papers agreeing to the association's boycott by club-wielding rebels. In the background a sack of feathers and a barrel of tar hang ominously from a post.

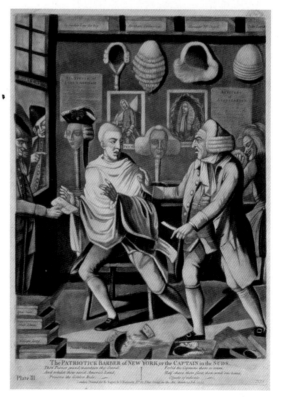

The PATRIOTICK BARBER of NEW YORK, or the CAPTAIN in the SUDS.

This cartoon by English artist Robert Dighton shows a barber refusing to finish shaving a customer after learning of his loyalist convictions. Called The Patriotick Barber of New York, or the Captain in the Suds, the verse underneath reads: "Then Patriot grand, maintain thy stand, / And whilst thou sav'st America's Land, / Preserve the Golden Rule, / Forbid the Captains there to roam, / Have shave them first, then send 'em home / Objects of ridicule." It was published by Sayer and Bennett in February 1775.

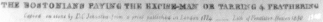

THE BOSTONIANS PAYING THE EXCISE-MAN OR TARRING & FEATHERING
Copied on stone by D.C. Johnston from a print published in London 1774. ... Lith. of Pendleton Boston 1830

The BOSTONIANS in DISTRESS.

This British political print, titled *The Bostonians Paying the Excise-man or Tarring & Feathering*, recreates the scene soon after the Boston Tea Party when citizens of Boston forced hot tea down the throat of John Malcolm, Boston commissioner of customs, after tarring and feathering him (a form of punishment used since the Middle Ages, victims often sustained burns from the hot tar). The Stamp Act is written upside-down on the tree behind, from which dangles a noose. While opposition to British taxes and other policies was widespread throughout the colonies, New England, and Boston in particular, was the seedbed of the revolution. The original version of this cartoon was printed in London in 1774 by Robert Sayer and John Bennett; this lithograph was published in Boston by the firm of Pendleton in 1830.

Titled *Bostonians in Distress*, this print was published in London in November 1774, several months after the closing of the port of Boston. It shows Bostonians held captive in a cage suspended from the Liberty Tree, a popular symbol of colonial revolt. Three British sailors standing in a boat feed them fish in return for a bundle of papers labeled "Promises." Around the tree and in the background are cannons and British troops.

ATLANTIC OCEAN

"The Declaration of Independence," historian D. W. Meinig wrote in *The Shaping of America: A Geographical Perspective on 500 Years of History* (1986), "was a claim to maturity. [The colonies] aspiration for a 'separate and equal station' among 'the Powers of the earth' was not a struggle for isolation but acceptance as a full member in the larger family of mature states." Asher B. Duran made this engraving depicting the signing of the Declaration of Independence in 1820, after the painting by John Trumbull (1817–18).

The Troops, the Battles

When the War for Independence began, the Americans had neither a professional army nor a navy. Each colony provided for its own defense through its local militia. The Continental Congress established a regular army in June 1775, and its development was an ongoing process throughout the war. About 250,000 American men served as regulars or militiamen during the course of the conflict, but there were never more than 90,000 serving at one time. By war's end, there were some 65,000 British troops involved, a third of whom were German Hessians hired by the British as mercenaries.

OPPOSITE TOP: On the night of April 18, 1775, the British sent seven hundred men to seize colonial munitions stored in the Massachusetts town of Concord; there was also a secret plan to arrest the rebel leaders Samuel Adams and John Hancock in Lexington, a few miles east of Concord. When, the next day, the troops entered the town of Lexington, they found about seventy militiamen waiting for them. Shots were fired and several of the militiamen were killed. The American Revolutionary War had begun. This print of the Battle of Lexington was created by François Godefroy and published in Paris around 1784.

OPPOSITE BOTTOM: The Battle of Bunker Hill (actually Breed's Hill), which took place on June 17, 1775, resulted in a Pyrrhic victory for the British. After three assaults, the king's forces finally overran the Americans' fortified earthworks. But before the battle was over the British had suffered more than one thousand casualties. "A few more such victories," English General Henry Clinton confided to his diary after the battle, "would have surely put an end to British dominion in America." E. Percy Moran painted this scene of the battle in 1909.

TOP RIGHT: As commander in chief of the American forces, George Washington's strategy was to take the British by surprise wherever and whenever he could. In this famous painting by Emanuel Leutze (1851), the man who would first hold together a tenuous army and then an infant nation crosses the Delaware while launching a surprise attack on Christmas Day 1776 against Hessian forces encamped at Trenton, New Jersey.

BOTTOM RIGHT: The American Revolution was also fought at sea, most notably in the engagement on September 23–24, 1779, between the *Bonhomme Richard*, a re-outfitted French merchant vessel that had been loaned to America by France, and the powerfully armed British ship HMS *Serapis*. After a deadly three-hour battle in the North Sea, in which nearly half of the American and British crews were killed, the men of the *Bonhomme Richard*, which was commanded by America's naval hero John Paul Jones, succeeded in boarding the *Serapis* and taking control of the ship. Balthasar Friedrich Leizelt engraved this print around 1780, after a painting by Richard Paton.

Stated most simply, it was a war characterized by a lack of necessary commitment by the British to adequately finance and carry out a conflict in a setting almost totally unfamiliar to its officers and troops. It was also marked by the brilliance of the undermanned American commander in chief George Washington in effectively maintaining a hit-and-run military strategy and avoiding a decisive British victory that could have spelled defeat. And, in the end, it was characterized by the aid, in the nick of time, of French ground and naval forces.

When, in the fall of 1781, the cornered British General George Cornwallis surrendered his army at Yorktown, Virginia, legend has it that his musicians struck up the old tune "The World Turned Upside Down." Whether it was played or not, the song was most appropriate, for it was both an end and a beginning: the end of the major portion of England's American empire, and the beginning of a whole new nation whose successful struggle for liberty and the type of government it would create would have a profound effect on societies throughout the Atlantic world.

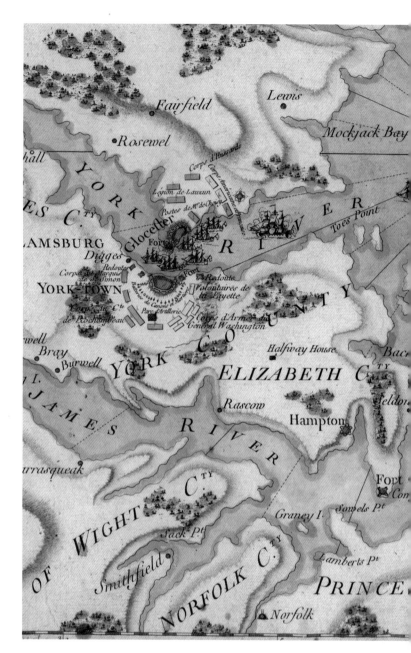

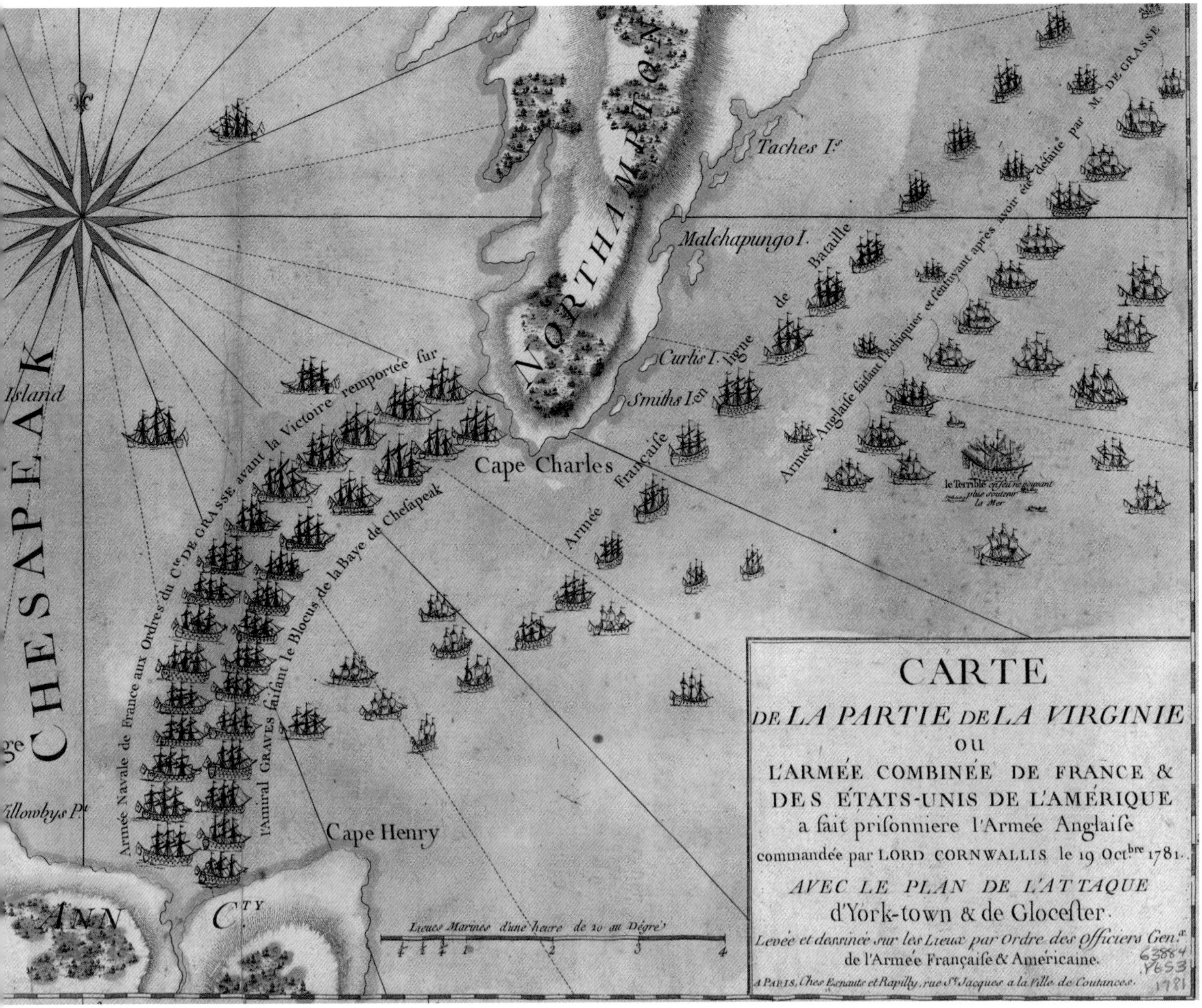
CARTE
DE LA PARTIE DE LA VIRGINIE
OU
L'ARMÉE COMBINÉE DE FRANCE &
DES ÉTATS-UNIS DE L'AMÉRIQUE
a fait prisonniere l'Armée Anglaise
commandée par LORD CORNWALLIS le 19 Oct.bre 1781.
AVEC LE PLAN DE L'ATTAQUE
d'York-town & de Glocester.
Levée et dessinée sur les Lieux par Ordre des Officiers Gen.x
de l'Armée Française & Américaine.
A PARIS, Chez Esnauts et Rapilly, rue St. Jacques a la Ville de Coutances.
CHESAPEAK
NORTHAMPTON
Cape Charles
Cape Henry
Taches I.
Malchapungo I.
Curtis I.
Smiths I.
Armée Française
Armée Anglaise faisant l'échiquier et s'enfuyant apres avoir été défaite par M. DE GRASSE
ligne de Bataille
Armée Navale de France aux Ordres du Cte DE GRASSE avant la Victoire remportée sur
l'Amiral GRAVES faisant le Blocus de la Baye de Chesapeak
le Terrible en feu ne pouvant plus soutenir la Mer
Lieues Marines d'une heure de 20 au Degré
Island
Willowbys Pt.

The surrender of British general George Cornwallis to the combined American and French forces led by General George Washington and General Comte de Rochambeau caused Great Britain to negotiate an end to the war and to its once proud empire in North America. This detail from a map published in Paris around 1781 by Esnauts and Rapilly shows the forces in the Battle of the Chesapeake (or the Battle of the Capes) on September 5, 1781. British ships led by Rear-Admiral Sir Thomas Graves were outnumbered and defeated by the French fleet led by Rear-Admiral Comte de Grasse. Because of the battle, Cornwallis's troops and weapons supply in Yorktown was cut off, leading to his surrender.

7

THE IMPACT OF THE AMERICAN REVOLUTION

A NEW MODEL FOR GOVERNMENT

English marine painter
William Clarkson Stanfield
painted this dramatic
scene of the Battle of
Trafalgar in 1836, thirty-one
years after the epic battle
in October 1805 that ended
Napoleon's plan to invade
Britain from the Atlantic.

THE IMPACT OF THE AMERICAN REVOLUTION

Liberté, egalité, fraternité, ou la mort! (Liberty, equality, fraternity, or death!)

—RALLYING CRY OF THE FRENCH REVOLUTION

The American Revolution resulted in far more than the separation of the American colonies from Great Britain. As important as the successful revolt itself was the equally revolutionary form of government that the founding fathers of the new United States created. It was a bold new system, a republican form of government based on liberty and the consent of the governed. Church and state were separated; power was delegated to the government through written constitutions. It became a model that inspired people in long-established European nations and in their South American and Caribbean possessions to aspire to this new ideal of self-governance.

In less than a half decade after the United States had been created, the constitutionalism of the infant nation spread across the ocean. France's 1789 Declaration of the Rights of Man and the Citizen, modeled directly after the Virginia Declaration of Rights, drafted in 1776, bolstered hopes for reform throughout the Western world. As Wim Klooster, in the introduction to his book *The Atlantic World: Essays on Slavery, Migration, and Imagination* (2004), points out: "The Chilean law of 1811 (created by the Chilean National Congress inaugurated on July 4, 1811), begins with the words 'All men have certain inalienable rights which the Creator has given them in order to assure their happiness, prosperity, and well being.'" And, as Klooster also documents: "The constitutions of Argentina (1819), Colombia (1821), and Mexico (1824) adopted the North American model of separation of powers."

THE ENLIGHTENMENT

It was a development inspired not only by the example set in America, but by the profound influence of an intellectual movement of the era known as the Enlightenment. Combined with the Scientific Revolution, which began in earnest in Europe in the early sixteenth century, the Enlightenment opened a path for independent thought and

OPPOSITE: The American Revolution and the government created for the new American nation provided the first lesson in successful revolt and the establishment of a republic for those who would take an active role in Europe and Latin America in attempting to achieve these same goals. The Virginia Declaration of Rights, written by George Mason in May 1776 and amended by Thomas Ludwell Lee and the Virginia Convention, served as a model for Thomas Jefferson in the opening paragraphs of the Declaration of Independence (shown here), as well as for James Madison in drafting the Bill of Rights (1789) and the Marquis de Lafayette in outlining the French Declaration of the Rights of Man (1789). Mason wrote: "all men are born equally free and independant [sic], and have certain inherent natural rights,...among which are the Enjoyment of Life and Liberty, with the Means of acquiring and possessing Property, and pursueing [sic] and obtaining Happiness and Safety." All of these men were inspired by seventeenth-century English philosopher John Locke, who stated in his *Second Treatise Concerning Civil Government* (1690) that "no one ought to harm another in his life, health, liberty, or possessions."

IN CONGRESS, JULY 4, 1776.

The unanimous Declaration of the thirteen united States of America.

When in the Course of human events, it becomes necessary for one people to dissolve the political bands which have connected them with another, and to assume among the powers of the earth, the separate and equal station to which the Laws of Nature and of Nature's God entitle them, a decent respect to the opinions of mankind requires that they should declare the causes which impel them to the separation.

We hold these truths to be self-evident, that all men are created equal, that they are endowed by their Creator with certain unalienable Rights, that among these are Life, Liberty and the pursuit of Happiness.— That to secure these rights, Governments are instituted among Men, deriving their just powers from the consent of the governed,— That whenever any Form of Government becomes destructive of these ends, it is the Right of the People to alter or to abolish it, and to institute new Government, laying its foundation on such principles and organizing its powers in such form, as to them shall seem most likely to effect their Safety and Happiness. Prudence, indeed, will dictate that Governments long established should not be changed for light and transient causes; and accordingly all experience hath shewn, that mankind are more disposed to suffer, while evils are sufferable, than to right themselves by abolishing the forms to which they are accustomed. But when a long train of abuses and usurpations, pursuing invariably the same Object evinces a design to reduce them under absolute Despotism, it is their right, it is their duty, to throw off such Government, and to provide new Guards for their future security.— Such has been the patient sufferance of these Colonies; and such is now the necessity which constrains them to alter their former Systems of Government. The history of the present King of Great Britain is a history of repeated injuries and usurpations, all having in direct object the establishment of an absolute Tyranny over these States. To prove this, let Facts be submitted to a candid world.

He has refused his Assent to Laws, the most wholesome and necessary for the public good.

He has forbidden his Governors to pass Laws of immediate and pressing importance, unless suspended in their operation till his Assent should be obtained; and when so suspended, he has utterly neglected to attend to them.

He has refused to pass other Laws for the accommodation of large districts of people, unless those people would relinquish the right of Representation in the Legislature, a right inestimable to them and formidable to tyrants only.

He has called together legislative bodies at places unusual, uncomfortable, and distant from the depository of their public Records, for the sole purpose of fatiguing them into compliance with his measures.

He has dissolved Representative Houses repeatedly, for opposing with manly firmness his invasions on the rights of the people.

He has refused for a long time, after such dissolutions, to cause others to be elected; whereby the Legislative powers, incapable of Annihilation, have returned to the People at large for their exercise; the State remaining in the mean time exposed to all the dangers of invasion from without, and convulsions within.

He has endeavoured to prevent the population of these States; for that purpose obstructing the Laws for Naturalization of Foreigners; refusing to pass others to encourage their migrations hither, and raising the conditions of new Appropriations of Lands.

He has obstructed the Administration of Justice, by refusing his Assent to Laws for establishing Judiciary powers.

He has made Judges dependent on his Will alone, for the tenure of their offices, and the amount and payment of their salaries.

He has erected a multitude of New Offices, and sent hither swarms of Officers to harrass our people, and eat out their substance.

He has kept among us, in times of peace, Standing Armies without the Consent of our legislatures.

He has affected to render the Military independent of and superior to the Civil power.

He has combined with others to subject us to a jurisdiction foreign to our constitution, and unacknowledged by our laws; giving his Assent to their Acts of pretended Legislation:

For Quartering large bodies of armed troops among us:

For protecting them, by a mock Trial, from punishment for any Murders which they should commit on the Inhabitants of these States:

For cutting off our Trade with all parts of the world:

For imposing Taxes on us without our Consent:

For depriving us in many cases, of the benefits of Trial by jury:

For transporting us beyond Seas to be tried for pretended offences:

For abolishing the free System of English Laws in a neighbouring Province, establishing therein an Arbitrary government, and enlarging its Boundaries so as to render it at once an example and fit instrument for introducing the same absolute rule into these Colonies:

For taking away our Charters, abolishing our most valuable Laws, and altering fundamentally the Forms of our Governments:

For suspending our own Legislatures, and declaring themselves invested with power to legislate for us in all cases whatsoever.

He has abdicated Government here, by declaring us out of his Protection and waging War against us.

He has plundered our seas, ravaged our Coasts, burnt our towns, and destroyed the lives of our people.

He is at this time transporting large Armies of foreign Mercenaries to compleat the works of death, desolation and tyranny, already begun with circumstances of Cruelty & perfidy scarcely paralleled in the most barbarous ages, and totally unworthy the Head of a civilized nation.

He has constrained our fellow Citizens taken Captive on the high Seas to bear Arms against their Country, to become the executioners of their friends and Brethren, or to fall themselves by their Hands.

He has excited domestic insurrections amongst us, and has endeavoured to bring on the inhabitants of our frontiers, the merciless Indian Savages, whose known rule of warfare, is an undistinguished destruction of all ages, sexes and conditions.

In every stage of these Oppressions We have Petitioned for Redress in the most humble terms: Our repeated Petitions have been answered only by repeated injury. A Prince, whose character is thus marked by every act which may define a Tyrant, is unfit to be the ruler of a free people.

Nor have We been wanting in attentions to our British brethren. We have warned them from time to time of attempts by their legislature to extend an unwarrantable jurisdiction over us. We have reminded them of the circumstances of our emigration and settlement here. We have appealed to their native justice and magnanimity, and we have conjured them by the ties of our common kindred to disavow these usurpations, which, would inevitably interrupt our connections and correspondence. They too have been deaf to the voice of justice and of consanguinity. We must, therefore, acquiesce in the necessity, which denounces our Separation, and hold them, as we hold the rest of mankind, Enemies in War, in Peace Friends.

We, therefore, the Representatives of the united States of America, in General Congress, Assembled, appealing to the Supreme Judge of the world for the rectitude of our intentions, do, in the Name, and by Authority of the good People of these Colonies, solemnly publish and declare, That these United Colonies are, and of Right ought to be Free and Independent States; that they are Absolved from all Allegiance to the British Crown, and that all political connection between them and the State of Great Britain, is and ought to be totally dissolved; and that as Free and Independent States, they have full Power to levy War, conclude Peace, contract Alliances, establish Commerce, and to do all other Acts and Things which Independent States may of right do.— And for the support of this Declaration, with a firm reliance on the protection of divine Providence, we mutually pledge to each other our Lives, our Fortunes and our sacred Honor.

John Hancock

Button Gwinnett
Lyman Hall
Geo Walton.

Wm Hooper
Joseph Hewes,
John Penn

Edward Rutledge.

Thos Heyward Junr.
Thomas Lynch Junr.
Arthur Middleton

Samuel Chase
Wm Paca
Thos Stone
Charles Carroll of Carrollton

George Wythe
Richard Henry Lee
Th Jefferson
Benja Harrison
Thos Nelson jr.
Francis Lightfoot Lee
Carter Braxton

Robt Morris
Benjamin Rush
Benja Franklin
John Morton
Geo Clymer
Jas Smith
Geo Taylor
James Wilson
Geo. Ross
Caesar Rodney
Geo Read
Tho M:Kean

Wm Floyd
Phil. Livingston
Frans Lewis
Lewis Morris

Richd Stockton
Jno Witherspoon
Fras Hopkinson
John Hart
Abra Clark

Josiah Bartlett
Wm Whipple
Saml Adams
John Adams
Robt Treat Paine
Elbridge Gerry
Step Hopkins
William Ellery
Roger Sherman
Sam'el Huntington
Wm Williams
Oliver Wolcott
Matthew Thornton

ANTOINE LAURENT LAVOISIER,
FERMIER GÉNÉRAL NÉ A PARIS LE 16 AOUT 1743.
Jugé le 16 floréal l'an 2.

Robespierre s'attachoit plus particulièrement à proscrire tous les hommes dont les talens, les vertus assuroient la vénération, les hommages de leurs contemporains et de la postérité. à ces titres il devoit proscrire Lavoisier. quel homme, fut en effet plus vertueux? quel homme mérita plus des sciences et des arts? toutes les branches des sciences mathématiques et phisiques eurent des droits sur ses veilles; et il sembloit destiné a contribuer également au progrès de toutes, lorsqu'une circonstance, telle qu'il ne s'en présente que rarement dans les fastes de l'esprit humain, décida son choix, l'attacha exclusivement à la Chymie, et le conduisit rapidement à l'immortalité. Nous parlons de la découverte si célèbre des fluides élastiques. Blak, Cavendish, Mackbride et Priestley venoient de faire connoître aux Physiciens un monde nouveau. Lavoisier s'empressa de répéter leurs expériences, de confirmer et d'étendre leurs résultats.

Un Chymiste distingué a comparé de la manière suivante Lavoisier et Priestley.». dans les ouvrages de Lavoisier tout est régulier et méthodique; on voit dans ses nombreux mémoires la série d'un immense travail, la même pensée-mère qui plane sur les détails, les lie, et les rapporte à un centre commun: dans Priestley une foule d'expériences, de découvertes, s'offre de toutes parts; vous êtes étonné par le nombre et la diversité des faits nouveaux, mais en même tems frappé de leur incohérence, de leur opposition, de leur contradiction.».

Traduit au tribunal révolutionnaire, Lavoisier demanda à ses juges, ou plutôt à ses bourreaux, quinze jours pour terminer des expériences nécessaires à un travail dont il s'occupoit depuis plusieurs années. Le féroce Cofinhal qui présidoit le tribunal, fit cette réponse barbare.». la République n'a pas besoin de Savans, ni de Chymistes». ainsi Lavoisier fut confondu dans la fournée des fermiers généraux. Il monta à l'échafaud d'un pas ferme; et mourut, comme il avoit vécu, en philosophe, en sage.

OPPOSITE: Regarded as the father of modern chemistry, Antoine-Laurent Lavoisier was a leading figure in pre-revolutionary France. Among his many discoveries, Lavoisier recognized the role of oxygen in the process of burning and combustion and that water was a compound of hydrogen and oxygen (he also coined the names of these elements). Lavoisier was also a member of the Ferme générale, a private tax agency that collected money for the Crown. Although he worked on tax reform, and was sympathetic to the Revolution, he was also hated by Jean-Paul Marat, the physiologist, radical journalist, and Jacobin leader whose bid for membership in the French Academy of Science had been denied in 1780 (Lavoisier was one of the academy members who had rejected Marat's application). This factor led to Lavoisier's beheading during the French Revolution in 1794. This French print, created shortly after Lavoisier's death, depicts his portrait and scenes of his arrest, below.

ushered in an era in which a seemingly endless amount of new knowledge in such fields as philosophy, politics, economics, ethics, mathematics, physics, and medicine burst forth. Embraced enthusiastically by the increasingly literate upper and middle classes on both sides of the Atlantic, the Enlightenment touched almost every area of civilized life.

Above all, the Enlightenment was a movement that advocated reason, as applied to aesthetics, ethics, logic, and, most significantly, government, as the means to lead the world out of inhibiting tradition, irrationality, superstition, and tyranny. At its heart was the consideration of what constituted the proper relationship between the citizen and the monarch or the state. Out of this exploration, led by such philosophers as Charles-Louis de Secondat, Baron de Montesquieu; François-Marie Arouet (Voltaire); Jean-Jacques Rousseau; David Hume; John Locke; and Thomas Jefferson, came the deep-seated notion that society is a contract between the individual and society and the state and that the individual has natural rights or, as they came to be expressed, "the rights of man."

THE FRENCH REVOLUTION

The tenants of the Enlightenment occasioned great debate, nowhere more so than in late eighteenth-century France, a country where the French aristocracy was very pleased with things as they were. And with good reason. The court of King Louis XVI lived a life of opulence that had not been seen since the days of ancient Rome. And, despite France's recent losses in her battle with England for empire, the nation was setting an unparalleled standard of achievement. French artists, architects, and craftsmen dominated creative expression. Europe's finest roads and canals were being built in France. Population and trade were increasing every year. French scientists, such as chemist Antoine-Laurent Lavoisier, astronomer Pierre-Simon, marquis de Laplace, and naturalist Georges-Louis Leclerc, comte de Buffon, were the envy of their counterparts throughout the world. As historian Bruce Lancaster documented in *The American Heritage History of the American Revolution* (1971), British politician Edmund Burke described all of these accomplishments as "something which awes and commands the imagination," concluding that his native England was "an artificial country; take away her commerce, and what has she?"

There seemed little question that the future belonged to France. But, underneath it all, there was trouble brewing, turmoil that would unleash revolutionary activity on the part of millions of French citizens whose lives in no way reflected all that France as a nation had achieved.

The immediate cause of the French Revolution was the serious financial crisis brought about by the out-of-control

Enlightenment Thinkers

Many historians believe that the Enlightenment was the point where reason replaced dogma as the basis for thinking. Central to the Enlightenment philosophers' achievements was the way in which their influence made it more possible than ever before for thinkers and writers to pursue the truth wherever it led without the threat of sanction for violating established ideas. Among those who helped create the framework for the American, French, and Latin American revolutions were the men depicted here.

John Locke

The work of influential thinker John Locke, who is shown here in a nineteenth-century print, was a catalyst for the Enlightenment movement. In addition to inspiring American patriots, his writings on government had a major influence on Voltaire and Rousseau, and his important 1690 publication *An Essay Concerning Human Understanding* was a prototype for empiricism.

Thomas Hobbes

English political philosopher Thomas Hobbes's most famous writings appeared in his book *Leviathan*, written in 1651. In the book, Hobbes argued in favor of a government in which a leader (preferably a monarch) was given great power and was obeyed under all circumstances. Hobbes also advocated the need for elected representatives of the people to act as liaisons to the monarchy, as well as safeguards against abusive regimes. While acknowledging that absolute rule was risky, Hobbes argued that it was far better to live in security under such a system than to live in a constant state of war. Although many disagreed with Hobbes, *Leviathan* was extremely important in setting the agenda for almost all the Enlightenment and other written political philosophy that would follow. This portrait is by John Michael Wright (ca. 1669).

Charles-Louis de Secondat

Charles-Louis de Secondat, Baron de Montesquieu, was one of the most influential of all the Enlightenment figures. His *The Spirit of the Laws* (1748) not only had an enormous impact on French society, with its emphasis on the individual's natural rights, but was used by American colonial leaders in challenging British authority. He is shown here in an eighteenth-century French profile portrait.

Voltaire

Philosopher, writer, essayist, and deist, the man who took the pen name Voltaire was a true Renaissance man. His widely read writings criticized both French political and social institutions and Christian Church dogma. This engraving of Voltaire was published on the frontispiece of an 1843 edition of his *Philosophical Dictionary* (1764).

Jean-Jacques Rousseau

Like many of the Enlightenment philosophers, Jean-Jacques Rousseau was a man of many talents. As a musician, he was both a successful composer and theorist. His novel, *Julie, ou la nouvelle Heloise (Julie, or the New Heloise)* (1761), was one of the best-selling works of fiction of the eighteenth century, and his *Confessions* (completed around 1770) is regarded as the birth of modern autobiography. In his passionately written treatise entitled *Social Contract, or Principles of Political Right* (1762) Rousseau raised the question of why man, who was born free, should be enslaved. This evocative portrait of Rousseau is by Scottish painter Allan Ramsay (1766).

David Hume

Philosopher, economist, and historian, David Hume was the most important figure of the Scottish Enlightenment. His initial fame came as a historian, and his six-volume *History of England* (1754–62) was the standard work on English history for some seventy years. At the heart of Hume's philosophical views was his belief that true knowledge comes only from the experience of events ("impressions of the senses") and that knowledge acquired in any other way is "meaningless," a theory that Albert Einstein later credited as being highly influential in his formulating his Special Theory of Relativity. Ramsay also painted this portrait of Hume in 1766.

spending of the French royalty, which, in effect, was the French state, and by the expenses incurring during French involvement in both the Seven Years' War and the American Revolution. Attempting to alleviate the problem, France's controller-general of the finances Charles Alexandre de Calonne proposed a uniform land tax as a long-term solution. Calonne was able to convince the king of his plan but the Assembly of Notables refused to go along, proclaiming that only a representative body such as the nation's Estates-General could impose new taxes (and they had not been convoked by a king since 1614). Convinced that Calonne was no longer effective, King Louis replaced him with Étienne-Charles de Loménie de Brienne, the archbishop of Toulouse. Brienne began instituting reforms and granting civil rights to various groups, including freedom of worship for Protestants. He also promised that the king would call together the Estates-General within five years. At the same time, he tried to push forward Calonne's plan for a uniform land tax.

When the Parlement of Paris opposed the tax, Brienne tried to disband that body and to collect the revenues without their approval. The result was huge uprisings in many places, which alarmed the creditors whose short-term loans were essential to the French treasury for their daily operations. When creditors began to withdraw their loans, Brienne resigned, and in 1789, the king was forced to convene the

OPPOSITE: Although highly popular when he first took the throne in 1775, Louis XVI came to be regarded by much of the French citizenry as the very symbol of a tyrannical government. This portrait was painted by Antoine-François Callet in 1789, at the start of the revolution. After the monarchy was abolished in 1792, in a negative application of the traditional nicknaming of French kings, Louis became derisively referred to as "Louis le Dernier" (Louis the Last).

BELOW: With one exception, the Tennis Court Oath was signed by every one of the 577 members of France's Third Estate. In taking the solemn vow, the members pledged "never to separate, and to meet whenever circumstances demand, until the constitution of the kingdom is established and affirmed on solid foundations." This engraving by Pierre Gabriel Berthault was printed soon after the assembly meeting at the tennis court.

237

Contrary to later, highly exaggerated accounts, the attack on the Bastille did not involve the release of hundreds of prisoners. Actually, only seven prisoners were freed—four forgers, two "lunatics," and a sexual offender. But the storming of the Bastille became a powerful and lasting symbol of the French Revolution. This French political cartoon, in two parts, from 1789 shows citizens with guns and pikes storming the Bastille (ABOVE) and parading the heads of "traitors" on pikes (OPPOSITE).

Estates-General, the French legislative body encompassing the first Estate (the clergy), the second Estate (the nobility), and the third Estate (the middle class and peasants).

When the Estates-General opened its meetings in Versailles on May 5, great debate arose over how much power each of these three bodies should have. On May 28, influential member and revolutionary Abbé Sieyès proposed that the third Estate should proceed by publicly declaring the power they intended to exercise. Not only did the third Estate do so, but on June 17, in an extraordinarily radical move, it declared itself the National Assembly—an assembly not of the Estates but of "the People." It then invited the other two estates to join it in this assembly but made it clear that with or without them, it intended to conduct the nation's business.

Outraged at the assembly's actions, Louis XVI ordered that the Salle des Etats, where the meetings were being held, be shut down. Undeterred, the assembly reconvened in the empty Royal Tennis Court, where on June 20, 1789, its members swore the Tennis Court Oath, by which they agreed not to halt their proceedings until they had given France a constitution. When news of this historic move reached the clergy, a majority of the members of that estate joined the assembly. Soon, forty-seven members of the nobility also joined. The king ostensibly recognized the assembly on June 27, although he began building up royal troops near Paris.

On July 9, fortified by messages of support from Paris and other French cities, the assembly reorganized itself as the National Constituent Assembly. Two days later, the king, influenced by the advice of the conservative members of his privy council and by his wife Marie-Antoinette, banished the reformist finance minister Jacques Necker and totally reconstructed the ministry. Believing this to be the beginning of a royal coup, much of Paris, including some of the military, erupted into open rebellion. On July 14, 1789, after heavy street fighting, the rebels stormed the Bastille, a prison that was, to many, a symbol of all the abuses that had taken place under the royal regime. The Bastille held great stores of gunpowder and arms as well; now mostly empty of prisoners, it was being used as an armory. There they killed the facility's governor and several of his guards. The bloodshed continued when, after returning to Paris's city hall, the mob captured the city's mayor, accused him of treachery, and assassinated him.

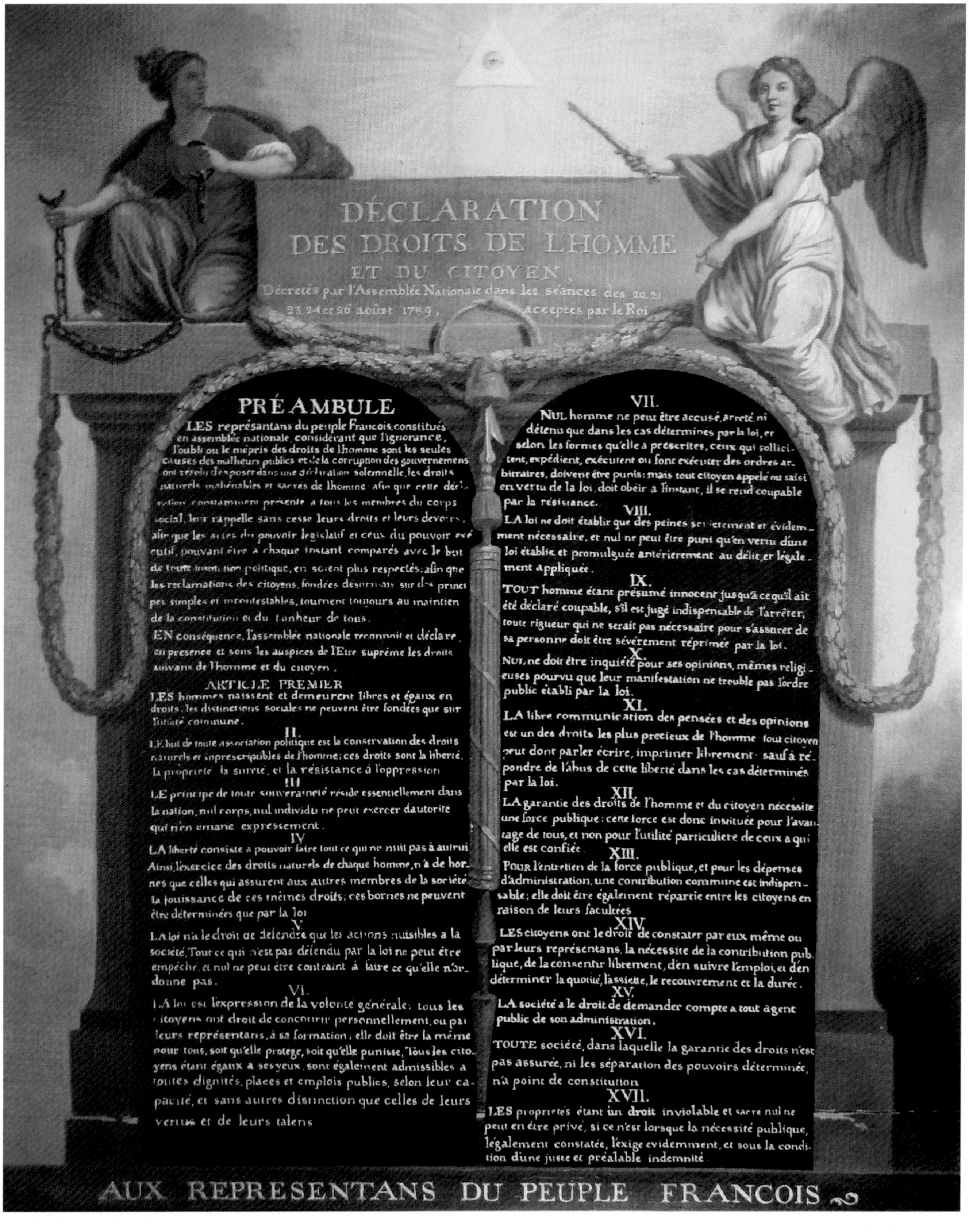
DÉCLARATION
DES DROITS DE L'HOMME
ET DU CITOYEN,
Décretés par l'Assemblée Nationale dans les séances des 20, 21
23, 24 et 26 aoust 1789, acceptés par le Roi
PRÉAMBULE
ARTICLE PREMIER
AUX REPRESENTANS DU PEUPLE FRANCOIS

OPPOSITE: This eighteenth-century French allegorical painting of the Declaration of the Rights of Man and the Citizen depicts liberty and reason as a French woman holding broken chains; a guardian angel on the top right points to the all-seeing eye, an ancient symbol often associated with masonry that was incorporated on the reverse of America's Great Seal in 1782 (where it was called the Eye of Providence). The figures sit atop the clauses of the declaration, which are designed to resemble the tablets of the Ten Commandments.

Alarmed by the events, Louis XVI and his military supporters backed down. The popular Marquis de Lafayette took command of the National Guard of Paris, and a new mayor of that city, Jean-Sylvain Bailly—who had been president of the Nation Assembly when the Tennis Court Oath was taken—was appointed. Many nobles, fearful that the reconciliation was temporary at best, began to flee the country. Others began plotting a civil war. By late July, insurrection again erupted, particularly in the rural areas where, in what became known as *la Grande Peur* (the Great Fear), a large number of chateaux were destroyed.

On August 26, 1789, using the United States Declaration of Independence as a model, the assembly published the Declaration of the Rights of Man and the Citizen. Like the American Declaration of Independence, it was not a constitution with legal powers, but a proclamation of principles at the heart of which were statements on basic human rights: "Men are born and remain free and equal in rights... the aim of all political association is the preservation of the natural and imprescriptible rights of man. These rights are liberty, property, security, and resistance to oppression." At the same time, the assembly was embroiled in what it saw as its main objective—drafting a new French constitution. It was a process marked by argument and debate among the various factions that had developed within the body. Some members pushed hard for a senate with members appointed by the king after they had been nominated by the people. Most of the nobles wanted an aristocratic upper house elected by members of their class. In the end, however, the popular party within the assembly won out. France was to have a single, unilateral assembly. The king would have only a "suspensive veto." He could delay the implementation of a law, but he could not block it completely.

In late 1790, a number of small counterrevolutionary uprisings broke out, led by supporters of Louis XVI, who tried in vain to enlist the support of the army in restoring the monarch's full powers. However, all of these efforts failed. By this time, Louis and the rest of the royal family had become truly fearful of their safety and their future. On the night of July 20, 1791, the family, disguised in clothing borrowed from their servants, fled the palace at Versailles. The next day however, the king was recognized in Varennes, in eastern France, and he and his family were arrested and taken back under guard to Paris, still dressed in their tattered servants' clothing. The assembly then provisionally suspended Louis XVI and ordered that he and the queen remain under guard as hostages in their former palace, the Tuileries.

With the king held prisoner and a constitution in place, the role of the monarch in this new government now became a pressing issue. Acting quickly, the various factions within the assembly reached a compromise, making the king little more than a figurehead by declaring that he would have to pledge allegiance to the constitution and would have to take an oath swearing that if he retracted this allegiance, or headed an army seeking to overthrow the assembly by force, or if he permitted an outside force to do the same, he would, in the eyes of the assembly, be abdicating his throne. The latter provision was in response to a real threat that had arisen in August 1791 when the Holy Roman Emperor, Leopold II; Frederick William II of Prussia; and Louis XVI's brother, the comte d'Artois, had taken up the king's cause and had declared that, if Louis was not granted his freedom and if the assembly was not dissolved, they would lead a military invasion of France. Ironically, since the French people had such deep resentment of the interference of foreign monarchs, the declaration actually placed Louis in even greater danger.

Events now moved at a rapid pace. On the night of August 10, 1792, insurgents attacked the Tuilieries and imprisoned

ABOVE: **French nineteenth-century artist Jean Duplessi-Bertaux recreated the scene of Louis XVI and his family unceremoniously brought back to Paris on June 25, 1791 after their failed flight to Varennes. Remarkably, while the royal family painstakingly disguised themselves by dressing in servants' clothing, they reportedly refused to ride in simple carriages and attempted to make their escape with an entourage in two large, ostentatious coaches.**

OPPOSITE: **This 1791 political cartoon about the French Third Estate depicts a cleric, an aristocrat, and a member of the Third Estate pulling on a rope tied to a bundle of papers including ones labeled** Nouvelle Constitution **(New Constitution) and** Voeux de la Nation **(Hopes of a Nation), which are held aloft by a female figure representing liberty. The caption reads** Ha je seront ben content quand j'aurons tous ces papiers la—le tresor tiré des ténébres **(loosely translated as "How wonderful it will be when all of these papers—these treasures are brought to light").**

Ha je seront ben Content quand j'aurons tous ces Papiers la

Le Tresor tiré des Ténébres.

A Paris mob storms the Tuileries palace, August 10, 1792; Duplessi-Bertaux reimagined the chaotic and bloody scene in his 1793 painting of the event.

the royals. Mobs of vigilantes broke into the prisons where they slaughtered some fourteen hundred victims. On August 13th, Louis was arrested and taken to an ancient fortress called the Temple, which had been converted into a prison. On December 11, the king was brought before the convention, where he was formally charged with having committed treason and crimes against the state. On January 15, 1793, by a vote of 693 to 0, Louis was found guilty of the charges made against him. Six days later, before a wildly cheering crowd, thirty-eight-year-old Louis XVI was executed. Nine months later, his queen, having also been found guilty of treason, followed him to the guillotine.

But the greatest carnage of the French Revolution was still to come. In July 1793 the Committee of Public Safety came under the control of Maximilien Robespierre, a member of the Committee of Public Safety, and the group he led, a polit-

ical club known as the Jacobins. Over the better part of the next two years, Robespierre and the Jacobins—under the aegis of the committee—unleashed their "Reign of Terror," executing more than eighteen thousand people. The slightest suspicion of opposition to the revolution meant death, either by the blade of the guillotine or by a beating at the hands of a mob. By 1794, Robespierre was even ordering the execution of ultra radicals and moderate Jacobins. Even Robespierre himself could not escape the slaughter. On July 27, 1794, he was arrested and executed by members of the Committee of Public Safety who rose up against him. Still the slaughter went on. After taking control of the government, the Girondists launched their own "White Terror" by executing even those Jacobins who had helped overthrow Robespierre.

Remarkable as it may seem, despite the years of chaos and carnage, the convention, in September 1795, managed

HELL BROKE LOOSE, OR, THE MURDER OF LOUIS.

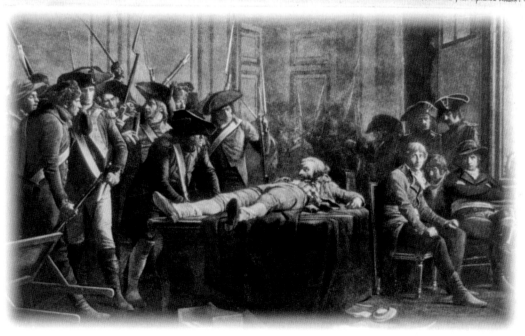

A REPUBLICAN BELLE.
A Picture of PARIS for 1794.

In this 1794 etching by English artist and political and social critic Isaac Cruikshank, a French revolutionary woman holds a pistol in one hand while she fires at a man lying on the ground. She wears a miniature guillotine around her neck; her clothing features a skull and a crossbones design, while in the background men bowl with skulls beneath the severed and bleeding head of Louis XVI. The picture is captioned "A republican belle—a picture of Paris for 1794."

to complete a constitution centered on a new form of government; called the Corps législatif, it was the first bicameral legislature in French history. The parliament was made up of 500 representatives and 250 senators. Executive power was placed in the hands of five elected directors, who formed the Executive Directory. The new government, however, met immediate opposition from remaining Jacobins and the significant number of royalists who were still dedicated to restoring the monarchy. The years 1796–97 saw the directory grow increasingly authoritarian, quelling all hints of opposition and suppressing Christianity. Almost from the beginning of the revolution, and despite the continued domestic turmoil, France had been involved in wars with foreign rivals, most notably Prussia and Austria. In the process, the army had become increasingly powerful, and its commander, General Napoleon Bonaparte, flush with overseas victories, had become more revered and more ambitious than ever before. On November 9–10, 1799, Bonaparte staged a coup, overthrowing the directory and establishing himself as dictator. Five years later he had himself proclaimed emperor.

Today, historians still disagree in their assessments of the complex, tumultuous French Revolution. Some, pointing to the "Reign of Terror" and the "White Terror," regard it as the precursor of modern totalitarianism. Others, while

Napoleon Bonaparte staged his coup at the Château de Saint-Cloud, a former royal residence overlooking the Seine, several miles west of Paris. The dramatic climax of the event was imagined by François Bouchot in this painting from 1840.

acknowledging this ominous aspect, emphasize the role the revolution played in continuing the precedents for such democratic institutions as elections, representative government, and constitutions first set in the establishment of the United States. What cannot be denied is that the French Revolution was a vital turning point in the history of the Atlantic world. As the first major social revolution, it signaled the transformation from an age of aristocracy to one in which the citizenry became the major force. What is also true is that, like the American Revolution, and despite its

failings, it had a far-reaching influence on other nations throughout the Atlantic.

Almost all of these societies were profoundly changed in one way or another by this new age of revolution. Some, particularly in Latin America, experienced dramatic, rapid transformations. In others, particularly in England, the changes, although momentous, were less severe and took place more gradually. Actually, the transformation that took place in Great Britain began almost immediately after the American War for Independence. The loss of the New

ABOVE LEFT: This highly romanticized and iconic painting by Jacques-Louis David (an active supporter of the French Revolution) is entitled *Napoleon Crossing through the St. Bernard Pass* (1801–5). It glorified Napoleon's victory over the Austrians in June 1800 at the Battle of Marengo, in North Italy. Napoleon is depicted on a charging stallion leading his troops across a snowy ridge. Most accounts say that in reality, he and his troops crossed the Alps on sure-footed mules. In 1805, Napoleon was crowned King of Italy.

Napoleon

As emperor, king, and conqueror, Napoleon Bonaparte was the dominant figure on the world scene for almost two decades. During the long series of wars fought throughout that period, known as the Napoleonic Wars, the armies of France, under his command, battled with almost every European power and, before the tide was turned against him, gained control of almost all of continental Europe.

BELOW LEFT AND INSET: The Battle of Trafalgar (October 21, 1805) in which a British naval fleet of twenty-seven vessels destroyed an allied French and Spanish fleet of thirty-three ships, was the most significant naval battle of the Napoleonic Wars. The heroics performed by the British commander Admiral Lord Horatio Nelson (shown in inset in a ca. 1799 portrait by Italian painter Leonardo Guzzardi) assured his place as England's greatest naval hero. The British victory solidified its rule of the seas, but Napoleon had already given up his plans to invade England and was focusing on completing his defeat of Britain's allies in Germany. The naval painting (1807) by Louis-Philippe Crépin captures the havoc of the battle. Nearly eight thousand men were killed and wounded, including Lord Nelson.

ABOVE: At the beginning of 1812, Russia's Tsar Alexander was pressured by Russian merchants and landowners to break the nation's shaky five-year alliance with France. They wanted to opt out of the blockade Napoleon had ordered against trade with Britain. In June, Napoleon responded by invading Russia with his Grande Armée, leading to an epic battle fought on September 7, 1812, at the small Russian town of Borodino, about seventy miles west of Moscow. Involving more than a quarter of a million soldiers in total, the Battle of Borodino was a Pyrrhic victory for Napoleon—the largest and bloodiest battle of the Napoleonic Wars, and one of the deadliest single-day battles in history. The battle cost the French more than thirty thousand dead and wounded, while the Russians suffered forty-five thousand dead and wounded. In this Russian nineteenth-century painting, a downcast Napoleon looks on as the decisive conquest he hoped for was denied him.

ABOVE RIGHT: Following Borodino, Russia's military commanders ordered a retreat all the way back to Moscow, forcing Napoleon to lead his troops further and further into the Russian interior. When the general entered the capital city on September 14, confident that its fall would force the Russians to negotiate a peace treaty, he quickly discovered that the Russians had ordered the city burned—as depicted here in this nineteenth-century Russian painting. A month later, with the deadly Russian winter fast approaching, Napoleon ordered his troops out of Moscow and out of Russia itself. It was a disastrous and humiliating two-month-long retreat, the culmination of a campaign in which it is estimated that the French suffered a staggering 575,000 casualties.

ABOVE: Encouraged by Napoleon's losses in Russia, the Allies (nations opposed to Napoleon) continued to grow in number until, by the fall of 1813, they included England, Russia, Prussia, Spain, Portugal, Sweden, and Austria. From October 16–19, 1813, they clashed with Napoleon's forces at the Battle of Nations (also known as the Battle of Leipzig). With over half a million troops involved, it was the largest battle Europe witnessed until World War I. Napoleon suffered another defeat, and by the time his army made its way back to France, it had been reduced to fewer than 100,000 men. In April 1814, the Allies forced Napoleon to abdicate, and he was exiled to Elba, a small island off the coast of Italy. Less than a year later he escaped, raised an army of more than 350,000 men, and attempted to gain revenge on the Allies. Currier and Ives published this print (ca. 1835–56) showing Napoleon's last stand on June 18, 1815, at Waterloo, in present-day Belgium, where his troops were overwhelmingly defeated by British forces. Imprisoned and exiled to the small South Atlantic island of Saint Helena, Napoleon spent the last six years of his life far removed from the glory that once was his.

World colonies was so devastating to both the Crown and the aristocracy that they never regained the primacy they enjoyed before the American Revolution. Well before the nineteenth century was over, English members of the middle class, many of whom had supported the American cause, acquired a power unimaginable before the events in the colonies had taken place. As historian J. H. Plumb so eloquently expressed in his book *England in the Eighteenth Century* (1950): "America acquired freedom; Britain moved toward a less privileged society... for the first time, she was made to realize that empire was more than trade and riches—that it was a complex problem of duties as well as rights."

WAR OF 1812

The nineteenth century started, however, with a war that some call America's "second war of independence." In 1812, only twenty-nine years after the American Revolutionary War officially ended, England and the United States went to war again. Among the major causes of the conflict was American outrage over the impressment of American sailors into the British navy and England's restrictions on neutral trade, as well as fears that Britain would ally with Native

LEFT : Master Commandant Oliver Hazard Perry is depicted in a ca. 1911 print by Percy Moran during the Battle of Lake Erie standing on the prow of a small boat, being transferred to the *Niagara* after his flagship, the *Lawrence*, was hit. His squadron of nine small vessels defeated his opponents, a British squadron of six (including two warships), shortly thereafter, securing Lake Erie for the United States. In a letter written to U.S. army general (and ninth U.S. president) William Henry Harrison regarding the British surrender, Perry famously wrote, "We have met the enemy and they are ours."

Americans on the expanding American frontier. The war (1812–15) was fought on both land and sea. On land, the American objective was to capture Canada and hold it hostage until England ceased its impressment policy and recognized American neutral trade rights. The United States, however, had only seven thousand poorly trained men in its regular army, and the attempt to invade Canada resulted in a quick defeat.

It was on the sea that the most dramatic battles of the war were fought, and it was on the sea that the Americans had considerably more success, even though the U.S. Navy had fewer than twenty vessels and no battleships—and were fighting the greatest maritime power in the world. The most famous American warship to emerge from the conflict was the frigate USS *Constitution* ("*Old Ironsides*"), which, on August 19, 1812, scored a major victory by defeating the British warship HMS *Gurrière* off the coast of Nova Scotia. In the fall, the USS *Constitution* defeated the HMS *Macedonian* in waters off Africa and then, in late December, followed up this victory by destroying the HMS *Java* off the coast of Brazil. The most important American naval victory took place on September 10, 1813, when American ships commanded by Master Commandant Oliver Hazard Perry defeated a British fleet on Lake Erie.

This 1816 print, published in Philadelphia, was accompanied by a description that read "A view of the bombardment of Fort McHenry, near Baltimore, by the British fleet... on the morning of the 13th of Sept 1814 which lasted 24 hours & thrown from 1500 to 1800 shells in the Night attempted to land by forcing a passage up the ferry branch but were repulsed with great loss."

From the beginning, the key British strategy had been the blockade of the American Atlantic coast and the carrying out of raids on American seaports (to which the Americans retaliated by commissioning privateers to raid British commercial ships). In August 1814, British troops launched an assault on Washington, D.C., in which they burned the Capitol, the Navy yard, and several other government buildings. After leaving Washington, the British moved up Chesapeake Bay and launched a heavy bombardment on Fort McHenry, guarding the city of Baltimore. The Americans, however, withstood the fierce shelling, leading to eyewitness Francis Scott Key's writing of the "Star Spangled Banner." With the signing of the Treaty of Ghent on Christmas Eve, 1814, the War of 1812 ended as it had begun, in a stalemate with no mention being made of either impressment or the trading rights of neutral nations.

LATIN AMERICAN INDEPENDENCE

In *Reisebilder* (*Travel Pictures*), the travel narratives that he wrote between 1826 and 1831, German author Heinrich Heine stated: "But what is the task of our time? It is emancipation—not just the emancipation of the Irish, the Greek, the Frankfort Jews, the East Indian Blacks and similarly oppressed peoples, but the emancipation of the entire world."

Nowhere could this movement toward freedom and the violence that often accompanied it be seen more clearly than in the French and Spanish possessions in the Americas.

It began in the French Caribbean colony of Saint-Domingue (Haiti) situated on the western third of the island of Hispaniola (Santo Domingo, which occupied the eastern two-thirds, was owned by Spain). Haiti had long been the jewel in France's overseas possessions. One of the richest colonies in the Americas, it produced half of all the sugar and coffee shipped to Europe and the United States. And, like all the Caribbean European possessions, it owed its wealth to the labor of slaves.

As physically removed as they were from their mother country, French planters, craftsmen, soldiers, and administrators in Haiti watched intently as the events of the French Revolution began to unfold. Many had long feared that they were sitting on a powder keg, vastly outnumbered by the slaves that they continued to treat with brutality. Now, all this talk of rights, liberty, and equality was bound to make matters worse.

And they did not have to wait long: in 1790, inspired by the revolutionary French assembly's Declaration of the Rights of Man and of the Citizen, the free mulattos and blacks in Haiti, some of them slave owners themselves, demanded the citizenship that the document had decreed. After this

" But what is the task of our time? It is ... the emancipation of the entire world. "

—Heinrich Heine, *Reisebilder*, 1826–31

demand was summarily rejected, a group of some three hundred men, led by wealthy mulatto Vincent Ogé, revolted—but Ogé was eventually defeated, captured, and executed. Yet even so, and against the wishes of the white Haitians, on May 15, 1791, the French National Assembly granted political rights to all free blacks and mulattos who were born of free mothers and fathers (a relatively small group). But the spark had been ignited. On August 22, 1791, an armed rebellion erupted, one in which one hundred thousand slaves, who outnumbered their French masters more than ten to one, joined the free blacks in the revolt.

Unlike both the American and the French Revolutions, the Haitian rebellion was staged by men and women who had been forced to endure the horrors of slavery for most of, if not all of, their lives. It was an uprising motivated as much by the desire for revenge as the desire for freedom. And it was almost unimaginably brutal. During the first three weeks of the revolt, slaves burned every Haitian plantation and murdered every Frenchmen they encountered. Those Frenchmen who managed to survive fled to the coastal towns from which they sent messages to France pleading for rescue.

What then ensued was one of the longest and most complex revolutions in history, a bloody thirteen-year succession of wars involving slaves, whites, free blacks, France, Spain,

and England. When it was finally over, Haiti would become the first independent black nation in the Western world.

The great hero of the long struggle was an ex-slave who, in time, would be regarded throughout Europe and America as one of the greatest figures of the revolutionary era. François-Dominique Toussaint L'Ouverture was actually a latecomer to the Haitian rebellion. A free black, he joined the insurgents as a medic in 1791 and quickly rose through the ranks. Had it not been for him, the revolution would, in all probability, have taken a very different turn.

Toussaint's real genius was in recognizing the fact that the revolution could not succeed unless two vital factors were addressed. One was that the insurgent slaves had to be both militarily and politically organized. The other was that throughout the revolution, the rebels would be caught between three rival European powers—France, which wanted to regain control of Haiti; and Spain and England, who viewed the revolution as a golden opportunity to seize control of the sugar and coffee-rich territory.

A charismatic and brilliant leader, Toussaint not only succeeded in organizing the rebels but managed to play each of the European powers off each other until he saw that the greatest opportunity lay in allying his forces with the French. By reaching an agreement whereby Haiti remained nominally a part of France but was governed by a counselship under his

Both the American Revolution and the ideals of the French Revolution spawned a spirit of freedom-seeking throughout the Spanish New World possessions. This symbolic revolutionary print (undated) exposed the plight of Mexican peasants.

ABOVE LEFT: In addition to effectively ruling Haiti as an autonomous entity, Toussaint L'Ouverture—shown here in a nineteenth-century engraving—overcame a succession of local rivals and, in 1801, led an invasion of neighboring Santo Domingo, where he succeeded in freeing all the slaves held there.

ABOVE RIGHT: The Battle of Ravine-à-Couleuvres, on February 23, 1802, was typical of the bloody engagements that took place in Haiti during the revolution; at this battle, the French forces led by General Charles Leclerc defeated the troops of freedom-seeking blacks led by Toussaint L'Ouverture. This illustration appeared in *The History of Napleon the First*, by French historian Pierre Lanfrey (1805–8).

control, Toussaint, for the better part of a decade, was able to maintain a delicate balance of harmony between the newly freed slaves and the French.

His control of the situation, however, was not to last. In 1802, newly crowned emperor Napoleon Bonaparte, determined to regain total French control of Haiti, dispatched his brother-in-law, Charles Leclerc, with more than twenty thousand soldiers to overthrow Toussaint. After leading his forces in waging guerrilla warfare against Leclerc's troops, Toussaint was able to negotiate peace, but his days as the virtual ruler of Haiti were over. His life did not have a happy ending. After a short year of retirement, he was tricked into a meeting with the French, where he was arrested and sent to France. In April 1803, the man who had been the true architect of the Haitian rebellion died in prison.

Toussaint's demise was not, however, the end of the cause for which he had so long labored. With French troops now in control, the struggle was taken up by another ex-slave, Jean-Jacques Dessalines. What followed was what some historians have described as a slaughter of noncombatants that would not be equaled until World War II. Desperate for victory, Leclerc executed whatever blacks he encountered. Dessalines

BELOW: **Upon helping to liberate Haiti, Jean-Jacques Dessalines—the first leader of an independent Haiti— was named governor for life in January 1804. Eight months later he crowned himself emperor and ruled over the new nation with** **an iron fist until he was killed in an 1806 overthrow led by the revolutionary Henri Christophe and Alexandre Sabès Pétion, who had served under Dessalines in 1802. Dessalines is shown here in an undated print.**

responded by committing atrocities on numerous French troops. When Leclerc was replaced by Donatien-Marie-Joseph Rochambeau—son of Jean-Baptiste, leader of the French forces during the American Revolution, the two-sided slaughter continued. It finally ended on November 18, 1803 when Rochambeau, having failed to obtain badly needed reinforcements from Napoleon, was forced to surrender his troops at the Battle of Vertières. On January 1, 1804, now-President Jean-Jacques Dessalines proclaimed Haiti a republic—the second republic of the Western hemisphere and the first black republic in the world.

The accomplishments of Toussaint L'Ouverture and his fellow revolutionaries in Haiti had deep, world-wide repercussions. Political thinkers and activists, intent on replacing oppression with liberty and equality, were energized by what had taken place on the Caribbean island. Soon the actions of two men, José de San Martín and Simón Bolívar, would impact a far larger territory and lead to the breakup of the Spanish empire in the New World.

José Francisco de San Martín Matorras was born in the small town of Yapeyú, Argentina, in 1778. The son of a Spanish official, he was sent to Spain where, after studying at the military academy in Madrid, he joined the Spanish army and rose to the rank of lieutenant colonel. In 1808 he fought with distinction in the Battle of Bailén against Napoleon's army that had invaded the peninsula.

The turning point in San Martín's life came during the time he spent in Cádiz following that battle. There he met South American officers who impressed him with their revolutionary beliefs and zeal. Soon he began attending lodges formed to promote independence, particularly in his native Argentina. In 1812, now deeply imbued with the revolutionary spirit, San Martín resigned his military commission and sailed to Argentina intent on joining the revolutionary forces being assembled there.

He did not have to wait long before becoming deeply involved. Soon after his arrival he was given command of the Granaderos cavalry, the best-trained of all the revolutionary units, and on February 3, 1813, he successfully led his troops against Spanish forces in the Battle of San Lorenzo, the first rebel victory in the Argentine War of Independence. Given the rank of general by the revolutionary provisional government, he was then named governor of the Argentine province of Cuyo, an appointment

ATLANTIC OCEAN

LEFT: **Before becoming the great champion of Latin American independence, José de San Martín had gained valuable military experience in Europe while serving in the Spanish army, fighting against the** French in such engagements as the Battle of Bailén (July 1808) and the Battle of Albuera (May 1811). **This is a rare daguerreotype of San Martín, taken in Paris ca. 1848.**

BELOW: **The Battle of San Lorenzo was the first armed engagement of the Argentine War of Independence. According to legend, during the battle, rebel sergeant Juan Bautista Cabral sacrificed his life to save José de San Martín, who had become trapped beneath his horse. In this 1903 work, Argentine painter Angel** Della Valle recreated the battle scene from 1813. Three years later the Argentine Declaration of Independence was drafted. The constitutional ideas embodied in the American Declaration of Independence and the U.S. Constitution inspired freedom-seekers throughout Latin America.

that brought him into contact with scores of refugees who had fled Spanish oppressions in neighboring Chile. It was another turning point in the life of the man who later became one of South America's most revered figures.

Ignoring the certainty of hardships and danger, San Martín formulated a plan for taking an army across the high and perilous Andes to liberate the Chilean people. In January 1817, he led his "Army of the Andes," comprised of approximately four thousand men, twelve hundred horses, and twenty-two artillery, across the mountains. José de San Martín's feat of taking a large and heavily equipped army over and through the Andes has been compared to the crossing of the Alps by Hannibal and by Napoleon Bonaparte. Just as they were completing their month-long trek, their advance was halted at a valley named Chacabuco. In the battle that followed, San Martín's forces, due in great measure to the actions of General Bernardo O'Higgins—whose cavalry troops succeeded in sweeping through the Spanish lines—won a total victory. Days later, San Martín and his liberators entered the city of Santiago de Chile.

Bernardo O'Higgins, the first supreme director to lead an independent Chilean state, is proudly depicted in full regalia in this nineteenth-century painting by Peruvian artist José Gil de Castro.

Bernardo O'Higgins Director Supremo de la República Chilena. Capitan General de este Primer Almirante de sus Esquadras, Presid.te del Consejo de la Legion de Mérito. y Grande Oficial de ella &&

The grateful Chileans then named San Martín supreme director of the country, but he turned down the position in favor of O'Higgins. It was more than a generous gesture, for San Martín had yet another goal in mind. He was now turning his attention to Peru, the last Spanish stronghold in the New World.

On August 20, 1820, a fleet of ships from the Chilean navy carrying an allied army was sent from Valparaíso to Paracas Bay in southern Peru. On September 7, a military force landed in Paracas and successfully attacked the coastal city of Pisco. San Martín's strategy was to liberate the country as much as he could through diplomacy, rather than militaristically, as he had done in Argentina and Chile. It was a strategy also based on the fact that on many fronts, Spanish control of the country had already been successfully challenged. In northern Peru, Simón Bolívar had overthrown Spanish authority, and he and his forces were making their way toward the capitol city of Lima. Insurgent Peruvian military commanders had also scored important, isolated victories. Several Peruvian ports had been blockaded. And throughout the country, landowners were engaged in spirited uprisings.

Confident that in the face of all these developments, authorities would negotiate Peruvian independence, San Martín met with various Spanish officials. All claimed that

they lacked the authority to negotiate such an historic agreement. Finally losing patience, San Martín dispatched his army by sail to the port of Ancón next to Lima. From there troops were sent to the southern coast and to the eastern hills, effectively isolating the capitol. On July 21, 1821, San Martín triumphantly entered Lima. On July 28, Peruvian freedom was formally declared (although the fighting was not over yet), and San Martín was voted "Protector" of the newly independent nation.

A few days earlier he had met with Simón Bolívar in Guayaquil, Ecuador. To this day, mystery surrounds what actually took place at their meeting. Some historians believe that the two liberators discussed the future of Latin

In *Atlantic History: Concepts and Contours* (2005), historian Bernard Bailyn described Simón Bolívar as "a true Atlantacist: born and bred in Caracas... educated in Europe and steeped in the writings of the European and North American Enlightenment." Gil de Castro also painted this portrait of Bolívar in the nineteenth century.

America. Others speculate that Bolívar asked San Martín to join him in defeating the remaining Spanish forces who refused to accept Peruvian independence. What *is* known is that shortly after Peru's parliament was assembled, San Martín resigned his command, left the country, and returned to Argentina where he took up the life of a farmer. In 1824, he moved to France where he spent the rest of his days in retirement. It had been a remarkable career—from Spanish officer to the agent of freedom in Argentina, Chile, and much of Peru, a journey of liberation rivaled only in Latin America by Simón Bolívar.

Unlike San Martín, whose earliest days gave little indication of the path his life would take, Simón Bolívar was imbued with a revolutionary spirit which he displayed while hardly out of his childhood. He was born Simón José Antonio de la Santísima Trinidad Bolívar y Palacios in Caracas, Venezuela on July 24, 1783. His aristocratic parents were extremely wealthy, and he received a privileged education from several specially selected tutors who marveled at the way the young man was so taken with the American achievement of independence and the type of government that its leaders had created.

Bolívar lost both his parents by the age of nine, and he was sent by his uncle to Spain to continue his education at age sixteen. En route to Europe he stopped off in Mexico City and

requested a meeting with the viceroy of New Spain, who was both shocked and alarmed that so young a man could argue so vehemently on behalf of Spanish-American independence.

In 1807 he returned to Venezuela and by 1808 began participating in the resistance movement. When the Spanish governor was expelled in 1810, Bolívar was sent on an unsuccessful diplomatic mission to England to try to gain support for the independent Caracas junta. The Venezuela War for Independence erupted in full after independence was declared in July 1811. A year later, when junta leader Francisco de Miranda was forced to surrender his troops, Bolívar was compelled to flee to Cartagena in New Granada (present-day Colombia). By this time, he was convinced that the greatest chance of throwing off the Spanish yoke lay in gaining assistance from neighboring New Granada. In 1813, after convincing New Granada's revolutionary leaders that by helping liberate Venezuela they would gain the same freedom for their country, he was given command of a large military force. On May 13, 1813, Bolívar led the invasion of Venezuela and by May 23 had taken the city of Merida. When, three months later, he defeated the Spanish army at Caracas, he was proclaimed *El Libertador*, a name that would stick with him for the rest of his life. This second independence of Venezuela was short-lived, however, as royalist supporters retook the region in June 1814.

But Bolívar was far from done. In 1814 he returned to New Granada, where a briefly established republican government had been overthrown by forces still loyal to Spain. Commanding Colombian nationalist troops Bolívar recaptured the city of Bogotá but then suffered reversals that forced him to flee the country. Determined to bring independence to Colombia, he traveled first to Jamaica and then to Haiti, seeking military aid from its president Alexandre Sabès Pétion—which he received after promising that he would free all the slaves in the territories he liberated.

Returning from Haiti with his reinforcements, he won a series of victories culminating, in 1819, in the decisive Battle of Boyacá. He then became instrumental in the creation of Gran Colombia, a federation of present-day Venezuela, Colombia, Panama, and Ecuador, and became its president.

Still his work was not finished. As San Martín had done some five years before, he turned his attention to Peru and took his army across the Andes. In 1824, at the battles of Junin and Ayacucho, Bolívar and his generals defeated the last remnants of Spanish opposition to Peruvian independence.

When, in 1825, the Republic of Bolivia was created in the former territory of Upper Peru—both to weaken the aristocracy that still existed there and to honor Bolívar—it seemed that his lifelong dream of South American independence and republicanism had been fully realized. The constitution he

ATLANTIC OCEAN

EQUATOR

Tropic of Capricorn

A New Map of
SOUTH AMERICA
From the
LATEST AUTHORITIES

drafted for new Bolivia was, in fact, a shining example of separation of power, freedom of religion, property rights, and rule of law put into practice. However, the South American unity that had also been part of his dream was not to be. By 1827, personal rivalries among leaders of the newly created independent nations brought turmoil and factional strife, and an assassination attempt was made on Bolívar's life in 1828. Now suffering from tuberculosis, Bolívar decided to leave the South America upon which he had had so great an impact and retire in Europe. But on December 17, 1830, just before setting sail, he succumbed to a final bout with his physical affliction.

CHALLENGING SLAVERY

The legacies left behind by Toussaint L'Ouverture, José de San Martín, and Simón Bolívar were momentous. Despite the inevitable turmoil and twists and turns that all the newly liberated nations would experience, both independence and constitutionalism had been introduced into places where oppression and tyranny had, from the beginning, been the hallmarks. In the process, hundreds of thousands of slaves had gained their freedom. And, with so much of the world having been involved in the issues of liberty and equality, the institution of slavery was increasingly being looked at in a new

light. "Slavery," as Bernard Bailyn wrote in his book *Atlantic History: Contours and Concepts* (2005), "would survive well into the nineteenth century (in Brazil until 1888), but while in all the years before it had seldom been seen as an overwhelming moral problem and a profound anomaly in Christian society, after the Revolutionary era, there was never a time when it was not seen as such, when it was not challenged and reviled...and not understood to be doomed."

The original patent for Eli Whitney's cotton gin, shown here, was issued in 1794. Any hope of slavery in the United States being peacefully abolished vanished when this machine made cotton production and slavery more profitable than ever. "[With this machine]," wrote Whitney in his petition for the patent, "two persons will clean as much cotton in one Day as a Hundred persons could [formerly] clean in the same time."

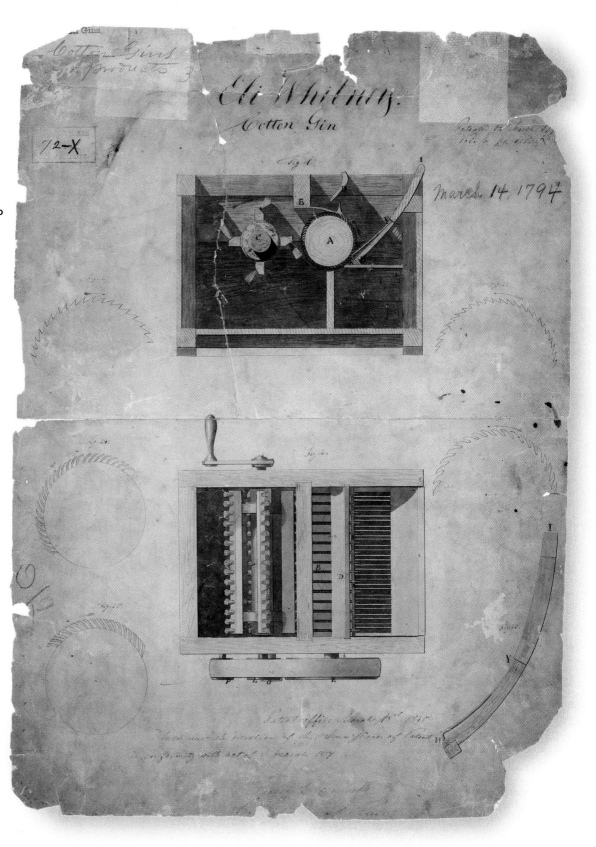

Indeed, in 1794 France abolished slavery, and in 1807 England outlawed the international slave trade. And, in that same year, the U.S. Congress voted to ban the importation of slaves. These actions, combined with the ideals of freedom and equality expressed in the American Constitution, bolstered the belief of many abolitionists that slavery in the United States might be outlawed. A combination of factors, however, conspired to dash these hopes.

The atrocities inflicted upon the white planters during the Haitian rebellion truly frightened the slave owners in the United States. Alarmed that similar occurrences might take place on their plantations, they began to exercise closer and harsher control over their slaves. More important was the fact that with the advent of the Industrial Revolution and the enormous growth in the worldwide textile industry, cotton, grown on the Southern plantations, became so profitable a crop that any chance of even the most benevolent planters releasing their hold on their slaves became virtually nonexistent.

The first federal census in 1790 revealed that there were 697,897 slaves in the United States. By 1810, due in great measure to the invention of the cotton gin, which made it far easier to process the raw cotton than ever before, the number of slaves had grown to 1.2 million. By 1850 more than 2.5 million slaves on the Southern plantations were producing three million bales of cotton each year. It was not only in Europe and other developed countries that the crop became so important. Cotton was the cornerstone of the development of New England textile manufacturing, which would become one of America's largest industries.

Despite the enormous importance to the economies of both South and North, however, there were those who were determined to bring an end to what they regarded as "that evil institution." Among the first stirrings of the abolitionist movement were the slave narratives, written by freed or escaped slaves detailing the horrors of their life in bondage. Immensely popular not only in the North, many were translated into French, German, Dutch, and Russian.

Religious groups, such as the Quakers and those headed by articulate, impassioned black preachers, took up the cause as did hundred of local and national abolitionist societies created to promote emancipation and aid fugitive slaves. Almost all of these societies had their own publications that attacked slavery as both a moral and political evil. And none was more vehement or unyielding in its approach than the antislavery newspaper the *Liberator*, published by the leading abolitionist William Lloyd Garrison. "On [slavery]," Garrison wrote in the *Liberator*'s first issue, published in 1831: "I do not wish to think, or speak, or write, with moderation. No! no! Tell a man whose house is on fire to give a moderate alarm; tell him to moderately rescue his wife from the hand of a ravisher; tell the mother to gradually

With slave holders and apologists alarmed at the events in places such as Haiti where slaves had won their freedom, images such as this were published in the United States, portraying slaves as being "contented" with their condition. In this ca. 1841 print drawn by a Northern Whig slavery apologist, Edward Williams Clay, "happy" slaves dance in the background while an elderly slave says, "God bless you massa! you feed and clothe us. When we are sick you nurse us, and when too old to work, you provide for us!"

RIGHT: The abolishment of slavery in the United States would come, but at a terrible price—the American Civil War (1861–65). The deadliest war in U.S. history, it tore the nation apart and left more than 600,000 dead and over 400,000 wounded. This *Harper's* *Weekly* cover of March 23, 1861, features nine officers at Fort Sumter, in South Carolina, one of four federal union-held forts left in the Confederacy in 1861. The fort was bombarded twenty days later and taken over by the Confederates, the first skirmish of the war.

ABOVE: This woodcut engraving of a male slave in chains appeared on the broadside publication of John Greenleaf Whittier's antislavery poem, "Our Countrymen in Chains." Widely distributed as a symbol of the antislavery movement, the original broadside contained the quotation, "England has 800,000 slaves and she has made them free. American has 2,250,000 and she holds them fast!!!"

extricate her babe from the fire into which it has fallen;—but urge me not to use moderation in a cause like the present. I am in earnest—I will not equivocate—I will not excuse—I will not retreat a single inch—AND I WILL BE HEARD."

Garrison was indeed heard. In areas of the South, brave and desperate slaves led ill-fated revolts. The Underground Railroad system was established to help those in bondage escape. Impassioned pleas continued. But cotton was too profitable; the Southern way of life too entrenched. In the end, in a country that had inspired the movement toward freedom throughout the Western world, it would take a devastating civil war to bring freedom to millions who labored in bondage within its own borders.

KEPLER

EXTRACT
OF MALT

KEPLER
SOLUTION OF
CODLIVER OIL
IN EXTRACT
OF MALT

10.116. — DARTFORD BURROUGHS WELLCOME & CO'S FACTORY

8

THE INDUSTRIAL REVOLUTION

MECHANIZATION AND THE ATLANTIC WORLD

This photomechanical
print ca. 1890 shows
a view of the Burroughs
Wellcome & Company's
pharmaceutical factory in
Dartford, an important
industrial center in Kent,
England.

BURROUGHS WELLCOME & Co.

THE INDUSTRIAL REVOLUTION

The story of civilization…is the story of…that long and arduous struggle to make the forces of nature work for man's good.

—L. Sprague de Camp, *The Ancient Engineers*, 1963

The late eighteenth and early nineteenth-century political revolutions that echoed throughout the Atlantic world were truly momentous. Yet there was another type of transformation that had its beginnings at approximately the same time, one with such dramatic and lasting effects that historians have compared it to the Neolithic revolution, that prehistoric period in which humans moved from hunting and gathering to agriculture and abandoned their nomadic way of life. Characterized by the accomplishments of scores of inspired inventors and tinkerers, the Industrial Revolution brought about changes that permanently affected almost the entire world. It began with the mechanization of the textile industries and the development of iron-making techniques, and it started in Great Britain.

There were many reasons why it was England that ushered in the Age of Industry. The enormous revenues that Britain received from its overseas colonies and the huge profits it made in its slave trade between Africa and the Caribbean gave England the financial resources to launch such an historic transformation. And it had an abundance of other resources as well. The huge amounts of coal, lead, iron, tin, copper, limestone, and waterpower located throughout northern England, the Midlands, South Wales, and the Scottish Lowlands were essential for the development and expansion of industry. And, despite its relatively small size, England had a dense population—a readily available labor supply that was also necessary for the transformation about to take place. Furthermore, England was the one European nation that had emerged from the Napoleonic Wars without having experienced economic collapse. Its large merchant fleet was still intact, a fleet that early on had gained experience in transporting goods from the nation's cottage industries to markets that had already been established.

OPPOSITE AND RIGHT: **Before the industrial transformation in the making of textiles took place, scenes such as this one inside an Irish dwelling were commonplace in Europe. Here, according to** the artist's caption, women are "spinning, reeling with the clock reel, and boiling the yarn." The print by Irish artist William Hincks is one of a series published in London in 1791.

TEXTILE MANUFACTURING

In the early eighteenth century, cottage industry was the foundation of Britain's vital textile production. Based on wool, it was carried out by individuals who spun and wove in their own homes or small shops. Cotton and flax were also processed in this way, but it was a much more difficult procedure and represented only a small portion of British output. Steadily, however, and due in great measure to the ever-increasing availability of raw cotton from the Caribbean and the southern United States, advances were made that would result in the mechanization of the British textile industry in general and in the manufacture of cotton goods in particular.

Among the earliest of these advancements was the roller spinning machine, patented by Lewis Paul and John Wyatt in 1738. Featuring two sets of rollers that traveled at different speeds, the machine was powered by the use of donkeys. Although Paul and Wyatt could not make their invention profitable and eventually went bankrupt, five of their machines were purchased by a man named Edward Cave who installed them in his fledging factory in Northampton, thereby establishing the world's first cotton-spinning mill.

The next step forward was accomplished by a local weaver named James Hargreaves, who lived in the village of Stanhill. As the story goes, Hargreaves's contribution began when his daughter accidentally knocked over his spinning wheel. Noticing that the spindle continued revolving, Hargreaves came up with the idea that several spindles could be worked off one wheel. (This is likely an early urban myth).

What is true is that around 1764, Hargreaves built what eventually became known as the spinning jenny (though there is some controversy as to whether Hargreaves simply refined a prototype created by Lancaster weaver Thomas Highs). The machine contained eight spindles rather than the one found on common spinning wheels. An operator, by turning a single wheel, could now spin eight threads at one time. It was a significant achievement, and it brought a response that would be encountered by other pioneer industrial inventors. For when Hargreaves began to sell his new machines, spinners from neighboring locales, fearful that the new device would put them out of business, descended upon his house and destroyed his machines. Undaunted, Hargreaves moved to Nottingham, where he built a small spinning mill. Unfortunately for Hargreaves, he didn't patent his device until 1770, and by that time others had copied his idea and had made improvements on the machine. By the time Hargreaves died in 1778, the capacity of the spinning jenny had been increased from eight to eighty threads, and more than twenty thousand machines were being used throughout Great Britain.

All of these early inventions, and others that soon followed, were, in their own right, historic, but none would have had the impact they engendered had it not been for a group of British entrepreneurs, and one man in particular, who capitalized on these achievements. Led by Richard Arkwright, these entrepreneurs encouraged the various inventors, financed many of their ideas, and protected their creations by patenting them. (In some cases, they actually stole the inventions.) Arkwright, a brilliant industrialist, was the first to bring the various early mechanized production processes together under a single roof, thereby creating the first real factories. And it was he who championed the steady advancements in the use of power—from horse to water to steam.

Along with his many entrepreneurial skills, Arkwright was also an inventor, although many of the creations with which he is credited were mainly the invention of someone with whom he allied himself. The youngest of thirteen children, he was born in the ancient English community of Preston in 1732. Because his parents could not afford to send him to school he was taught to read and write by one of his cousins. After a short stint as a barber's apprentice, the young but ambitious Arkwright started his own wig-making business, which required him to travel throughout the country.

Arkwright's life took a dramatic turn when, on a 1767 business trip, he met John Kay who, along with Thomas Highs, had built a prototype for an improved spinning machine that worked with a system of rollers. Learning that the inventors had run out of money, Arkwright, whose wig-making business was prospering, offered to hire Kay, with whom he was particularly impressed, to continue work on the machine. Realizing that the inventor also needed physical help with his ambitious project, Arkwright then hired other local craftsmen, and soon the team produced what became known as the spinning frame. Featuring three sets of paired rollers that turned at different speeds, the machine was able

OPPOSITE: Hincks also depicted the interior of an early Irish linen textile mill, where men are "winding, warping with a new, improved warping mill, and weaving."

ABOVE: "This plate," Hincks wrote in his caption to this image, "represents a perspective view of a scutch mill, with the method of breaking the flax with [grooved] rollers, and scutching it with blades fixt on a shaft, both turn'd by the main wheel; great improvements in the method of breaking and scutching the flax."

BELOW: This diagram of Arkwright's spinning frame appeared in a London publication by Richard Marsden titled *Cotton Spinning: Its Development, Principles and Practice* (1884). Thanks to the increased productivity that machines like this one enabled, by the early 1800s, manufactured cotton goods became the dominant British export, and England had replaced India as the world's leading supplier of cotton goods.

RIGHT: Richard Arkwright staffed his factories by encouraging families to move to the villages near them. As an incentive he is said to have provided them with a week's vacation a year, but only if they promised not to leave the village. He had other rules as well, including the dictum that any worker caught whistling within the factory was to be fined one shilling. This nineteenth-century print is by James Posselwhite, after a drawing by Joseph Wright.

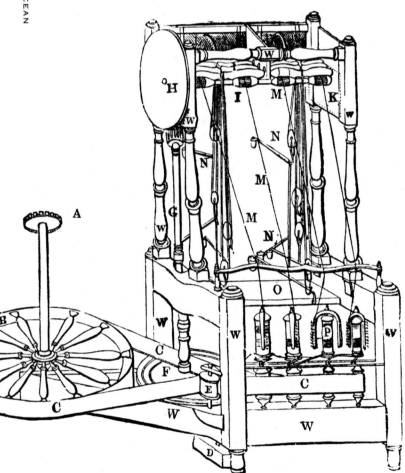

to produce a thread that was far stronger than Hargreaves's spinning jenny was able to make.

Encouraged by this giant step forward in textile production, Arkwright then expanded his business by acquiring needed capital from a Nottingham bank and forming a partnership with two fellow entrepreneurs, Jedediah Strutt and Samuel Need. Realizing that the spinning frame was too large to be powered by hand, the partners first tried powering it with horses. When this proved inadequate, they decided to set up a large factory next to the River Derwent, where they constructed a huge waterwheel. Soon the machine became known as the water frame. (Arkwright went on to patent the water frame as his own invention; the patent was legally rescinded in 1785).

The ambitious and visionary Arkwright was far from finished. His next goal was to expand operations by building several other factories, a plan that he was forced to carry out on his own when, in 1781, Need died and Strutt, after arguing that Arkwright was moving too quickly, pulled out of the partnership. Moving ahead, Arkwright built factories in

BELOW: Historians and archeologists believe that the first use of iron occurred around 4000 BCE in ancient Egypt and Sumer, where small objects such as the tips of spears and decorative ornaments were made from iron recovered from meteorites.

This image of medieval ore smelting is from *De re metallica* (*On Metallic Matters*), by Georgius Agricola, a German scientist and the so-called father of minerology, published posthumously in 1556.

Lancashire, Staffordshire, and Scotland, all of which became immensely profitable. His innovations continued when he powered the machines in each of these facilities with the revolutionary steam engine that had been recently developed by James Watt and Matthew Boulton (see this chapter, "Steam Power"). By the time he died in 1792, Richard Arkwright employed more than nineteen hundred people, many of them child laborers, and had become one of the wealthiest men in England.

IRON-MAKING

The advancements made in the manufacture of textiles would be accompanied by an equally vital revolution in iron-making. As Doug Peacock of the British website *Cotton Times* put it, "If textiles fueled the Industrial Revolution, iron was the scaffolding on which it was constructed." It was iron that formed the framework of the textile machinery and the factories in which they were housed. And it was iron that spurred the development of thousands of other machines and enabled the building of railways and ships that would move manufactured goods and people around the world as never before.

The production of iron was not new to Great Britain. It had been produced by the Celts as early as the fifth or sixth centuries BCE, and later by the conquering Romans

A dramatic scene of Coalbrookdale at night, painted by English artist Philip James de Loutherbourg in 1801; the name Coalbrookdale became synonymous with early iron manufacturing, and scenes such as this one became symbolic of the Industrial Age. Along with their major operations at Coalbrookdale, the Darbys also established iron-making centers in South Wales, Scotland, and Staffordshire.

(between 43 and 410 CE) in a type of furnace known as a bloomery. The first significant advancement came in the late fifteenth century when the blast furnace, which operated by air being forced into the fire by bellows, was introduced in England. It was not, however, until the use of coal instead of wood was established that the real transformation in iron-making began. In 1678, Sir Clement Clerke and others began smelting iron in coal-reverberating furnaces called cupolas, in which iron ore was heated indirectly by flames deflected downward from the furnace's roof. The flames played on the ore and reduced the oxide to metal while at the same time preventing impurities in the coal from migrating into the iron.

> " *If textiles fueled the Industrial Revolution, iron was the scaffolding on which it was constructed.* "

—Doug Peacock, *Cotton Times*, 2008

It was a giant step forward, but the most important steps lay ahead. And they were largely taken by one family—the iron-making Darbys. The son of a Quaker farmer, Abraham Darby I was born in Wren's Nest, near Dudley, in about 1678. In 1704, during a visit to Holland, he became fascinated with metal-making, and when he returned to England, he brought back with him several Dutch experts who helped him establish a brass foundry in Bristol. In 1709, he turned his attention to iron and moved to Coalbrookdale in Shropshire, where he acquired an ironworks. It was here that Darby perfected his historic technique for smelting iron ore by using coke (the hard, dry substance produced by heating coal to an extremely high temperature in the absence of air). It was here that by using coke—which, unlike coal, contained no impurities—Darby's furnaces produced the highest quality iron that had ever been made. And it was here that he turned Coalbrookdale into the cradle of the iron-making industry.

When, in 1717, Abraham Darby I died at thirty-nine, the operations at Coalbrookdale passed into the hands of Abraham Darby II. It was he who, according to his employees, discovered how to make wrought iron from coke-smelted ore, an advancement that made the iron malleable so that it could be rolled out. Darby II, unfortunately, left no records of his discovery nor did he patent it, so that honor later fell to an iron-maker named Henry Cort.

Darby II was succeeded, after his death in 1763, by Abraham Darby III who, along with carrying on the family tradition of improving iron-making techniques, proved to be one of the most sympathetic and generous employers of the Industrial Age. He became known for paying higher wages than other factory owners, for supplying unusually good housing conditions for his workers, and for buying up farms during food shortages so that his employees would be adequately fed.

Darby III's greatest achievement was the construction, in 1779, of the worlds' first cast-iron bridge, a one-hundred-foot structure that spanned the River Severn at a spot that became known as Ironbridge. Although Darby III passed away at forty-one, members of the Darby family continued to manage the Coalbrookdale Company until 1849. They carried on the Darby tradition of advocating the use of iron for almost everything from houses to pavements (the curbstones in the village of Ironbridge are still made of iron). And the iron produced at Coalbrookdale made possible the earliest development of the steam engine—the single most important invention of the Industrial Revolution.

STEAM POWER

"Steam," the editor of *The New York Mirror* exclaimed in 1828 "the tiny thread that sings from the spout of a tea kettle, that rises from our cup of shaving water, suddenly steps forth…and annihilates time and space." He was right. Steam, the most effective power source yet devised, indeed stepped forth and changed almost everything connected with the Age of Industry.

The textile industry was among the first to reap the benefits of the power of the steam engine. Although many mill owners with small-scale machinery continued to rely on wind or water power, those who turned to steam to drive larger machines quickly discovered that their productivity was greatly enhanced. The steam engine had an even greater positive effect on the iron-making industry, particularly as far as the mining of coal was concerned. Before the steam engine, coal, now in greater demand than ever because of the rise of iron-making and the introduction of coke, was most commonly surface mined; the mined veins were close to or on the surface of the ground. Sometimes, if conditions in the soil were favorable, somewhat deeper mining could take place by means of an opening driven into the side of a mountain or hill. Some shaft mining was also carried out, but this practice was highly limited because of the considerable problem of removing water in the shaft that appeared from deep within the earth or inundated the shaft after heavy rainfall. The power of the steam engine not only removed this problem but enabled shafts to be driven much deeper, providing access to larger deposits of coal. Along with these and other immediate benefits, the steam engine eventually led to a Transportation Revolution as profound and far-reaching as the Industrial Revolution that had spawned it.

The man credited with being the first to develop a workable steam engine for industrial use was Thomas Savery, a member of a well-known Devonshire family. Educated as a military engineer, Savery was an inveterate tinkerer whose efforts turned serious when he devised a unique arrangement of paddle wheels for propelling vessels in calm weather. His greatest contribution, however, came in response to the engineering difficulties encountered by British coal mine operators in keeping water out of their mines, a condition that some operators attempted to keep under control by employing up to five hundred horses to draw the water up in buckets.

After much experimentation, Savery developed what he called the "Miner's Friend" or, as some later called it, the "Fire Engine." In 1698, he demonstrated a model of his device to King William III and his court, who were so impressed with the invention that Savery was almost immediately awarded a patent, one which prophetically indicated

A Land and People Transformed

The Industrial Revolution brought about unprecedented changes in the way people worked, transported themselves, and lived. One of the most visible signs of the transformations that took place was the alteration of the landscape—*and the home*—in those nations increasingly involved in what would become known as the Industrial Age.

TOP: **Before the Age of Industry and the advent of the factory system, European artists' depictions of the landscape commonly featured peaceful, often pastoral scenes. This painting of the English countryside,** *The Cornfield*, **was created by John Constable in 1826.**

ABOVE: **By 1830, when German artist Carl Blechen painted this scene,** *Mill in Eberswalde*, **the factory had made its appearance even in remote rural areas.**

RIGHT: **By the late 1850s, towns like Sheffield, England, had become industrial centers, the home of companies such as the one featured in this ca. 1856 print—John Martin & Co., a steel-manufacturing and iron-exporting concern.**

ABOVE LEFT: The products of the Industrial Revolution not only enhanced the economies of nations on both sides of the Atlantic but also made daily life—and household chores—easier in countless ways. Old methods of doing things gradually gave way to the new. This painting by Jean-François Millet, *Peasant Woman Baking Bread* (1854), demonstrates the age-old method of baking bread in a hearth oven. By the twentieth century, commercial bakeries began to supplant home baking in most industrialized countries.

ABOVE RIGHT: Toward the end of the nineteenth century, most middle-class homes in urbanized areas had running water, such as in this kitchen in a chromolithograph published by American printer Louis Prang ca. 1874. Note the large, ornate cast-iron wood-burning stove, soon to be replaced in most homes by gas stoves in the early twentieth century.

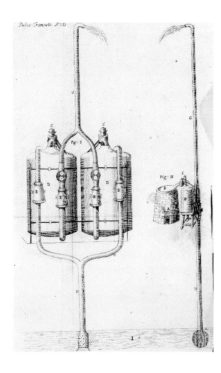

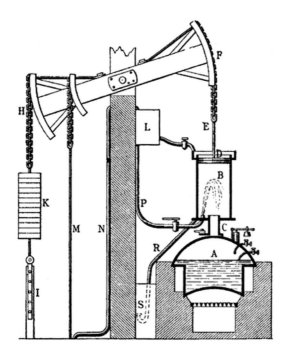

uses for the steam engine other than emptying the mines of water. It read: "A grant to Thomas Savery of the sole exercise of a new invention by him invented, for raising of water, and occasioning of motion to all sorts of mill works, by the important force of fire, which will be of great use for draining mines, serving towns with water, and for the working of all sorts of mills, when they have not the benefit of water nor constant winds."

Although Savery's engine was a major advancement, it was never powerful enough to deliver what its patent promised. But it provided a vital platform upon which others could build. The real breakthrough came in 1712 when blacksmith/plumber/tinsmith/lay preacher Thomas Newcomen built a steam engine much more powerful than that of his onetime partner Savery. Unlike Savery's engine, which had no piston and cylinder and generated about one horsepower, Newcomen's had both components and delivered five times more power. By 1725, Newcomen's device was in common use with more than one hundred of the engines having been installed throughout the British mining regions. They would remain the main method for draining the mines for almost the next fifty years.

The greatest achievement, however, was yet to come, an advancement so momentous that it transformed the world of work and, as several historians have expressed it, "gave us the modern world." It was this invention, developed by Scotsman James Watt, that took the steam engine out of the coal fields and into the factories, where it revolutionized textile production and made it possible for factories, no longer dependent upon water power, to be located anywhere. It was the Watt engine that led to the Transportation Revolution, soon to be evidenced by the locomotive and the steamboat.

The son of a merchant, James Watt was born in Greenock, Scotland in 1736. When he was nineteen he moved to Glasgow, where he studied instrument-making. In 1757, he established his own business and soon earned a reputation as a highly accomplished and innovative engineer. His life and that of the world was changed dramatically when, in 1763 he was sent a Newcomen steam engine to repair. As he worked on it, he realized that he could not only fix it, but could make it better. After spending several months experimenting with different approaches, he created an engine that cooled the used steam in a condenser separate from the main cylinder, making the device much more efficient and powerful.

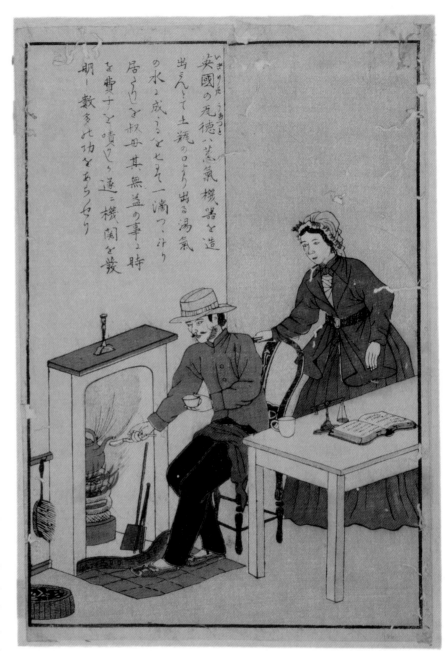

James Watt's invention of the steam engine that changed the world brought him international fame. In this Japanese print ca. 1850, depicting Watt's inspiration for his invention, Watt collects steam from a boiling kettle while his aunt rebukes him for his "nonsense."

MR. WATT'S DOUBLE STEAM ENGINE from his SPECIFICATION of 1782.

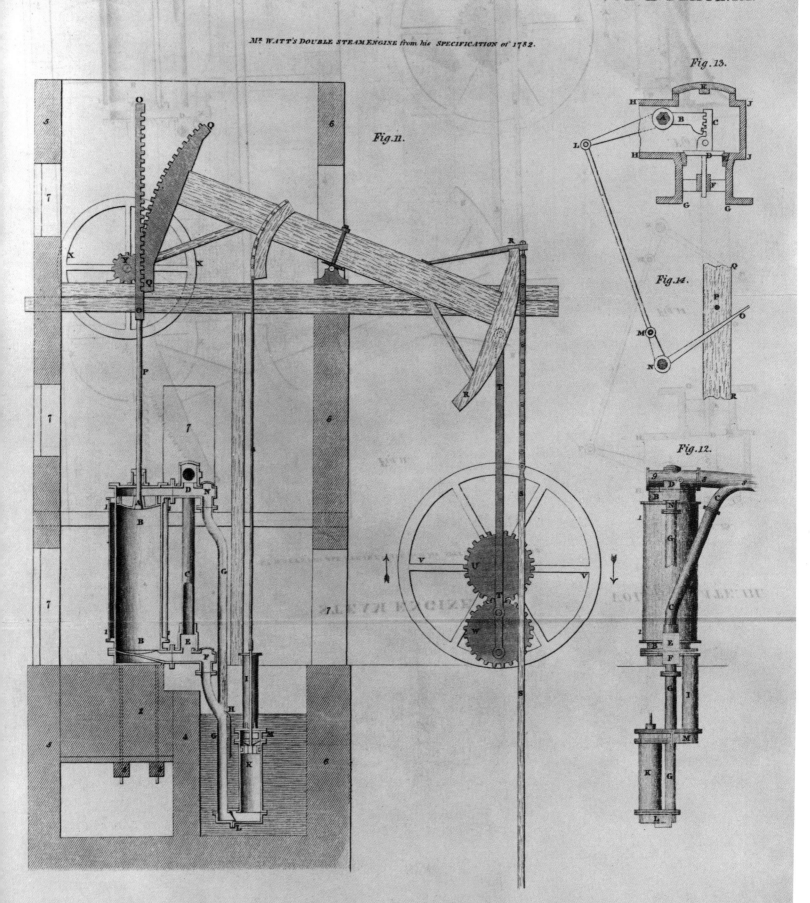

Fig. 11.

Fig. 13.

Fig. 14.

Fig. 12.

OPPOSITE **This diagram of James Watt's double steam engine was reproduced in *A System of Mechanical Philosophy* (1822), by Scottish inventor and physicist John Robison. The inscription on Watt's statue in London's Westminster Abbey includes the words:** *enlarged the resources of his country increased the power of man and rose to an eminent place among the most illustrious followers of science and the real benefactors of the world.*

Watt knew that he was on to something important, but he also realized that in order to fully develop and produce his new engine he needed considerable funding. He found it in the person of Birmingham businessman Matthew Boulton and, for the next eleven years, Boulton's factory produced and sold Watt's steam engines, mainly to coal mine owners. These businessmen found the machines to be more than four times more powerful than the Newcomen engine they had for so long been using.

Watt's greatest accomplishment, however, was yet to come. In 1781, after continuous experimentation, he created a revolutionary rotary-motion steam engine. Unlike his earlier invention, which was mostly used for pumping out mines, this new engine could be used for powering almost every type of machinery. Among the first to recognize the significance of this new engine was Richard Arkwright who, by 1783, was using the rotary engine in all of his factories. Other mill owners soon followed Arkwright's lead, and by 1800, more than five hundred of the machines were in use throughout Great Britain.

Watt had been granted a patent for his invention by Parliament, and for the next twenty-five years, the Boulton and Watt Company enjoyed what amounted to a monopoly on the engine's production and sale. Its use not only fueled the transformation in the way goods were made and people moved about, but also made possible another vital aspect of the Industrial Age—the manufacture of machine tools, without which machinery, including the steam engine itself, could not have been made.

THE IRON HORSE

Of all the machines that were made, none epitomized the era more dramatically than the mechanical marvel that became the very symbol of the age itself—the locomotive. Without the advances in mining, iron-making, and the delivery of steam power, the development of the machine that poet Walt Whitman described in *Leaves of Grass* (1900) as "Type of the modern! emblem of notion and power! pulse of the continent!" would never have been possible. And, as was the case with all the technological steps forward, the "iron horse" was the result of the ingenuity and skill of a number of determined, often driven individuals. The first was Richard Trevithick. A giant of a man, known for his athletic prowess, Trevithick was born in Cornwall in 1771. He began his career as a mining engineer and early on developed a successful high-pressure engine for raising ore and refuse from the mines. But his real dream was to build steam-driven vehicles. By 1796 he had succeeded in constructing a prototype miniature locomotive that operated when a red-hot iron was

> " *Type of the modern! emblem of notion and power! pulse of the continent!* "

—Walt Whitman, *Leaves of Grass*, 1900

288

ATLANTIC OCEAN

inserted into a tube beneath a boiler filled with hot water, causing steam to rise and set the engine in motion.

In 1801, Trevithick realized an even greater accomplishment when he built a full-size steam road carriage. On Christmas Eve of that year, he startled onlookers by loading several of his friends into what he called the *Puffing Devil* and taking them first up a hill and then on to a nearby town. Although three days later the carriage overheated and was destroyed, and a larger steam-drum carriage that he built two years later was too expensive to be commercially viable, many historians regard the *Puffing Devil* as the historic forerunner of the automobile.

Undeterred by his failure to create a successful steam carriage, Trevithick turned his attention back to the development of a workable locomotive. And, with the backing of a prosperous ironworks owner, he succeeded in producing the world's first steam engine to successfully run on rails. It was also the first locomotive in which the exhaust steam was directed up the chimney, which drew the hot gases from the fire more powerfully through the boiler. In February 1804, Trevithick accomplished the then-astounding feat of using his new locomotive to haul ten tons of iron, seventy passengers, and five wagons on a journey from an ironworks to a canal some nine miles away. During the trip the locomotive reached the hitherto unheard of speed of five miles per hour.

But, once again, it was a one-time triumph. Each time Trevithick tried to repeat such a journey, the seven-ton steam engine broke the cast-iron rails.

He made one last grand attempt. In the summer of 1808, after having built a new engine he named *Catch Me Who Can*, Trevithick built a circular railway and, for the fare of one shilling, offered the public rides on his locomotive which, thanks to improvements he had made, reached speeds of twelve miles per hour. But, after two months of successful circular trips, his old problem reemerged.

The rails began breaking, and a discouraged Trevithick was forced to turn to other endeavors. He had not realized his dream, but he had set so much of the groundwork for the realization of team locomotive-driven railway lines that, in many transportation circles he is regarded as the father of the locomotive.

Another man, however, earned the title "father of the railways." George Stephenson was born near Newcastle-upon-Tyne in 1781. His father was an engine keeper in a coal mining company (called a *colliery*), and the young Stephenson developed a keen interest in all things mechanical. Denied a formal education, he attended night school where he learned to read and write, and early on he studied the works of both Trevithick and Watt.

In 1802 he became a colliery engineer, devoting all his spare time to taking engines apart to discover how they

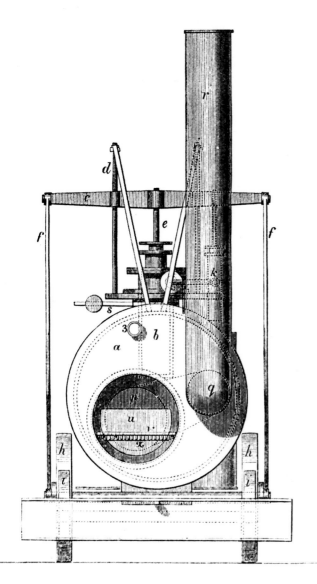
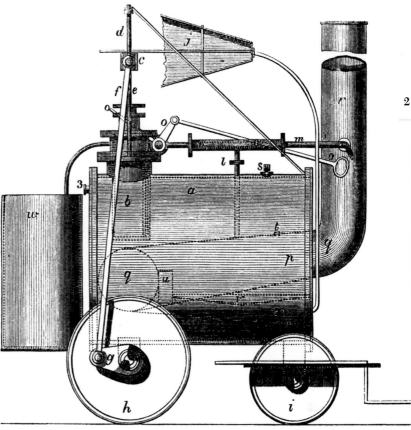

worked. In 1813, he convinced the colliery manager to let him attempt to build a locomotive. The result was the *Blucher*: although sluggish and unreliable, it utilized two vertical cylinders set into the boiler, which permitted it to pull thirty tons up a grade at four miles per hour. Most important, rather than using a cogged rack-and-pinion system, it was the first successful flanged-wheel locomotive.

Over the next several years, Stephenson continued to build new locomotives, more than sixteen in all, continually adding improvements, including connecting rods that drove

This plan of Richard Trevithick's first passenger-carrying, common-road locomotive, from 1801, shows side and front views of the steam locomotive. The two front wheels (labeled *i*) were called the "steering wheels"; turned by a rod, they guided the locomotive. The back wheels were the "driving wheels." The illustration appeared in *Life of Richard Trevithick, with an Account of His Inventions* (1872), by his son Francis.

An engraving from 1826 depicts rear and side views of George Stephenson's steam locomotive and railroad cars of the Stockton and Darlington Railway. The noted American engineer and architect William Strickland included this illustration in his "Reports on Canals, Railways, Roads, and Other Subjects, Made to the Pennsylvania Society for the Promotion of Internal Improvement" in 1826. The year before, the society had appointed Strickland as their agent and sent him to Europe to gather information on the construction of inland navigation systems, especially railroads. The society's 1826 annual report reprinted their letter of instruction to Strickland, which included this directive: "Locomotive machinery will command your attention. This is entirely unknown in the United States and we authorize you to procure a model of the most approved locomotive machine at the expense of the Society."

the wheels directly and chains that coupled the wheels together. By this time he had earned the respect of the colliery owners to such an extent that he was given the responsibility of constructing an eight-mile railway line from Hetton to Sunderland.

In 1821, Parliament passed an act authorizing a company owned by Edward Pease to build a horse railway that would link the towns of Darlington and Stockton, a span of twenty miles. Stephenson arranged a meeting with Pease and, after showing him his *Blucher* at work, convinced him that he should build a locomotive-powered railway instead. Fortunately for Stephenson, a short time after this agreement, John Birkinshaw, an engineer at the Bedlington Ironworks introduced a new method of rolling wrought iron rails in fifteen-foot lengths. Stronger than any previously developed rails, they assured that Stephenson's project would not meet the fate suffered by Trevithick.

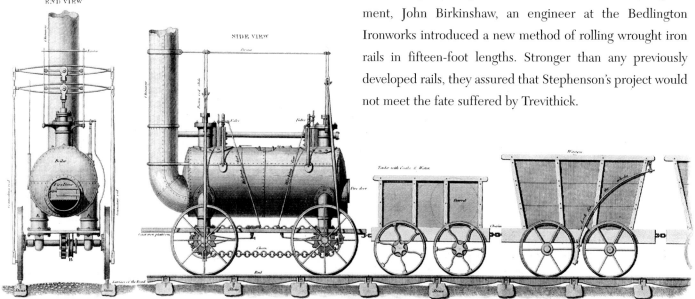

G. STEPHENSON'S PATENT LOCOMOTIVE ENGINE.

A train makes its way out of Berlin and into the German countryside in a painting by Adolf von Menzel, *The Berlin-Potsdamer Railway* (1847). Beginning in 1835 with a locomotive built by the Stephensons for a line that ran out of Nuremberg, the German railroad system grew rapidly. In 1843, the Rheinische Eisenbahn, operating between Cologne in Prussia and Antwerp in Belgium, became the world's first international railway line.

The engine created by Stephenson and his son Robert, who was now working with him, was originally called *Active*, but was soon renamed *Locomotion*. On its first run in 1825, it carried more than five hundred passengers and hauled a load of about thirty tons. Averaging eight miles per hour, it reached speeds as high as twelve miles per hour. It was a historic accomplishment, the world's first steam-driven passenger railway. And it caused a sensation, one vividly described by John Sykes, an eyewitness to the event, in his 1833 book *Local Records; Or, Historical Register of Remarkable Events: Which Have Occurred in Northumberland... with Biographical Sketches of People of Talent, Eccentricity and Longevity*:

> The novelty of the scene and the fineness of the day had attracted an immense concourse of spectators, the fields on each side of the railway being literally covered with ladies and gentlemen on horseback, and pedestrians of all kinds. The train of carriages was then attached to a locomotive engine, built by George Stephenson, in the following order: (1) Locomotive engine, with the engineer (Mr. George Stephenson) and assistant. (2) Tender, with coals and water; next, six wagons, laden with coals and flour; then an elegant covered coach, with the committee and other proprietors of the railway; then 21 wagons, fitted up for passengers; and last of all, six wagons laden with coal, making altogether, a train of 38 carriages. By the time the cavalcade arrived at Stockton, where it was received with great joy, there were not less than 600 persons within, and hanging by the carriages.

In 1829, the success of the Darlington and Stockton line earned George and Robert Stephenson an even bigger assignment—the construction of a thirty-six-mile railway between Liverpool and Manchester, linking Britain's greatest industrial region with one of its greatest seaports. The *Rocket*, the loco-

The seemingly far-fetched notion of "free-running steam carriages" occasioned both satire and ridicule. This 1831 drawing by English artist H. T. Aiken titled "A View in Whitechapel Road," featured two large steam-driven carriages named "The Infernal Defiance" and "The Dreadful Vengeance."

motive designed to run on this line by Robert Stephenson, was twice as fast as *Locomotion I* and was the most reliable and easiest to operate engine of its day.

TECHNOLOGY BOOM

Based on their accomplishments, the Stephensons became the world's most respected and renowned locomotive and railway builders. News of their achievements traveled across the Atlantic to America, to a nation just beginning to realize the importance of its own industrial potential. The dissemination of innovative technologies had begun long before the Stephensons' successes, and knowledge was shared in numerous ways: Whenever a trained worker moved from one

employer or one locale to another, he typically shared new techniques he may have learned; also, throughout the Industrial Revolution, individuals and groups engaged in study tours in which they traveled from one manufacturing facility to another, gathering technical knowledge. Some countries, most notably France and Sweden, sponsored study-touring for civil servants and technicians

Cutting-edge technologies were also transferred by members of informal philosophical (natural science) societies. The most famous of these was Birmingham's Lunar Society, whose members included James Watt, Matthew Boulton, and Joseph Priestly, one of the pioneers in the field of electricity. Those who actively corresponded with the society included Richard Arkwright, Benjamin Franklin,

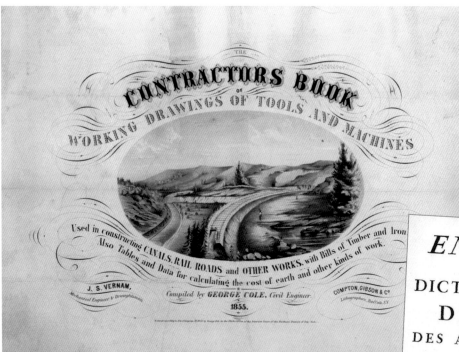

ABOVE: The so-called Second Industrial Revolution, spearheaded in the United States and Germany by knowledge transferred from Europe, was aided by the publication of books and manuals such as this *Contractor's Book of Working Drawings of Tools and Machines Used in Constructing Canals, Railroads, and Other Works*, compiled by civil engineer George Cole and published in Buffalo, New York, in 1855.

RIGHT: From 1751 to 1772, French writer Denis Diderot oversaw the publication of the immense work the *Encyclopédie ou Dictionnaire raisonné des sciences, des arts et des métiers* (*Encyclopedia, or a systematic dictionary of the sciences, arts, and crafts*). The encyclopedia includes 17 volumes of text, 11 volumes of plates, and over 18,000 pages containing 72,000 articles written by more than 140 contributors, including his co-editor until 1757, French scientist and mathematician Jean le Rond d'Alembert. The encyclopedia included thousands of detailed entries regarding the technical advancements that had been made throughout Europe. Diderot's encyclopedia was much more than a reference work though; a prominent Enlightenment political philosopher as well, the volumes encapsulated the thoughts and beliefs of the Enlightenment movement (with contributions from thinkers such as Voltaire, Rousseau, and Montesquieu), fomenting the seeds of the French Revolution.

By saving considerable capital, effort, and time by modeling their factories after those that had developed in England, and by investing more heavily in science and pure research, Germany replaced Great Britain as Europe's primary industrial nation during the Second Industrial Revolution. This painting from 1910 depicts the Zeiss Company optical lens factory complex, located in Jena.

294

> *"Until we manufacture more, it is absurd to celebrate the Fourth of July as the birthday of our independence."*
>
> —*Boston Gazette*, 1788

The building of canals that was an integral part of the Industrial Age facilitated the movement of raw materials from ocean-going vessels to the factories and finished products to the ships. This scene, painted by an anonymous artist in 1823, depicts London's busy Regent Canal, which linked the earlier-built Grand Junction Canal with the Thames.

Thomas Jefferson, and many people who were interested in sharing new technological ideas.

Perhaps most important of all were the publications devoted to descriptions of new inventions and methods. Encyclopedias such as Abraham Rees's *Cyclopaedia* and John Harris's *Lexicon technicum* contained a wealth of information. One of the most widely read of all was Denis Diderot's *Encyclopédie*, which through beautifully rendered engravings explained in detail how manufacturing was carried out in various foreign nations.

By 1800, these sources were joined by the appearance of periodicals devoted to technology and manufacturing, which described newly granted patents and included reports by individuals who had been engaged in study tours.

The continual transfer of all this knowledge had profound global effects and resulted in what historian Anthony Wallace in his book *Growth of an American Village in the Industrial Revolution* (1978), has termed "the international fraternity of mechanicians." It resulted also in what is regarded as the Second Industrial Revolution (ca. 1865–1900), an era in which nations outside of England became heavily industrialized, one in which technological leadership passed from Great Britain to the United States and Germany.

Just as conditions in England had been right for the nation to usher in the First Industrial Revolution, by the late eighteenth century all of the elements were beginning to coalesce for the United States to assume a leadership role in the second. The huge nation was expanding from coast to coast. Enormous mineral deposits lay beneath its soil. No nation had more major rivers or seaports. And no other country was as free of government restrictions on trade and manufacturing as was the United States, an advantage that had not escaped the attention of the nation's secretary of the treasury, Albert Gallatin, who, in his 1810 report to the U.S. House of Representatives, wrote:

> No cause, indeed, has, perhaps, more promoted in every respect, the general prosperity of the United States than the absence of those systems of international restrictions

and monopoly which continue to disfigure the state of society in other countries. No law exists here, directly or indirectly, confining man to a particular occupation or place, or excluding any citizen from any branch, he may, at any time, think proper to pursue. Industry is, in every respect, perfectly free and unfettered, every species of trade, commerce, art, profession and manufacture, being equally open to all, without requiring any previous regular apprenticeship, admission, or license.

Yet despite all of these advantages and all the progress that had been made in the still young nation, there were many who decried the fact that the country had fallen so far behind its former mother country as far as industrialization was concerned. "Until we manufacture more," the *Boston Gazette* exclaimed in 1788, "it is absurd to celebrate the Fourth of July as the birthday of our independence."

However, this would all change, and ironically it began in duplicity. In the same year that the *Boston Gazette* had published its lament, a stocky, fair-haired young Englishman named Samuel Slater read a Philadelphia newspaper account of how a man had received a £100 bounty for having designed a textile machine. Here, thought Slater, was real opportunity, and he was determined to take advantage of it. He was certainly prepared, having served an apprenticeship

29211   Slater Mill, First Cotton Mill in United States, Pawtucket, R. I.

As had earlier taken place in Europe, the landscape of the United States was also transformed by the Industrial Age. This stereograph, taken in 1927 by the Keystone View Company, shows the original Slater Mill in Pawtucket, Rhode Island— the first water-powered textile mill in America. Samuel Slater, in an essay included in *Documents Relative to the Manufactures in the United States*, an 1833 report by U.S. secretary of the treasury Louis McLane, wrote: "If the people of this country desire to be a civilized and powerful people, they must cultivate and promote those arts of life which form the elements of civilization and power. An exclusively pastoral agricultural nation can never be formed into a polished or a powerful community."

under Richard Arkwright's partner Jedediah Strutt, who had passed on to the young lad many of Arkwright's trade secrets. The fact that British law forbade the emigration of engineers did not faze him. He needed no plans or drawings; he carried all of Arkwright's secrets safely stored within his head.

Convincing custom officials that he was a simple farmer, Slater sailed for America, where he was hired by Quaker merchant Moses Brown, who was about to erect his own textile mill outside of Providence, Rhode Island. Slater oversaw its construction based on the Arkwright designs in his memory. The result, in 1793, was the first water-powered textile mill in America. In 1798, after having built a second mill as Brown's partner, Slater struck out on his own and constructed a much larger factory. It was the beginning of the spread of what became known as the "Slater system," a network of thirteen textile mills that made Providence and the neighboring Blackstone Valley "the nation's nursery of manufacturing."

While Samuel Slater was a man with a plan, Oliver Evans was a man with a vision. He had never heard of either Thomas Newcomen or James Watt, yet he invented the most effective steam engine yet devised, one that enabled the United States to overtake Great Britain in the development of the railroad and was instrumental in the introduction of the automobile.

Evans was born in Newport, Delaware, in 1755 and, at the age of fourteen, was apprenticed to a wheelwright. His first invention came in 1777 when he created a machine that improved the carding of wool. An even more important invention soon followed when he devised an automated gristmill that operated by means of a series of bucket elevators and conveyor belts.

His greatest contribution, however, came in 1804, when he patented a high-pressure steam engine that was lighter and capable of delivering more power than any that had ever been built. He did so with a specific vision in mind, for he was convinced that the steam engine would eventually propel people over land faster and for greater distance than anyone had yet imagined. "The time will come," he stated, in his pseudonymous book *Patent Right Oppression Exposed* (1813) "when carriages powered by steam will travel almost as fast as birds fly, fifteen or twenty miles an hour."

In 1805, Evans created his most intriguing invention. Granted a commission from the Philadelphia Board of Health to build a dredge employing his newly invented steam engine, he constructed an enormous contraption that he called the *Oruktor Amphibolos* (Amphibious Digger). Thirty-feet long, the fifteen-ton vehicle was powered by Evans's five-horsepower engine. It was never terribly effective as a dredge, but when Evans drove it through Philadelphia streets on his way to the harbor, the *Oruktor Amphibolos* became America's first self-powered land vehicle.

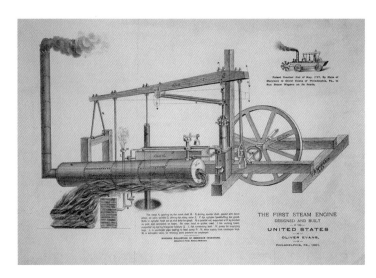

LEFT: The inscription on the lower right of this lithograph by Thomas Arnold McKibbin reads: "The first steam engine designed and built in the United States by Oliver Evans of Philadelphia, PA, 1801." Evans expressed what he perceived to be a lack of sufficient glory—and funding—befitting his status as an inventor, as well as frustration over patent infringement, when he dourly titled his second book *The Abortion of the Young Steam Engineer's Guide* (1805). A quote attributed to him during this period reads: "He that studies and writes on the improvement of the arts and sciences labours to benefit generations yet unborn, for it is not probable that his contemporaries will pay any attention to him."

BELOW: As early as the 1830s, Oliver Evans's *Oruktor Amphibolos* was being hailed as the world's first successful steam land carriage. This illustration appeared in the July 1834 issue of *The Boston Mechanic and Journal of the Useful Arts and Sciences.*

Elias Howe did not invent the sewing machine—that honor belongs to Walter Hunt. But the refinements that Howe brought to the machine made it one of the most useful inventions in history and profoundly changed the way clothing was made and the type of clothing that was worn.

This fanciful advertisement for the Empire Sewing Machine Co., ca. 1870, depicts the scenes of sewers using their machines as a sign of progress, alongside the steam locomotive also featured—contrasted with the hand sewers and the horse-drawn carriage.

The contributions of Samuel Slater and Oliver Evans were but part of the cascade of inventions and advancements that characterized the emergence of the United States as an industrial power, advancements that included Eli Whitney's introduction of interchangeable standardized parts in his musket factory in the early 1800s, the forerunner to the assembly line, and Elias Howe's enhancement of the sewing machine in 1846, which revolutionized the manufacture of clothing.

Perhaps nothing better illustrates the industrial progress that took hold in the United States than the transformation of the American farm, particularly in the vast prairie lands. Thanks to inventors such as John Deere and Cyrus McCormick, and the development of such marvels as mechanical reapers, threshers, binders, and combines, by the 1880s, the same American farm family that had once struggled to cultivate two acres of land a day was able to plant and harvest more than one hundred.

By the late nineteenth century, the United States was the world leader in the development of the railroad. It began in 1828, when the fledging Delaware and Hudson

Like the locomotive, farm machinery, most notably the mechanical reaper patented in 1834 by Cyrus McCormick, and the combine, patented in the same year by Hiram Moore, became visible symbols of both the Age of Machine and industrial progress. This chromolithograph (ca. 1859) by American artist Edwin Forbes illustrates men using the new reaper at the Lagonda Agricultural Works in Springfield, Ohio. Combines are shown in the small insets at the bottom of the image.

With the advent of the
Industrial Revolution,
mills were no longer reliant
on water power. As
historian Anthony F. C.
Wallace wrote in *Rockdale:
The Growth of an American
Village in the Early
Industrial Revolution*
(1978), once "the reliable
steam-driven factory could
be...placed alongside
a railroad beside a harbor,
within a great city...the
wilderness lost its
plausibility as a site for
industry." This 1881
chromolithograph by
Charles Hart after William
Porter shows the Eaton,
Cole & Burnham Co. factory
complex in Bridgeport,
Connecticut, on the Long
Island Sound. The company
manufactured brass and
iron fittings and tools.

THE INDUSTRIAL REVOLUTION

TESTING RAIL

ROLLING A RAIL

SAWING A RAIL

THE CONVERTERS

WATCHING THE CONVERTERS

Genuine Conne...lle Coke

VIEW OF DRAVO WORKS.

VIEW OF TROTTER SHAFT.

MINING COAL.

5000 OVENS. CAPACITY 8750 TONS DAILY.

Process of Manufacturing Coke at the Works of the

H.C. FRICK COKE COMPANY,

CONNELLSVILLE COKE REGION PENN'A
POST OFFICE, PITTSBURGH PA.

Watering and Drawing Coke.

OPPOSITE: Workers toil in a Pittsburgh steel-making plant in an engraving by Alfred Rudolph Waud. The image appeared in the *Harper's Weekly* of March 25, 1876, to illustrate an article on the Bessemer process. In 1855, English engineer Sir Henry Bessemer patented the process of mass-producing steel from pig iron by introducing air into the fluid metal to remove carbon and other impurities. Bessemer wrote in *Sir Henry Bessemer*

F.R.S.: An Autobiography (published posthumously in 1905): "I had an immense advantage over many others dealing with the problem under consideration, inasmuch as I had no fixed ideas from long-established practice to control and bias my mind, and did not suffer from the general belief that whatever is, is right." The Bessemer process was further refined by English metallurgist Robert Forester Mushet, who laid the first steel rails in Derby Station in 1857.

ABOVE: This late nineteenth-century print depicts the works of the H. C. Frick Coke Company in the Connellsville district of Pittsburgh, an area rich in high-quality coal deposits that became a major center of coke production. Coke, increasingly used by iron and steel manufacturers at the time, was transported by water or rail to iron furnaces across the country.

The perfection of the steel-making process made possible the construction of structures such as the combined Eads road and railway bridge over the Mississippi River connecting St. Louis and East St. Louis, Illinois. When completed in 1864, the bridge, the first to be constructed using steel as the primary structural material, was the longest arch bridge in the world—including the approaches on both sides, it reaches an overall length of 6,442 feet. This chromolithograph of the bridge was printed in 1874.

By 1869, the United States had been connected coast to coast by steel rails. No area was too remote or too challenging for those who built the railroad. Among the most spectacular of their accomplishments is the Georgetown Loop, which spans Colorado's Clear Creek. Completed in 1884, the tracks scaled an elevation of 640 feet over mountainous terrain and steep canyons. It was an engineering marvel that became a major tourist attraction and is still operable today. A photochrome print from ca. 1899 shows a breathtaking view of the loop.

Canal Company ordered the first of three locomotives from George and Robert Stephenson's company for hauling coal from the mines of Carbondale, Pennsylvania, to the site of a canal that the firm was building some thirty miles away. By 1860, some thirty thousand miles of track had been laid in the United States. Nine years later, the entire nation was linked by rail, leading philosopher Henry David Thoreau to exclaim in *Walden* (1854) that "When I hear the iron horse make the hills echo with his snort like thunder, shaking the earth with his feet, and breathing fire and smoke from his nostrils…it seems as if the earth had got a race now worthy to inhabit it."

Before the nineteenth century was over, American inventors, such as George Westinghouse, Alexander Graham Bell, the incomparable Thomas Edison, and scores of others, revolutionized not only the worlds of industry and transportation but the world of communications as well. A century that had begun with the United States relying on England and Europe for its manufactured products and technological ideas ended with America emerging as the world's greatest exporter of machine-made products and innovative ideas.

And it had come about in a significantly different manner from the transformation that had occurred across the Atlantic. The American Industrial Revolution had taken place in a still-fledgling nation unhampered by old beliefs and ancient traditions, a nation that celebrated ingenuity and that, for the most part, embraced change. As D. W. Meinig

observed in *The Shaping of America* (1993), "the real American system of manufacture was something more than the efficient use of machines to produce machines, it involved a new scale of production and an inventiveness, an openness, an avid national commitment to create an environment in every way congenial to capitalistic enterprise." Historian Thomas Cochran perhaps put it best in his book *Frontiers of Change: Early Industrialism in America* (1981). "Europe," he wrote, "modified industrialism to fit its various cultures... American culture more readily changed to suit new conditions."

This 1874 lithograph by printmaker Otto Krebs depicts a bird's-eye view of the cities of Pittsburgh, Birmingham, and Allegheny City, Pennsylvania, at the junction of the Monongahela and Allegheny rivers. When this lithograph, showing the presence of factories, bridges, and steamboats, was drawn in 1874, the United States was well on its way to becoming an industrial giant.

Grand Exhibitions

From cottage industry to teeming factories; from scarcity of goods to the greatest proliferation of products the world had ever known; from plodding, overland transport to travel by train at more than a mile a minute—the Industrial Revolution altered the world. On both sides of the Atlantic, "progress" was the watchword, most clearly evidenced by the giant exhibitions and expositions organized to both showcase and celebrate all that had been and was being accomplished.

The first great exhibition organized to hail industrial progress was held in Hyde Park in London in 1851. Held in an enormous iron-framed building with over a million feet of glass named the Crystal Palace, the exhibition featured some thirteen thousand exhibits including such diverse industrial marvels as the world's most advanced mechanical loom, an envelope machine, sophisticated tools, newly developed kitchen appliances, steel-making displays, and farm machinery. During the four-and-a-half-month life of the exhibition—the forerunner of a series of similar events that took place during the last half of the nineteenth century—more than 6,200,000 visitors made their way to the Crystal Palace.

ABOVE: The lithograph, ca. 1851, illustrates visitors perusing the exhibits in an interior hall of the palace.

LEFT: The photograph, taken by Philip Henry Delamotte around 1854, shows the vast structure after it was moved to its new location in Sydenham Hill (the palace was destroyed by fire in 1936).

ABOVE: The World's Columbian Exposition was held in Chicago in 1892–93 to celebrate both industrial progress and the four-hundredth anniversary of Christopher Columbus's discovery of the New World. Covering more than six hundred acres, the exposition was a proud demonstration of America's emerging industrial greatness in the same way that the Crystal Palace Exhibition heralded England's leadership of the industrial world in 1851. Among the features of the Columbian Exhibition was a building introducing the public to electrical power. Currier & Ives published this bird's-eye view lithograph of the exposition grounds ca. 1892.

RIGHT: At the heart of all the exhibitions and world's fairs were the displays of machinery, none more spectacular than the Corliss steam engine. Patented by American engineer George Henry Corliss in 1849, a gigantic seventy-foot-tall double Corliss engine was exhibited at the Centennial International Exhibition of 1876 (a fair held in Philadelphia celebrating the one-hundredth birthday of the United States). "The Corliss engine does not lend itself to description;" wrote American author and literary critic William Dean Howells in an *Atlantic Monthly* essay in July 1876, "its personal acquaintance must be sought by those who would understand its vast and almost silent grandeur. It rises in the center of the huge structure, an athlete of steel and iron…Yes, it is still in these things of iron and steel that the national genius most freely speaks…" In May 1876, *Harper's Weekly* reproduced this engraving, made after a sketch by Theodore R. Davis, showing visitors gawking at the colossus as President Ulysses S. Grant and Emperor Dom Pedro of Brazil start the engines on the first day of the exposition.

9

NEW SHIPS, NEW COMMERCE

A NEW AGE OF ATLANTIC TRADE

Currier and Ives created
this print of the
impressive steamships
Egypt and *Spain* in 1879.

NEW SHIPS, NEW COMMERCE

When trade is at stake, you must defend it or perish.

—WILLIAM PITT, EARL OF CHATHAM, SPEECH TO THE HOUSE OF COMMONS, 1739

At 10:00 A.M. on January 5, 1818, during a heavy snowstorm, the 424-ton sailing vessel *James Monroe* sailed out of New York Harbor. Bound for Liverpool, she carried in her hold 1,500 barrels of apples, 860 barrels of flour, some 70 bales of cotton, 14 bales of wool, an assortment of live hens, pigs, cows, and sheep, and a large sack of mail. On the surface, it seemed nothing more than an ordinary sailing, not unlike any of the tens of thousands that had originated in New York's bustling harbor since colonial times. But, as evidenced by the throng of onlookers who had braved the snow to witness the departure, this was a special event. The curious had been drawn to the dock by advertisements in the New York newspapers proclaiming that, beginning on that day, Quaker merchant Isaac Wright and his partners, including Jeremiah and Francis Thompson and Benjamin Marshall, would be sending ships of his newly established Black Ball Line across the Atlantic to Liverpool not on the whim of wind or tide but at an exact time according to a set schedule. And—most startlingly of all—his ships would sail

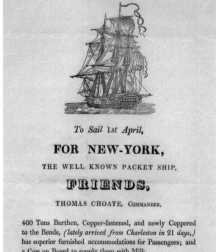

To Sail 1st April,

FOR NEW-YORK,

THE WELL KNOWN PACKET SHIP,

FRIENDS,

THOMAS CHOATE, COMMANDER,

400 Tons Burthen, Copper-fastened, and newly Coppered to the Bends, *(lately arrived from Charleston in 21 days,)* has superior furnished accommodations for Passengers; and a Cow on Board to supply them with Milk.

Shippers and Passengers are requested to have Goods or Luggage, intended for this Vessel, at Greenock, by Saturday, the 29th, at farthest.

For *Freight* or *Passage*, apply to Messrs. STEVENSON, MILLER, & Co. Greenock; the CAPTAIN on board; or here, to

JOHN FYFE & CO.

GLASGOW, *11th March*, 1823.

A. Young, Printer.

at their appointed time whether or not they had a full load of cargo or passengers.

It was unheard of. All merchant ships waited for full holds and a full complement of passengers before setting sail. And they certainly did not leave until the winds, the tides, and the skies were favorable. The delay could be as long as two weeks. Sometimes even longer.

It was a bold and venturesome move, and, for the next three decades, it was an enormous success as merchants and manufacturers on both sides of the Atlantic—now able for the first time to rely on scheduled deliveries—embraced this new dimension in ocean shipping. Time-pressed passengers, taking advantage of reliable departures and arrivals, also flocked to the ships in increasing numbers.

PACKET SHIPS

By the end of its first year of operation in 1818, the Black Ball Line boasted four packets, each of which had made three round trips between New York

The notions of ships not sailing with the tide and without a full cargo were, in the words of historian Melvin Maddocks (in *The Atlantic Crossing*, 1981), "as breathtakingly simple as the past was turmoiled." Sailing, no matter what the conditions, often presented real problems. These packet ships were caught in a hurricane in the waters near Liverpool, depicted here in an 1839 print after a painting by British artist Samuel Walters.

and Liverpool. The revolutionary line eventually became so steeped in maritime lore that a century later the watch on scores of sailing vessels was called with the cry "Arise and shine for the Black Ball Line." Success, of course, bred competition, and, in 1821, two other transatlantic packet lines, the Red Star Line and the Swallowtail Line, were established. In the next two decades, other lines followed, most notably

OPPOSITE: This poster announced accommodations aboard the "well-known packet ship *Friends*," which was to sail from Greenock, Scotland, to New York on April 1, 1823. Passengers were promised "superior furnished accommodations," as well as "a cow on board to supply them with milk."

Bending the Foresail &c.

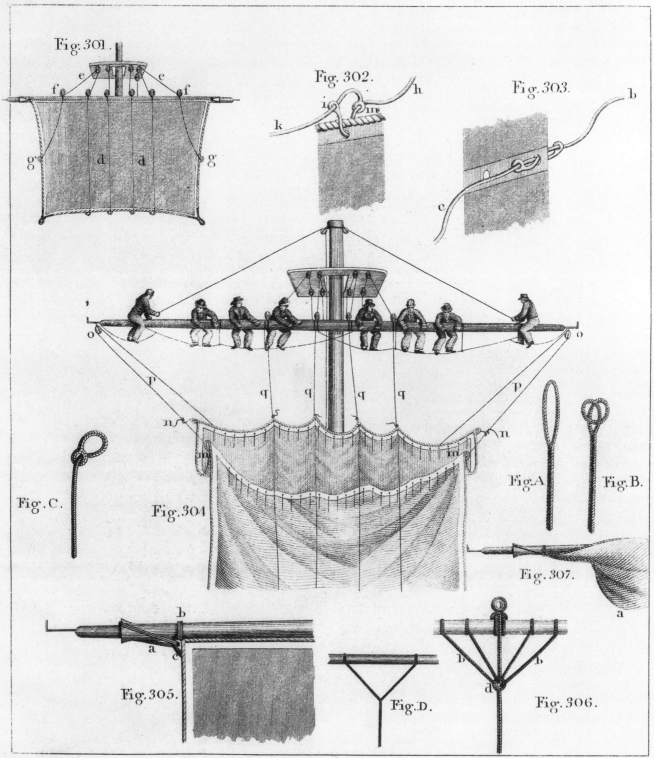

Fig: 301.

Fig. 302.

Fig. 303.

Fig. C.

Fig. 304.

Fig.A.

Fig.B.

Fig. 307.

Fig. 305.

Fig.D.

Fig. 306.

Young & Delleker Sc.

OPPOSITE: The rapid growth of the packet trade, and the increasing number of ships it spawned, placed a shortage on the number of qualified seamen available to man the vessels. These illustrations are from *The Young Sea Officer's Sheet*

Anchor: Or a Key to the Leading of Rigging and to Practical Seamanship (1808) by British maritime expert Darcy Lever, intended, as the manual stated, "to induce many to study the profession."

BELOW: The April 12, 1856, edition of *Frank Leslie's Illustrated Newspaper* included a story about the destruction of the packet-ship *John Rutledge* by an iceberg two months earlier. There was only one survivor.

Edward Collins's Liverpool Line, also known as the "Dramatic Line" because its ships were named after dramatists and actors.

As historian Melvin Maddocks wrote in the book *The Atlantic Crossing* (1981): "These vessels and others like them clearly deserved a name of their own and the public gave them one. The term 'packet'—heretofore applied indiscriminately to miscellaneous ships that carried cargoes [including mail] bundled in packets—came to signify a ship that sailed on schedule." A packet typically measured about 120 feet in length and was some 28 feet wide. Its three masts carried as much canvas as they could handle, while its hold, some 14 feet deep, could transport more than 3,500 barrels of cargo. More than any other vessels that had preceded them, packets combined strength, capacity, and speed.

And, given their devotion to schedule, it was speed that was of the essence. On that first packet voyage in 1818, it took the *Monroe's* Captain James Watkinson twenty-eight days to reach Liverpool. The ship's sister packet, the *Courier*, which had departed Liverpool at approximately the same time and had become caught up in raging seas, had taken six terrifying weeks to reach New York. Only six years later, Captain Pitkin Page completed the Atlantic crossing in thirteen days and fourteen hours. And, in 1840, despite the fact that because of prevailing winds and currents it took sailing vessels longer to

The piers along New York City's South Street were appropriately known as Packet Row. After visiting the area in 1842, author Charles Dickens wrote in *American Notes* (1842) that the bowsprits of the packets "almost thrust themselves into the windows" of the buildings across from the piers. This nineteenth-century print shows New York's bustling South Street Seaport.

cross the Atlantic from Europe to America than from the New World to the Old, the *Siddons*, under the command of Captain Nathaniel B. Palmer, made the westward crossing in the then-startling length of fifteen days.

Along with the ships themselves, these accomplishments were also due to the skill and daring of the packet captains. Willing to take almost any risk to arrive in port on time, the packet captains achieved heroic status on both sides of the Atlantic. Newspapers acclaimed each record crossing, mentioning the captain's name far more prominently than that of the ship. In *Men, Ships, and the Sea* by Alan Villiers (1962), one newspaper is said to have proclaimed that "The *Queen of the West* is the noblest work of man, and her commander...the noblest work of God!" Not to be forgotten were the special challenges faced by a packet's crew. "Aboard those liners," wrote Herman Melville in his book *Redburn: His First Voyage* (1849), "the crew have terrible hard work, owing to their carrying such a press of sail in order to make as rapid passages as possible, and sustain the ship's reputation for speed." Melville, who, in 1839 sailed on a packet as a ship's boy, might have added that this "terrible hard work" involved the dangerous practice of maintaining full sails even during the fiercest storms.

It all came at a terrible price. The mania for speed at any cost exacted a heavy toll on both ships and humans. In 1847, all of the officers aboard the Black Ball Line's *Columbia* were

Claude Joseph Vernet

Arguably more than any other subject, the romance and adventure of ships and the sea captured the attention of artists throughout the Atlantic world. One of the most talented of all the acknowledged masters of this extraordinarily popular subject was the eighteenth-century French painter Claude Joseph Vernet. He was only fourteen when he painted alongside his father, who was a successful decorative artist. But it was a trip he took to the Marseilles seaside and a voyage to a port on the Tyrrhenian Sea that led to the maritime art career that occupied him for the rest of his life. After finding employment in the studio of Italian marine painter Bernardino Fergioni, where his work attracted great attention, he struck out on his own. For the next twenty years, while living in Rome, Vernet produced acclaimed paintings of ships and the sea. In 1753 he was recalled to Paris by royal command, and it was there he painted the series of French seaports for which he is best known.

ABOVE: *The Calm*, 1734, shows fishermen working on the shore of the Mediterranean. Of Vernet's work, the *Encyclopedia Britannica* of 1911 noted: "Perhaps no painter of landscapes or sea-pieces has ever made the human figure so completely a part of the scene depicted or so important a factor in his design."

BELOW: *The Interior of the Port of Marseille*, 1754, depicts the bustling scene at the docks of this major European shipping center. Vernet's series of paintings of the ports of France were immensely popular both with the public and the French aristocracy.

TOP: *View of the Port of Toulon*, 1755. Today Vernet is widely regarded as the leading French landscape painter of the eighteenth century.

ABOVE: *View of the Port of Cette*, 1757. "Others may know better," Vernet is legendarily said to have declared, "how to paint the sky, the earth, the ocean; no one knows better than I how to paint a picture."

The crew have terrible hard work, owing to their carrying such a press of sail in order to make as rapid passages as possible.

—Herman Melville, *Redburn: His First Voyage*, 1849

killed in a ferocious winter storm. Six years later, almost a hundred of the 922 emigrants sailing on the *Constellation* were buried at sea; the cramped, squalid conditions were likely exacerbated by a cholera outbreak. Some packets simply vanished, their names listed in the marine columns under the dreaded title "Went Missing"—the *Ocean Queen* with 90 passengers and a crew of 33 aboard; the *Driver* carrying 372 passengers and crew.

Still, in spite of all these perils, the packets changed the whole nature of ocean shipping and the Atlantic connection. And they set the stage for an even faster type of vessel—the clipper ships, the greyhounds of the sea.

CLIPPER SHIPS

Speed and profit—the essential ingredients of merchant shipping in the midst of an industrial revolution. And no ships of their day better delivered both than the clippers. They were a natural development, an outgrowth of the passion for speed on the seas that the packets had engendered. They were the perfect vessels for their age—moving goods and people in record time, meeting the intense competition of the new trade with China that had developed, and eventually transporting frantic treasure seekers from throughout the world to newly discovered gold fields in the far American West.

Unlike the packets, whose rigid schedules kept them tied to specific destinations, clippers would go anywhere that profit beckoned. They were not only the fastest ships that had ever been built but were also widely regarded as the most beautiful. As long as 208 feet and sporting knifelike bows, their most striking feature was their towering masts laden with canvas, masts so tall that an admiring public endowed them with such nicknames as "moonrakers," "cloud dusters," "skyscrapers," and "stargazers." The popular adulation that the clippers received was unparalleled, inspired both by the beauty of the vessels and admiration for the skill required to operate and control them. It could be seen each time a new ship was launched. When, for example, the *Great Republic* was ready to make its maiden voyage in 1853, more than thirty thousand people jammed the docks at East Boston where, as one newspaper reported, the ship was launched "amid the roar of artillery, the music of bands, and the cheers of the multitude."

No one really invented the clipper ship; it evolved from the topsail schooners that were developed in Chesapeake Bay before the American Revolution, vessels that made their mark during the War of 1812 when their speed enabled them to outrun the British blockade of Baltimore. Historians differ as to when the first real clippers were built, but most believe that it began with the construction, in 1845, of the streamlined, three-masted, 750-ton *Rainbow*, designed by John W.

LEFT: Donald McKay began his career at a tender age when he was apprenticed to renowned New York shipbuilder Isaac Webb. McKay was forced to work a six-day, seventy-hour week by his harsh employer, but the knowledge he acquired proved invaluable. During the American Civil War, McKay built several vessels for the Union navy. This undated portrait was engraved by W. G. Jackman.

BELOW: The *Great Republic* was the largest clipper ever built—335 feet long, 53 feet wide, with a hold 39 feet deep. Unfortunately for shipbuilder Donald McKay, the ship burned to the waterline at her berth in New York on December 26, 1853, one day before she was to make her maiden trans-Atlantic voyage to Liverpool. McKay rebuilt her, but she never brought in enough revenue to cover the cost of her building and rebuilding. Currier published this print, ca. 1855.

Griffiths and constructed by New York shipbuilders Stephen Smith and John Dimon.

By this time, the need for ships capable of delivering raw materials and manufactured goods with unprecedented speed was greater than ever, and, over the next decade. Bold and innovative American shipbuilders, such as William Webb, George Steers, Samuel Hall, Jacob Westervelt, and David Brown, built vessel after vessel. One man, however, outstripped them all, a master at his craft whose name would become synonymous with the clipper ship.

He was Donald McKay. Born in Nova Scotia in 1810, as a young man he apprenticed with shipbuilders in New York City.

McKay opened his own shipyard in Newburyport, Massachusetts, in 1841 and then moved to East Boston in late 1844, where he built thirty-two of the fastest, most beautiful, and best-known clipper ships ever constructed. Along with his obvious shipbuilding talents, McKay was a perfectionist who was never satisfied with his latest accomplishment. In 1864, even after he had astounded the world with the quality and performance of his ships, he stated to the *Boston Daily Advertiser* that "I never yet built a vessel that came up to my own ideal. I saw something in each ship which I desired to improve upon."

Along with the considerable fame he personally achieved, McKay's clippers became legendary in their own time.

The great challenge that most clipper ship captains experienced was that of rounding the always perilous Cape Horn. Here, the clipper *Red Jacket* is depicted making her way through the icy waters off the horn in August 1854, carrying a cargo of wool from Australia to Liverpool. The print was published by Nathaniel Currier in 1855.

Mariners loved to describe his 4,555-ton *Great Republic* as having masts so high that sailors who were youngsters when they first climbed them had turned into doddering old men by the time they came down. And while none of McKay's ships may have measured up to his lofty ideals, they certainly met almost everyone else's.

Mariners on both sides of the Atlantic were astounded when, in 1851, on her maiden voyage, *Flying Cloud*, the vessel that came to be known as the "Queen of Clippers," sailed around Cape Horn and passed the Golden Gate in an unheard of eighty-nine days and twenty-one hours. And she did it in midwinter, making eighteen knots, even during heavy squalls. A year later, McKay's *Sovereign of the Seas*,

despite enormous seas, furious winds, icy rain, and snow, made it to California in an equally astounding 103 days. Arthur H. Clark, a former clipper captain and maritime historian, recalls McKay's opinion of the ship in *The Clipper Ship Era* (1910): "A pretty good ship, but I think I can build one to beat her." Which he did, and more than once. On March 1, 1854, McKay's *Lightning* sailed 436 miles, the longest single-day distance recorded by a sailing vessel, a record that still stands today.

It was not only McKay's clippers that set new records for speed. The *Sea Witch*, despite encountering a monsoon, made the return voyage from China to New York in an unprecedented eighty-one days. The *Dreadnought* regularly

The most famous of Donald McKay's clippers, the *Flying Cloud* continually broke speed records including its 1851, sixteen-thousand-mile voyage from New York to San Francisco, which it accomplished in eighty-nine days and twenty-one hours, a record that stood until 1989. Extremely unusual for the times, the navigator of the *Flying Cloud* was a woman. Eleanor Creesy had studied ocean currents, weather patterns, and astronomy since her childhood in Marblehead, Massachusetts. Her husband, Josiah Perkins Creesy, was the ship's captain. Nathaniel Currier dedicated this 1852 print of the *Flying Cloud* to Grinnell, Minturn & Co, who purchased the clipper before the building of the ship was finished.

112 DAYS TO SAN FRANCISCO.

MERCHANTS' EXPRESS LINE OF CLIPPER SHIPS.

Dispatching the Greatest Number of Vessels!

SMALLEST, SHARPEST AND FASTEST VESSEL NOW UP!

THE MAGNIFICENT OUT-AND-OUT CLIPPER SHIP

WHITE SWALLOW

BUNKER, Commander, is now rapidly loading at PIER 16 E. R.

This splendid vessel, having made *very short passages*, and delivered her cargo in *unexceptionable order*, has established a reputation that will ensure *immediate dispatch.*

RANDOLPH M. COOLEY, 88 Wall Street,

Agents in San Francisco, MESSRS. DE WITT, KITTLE & Co.   (PONTINE BUILDING.)

NESBITT & CO., PRINTERS.

This ca. 1850s card announced a 112-day trip from New York to San Francisco on the "magnificent out-and-out clipper ship" the *White Swallow.* As the fame of the clipper ships spread, European shipbuilders began constructing their own clippers, particularly the English, who employed the vessels in transporting wool and tea.

> " *Last trip I astonished the world…This trip I intend to astonish God almighty.* "

—Captain James Nicol "Bully" Forbes, from *The Colonial Clippers* (1921), by Basil Lubbock

eclipsed the transatlantic sailing record. Captain James Nicol "Bully" Forbes sailed the *Marco Polo* from Liverpool to Melbourne in seventy-six days. According to Basil Lubbock's book *The Colonial Clippers* (1921), Forbes boasted to his passengers: "Last trip I astonished the world…This trip I intend to astonish God almighty."

Well into the 1850s, the clipper ships, some of them the largest merchantmen in the world, displayed their speed around the globe. Along with their use in the China trade, clippers sailed from Boston or New York to San Francisco and from there to Hong Kong, where British merchants paid a handsome price to have the vessels carry their tea to London. Other clippers, some of them British-built, transported fruit and coffee from the West Indies and South America to the United States and England. Because of their speed, clippers also became involved in activities that can best be described as despicable. Those involved in the now-illegal slave trade found the vessels ideal for outrunning or eluding authorities on the high seas. So too did smugglers as well as opium dealers who, by shipping the narcotic from India to China and loading the return clippers with silver specie, gave a whole new meaning to the China trade.

The speed records that the clippers continually established would, in themselves, have gained them sufficient glory. But a totally unexpected event provided the impetus for even greater fame. On the morning of July 24, 1848, as a miner named James Marshall was digging in the California hills above the sleepy, small settlement called San Francisco, something glittering captured his attention. "My eye was caught by something shining in the bottom of the ditch…," the miner later recalled. "I reached my hand down and picked it up; it made my heart thump, for I was certain it was gold…Then I saw another." Word of Marshall's discovery spread throughout the United States and across the Atlantic. Thousands headed for California, hoping to strike it rich. "The field is left unplanted, the house half built, and everything neglected but manufacture of shovels and pickaxes," wrote a reporter in the 1848 *California Star*, quoted in Marshall B. Davidson's *Life in America* (1951).

Determined to get to the gold fields before the treasure ran out, prospectors boarded fishing boats, whaling vessels, even crude ferries. Those fortunate enough to be able to afford the fare turned to the clippers, the fastest ships afloat. By this time, newly built clippers were speedier than ever. They were also larger and able, with some tragic exceptions, to withstand the pounding they took in the voyage through the treacherous waters around Cape Horn, which represented the quickest route to the gold. Pushing their vessels to the limit, clipper ship captains regularly brought passengers and equipment to California in record time. By the time the

> " *My eye was caught by something shining in the bottom of the ditch..., I reached my hand down and picked it up; it made my heart thump, for I was certain it was gold...Then I saw another.* "
>
> —California Miner James Marshall, July 28, 1848

OPPOSITE: The clippers not only carried frantic treasure-seeking passengers to the gold fields of California but also the enormous amounts of cargo needed to sustain the tens of thousands who had poured into the area. Clipper ship owners, aware that they had the suppliers of the cargo at their mercy, greatly inflated their freight rates. This cartoon print published by Nathaniel Currier around 1849 is titled *The Way They Go to California*. It shows men jumping from the dock crowded with prospectors holding picks and shovels, eager to reach the departing clipper ship. A crowded airship and a man on a rocket fly overhead.

BELOW: Whaleships off Greenland are depicted in an undated print. As early as the late 1600s, Dutch whalemen, along with those from France and England, were pursuing whales in what became known as the Greenland Fishery. By the 1850s, the United States had become the premier whaling nation, particularly the Massachusetts town of New Bedford, about fifty miles south of Boston. "They hug an oil-cask like a brother," Boston-born author/philosopher Ralph Waldo Emerson wrote of New Bedford whalers in his essay entitled "Boston" (published posthumously in *Natural History of the Intellect*, in 1893).

gold ran out in about 1864, the voyage, which in the early 1840s had taken some two hundred days, had been reduced to less than one hundred.

The packets and the clipper ships were the very epitome of the Age of Sail. At the same time, however, there was a much less romantic type of vessel plying the oceans of the world, one that time and again would bring its owners and captains even greater rewards, one that would make an enormous contribution to ways of life in the last half of the nineteenth century, and one that, in the process, would greatly expand the physical knowledge of the Atlantic world.

whalebone was turned into the corset stays that allowed women to attain their stylish appearance. Whalebone was also fashioned into clothespins, carriage frames, pie cutters, and hundreds of other products.

The average whaleship was about one hundred feet long and had a carrying capacity of more than three hundred tons. It was not built to look sleek or outrace other ships. Rather it was designed to provide ample space for cutting up and boiling down the enormous whales and for storing as many barrels of oil and as many bundles of whalebone in its hold as possible. At sea, a whaling vessel was distinguished by its slow speed, its lookouts standing high in its masts, its whaleboats

WHALESHIPS

From approximately 1815 to 1860—the golden age of American whaling—thousands of whalemen, many of them more boys than men, risked their lives on whaleships to hunt the greatest creatures on earth. Whales were an extremely profitable catch in the nineteenth century: their blubber provided the oil that lit the lamps of the world and lubricated every type of machine; and

This panoramic 1871 print, after a drawing by Benjamin Russell, illustrates whalers in the Arctic Ocean in various stages of catching and processing right (or baleen) whales. At far left, skiffs tow a whale to a ship; at left of center whalers begin loading blubber onto the ship; at right of center a full boat heads home; in the right foreground a whaler lances a whale; behind them a ship takes in a whale head; and to the far right a ship boils its last whale.

This rare photograph from 1864 depicts a whaling camp on the coast of Labrador.

A harpooner prepares to thrust his killing lance into a right whale in a late nineteenth-century Currier and Ives print. "Never in all of man's history," wrote whaling historian Everett S. Allen in *Children of the Light: The Rise and Fall of New Bedford Whaling and the Death of the Arctic Fleet* (1973), "has there been anything comparable to whaling in terms of what it demanded of those afloat who pursued it, or of the vessels in which they sailed."

hanging from its sides, and the smoke often billowing from its brick furnace called a "tryworks," where the oil from the whale's blubber was extracted. If a whaleship was in the middle of a successful voyage, it could also be identified by the smell of the oil that emanated from it, leading other types of mariners to exclaim, "You can smell a whaleship long before you see it."

Until the beginning of the 1860s, the greatest hunt for whales took place in the Pacific, the home of the oil-rich sperm whale. But in 1859, oil was discovered in the ground in Titusville, Pennsylvania. Soon whale oil, as the fuel that lit the lamps and lubricated the machinery of the world, gave way to oil pumped from deep within the earth. There was, however, another product of the whale that remained in great demand. Whalebone, used in making buggy whips, carriage wheels, pie cutters, clothespins, and, most importantly, corset stays, was an extremely valuable product. With the need for whale oil

diminished, whalemen turned their attention to the waters of the North Atlantic where the immense amounts of bone that could be extracted from that region's bowhead whales became their main target.

From the beginning, Dutch, British, French, and American whalers sailed the world. They were the first to sail into Japanese ports and were instrumental in opening up that long-isolated nation to foreigners. As they pursued the whale from Africa to Brazil, from the Azores to Chile, they discovered more than four hundred islands. And it was they who gave the world its first knowledge of the Gulf Stream and unlocked many of the age-old secrets of currents and tides. As author Richard Ellis wrote in his book *Men and Whales* (1999), "In their search for [whales] the roving whalers opened the world, much as the explorers of the sixteenth century had done in their quest for the riches of the Indies."

THE NORTHWEST PASSAGE AND THE SEARCH FOR JOHN FRANKLIN

The whalemen who turned their attention to hunting the bowhead were not the only ones carrying out a passionate quest. At the same time, another unique breed of men was venturing into Arctic waters pursuing the same goal as that of the sixteenth-century explorers. For more than four hundred years, the British in particular, beginning with the voyage of John Cabot and continuing with the journeys of such legendary seekers as Martin Frobisher, John Davis, Luke Foxe, Thomas James, and Henry Hudson, had been searching for a Northwest Passage through the Arctic to the riches of the East.

Beginning in 1819, England launched its most intensive effort and, for the better part of the century, sent more than thirty expeditions seeking the fabled route. When, in the mid 1850s, an expedition led by the world's most famous explorer John Franklin, completely disappeared, Britain launched an equal number of expeditions in what amounted to the greatest search and rescue effort in history. In the end, Franklin and his men were not found alive. And, though vital links in the passage were discovered, it was also proven that the waterway, frozen over for most of the year, had never been a viable route to the East. But, like the whalers, the intrepid seekers of the passage made discovery after discovery and, through the maps and charts they drew and the accounts they wrote, provided the world with knowledge of an enormous part of the Atlantic world that had previously been unknown.

The whalemen and explorers who sought the Northwest Passage had much in common. Aside from the extraordinary courage and determination they displayed in braving the most challenging waters of the world, they were both responsible for gathering the first information about the vast Arctic region. Many former whalemen served as crewmen and officers on passage-seeking expeditions, and one whaling captain, William Penny, commanded a Royal Navy expedition that made important discoveries about the fate of John Franklin and his men.

OPPOSITE: Although the Northwest Passage proved to be a nonviable passage, other historic discoveries were made. Here British naval explorer James Clark Ross and his men celebrate Ross's discovery of the Magnetic North Pole on June 1, 1831. He was the nephew of famed Scottish Arctic explorer Sir John Ross and accompanied his uncle on a harrowing 1829–33 expedition. This engraving appeared in an 1835 book about Sir John, *The Last Voyage of Capt. John Ross, Knt., R.N., to the Arctic Regions . . .* (1835), by Robert Huish. John Ross's last Arctic voyage was actually in 1850, to search for his friend John Franklin.

BELOW: All of those who were part of Arctic expeditions knew that they would have to spend at least one winter trapped in the ice. Some were imprisoned for two or even three winters. The crew of the HMS *Investigator*, on a mission to search for John Franklin (and the passage), became entrapped for two full years (1851–53). This dramatic image of the iced-in ship was created in August 1851 by Lieutenant Samuel Cresswell, a gifted artist and crew member.

The men of the HMS *Resolute* and *Intrepid* embark on a sledging journey on a mission to rescue the crew of the trapped *Investigator* in the spring of 1853. In one of maritime history's greatest true stories, the *Resolute* became iced in herself, and in 1854 was abandoned by an irresponsible commander. The *Resolute* eventually broke free and then sailed twelve hundred miles east on her own to the Davis Strait where an American whaling captain discovered her in September 1855 and brought her back to the United States. The ship was then refurbished and given back to England as a gift from the American government in 1856. When the *Resolute*'s sailing days were over, Queen Victoria ordered that the best timbers from the vessel be made into a magnificent desk which was then presented to President Rutherford B. Hayes in 1880. Since that time the desk has served most American presidents and sits in the Oval Office today.

LEFT: The men who sought the Northwest Passage were astounded by what they encountered when they first entered interior Arctic waters. Some were amazed at the majesty and incredible beauty of the icebergs. Explorer Elisha Kent Kane, in his book *The United States Grinnell Expedition in Search of Sir John Franklin: A Personal Narrative* (1854) wrote: "An iceberg is one of God's own buildings, preaching its lessons of humility to the miniature structures of man." Others, however, could not help but be swept by feelings of anxiety. The American physician and polar explorer Isaac Hayes wrote of icebergs in his memoir *The Open Polar Sea: A Narrative of a Voyage of Discovery Towards the North Pole . . .* (1869): "They seemed to be endless and numberless, and so close together that at a little distance they appeared to form upon the sea an unbroken canopy of ice . . . Had we been in the centre of the Black Forest, we could not have been more absolutely cut off from seeing daylight. As the last streak of the horizon faded from view between the lofty bergs behind us, the steward (who was of a poetical turn of mind) came from the galley, and halting for an instant, cast one lingering look at the opening, and then dropped through the companion scuttle, repeating from the Inferno: 'They who enter here leave hope behind.'" This engraving of icebergs near was made after a sketch by Kane for his bestselling book *Arctic Explorations: The Second Grinnell Expedition in Search of Sir John Franklin, 1853, 54, 55* (1856).

Yachting

No ocean has experienced more commercial activity or more competition for control of this activity than has the Atlantic. But the Atlantic has long been the site of noncommercial activity as well, some of it as competitive as the rivalries between the packet and clipper ship companies. Yachting is believed to have started in the Netherlands sometime in the seventeenth century, and, by the last half of the 1800s, it was extremely popular throughout the Atlantic world, whether it involved cruising Atlantic waters or engaging in spirited long- or short-distance races.

LEFT: On August 22, 1851, the New York Yacht Club's schooner the *America* defeated fourteen British yachts in the Hundred Guinea Cup, a fleet race around the Isle of Wight organized by the Royal Yacht Squadron. The race was thereafter dubbed the America's Cup, which continues to be the epitome of all racing by sail. This engraving accompanied a story on the race in the August 30, 1851 edition of the *Illustrated London News*.

BELOW: A print by Currier and Ives (first published in 1872) depicts a squadron of yachts in Newport, Rhode Island, considered by many to be the sailing capital of the world.

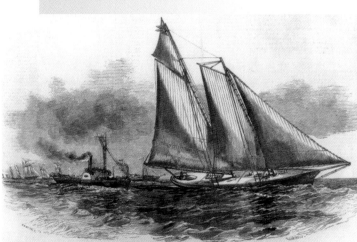

RIGHT: An almost three-dimensional photochrome from ca. 1890–1900 captures yachts starting out from Yarmouth, England.

TOP: Pennsylvania-born engineer/inventor Robert Fulton, seen here in a ca. 1874 engraving, was the first to build an effective commercial steamboat.

ABOVE: A "monster moving on the water, defying the winds and tides, and breathing fire and smoke." According to George Dodd's book *Railways, Steamers, and Telegraphs* (published in Edinburgh in 1867), that is how one observer described Robert Fulton's *Clermont* as it made its thirty-two hour historic voyage along the Hudson on August 17, 1807. According to a July 1909 report in the New York *Evening Sun*, another eyewitness raced home to tell his wife that he had "seen the devil on his way to Albany in a sawmill." This engraving appeared in an 1871 book by James D. McCabe, Jr., entitled *Great Fortunes, and How They Were Made or the Struggles and Triumphs of our Self-Made Men*.

> " *[Steam]...will diminish the size of the globe...Human beings will become one single people, one nation, one mind, one heart.* "
>
> —Editor, *New York Mirror*, 1810

STEAM VESSELS

The glory days of the packets and the clipper ships represented a unique chapter in maritime history. But by the end of the second decade of the 1800s their days were numbered, brought to an end by iron and steam—the inventions that had both fueled and epitomized the Industrial Revolution. Soon a whole new type of ocean-going vessel began to dominate the sea lanes. Eventually, even some whaling vessels and Northwest Passage–seeking ships were propelled by steam.

Even before Thomas Savery and Thomas Newcomen introduced their early engines, there had been visionaries who had predicted that one day ships would be steam-driven. One of the first was the Frenchman Salomon de Caux, who theorized in the early 1600s that if steam had sufficient force to drive water up a tube, it probably some day could power a ship. And as noted in *The Century of Inventions*, by Edward Somerset, Marquis of Worcester (1663), in 1618, Englishmen David Ramsey and Thomas Wildgoose are credited with having thought of steam when, soon after de Caux put forth his theory, they patented an invention that took advantage of "newe apte forces" with the potential to "make boates runn upon the water as swifte in calmes, and move safe in stormes, than boates full sayled in greate wyndes." It was not until James Watt had developed an effective steam engine in 1765, James Pickard had invented a system

employing a rod and crank in 1780, and Robert Fulton had made the first successful steamboat run up the Hudson River in 1807 that steam on the sea would become a reality. Once all that happened, however, it became apparent that a turning point in history had been achieved. "What is this steam going to lead to?" the editor of the *New York Mirror* asked in 1810. "Till now man has been bound to a single spot like an oyster, or a tree…[steam] is going to alter, to a degree far more remarkable than any previous change, the condition of mankind…*steam is union*. It connects minds…It will diminish the size of the globe…Human beings will become one single people, one nation, one mind, one heart." The steamboat, of course, never reached all those lofty heights, but it did, almost immediately, and particularly in America, transform the way goods and people moved on inland waters.

By 1827, the editor of the *New York Mirror*, amazed at the number of steamboats that were plying the waters of the Hudson River declared, "The amount of travel from one important commercial place to another in our country has lately increased to an astonishing degree…the bringing of such a number of steamboats on [the Hudson] seems to have multiplied rather than diminished the number of passengers in each. Each new boat is immediately filled, and yet the decks of the old ones seem only to swarm with additional numbers."

It was nothing compared to what developed on the Mississippi and the other great rivers of the American West

The steamboat was born on American eastern waters, but by 1815 the editor of the Cincinnati *Gazette* would declare, "The invention of the steamboat was intended for us. The puny rivers of the East are only as creeks, or convenient waters on which experiments may be made for our advantage." By 1846, Mississippi steamboats, shown here docked at the New Orleans harbor in a ca. 1884 print published by Currier and Ives, were already carrying ten million tons of freight a year—double the foreign commerce of the United States—up and down the river. By 1860, more than thirteen million 500-pound bales of cotton had been loaded onto outbound vessels, most headed for Great Britain or France.

where steamboats, along with becoming the principal mover of people, transported so many goods that, within decades, the tonnage on western rivers moved by steamboat exceeded that of the entire British merchant marine. It was indeed a historic development. But still few could imagine that the day was so close at hand that a ship, powered solely by steam could make its way across the Atlantic Ocean. Yet it happened.

On April 23, 1828, those living or working near the New York docks were treated to an astounding sight. Belching clouds of smoke, the British steam vessel *Sirius* suddenly appeared in the city's bustling harbor, having made the journey from Ireland in just nineteen days. "The news of the arrival of the steam-driven Sirius spread like wildfire," the *New York Times* exclaimed, "and the [Hudson River] became literally dotted with boats conveying the curious to and from the [strange ship]. There seemed to be a universal voice of congratulation, and every visage was illuminated with delight."

As if this excitement were not enough, another extraordinary event took place even while New Yorkers were coming to grips with the sight of the *Sirius*. Within an hour of the *Sirius*'s arrival, another steam-driven vessel entered the harbor. And, unlike the *Sirius*, this was no small ship. It was the 1,320-ton *Great Western*, which had left Bristol four days

after the *Sirius* had departed from Cork and had crossed the Atlantic in fifteen days. "Whilst all [the commotion over the *Sirius*] was going on," the *New York Times* reported, "suddenly there was seen over Governor's Island, a dense black cloud of smoke, spreading itself upwards, and betokening another arrival. On it came with great rapidity, and about 3 o'clock its cause was made fully manifest to the multitudes. It was the steamship *Great Western*...This immense moving mass was propelled at a rapid rate through the waters of the Bay; she passed swiftly and gracefully around the *Sirius*, exchanging salutes with her, and proceeded to her destined anchorage in the East River. If the public mind was stimulated by the arrival of the *Sirius*, it became intoxicated with delight upon view of the superb *Great Western*."

Superb she was—263 feet long with her hull trussed with iron and wood and sheathed entirely in copper beneath the waterline. Her immense bunkers held 800 tons of coal, a necessity since it required 30 tons of coal a day to keep up the pressure in her four enormous boilers. She was truly revolutionary, unlike anything that ocean goers had even encountered. The Canadian humorist Thomas Chandler Haliburton described what the ride must of felt like from a passenger's point of view in his best-selling collection of short stories *Life in a Steamer: The Letter-Bag of the Great Western* (1840): "How this glorious steamer wallops and gallops and flounders along! She goes it like mad...puffing like a porpoise, breasting the waves like a sea horse, and, at times, skimming the surface like a bird."

The *Great Western* was the brainchild of one of the most fascinating men of his or any other era. Both a genius and a true visionary, Isambard Kingdom Brunel had, before designing the *Great Western*, been Great Britain's leading creator of railroad systems and one of its premier bridge builders. It was as a pioneer of the steamship, however, that he achieved his greatest success and his greatest failure.

In 1845, Brunel built his second ocean-going steam vessel, a ship even more revolutionary in its design than the *Great Western*. The 322-foot *Great Britain* was the world's first large screw-propelled steamer. More astounding to those who first viewed her, she was the first iron ship to cross the Atlantic. "An enormous vessel, made of iron? Surely it would sink like a rock," exclaimed Brunel's critics. But it didn't, and for thirty years it carried passengers and freight between the British Isles and Australia. The *Great Britain* was then used as a mammoth facility to store coal in the Falkland Islands before ending her days by being beached, almost one hundred years after she had been launched.

OPPOSITE: In assessing the attributes that engineers should possess, the 1909 *British Encyclopaedia* stated that "it is requisite that, besides being ingenious, they should be brave in proportion." Isambard Kingdom Brunel was both brave and ingenious. He was also a true visionary. According to a 1958 lecture by Brunel's biographer, Lionel Thomas Caswall Rolt, at the Brunel College of Technology in London, Brunel offered this response to an 1847 proposal by the Royal Commission on the Application of Iron to Railway Structures to regulate the design of bridges: "In other words, embarrass and shackle the progress of improvements of tomorrow by recording and registering as law the prejudices and errors of today." Brunel strikes a pose in front of ship anchor chains in this 1857 photograph by Robert Howlett.

BELOW: The Great Eastern was a sexy brand in 1860, inspiring a New York company to come out with Great Eastern tobacco, prominently featuring the ship in its advertising.

Brunel's most extraordinary undertaking, however, was yet to come. He called it the *Great Eastern*, and it was a marvel of the age—693 feet long, 22,500 tons. Because no means of providing enough steam to adequately propel such a behemoth existed, Brunel equipped the ship with 58-foot paddle wheels powered by 1,000-horsepower engines and a 24-foot propeller, which was turned by a 1,600-horsepower engine. The ship had six towering masts that could accommodate 6,500 square yards of sail.

No ship like her had even been built, and construction took over six years. Launching her presented even greater difficulties. Because she was too big to be launched stern first, the *Great Eastern* was constructed parallel to the river upon which she was to be floated. But when, on November 3, 1857, the first attempt at launching her took place, the rails down which she was to slide buckled under her immense weight, a windlass disintegrated, and enormous chains snapped like twigs.

When, after three months of attempted launchings, an unusually high tide finally floated the vessel yet another disaster lay immediately ahead. During her trial runs, one of the *Great Eastern*'s mammoth boilers exploded, killing five men. Brunel, his health already weakened by the travails of eight years of construction and attempted launchings, was decimated by the latest tragic setback. Soon after learning about what had happened, he suffered a stroke and died on September 15, 1859.

The *Great Eastern* was five times the size of any vessel of her day. She was christened with the name *Leviathan* but those who believed that she was too big to ever float gave her the derisive nickname "Leave-her-high-and-dryathan." After being refinanced by the Great Ship Company in 1858, she was renamed the *Great Eastern*. Currier and Ives published this print of the behemoth around 1858.

By the third quarter of the 1800s, regular transatlantic steamship service had become both a reality and a profitable venture for many of the lines. This ca. 1889 card advertisement for the State Line announced its service between the United States and Glasgow, Belfast, Dublin, Londonderry, and Liverpool. The insets highlight the vessel's elegant dining room and the joys of lounging on the ship's deck under moonlight.

The *Great Eastern* carried on. In 1860 she made her first Atlantic crossing, creating as much of a sensation in New York as had the *Sirius* and the *Great Western*. But Brunel had built her well before her time, and the days when the demand for ocean travel would justify the construction of a ship designed to carry four thousand passengers were still a half-century away. Fate, however, had a very different role in store for the vessel. As the ship that was instrumental in the laying of the Atlantic cable, the first great telecommunications link between Europe and America, the *Great Eastern* became one of the most important ships in history.

Meanwhile, other ocean-going steamships, many built to transport passengers in luxury, were making regular runs back and forth across the Atlantic. Within ten years of the *Sirius*'s and the *Great Western*'s crossings, England's Cunard Line was dominating service between Liverpool and New York and Boston. Its first great challenge came from America's Collins Line, owned by Edward Collins.

By 1838, Collins's Dramatic Line of packet ships had overtaken Isaac Wright's Red Ball Line. But from the moment that Brunel's *Great Western* had steamed into New York, Collins had seen the future. According to author Rufus Rockwell Wilson in his *New York: Old & New: Its Story, Streets, and Landmarks* (1902), Collins remarked to a friend that "there is no longer chance for enterprise with sails,—it is steam that must win the day." Over the next decade Collins sold all his packets and began building a steamship line. In order to compete with the Cunard Line, he constructed four ships—the *Atlantic*, the *Arctic*, the *Baltic*, and the *Pacific*—that were faster and more luxurious than any of the Cunard vessels.

Fortune, however, was not kind to Edward Collins. In 1854, the *Arctic* was rammed and sunk off Newfoundland. Included in the 321 passengers who lost their lives were Collins's wife

Atlantic Cable

The *Great Eastern* attained its greatest glory as the ship that was instrumental in laying the Atlantic Cable, the first great communications link between the Old World and the New. The driving force behind the laying of the cable was American businessman and financier Cyrus West Field. In 1858, Field's American Telegraph Company successfully laid the first Atlantic telegraph cable between Ireland and Newfoundland, but three weeks after the task was completed the cable broke. In 1865, Field tried again, this time with a newly formed Anglo-American Telegraph Company, and this time using the *Great Eastern*, her huge interior stripped of cabins and saloons, to carry the more than three thousand miles of thick cable. This time the cable held. The first message sent across the Atlantic via the initial cable took over seventeen hours to transmit. The new cable, enhanced by advancements in both cable manufacture and methods of sending messages, transmitted eight words a minute.

TOP: In this allegorical print hailing the Atlantic cable as "The Eighth Wonder of the New World," Neptune rests in the foreground while a lion representing Great Britain holds one end of the cable and an eagle symbolizing the United States holds the other. At the top of the print is a likeness of Cyrus Field. It was published by Kimmel and Forster in 1866.

RIGHT: The transatlantic cable occasioned celebration on both sides of the ocean. This sheet-music cover for a song titled "Atlantic Telegraph Polka" shows the *Niagara* and the *Agamemnon*, the two ships that aided the *Great Eastern* in the laying of the cable. The lithograph, created by J. H. Bufford, was published ca. 1858.

Even though the Age of Sail was being rapidly replaced with an Age of Steam, many liners continued to carry sails, such as the Cunard Line's *Oregon*, shown here in a ca. 1884 Currier and Ives print. Sails not only boosted the speed capacity of the vessels, but served as backup in the event of boiler mishap or failure. Despite intense competition, England's Cunard Line—up to the advent of the superliners—ruled the transatlantic steamship trade. Much of the line's success was due to the superior training that all of the Cunard's officers received. "The Cunard people would not take Noah himself," Mark Twain is said to have declared, "until they had worked him up through all the lower grades and tried him ten years."

Union officers proudly pose on the deck of the USS *Monitor* some time between 1861 and 1865.

and two children. Two years later, the *Pacific* vanished at sea. These tragedies, combined with problems in maintaining a government mail subsidy for his fleet, spelled the doom of Collins's line. For the next half-century, the ships of the Cunard and other British lines and those from France and other European countries dominated transatlantic steamship service. It was a service that included not only the transportation of goods and passengers seeking pleasure or business on both sides of the Atlantic, but a very different kind of passenger as well—Europeans who, like the New World colonists more than a century earlier, left almost everything they had behind to seek a new life more than three thousand miles away.

IRONCLADS

The advent of steam on the sea revolutionized not only transportation but the nature of naval warfare. Combined with advancements in iron-making technology, steam led to the introduction of vessels known as *ironclads*.

As naval historian Richard Hill wrote in his book *War at Sea in the Ironclad Age* (2006): "The [ironclad] had three chief characteristics: a metal-skinned hull, steam propulsion and a main armament of guns capable of firing explosive shells. It is only when all three characteristics are present that a fighting ship can properly be called an ironclad."

The first battle between ironclads was the engagement between the CSS *Virginia* (originally the USS *Merrimack*) and the USS *Monitor* in 1862 during the American Civil War. The first fleet battle involving ironclads was the Battle of Lissa in 1866, fought in the Adriatic Sea between the Austro-Hungarian and Italian navies. The Austrians employed seven ironclads in the battle while the Italian fleet included twelve armored, steam-powered vessels. Historians characterize the battle between the *Virginia* and the *Monitor* and the Battle of Lissa as the beginning of modern naval warfare.

ABOVE: This ca. 1889 print entitled *Battle between the* Monitor *and* Merrimac, published by Kurz and Allison in Chicago, depicts the dramatic scene at the Battle of Hampton Roads (also known as the Battle of the Ironclads) on March 8–9, 1862, the first fight between two ironclads off the coast of Virginia.

RIGHT: Five Union ironclads took part in the Battle of Fort Hindman (or the Battle of Arkansas Post), fought from January 9–11, 1863, near the mouth of the Arkansas River, as part of the Vicksburg campaign. This Currier and Ives print of the scene was published approximately 1864 to 1907.

10

THE GREAT TIDE OF IMMIGRATION

A HISTORIC TRANSFER OF CULTURES

Immigrants arrive at
Ellis Island, ca. 1911.

THE GREAT TIDE OF IMMIGRATION

It wasn't only our battered suitcases and our dreams we brought.
We brought the old world with us on our backs.

—REMINISCENCES OF POLISH IMMIGRANT LOUIS SAGE, IN 1950 INTERVIEW WITH THIS AUTHOR

If America did not exist," one late nineteenth-century Italian immigrant exclaimed, "we would have had to invent it for the sake of our survival." (Leslie Allen, *Liberty: The Statue and the American Dream*, 1985) As was the case with millions of others, the reasons for his becoming part of what became the largest human migration in history had been long in coming.

One of the main factors was the enormous increase in the European population that took place in less than a century—from 140 million people in 1750 to 250 million by the 1840s. As the numbers increased, peasant families were constricted into increasingly smaller plots of land by powerful landlords, who were anxious to reap profits by creating larger farms to feed the growing cities. Soon, an alarming number of the peasants found themselves unable to subsist. They were joined in their plight by legions of artisans whose special skills—passed on from father to son and mother to daughter for generations—had earned them both a livelihood and a respected place in society. Now, however, scores of the goods they had so expertly handcrafted were being produced by the machinery of the Industrial Revolution. Thousands of these artisans found themselves out of work, forced to move to the cities and work in factories, where low wages, drudgery, and the loss of their personal independence resulted in a sadly diminished quality of life.

MASS EXODUS

Devastating as they were, none of these problems compared to the series of famines that, beginning in the 1840s, descended upon various European nations. Nowhere was the situation more desperate than in Ireland where, in 1845, a fungus destroyed the potato crop, the single food staple upon which the poorer classes of the country depended for survival. By the time the disease began to abate in 1849, more than a million Irish men, women, and children had starved to death. Susan Campbell Bartoletti recounts this eyewitness observation in her 2001 book *Black Potatoes: The Story of the Great Irish Famine, 1845–1850*: "The wretched people," observed a traveling Irish priest, "were seated on the fences of their decaying gardens, wringing their hands and wailing bitterly the destruction that had left them foodless."

OPPOSITE: **Bridget O'Donnel, the impoverished Irish woman in this sketch, had a tragic story to tell—unfortunately not that uncommon in a famine-racked Ireland. The image appeared in the *Illustrated London News* of December 22, 1849, accompanied by this quote: "We were put out last November. We owed some rent. I was at this time lying in fever... They commenced knocking down the house, and had half of it knocked down when two neighbors... carried me out. I was carried into a cabin and lay there for eight days... The whole of my family got the fever and one boy thirteen years old died with want and with hunger while we were lying sick."**

LEFT: **Many factors converged—severe weather and drought, governmental policies, lack of new agricultural advancements—to cause a disastrous famine in Russia in 1891–2. The famine affected millions; almost 400,000 died of starvation and disease. This engraving appeared in the *Illustrated London News* in 1892. The caption reads "Famine-stricken villagers who have left their homes, on the way to St. Petersburg."**

RIGHT: **Natural disasters have also displaced hundreds of thousands. The most destructive earthquake to hit Europe, with a 7.5 magnitude on the Richter scale, hit Messina Strait, between Sicily and Calabria, on December 28, 1908, killing almost 200,000 Italians. Here, homeless survivors of the quake wait for assistance. Some people were relocated to other towns in Italy; many emigrated to America.**

This print titled *The Eviction: A Scene from Life in Ireland* shows a group of tenants in despair after being forcibly evicted from their homes on land largely owned by British absentee landlords. The ca. 1871 print is a reproduction of an earlier painting by American artist William Henry Powell.

It was not only in Ireland that famine struck. Years after the great migration to America was over, the mayor of an Italian town was asked where documents could be found to help explain why so many people had left Italy and had braved the Atlantic voyage. "What documents?" the mayor replied. "Documents? They left because they were *morti di fame*— dying of hunger." (*La Storia: Five Centuries of the Italian American Experience*, by Jerre Mangione and Ben Morreale [1992]). A quote from the archives of the Iowa State Historical Society by a Polish youngster put it more personally: "We lived through a famine," he explained, "[so] we came to America. My mother said she wanted to see a loaf of bread on the table and then she was ready to die."

There were other important reasons for the mass exodus as well. Despite the notions of liberty and equality that both the American and French revolutions had spawned, oppressive governments in countries such as Russia, Germany, and Turkey had denied freedom of religion, freedom of speech, or other rights and had brutally put down rebellions aimed at bringing about reform. In Russia and Poland, massacres called *pogroms* erupted. Designed to eliminate minority groups who lived within their borders—particularly Jews— some of these pogroms were carried out by the governments of these two countries; others were unofficially endorsed by them. "We had taken shelter in the attic of a house because

OPPOSITE: The persecution of Jews in nations throughout Europe captured worldwide attention. A pogrom that took place in April 1903, in Kishinev, Russia, incited international outrage. Approximately 49 Jews were killed, 92 severely wounded, and 500 injured; 700 houses and 600 businesses were looted and destroyed. In this ca. 1904 cartoon for *Judge* magazine by American political cartoonist Emil Flohri, created in response to Kishinev, an elderly Jewish man carrying a huge sack labeled "oppression" leads fellow Jews away from their village, which was burned by Russian soldiers. An outraged President Theodore Roosevelt stands on a hill, chastising Nicholas II. The print is captioned "Stop your cruel oppression of the Jews."

LEFT: Between 1914 and 1918 the Ottoman government carried out the systematic genocide of the Armenian population in the Ottoman Empire. It is estimated that between 600,000 and 1.5 million Armenians died through mass killing, forced starvation marches, and of exhaustion and disease in deportation or concentration camps. This ca. 1915 photograph captures the despair on the faces of a deported Armenian mother and her children. Tens of thousands of Armenians emigrated to the United States during this time.

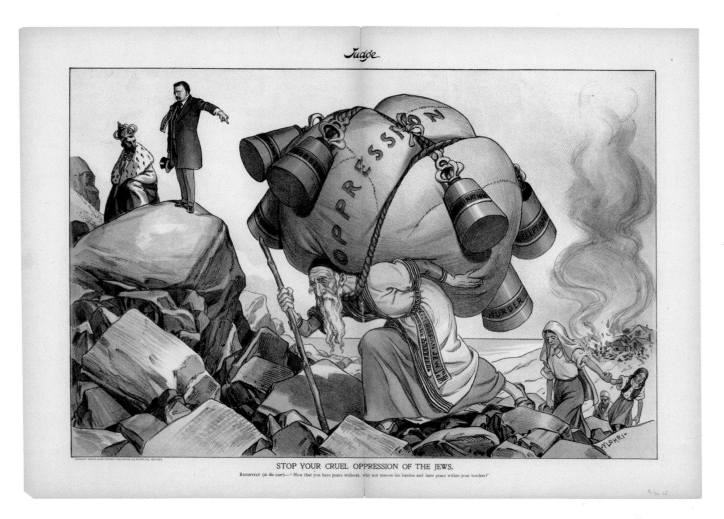

STOP YOUR CRUEL OPPRESSION OF THE JEWS.

Roosevelt (*to the czar*)—"Now that you have peace without, why not remove his burden and have peace within your borders?"

a pogrom was raging in our town, and we were hiding from the mob," Russian Jewish youngster Sophie Turpin later wrote. "My father at that time was in the cheese business…and he had his long cheese knife. He decided that before he and his family were killed he would kill as many of the attackers as he possibly could. It was up in that attic, surrounded by his terrified family, that my father vowed that he would leave this accursed Russia and make a new life for himself and his family in America" (Archives of the Iowa State Historical Society).

So to America they came, both pushed by desperate situations and pulled by the promise of a country that, by the early 1840s, was being hailed as a golden land of freedom and

opportunity, a nation that Thomas Paine in his 1776 political pamphlet *Common Sense* had earlier described as an "asylum for the persecuted lovers of civil and religious liberty from every part of Europe." They came in waves; according to the Time/Life Books volume *Immigrants: The New Americans* (1999), more than five million of them arrived between 1840 and 1880, an influx slightly greater than the entire population of the United States in 1790. Most emigrated from northern and western Europe—Scandinavians who settled in the American Midwest; Germans who established enclaves in New York, Baltimore, Cincinnati, St. Louis, and Milwaukee; and British and Irish who poured into Boston, New York, and other northeastern communities.

Immigrants in the Media

Although many of those heading for America had received letters from relatives who had already migrated there, the vast majority of emigrants were bound for a new land about which most knew absolutely nothing—but they were willing to risk everything to escape the conditions in their native lands. The new settlers discovered soon after arriving that the people of the United States were divided in opinion as to whether the enormous influx of foreigners was a positive or negative development for the nation. Throughout the latter half of the 1800s, and well into the first decade of the 1900s, newspapers in general and cartoonists in particular expressed their strong opinions on the subject.

AMERICAN CITIZE

We appeal to you in all calmness. Is it not time to pause? Already the enemies of our dearest institutions, like the foreign spies They are disgorging themselves upon us, at the rate of HUNDREDS OF THOUSANDS EVERY YEAR! They aim at nothing sh

A PAPER ENTITLED THE

IN FAVOR OF
The protection of American Mechanics against Foreign Pauper Labor.
Foreigners having a residence in the country of 21 years before voting.
Our present Free School System.
Carrying out the laws of the State, as regards sending back Foreign Paupers and Criminals.

OPPOSED TO
Papal Aggression & Roman Catholicism.
Foreigners holding office.
Raising Foreign Military Companies in the United States.
Nunneries and the Jesuits.
To being taxed for the support of Foreign paupers millions of dollars yearly.
To secret Foreign Orders in the U. S.

We
taxes h
in the
interfer
are for
nations
our reli
bor. W
speech.

☞ The PATRIOT is Published by J. E. Farwell & Co., 32
And for Sale at the Periodical Depots in this place. Sin

s!
an horse of old, are within our gates.
uest and supremacy over us.

RIOT.

burdened with enormous
igners. We are corrupted
of our youth. We are
h in our government. We
nto collisions with other
Ve are tampered with in
We are injured in our la-
assailed in our freedom of

gress St., Boston,
copies 4 Cents.

ABOVE: This 1852
advertisement announced
the publication of the
American Patriot, one of
many newspapers
vehemently opposed to
allowing "foreigners" into
America. The text of the
announcement lists the
many reasons why the
newspaper's editors were
convinced that immigrants
were a serious threat to
native-born Americans and
to the nation itself.

THE IMMIGRANT.

OPPOSITE BOTTOM: The
earliest mention of Uncle
Sam as a national
personification of the
United States was during
the War of 1812. However
the first illustration of the
white-haired, white-goateed
figure dressed in a red,
white, and blue suit and top
hat did not appear until
1852, when Frank Bellew
added the character to a
cartoon for the New York
Lantern. In this 1880
political cartoon for *Puck*
magazine, by Joseph
Keppler, Uncle Sam stands
at the door of the "U.S. Ark
of Refuge," warmly
welcoming immigrants
from many nations while
the cloud of war from which
many of them were fleeing
hangs in the distance.

ABOVE: *Judge* magazine
published this cartoon
by Gillam Victor around
1903. It is captioned,
"The Immigrant. Is He
an Acquisition or a
Detriment?" Various
characters hold signs with
their views on immigrants,
including a politician at far
right ("He makes votes for
me"), a worker at center
right ("He cheapens labor"),
and an industrialist tipping
his hat at center left ("He
gives me cheap labor").

BELOW: This cartoon by
William Allen Rogers,
expressing concern for
American jobs, was
published on the
September 29, 1888, cover
of *Harper's Weekly*—one
of America's most widely
read magazines in the
nineteenth century.
The label under
the immigrant reads
"Imported, Duty Free,
by Trust, Monopoly
& Co. to compete with
American labor."

IMPORTED, DUTY FREE,
by
TRUST, MONOPOLY & CO.
To compete with
AMERICAN LABOR.

Famine, poverty, persecution, denial of religious and political freedom—they were all reasons why millions of Europeans left their homelands and emigrated to America. For most, the most traumatic part of the frightening experience was saying farewell to relatives and friends, whom they knew they would never see again.

"I'll never forget that parting," Polish immigrant Lillian Krames related in an interview with this author, long after she settled in America, "the sad memory of it has remained with me all my life." This ca. 1883 American print was done after a painting by German artist Christian Ludwig Bokelmann.

Beginning in 1880 a great shift occurred when an even larger flood of newcomers came from eastern, central, and southern Europe—Russians, Poles, Austro-Hungarians, Greeks, Ukrainians, and Italians. In 1880 less than twenty percent of the 250,000 Jews living in New York had come from Eastern Europe. In the next forty years, the number grew to 1,400,000. That was one-fourth of the city's entire population. In the first quarter of the 1900s, more than two million Italians arrived. By the time the human tide was interrupted in 1914 by World War I, some thirty-three million people had fled their native lands, risking all to start life anew across the ocean.

THE JOURNEY OF THEIR LIVES

The challenges began even before they first set eyes on the Atlantic, with the heart-wrenching farewells to relatives and friends. "I can remember only the bustle and bristle of those last weeks in Pinsk...the embraces and the tears," Russian immigrant Golda Meir later wrote in her autobiography *My Life* (1975). "Going to America then was almost like going to the moon...We were all bound for a place about which we knew nothing at all and for a country that was totally strange to us."

The majority of emigrants lived far from the sea. Most had never seen a ship, let alone the ocean. Their great journey

This photochrome of the
harbor at Bremen, Germany,
was taken around 1900;
countless immigrants saw
this same scene—their last
view of Europe—before
sailing to America.

From the early 1850s, when immigration began in earnest, newspapers realized that this transfer of people, cultures, and ways of life from the Old World to the New was a story that demanded attention. This illustration, titled "Leaving Old England for America" appeared in the January 22, 1870, issue of *Harper's Weekly*.

began with an internal migration, by foot, horse cart, or, if fortunate, train, from the impoverished villages of the interior to such distant seaports as Liverpool, England; Antwerp, Belgium; Le Havre, France; or Bremen and Hamburg in Germany. "My father..." an Italian emigrant was recalled as saying in *La Storia: Five Centuries of the Italian American Experience*, "put my valises on the old mule, Old Titi, and we went up to the railroad station. It was pitch dark, early in the morning, the streets were empty... My father did not speak all the way to the train. I don't know when he said it to me, my father, he said, 'Make yourself courage.' And that was the last time I saw my father."

The scene on the docks as the emigrants boarded the ships could only be regarded as high drama. For some, it was an occasion filled with hope. "So at last I was going to America, really, really going at last," a Russian girl named Mary Antin later wrote in her book *The Promised Land* (1912). "The boundaries burst. The arch of heaven soared. A million suns shone out for every star. The winds rushed in from outer space, roaring in my ears. America America." For others, the departure of their countrymen signaled a mournful transition. "They go aboard," Minnesota historian Theodore C. Blegen wrote in his book *Norwegian Migration to America, 1825–1860* (1931): "the old man stands motionless on the shore gazing at the ship, like Mother Norway herself

As those who took part in the "greatest mass migration in history" arrived in New York, photographers were present to record the scene. Here, a group of eastern European emigrants huddle on the deck of the S.S. *Amsterdam*. The photograph was taken in 1899 by noted photographer Frances Benjamin Johnston, one of the first female photojournalists in the United States.

lamenting the going of her children." For most, it was a bewildering time. "Well, we're off to America," stated one of the characters in a ca. 1900 short story by Russian author Sholem Aleichem. "Where it is I don't know. I only know it's far."

Before the 1850s, almost all those who uprooted themselves and journeyed to America traveled in sailing vessels, many of them packet ships refitted for the emigrant trade. By the 1860s, however, most were making the voyage by steamship. But whether they crossed the Atlantic by sail or by steam it was for most a terrifying, life-threatening voyage that they would never forget.

The vast majority were far too poor to afford either a first- or a second-class ticket. Instead, they were crammed together far below decks in that dim, damp section of the ship called steerage, where, as a 1911 U.S. Immigration Commission report to President William H. Taft stated, conditions, to say the least, were horrendous: "The unaccounted vomit of the seasick, the odors of the not-too-clean bodies, the reek of food, and the awful stench of the nearby toilet rooms make the atmosphere in steerage such that it is a marvel that human flesh can endure it," exclaimed the report. "Most immigrants lie in their berths for most of the voyage, in a stupor caused by the foul air. The food often repels them…It is almost impossible to keep personally clean. All of these conditions are naturally aggravated by the crowding."

Added to their miseries were the fierce ocean storms that were commonly part and parcel of any Atlantic crossing. Remembering one of these storms, a Balkan immigrant, one of the almost one thousand travelers packed aboard an immigrant steamship spoke of "the howling darkness, the white

For hundreds of thousands of emigrants, the trip across the Atlantic, huddled in the cramped, dimly lit storage quarters beneath the deck, was the most terrifying experience of their lives, particularly during the inevitable storms that erupted during the voyage. "The storm was so great," recalled English immigrant Agnes Howerbend (Ellis Island Oral History Project). "Two people had died. I don't know how they did. But I well remember father at the funeral on deck, each one of us in hand. I turned around and they were throwing caskets overboard into the ocean...I remember that vividly." On May 10, 1855, *Frank Leslie's Illustrated Newspaper* published this dramatic print, which was captioned "Between decks of an ocean steamer during a storm— shipping a heavy sea."

This image was captured by one of the great masters of the medium, Alfred Stieglitz, and is today regarded as one of the most compelling photographs ever taken. It was the American photographer's favorite work. Entitled *The Steerage* (1907), Stieglitz shot the picture while sailing first-class with his family on the *Kaiser Wilhelm II*. Bored and irritated with the company on the upper decks, he ventured down to steerage, came across this throng of deported immigrants forced to make the return trip home, and made history.

rims of the mountain-high waves speeding like maddened dragons toward the tumbling ship." (Ellis Island Oral History Project) Young Irish immigrant Bertha Devlin had her own terrifying experience. "Oh, God, I was sick," she recalled. "Everybody was sick. I don't ever want to remember anything about that old boat. One night I prayed to God that it would go down because the waves were washing over it. I was that sick, I didn't care if it went down or not. And everybody else was the same way."

ISLAND OF HOPE, ISLAND OF TEARS

From the very beginnings of the waves of immigration, the greatest portal to America by far was New York. Until 1855, those who disembarked were free to enter without any examinations or restrictions. But with the arrival of millions of Irish fleeing the effects of the potato famine—the majority coming through New York Harbor—both the state and the city of New York became aware that something had to be done to keep "foreigners" from contaminating the native population. The result was the establishment of an immigration depot at Castle Garden, located at the tip of Manhattan. Between 1855 and 1890, approximately eight million immigrants, nearly seventy percent of the newcomers, were processed at this depot. By 1890, however, when it became apparent that

Immigrants pack the deck of the S.S. *Patricia*, the ocean liner taking them to America, in December 1906, in this photograph by maritime photographer Edwin Levick. "Let them all come," wrote philosopher/writer Ralph Waldo Emerson in his 1845 journal (published as the *Journals of Ralph Waldo Emerson* in 1909–14). "The energy of Irish, Germans, Swedes, Poles...and all the European tribes...will construct a new race, a new religion, a new state, a new literature."

TOP: This chaotic scene of immigrants at Castle Garden registering after arrival appeared in the *Frank Leslie's Illustrated Newspaper* of January 20, 1866.

RIGHT: Originally built as a fort to protect New York Harbor during the War of 1812, Castle Garden (the large round structure in the center foreground of this picture) served as an immigration depot from August 1, 1855 to April 18, 1890. In 1824 it became a cultural center, housing operas and plays, and in 1896 was transformed again into the first New York aquarium. The castle, now part of the U.S. national parks system, became a national monument in 1946. This bird's eye view of the castle and New York harbor was published by Currier & Ives ca. 1892, several years after the federal government founded Ellis Island. Ellis Island is the small island with the yellow building to the lower right of the Statue of Liberty.

ABOVE: This undated photograph captured the exhausted expressions of a family waiting at Ellis Island for the next stage in their journey, all of their worldly goods in a bag on the father's back.

RIGHT: A Russian emigrant stands at the door of Ellis Island in this photograph by R. F. Turnbull, ca. 1895. "I had no idea what to expect at that place," recalled Louis Sage. "I only knew that it was the only way to get into America."

> *" The questions they asked were really simple, and the puzzles they had us complete were pretty easy. But the poor fellow beside me was really confused by it all and I always wondered whether he made it out of that scary place. "*
>
> —Slovakian immigrant Abraham Krames

the small facility could not adequately handle the ever-increasing torrent of arrivals, the federal government stepped in and erected and took control of a huge new immigration station at Ellis Island. It would be here that more than twelve million immigrants were subjected to the physical, mental, and legal examinations designed to determine whether or not they were fit to enter America or whether, as was many times the case, they were to be sent back to their native land on the next available ship.

The laws of the United States were clear as to who should not be admitted into the country. In 1875, a law was passed barring prostitutes, convicts (except those charged with political offenses), and "coolies" (Chinese contract laborers) from entering. The Immigration Act of 1882 widened the banned list to include "lunatics" (the mentally disabled) and "public charges" (paupers). Also passed in 1882 was the Chinese Exclusion Act, which placed a ten-year moratorium on Chinese labor immigration. Three years later, the Alien Contract Labor Law banned contract laborers (except professional singers and actors, artists, educators, ministers, domestic servants, and some specialized categories of skilled laborers). And the Immigration Act of 1891 updated the 1882 act by specifically excluding "persons suffering from a loathsome or a dangerous contagious disease," polygamists, and those who were accused of "moral turpitude."

For most of the millions who passed its halls, the Ellis Island experience was both bewildering and frightening. The majority could not speak English and had to rely on overworked interpreters to gain any understanding of what was taking place. The sight of the uniformed inspectors was particularly frightening. "They terrified me," stated Polish immigrant Louis Sage. "I had come all this way to escape the men in uniforms who had destroyed our lives back home." And always there was the very real fear of failing one of the examinations and being returned to the horrors from which they had fled.

The first series of tests involved the physical examinations designed to exclude those whose physical condition might prevent them from finding employment in America or cause them to become a burden to society. Doctors checked for obvious diseases, for physical deformities, and for such disorders as lameness and shortness of breath. The most traumatic of the physical tests, however, were the eye examinations. The great flow of emigration took place at a time when a disease of the eyes known as trachoma had, for years, been spreading throughout southern and eastern Europe. Highly contagious, it often resulted in blindness and, more than any other condition, was the ailment that immigration officials feared most—so much so that in 1895 the Commissioner General of Immigration, in his annual report, warned that if trachoma

Statue of Liberty

LEFT: Before it was shipped to America and placed in New York Harbor, parts of the statue were put on display elsewhere in America. This stereograph shows the monument's torch and part of its arm (finished earlier than the rest of the statue), which were a featured attraction at the 1876 Centennial Exhibition in Philadelphia.

As the immigrants entered New York Harbor, many were astounded to see an enormous statue of a majestic woman bearing a huge torch in her hand. It was the Statue of Liberty, a gift from the people of France to the people of the United States, a symbol of the two nations' commitment to the principles of liberty. Created by French sculptor Frederic-Auguste Bartholdi, who endowed it with its formal title *Liberty Enlightening the World*, the 151-foot and one-inch statue standing on an 89-foot pedestal upon a 65-foot foundation was officially unveiled on October 28, 1886.

RIGHT: It took twelve years for Bartholdi and his workers, assisted by the famed French engineer Gustave Eiffel, to complete the statue, which was assembled in France and then dismantled and sent to New York in 214 enormous crates. This etching, done for the January 19, 1884, issue of *Harper's Weekly*, shows an almost final statue still housed in scaffolding. Before its dismantling, it stood on display in France and attracted legions of admiring viewers. The statue was completed in June 1884 and arrived in New York a year later.

LEFT: Crowds on steamboats in New York Harbor celebrate the Statue of Liberty's dedication on October 28, 1886. The statue is dramatically wreathed in smoke from the steamship stacks and the inaugural fireworks. This photograph was taken from the steamer *Patrol*.

BELOW: Immigrants' first sight of the Statue of Liberty represented their first realization that they had arrived in America. The Ellis Island Oral History Project has many recollections of this moment: "The bigness of Mrs. Liberty overcame us," an Italian immigrant wrote. "No one spoke a word, for she was a goddess and we knew she represented the big, powerful country which was to be our future home." Others had no idea what the statue represented. "When we arrived in New York Harbor," recalled German immigrant Estelle Miller, "my brothers and I ran out to see [the enormous statue]. One man said, 'Don't you know? That's Columbus.'" This engraving was in the July 2, 1887, issue of *Frank Leslie's Illustrated Newspaper*.

A sea of bewildered and anxious faces in a waiting area at Ellis Island. They had almost no idea of what lay ahead of them, and most were unable to speak their new land's language.

should make its way into the United States through the European newcomers, future Americans would be rendered "sightless" and the United States would become "the hospital of the nations of the world."

Following the physical examinations, the newcomers were then herded into another section of Ellis Island's mammoth Registry Room, where they were put through a series of tests aimed at detecting signs of insanity, neurosis, or any form of mental illness. "The questions they asked were really simple, and the puzzles they had us complete were pretty easy," recalled Slovakian arrival Abraham Krames. "But the poor fellow beside me was really confused by it all and I always wondered whether he made it out of that scary place." English newcomer Florence Norris had a different reaction to the mental tests. "[The inspector] asked me a lot of silly questions," she later stated. "You know what I mean? About America, if I knew all about America. Well, I didn't know any-thing about America." (Ellis Island Oral History Project)

It was indeed scary and confusing, but through it all some of those being questioned managed to keep the spirit that had brought them so far from home intact. "They asked us... 'How much is two and one? How much is two and two?'" remembered Polish newcomer Pauline Notkoff. (Ellis Island Oral History Project) "But the next girl, also from our country, went and they asked her, 'How do you wash stairs,

OPPOSITE: An undated photograph shows immigrants nervously waiting to be examined. "My greatest fear," stated Irish emigrant Sophie Connangton, "was that I'd miss hearing my name when it was called and that I'd never get out of that building." (Ellis Island Oral History Project)

ABOVE: An Ellis Island inspector checks a woman for trachoma in 1907. The inspectors, doctors, and other officials had an enormously difficult task. Most tried to be patient and compassionate, but, as Frank Martocci, a U.S. Immigration interpreter and legal inspector put it, "We were often overwhelmed by that rising human tide." (Ellis Island Oral History Project)

BELOW: Immigration mandates stated that an unescorted female was not to be allowed entry into America. Thousands of women, like those being questioned here, spent months, even as much as a year, waiting for a male relative or sponsor to appear at the depot and prove that the woman would be provided for.

OPPOSITE: The saddest of all places at Ellis Island were the detention cages, where emigrants who had failed their examinations waited to be deported. This photograph from 1902 depicts deportees on the roof, getting some air. Speaking of those who were sent back to where their long journey had begun, Ellis Island Commissioner Henry H. Curran (1923–26) wrote in his autobiography *From Pillar to Post* (1941): "I could only watch them go. Day by day the [ferries] took them…back to the ships again, back to the ocean, back to what?"

passenger to another to help out those who didn't have it. And this had to be done with a quick motion of the hand."

Surprising as it may seem, the most potentially disastrous of all the questions asked during the legal examination was the simple query: "Do you have a job waiting for you in the United States?" The 1885 Alien Contract Labor Law had been passed in great measure due to pressure exerted by organized labor groups such as the Knights of Labor, who were determined to prevent immigrants from taking jobs away from natural-born Americans. Organized labor's main target was foreigners who had signed an employment contract with an American employer in exchange for having their passage paid across the Atlantic. The law placed thousands of already confused newcomers in a bewildering position. Any newcomer could be denied entry into America if an inspector felt he was unlikely to find employment. Yet he could also be excluded if, in exchange for passage, he had signed a contract making him certain of having a job. Back in the old country, many of the emigrants had been warned of this perplexing

IMMIGRANTS AT ELLIS ISLAND.   8109-15

contradiction. "Remember," they had been told, "you have no job waiting for you, and you paid your own way." Many of the newcomers, however, simply did not understand what they were being told. And many others who did understand the warning simply could not grasp the logic of lying when there didn't seem to be any reason for doing so. The result was that thousands of those who had thought themselves among the most fortunate of all the emigrants by having a job waiting for them were sent directly back to the lands from they which they had fled.

In the end, ninety-eight percent of all those who passed through Ellis Island were admitted into the United States. At first glance the two percent who were barred from entering seems almost negligible. But the percentages are misleading. Given the millions who were examined, two percent represented more than 250,000 people for whom the immigration station had become known as an island of tears rather than an island of hope. It is no wonder that years after the depot was closed down, workmen restoring the facility as a national landmark

The vast majority of the newcomers passed the tests and were allowed entry. Released from the Ellis Island facilities, most—such as this family—waited for the ferries that would take them across the harbor into New York, gazing with expectation and no little amount of trepidation at what lay ahead.

found, under several layers of paint, an inscription written by one who had gone through the examination ordeal. "Why should I fear the fires of Hell?" it read. "I have been through Ellis Island."

OUT INTO AMERICA

They had survived the treacherous ocean voyage and the ordeal of Ellis Island, but now, for most, the greatest challenge of all lay ahead. According to *Immigrants: The New Americans*, a full one-third of all the millions of emigrants settled in New York. The great majority had never been in a city, let alone the largest in the world. From the moment the Ellis Island ferries had deposited them in the teeming metropolis most had been thunderstruck by what they encountered. "I was simply astounded by the sight of the buildings," Lillian Berger remembered during a 1950 interview with this author. "To me, they looked like mountains. Did people really live and work in them? And the bridges. I couldn't imagine myself ever being brave enough to set foot upon them. Most of all it was the noise. The screeching of those tracks that ran right down the middle of the street. And the crowds of people. One hardly had room to walk."

An even greater shock awaited them. Most of the newcomers were extremely poor; most had no choice but to rent rooms in buildings erected by greedy landlords to take advantage of the hordes that were arriving every day. Called tenements—and designed to cram as many people into them as possible—they were typically five to seven stories high and were lined up one after another, block after block. Partitioned into tiny rooms, most no larger than eleven by eleven feet, each of the dark, dreary buildings housed up to thirty-two families. As reported in *Immigrants: The New Americans*, by the 1890s, some 1,335,000 people lived in New York's 39,138 tenement buildings, making the city's immigrant sections the most densely populated places in the world.

For the immigrants, the tenements were the furthest from what most had been led to believe life in America would be like. As poverty-stricken as they had been back home, the

The majority of emigrants had never been in the center of a large city. Almost none had ever seen a trolley. All were astounded at the size of the New York buildings. "Oh my God," exclaimed newcomer Lillian Berger. "It was a different world and I could never imagine myself being part of it." This ca. 1900 photograph looks up bustling Broadway from Dey Street.

rural areas from which they had fled were filled with trees, fresh air—and sunshine. Young Russian immigrant Anzia Yezierska was one of those whose family had moved into a tenement on the Lower East Side of New York City. Yezierska, who was able to escape tenement life and pursue a career as an author, recalled her difficult childhood in the book *Hungry Hearts* (1920): "Again the shadow fell over me. In America were rooms without sunlight; rooms to sleep in, to eat in, to cook in, and a door to shut people out, to take the place of sunlight. Or would I always need the sunlight to be happy? And where was there a place in America for me to play? I looked out into the alley below and saw pale-faced children scrambling in the gutter. 'Where is America?' cried my heart."

It could not have been a more difficult beginning to the pursuit of a dream. Yet the immigrant experience grew to be one of the most inspiring of all stories. The majority overcame the squalid living conditions, the ridicule they commonly received from the native-born population, and the countless other slights and hardships. They did whatever it took to survive and to provide their children with a better life.

Thousands went to work in New York's garment district in small factories known as sweatshops, where they toiled for long hours for minimum pay. Others eked out meager livings by turning their overcrowded tenement rooms into "home sweatshops," where the entire family sewed clothing, assembled cheap jewelry and artificial flowers, or rolled cigars. They had come to America with their heads filled with stories

OPPOSITE: An Italian mother and her baby inside their New York tenement, photographed around 1890 by Jacob Riis, the pioneering Danish-American photographer and social reformer. Riis's groundbreaking book, *How the Other Half Lives* (1890), exposed tenement and slum conditions and ultimately helped spur housing reform. This image was engraved for reproduction in the earlier editions of the book, which due to the limits of technology included mostly engravings drawn after his photographs and small, blurry halftone reproductions.

ABOVE: Fortunately for the immigrants, there were individuals and societies shocked by the newcomers' living conditions and concerned over their welfare. This photograph of a Jewish arrival honoring the Sabbath in the tenement cellar in which he lived on Ludlow Street, was taken by Riis, himself a Danish immigrant.

RIGHT: Riis took this iconic photograph of immigrants sewing clothing in the Ludlow Street tenement "sweatshop" around 1899. "We did what we had to do," Louis Sage recalled, "there were millions of us and for most of us the only way up was through hard work."

OPPOSITE: Children play amid the rubble of the back "yard" of a tenement, February 1912, in a photograph taken by Lewis Hine, the acclaimed photographer for the National Child Labor Committee (NCLC), an anti–child-labor advocacy group that was founded in New York City in 1904. Hine's photographs were influential in building momentum toward banning child labor, but the NCLC were not victorious until 1938, when the Fair Labor Standards Act was passed, and for the first time, minimum ages of employment and hours of work for children were regulated by federal law.

TOP RIGHT: Boys play checkers on a New York City street curb in this ca. 1908–15 photograph.

RIGHT: Hine took this photograph of a row of tenements on Elizabeth Street in March 1912. The tenements housed many families with children who worked alongside their parents on the finishing of clothes for the garment industry.

Hine toured New York City, and elsewhere in the country, photographing conditions of children at work. The portfolio on these pages shows examples of a few of his hundreds of pictures of families working in home sweatshops. The photographs were all taken from 1908–12. As Italian emigrant Stefano Villani was quoted in the Ellis Island Oral History Project: "It was long, dull, laborious work, but we all did it, even six-year-old Joseph. We were determined to make it and to give our children a better life than we had known."

CLOCKWISE FROM TOP LEFT:

The Malesta family of New York's Sullivan Street makes silk flowers at their table for six cents a gross. The boys work after school until eleven in the evening and on Saturdays.

The Romana family makes dresses for dolls on Thompson Street.

A family picks nuts in their dirty basement tenement.

A family rolls cigarettes in their home.

CLOCKWISE FROM TOP LEFT:

TOP LEFT: **A Jewish family works on garters in their tenement home kitchen.**

TOP RIGHT: **The Ceru family live in a crowded attic in a tenement on Thompson Street, where they assemble artificial leaves.**

BOTTOM RIGHT: **On the stoop of a Boston tenement, families and neighbors (mostly children) work on tags.**

BOTTOM LEFT: **The Cottone family do garment finishing, making about two dollars in a good week.**

Hine's caption for this 1911 photograph read "Noon hour in the Ewen Breaker, Pennsylvania Coal Co., South Pittston, Pennsylvania." His notes indicated that not one of the child miners in the picture was over the age of eleven.

ATLANTIC OCEAN

of the riches they would easily acquire. In *La Storia: Five Centuries of the Italian American Experience*, one Italian newcomer is said to have explained that "in the old country they used to say that America was a rich and wonderful place—so rich you could pick gold up in the street. And I believed it." It did not take long for reality to set in. As another immigrant later stated, "We thought the streets were paved with gold. Most weren't even paved. We paved them." (*Ellis Island: Gateway to a Dream*, Pamela Reeves, 1991)

They worked extraordinarily hard, made enormous sacrifices—and also discovered the one true avenue for providing their children with a far better future than they had enjoyed. "For the immigrant children, the public schools are the sluiceways into Americanism," wrote Howard B. Grose in his book *Aliens or Americans?* (1906). In most of the nations from which the immigrants had come, there was no such thing as free public education. Most families could not afford to send their children to school. But in America, education was open to all. "A little girl from across the alley came and offered to [take us] to school," Mary Antin wrote in *The Promised Land*. "This child who had never seen us till yesterday, who could not pronounce our name...was able to offer us the freedom of the schools...No applications made, no questions asked, no examinations...no fees. The doors stood open for every one of us. The smallest child could show us the way."

Labor and Humanity

Children operating dangerous machines in a textile mill.

Hine titled this 1908 picture "Bill, a carrying-in boy... Gets eighty cents a day or night." Bill worked in a glass works in Marion, Indiana.

The millions of immigrants who arrived in America in the last half of the nineteenth century came at a time when the nation was fully engulfed in industrial transformation. While many hailed what was taking place as the beginning of an interrupted march to a bright new world, others, such as technology historian Lewis Mumford, saw it differently. "Western society," wrote Mumford in his two-volume book *The Myth of the Machine* (1967–70) "has accepted as unquestionable a technological imperative that is quite as arbitrary as the most primitive taboo: not merely the duty to foster invention and constantly create technological novelties, but equally the duty to surrender to these novelties unconditionally, just because they are offered, without respect to their human consequences." Mumford knew of what he wrote. There was indeed a price to industrial progress. And nowhere could it be seen more clearly than in American factories and mines, where the combination of an insatiable demand for labor and the desperate financial plight of many immigrant families led to the full-time employment of children, many younger than ten years of age.

The practice of child labor did not originate in America; it began with the first factories established by Richard Arkwright at the birth of the Industrial Revolution. By the time that industrialism swept the United States, photographers, most notably reformer Hine, would capture disturbing images such as these.

A boy operates a dangerous boring machine in a handle factory in Denison, Texas, in a 1913 photograph by Hine; at the time the picture was taken the boy was recovering from an accident in which his hand was badly mauled by the machine.

A 1913 Hine photograph of children working in a canning factory in Bluffton, South Carolina; the seven-year-old girl in the foreground shucked three pots of oysters a day.

Two boys are on their way to work at 5 P.M. at a glass factory in Pittsburgh, photographed by Hine in 1913.

LEFT: In this classic Riis photograph ca. 1892, immigrant children in the Mott Street Industrial School, in New York City, pledge allegiance to the flag of their new country—a pledge that was first recited in 1892, the year that Ellis Island opened its doors.

Commenting on the way in which free public education was permitting immigrant youngsters to adapt to their new land far better than their parents, a columnist in the *Jewish Daily Forward* concluded, "In America, the children bring up the parents."

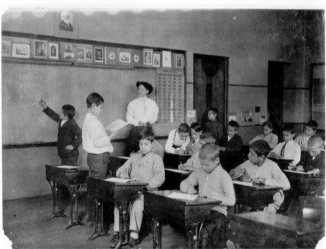

ABOVE: A class of immigrant children during a spelling lesson at the Washington School in Boston, photographed by Hine in 1909.

As the children became increasingly educated, not only in the language but in American ways, a unique phenomenon developed. Gradually in many families an unprecedented role reversal took place as the young people assumed responsibilities that their parents, who did not know how to deal with people or institutions outside their immediate neighborhoods, could not handle. "I was the one who always went down to the coal company to complain about the bill," an Italian youngster stated (*La Storia: Five Centuries of The Italian American Experience*). "And I was the one who dealt with the landlord. I could read the bills and the contracts and I could speak English to these people. I became, in a very real sense, the junior father of our family."

The hordes of newcomers who made New York their home created ethnic neighborhoods in many ways little distinguishable in language, foods, and traditions from the towns and villages from which they had come. The millions who boarded trains and fanned out across America created their own ethnic enclaves—Czechs and Poles in Chicago and Cleveland, Greeks in Detroit and Chicago, Armenians in Los Angeles and Boston, Ukrainians in Chicago and Pittsburgh.

Millions from Norway, Sweden, Denmark, Finland, Germany, and Russia journeyed halfway across the continent determined to start their new lives on the vast American plains. They had much in common. Most had been farmers in the Old

More than any other factor, it was free public education that enabled immigrant children to eventually build successful lives in America. This poster from 1936, which included Yiddish text, announced the opportunity for adult newcomers to learn English. Note how the announcement makes a special point of stating, "Learn to speak, read, and write, the language of your children."

The Neighborhood

The various immigrant groups that made New York their home settled together in neighborhoods that, in many ways, more resembled Europe than America. By 1910, Jewish author Alfred Kazan wrote that New York's "Rivington Street was only a suburb of Minsk." A newly arrived Irishman, first encountering a neighborhood in which his countrymen had settled, exclaimed that "it's for all the world like Cork." (*Immigrants: The New Americans*). And Jacob Riis proclaimed in his important work *How the Other Half Lives* (1890) that a section of New York's East Side resembled "Jerusalem in its palmiest days." It was true not only of New York, but of other American cities as well. Wherever an ethnic group settled in sufficient numbers, a newspaper in its native language was certain to be published. By 1917, more than 1,300 foreign-language papers had made their appearance.

ABOVE: Jewish immigrants in front of a synagogue in New York's Lower East Side. "Was this the America we sought?" asked one newcomer, as quoted in *Immigrants: The New Americans* (1999). "Or was it only a circle that we had traveled, with a Jewish ghetto at its beginning and its end?"

TOP: No matter what the section, New York's teeming ethnic neighborhoods were alive with the sounds, smells, foods, and other products that had been transferred from the Old World to the New. Here is an outdoor market in the Jewish district on the Lower East Side around 1907.

BELOW: A *Harper's Weekly* feature from the June 5, 1869, issue celebrated the completion of the Pacific Railroad; the meeting of the Union and Central Pacific lines.

FOLLOWING PAGES: This Currier & Ives print from 1874 portrays the excitement created by the "American Railroad Scene," as the image is captioned.

HARPER'S WEEKLY. [JUNE 5, 1869.

MPLETION OF THE PACIFIC RAILROAD—MEETING OF LOCOMOTIVES OF THE UNION AND CENTRAL PACIFIC LINES: THE ENGINEERS SHAKE HANDS.
[PHOTOGRAPHED BY SAVAGE & OTTINGER, SALT LAKE CITY.]

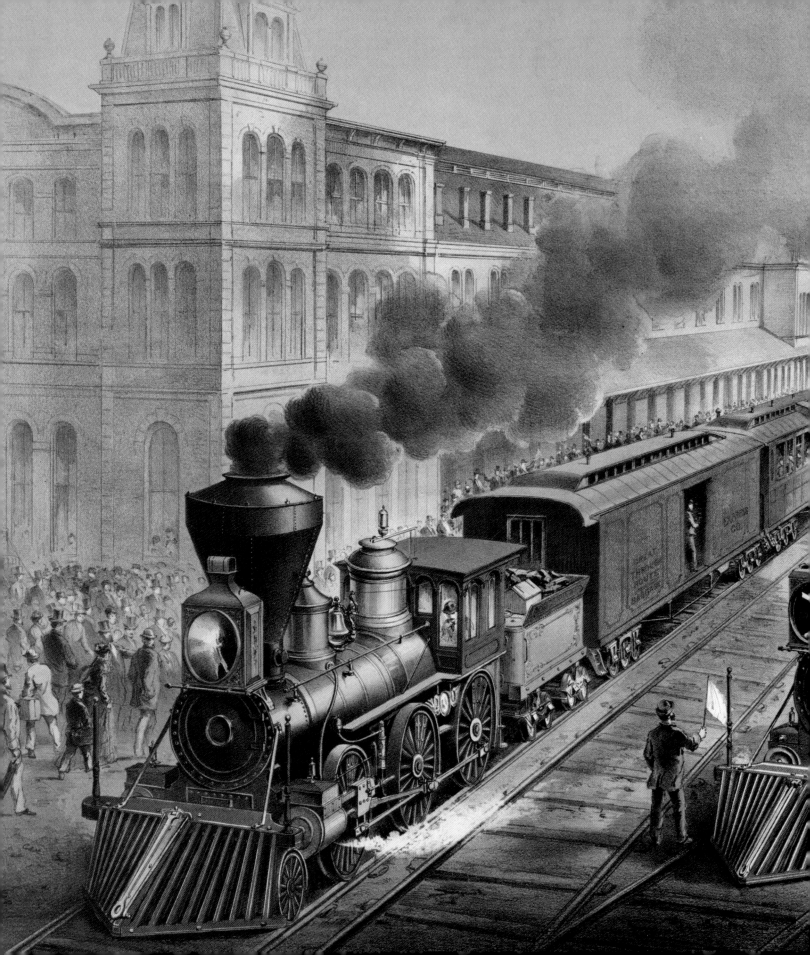

COMBINED HARVESTER &

W & RAYM

An early twentieth-century photograph of farmers on their harvester/thrasher. "Once," wrote historian Oscar Handlin in *The Uprooted: The Epic Story of the Great Migrations That Made the American People* (2002), "I thought to write America's immigrant story. Then I discovered that the immigrants *were* America's story. By following in the tradition of the earliest settlers who had braved the Atlantic crossing and who had overcome momentous obstacles, the nineteenth century immigrants, like these newcomers filling the once-barren prairie with crops, helped build a nation and, in the process, turned America into a nation of nations."

factories, mines, and construction trades that were turning the United States into an industrial giant, added their own invaluable contributions. By 1910, immigrants made up more than half of the American industrial workforce. Leading New York representative Samuel McMillan championed the immigrants in a 1908 speech to Congress: "Where would your mines have been dug and worked, where would your great iron industries and constructions...have been were it not for the immigrants?...It is the immigrant that bears the burden of hard labor...and has contributed his full share to the building up of our great country."

By the time the mass migration was halted by the world's first global war, whole cultures had left their ancient roots behind and had transferred them across the Atlantic, where they in turn would be transformed. The immigrants had come from every Old World nation, every class, every religious persuasion. As one late-nineteenth-century newspaper reported, "There had been nothing like [the diversity that had arisen in America] since the encampments of the Roman Empire" (*Liberty: The Statue and the American Dream*). As Herman Melville inspiringly pronounced in his book *Redburn: His First Voyage, Being the Sailor-Boy...* (1849), "We are not a nation, so much as a world." More precisely, it had been another major step in the development of an Atlantic world.

11

THE
ATLANTIC
WORLD
CONFIRMED

THE TWENTIETH
AND TWENTY-FIRST
CENTURIES

Passengers aboard the
Norddeutscher Lloyd
line's SS *König Albert*
stroll the promenade
deck at sunset, ca. 1905.

THE ATLANTIC WORLD CONFIRMED

The Atlantic basin is our home.

—LEONARD OUTHWAITE, *The Atlantic: A History of an Ocean* (1957)

The rich and varied cultures, ideas, and ways of life that the nineteenth-century immigrants brought with them from the Old World to the New represented one of the final stages in the making of the Atlantic world. The events that took place in the twentieth century and in the early years of the twenty-first made the notion of an acknowledged Atlantic community a full reality. It began with the introduction of the largest and greatest transatlantic passenger and commercial ships ever built. Just as the discovery of new worlds in the fifteenth and sixteenth centuries was occasioned by rivalries between the great European powers, so too did competition over transatlantic travel and shipping lead to the construction of the first true ocean liners.

SUPERLINERS

As the nineteenth century entered its final decade, Kaiser Wilhelm II of Germany, determined to wrest dominance of the Atlantic away from Great Britain, ordered the building of the world's first superliner. The result was the 655-foot-long SS *Kaiser Wilhelm der Grosse* which, when launched on May 4, 1897, boasted a passenger capacity of slightly under two thousand people. Stung by the appearance of the German vessel, which caused a worldwide sensation, the British government responded in 1903 by subsidizing Cunard to construct the two largest ships since Isambard Brunel's *Great Eastern*. The RMS *Mauritania* and the RMS *Lusitania* (both almost 32,000 tons and 762 feet long) made their maiden voyages in 1907. For the next seven years, the *Mauritania*, which continually broke transatlantic speed records, and the *Lusitania*, engaged in a friendly rivalry that together earned them the nickname the "Atlantic Ferry."

The success of the two Cunard ships served to intensify the heated competition for the Atlantic trade. The Holland America Line built the SS *Rotterdam IV* (launched in 1908); the French Line, or Compagnie Générale Transatlantique, constructed the SS *France* (1912); England's White Star Line launched three aptly named superliners, the RMS *Olympic* (1910), the RMS *Titanic* (1911), and the RMS *Britannic* (1914); and Germany

16536. P. Z. - NORDDEUTSCHER LLOYD
DAMPFER "KAISER WILHELM DER GROSSE" RAUCHZIMMER

These photographs show
a full starboard view of
the SS *Kaiser Wilhelm
der Grosse* (OPPOSITE), and
the liner's elaborately
decorated smoking cabin
(ABOVE), ca. 1897.

Elegantly dressed crowds gather on the dock in New York City on September 13, 1907, to greet the RMS *Lusitania* after her maiden voyage from Liverpool, England.

The spacious decks of the liners (the *Olympic* and the *Titanic*'s decks were more than 880 feet long and 93 feet wide) provided passengers with the opportunity to stroll or jog for exercise as they made the Atlantic crossing, and they also were the setting for all types of games and events. Here passengers on the RMS *Mauretania* watch as youngsters jump rope.

countered with the introduction first of the mammoth *Imperator* (1912), and then the even larger *Vaterland* (1913). These were more than gigantic vessels, they were the new wonders of the sea. As they continually competed for the Blue Riband—the coveted prize for the fastest Atlantic crossing—and as they reduced the crossing time to well under one week, the superliners replaced the locomotive as the prime symbol of the extraordinary and seemingly endless scientific and technological progress that had begun with the Industrial Revolution.

And they were not only fast; they were the most luxurious ships that had ever plied the ocean. Their elegantly appointed dining rooms, complete with marble pillars and crystal chandeliers, served lavish twelve-course meals. After dinner, passengers could attend nightclubs, concerts or dances held in ballrooms every bit as beautiful as those found in the world's greatest hotels. There were indoor and outdoor pools, beauty parlors, barber shops, smoking lounges, shops of every description, even kennels and elevators. For the active minded, there were fully equipped gymnasiums and deck sports that included golf, tennis, skeet shooting, and shuffleboard. More sedentary passengers could lounge on the decks or stroll along their enormous expanse or enjoy the comforts of each ship's well-stocked, plush library. And all first-class passengers could retire for the night to lavish multiroomed suites.

The luxury liners were built for the wealthy, and they came with a huge price tag, both in their construction and in first-class fares. Ironically, however, it was not the first-class passengers who made them so profitable. Built at a time when the mass migration of Europeans to America was fully underway, it was the millions of immigrants traveling with the cheapest tickets in the no-frills steerage section of each vessel who, by their sheer numbers, brought the liner companies the greatest revenues.

A sister ship of the RMS *Titanic*, the RMS *Olympic*, like the *Titanic*, was built by England's White Star Line to compete with Cunard's *Lusitania* and *Mauretania* for supremacy of the transatlantic trade. As the ca. 1909 photograph shows, the ships were built at the same time, side by side, in a Belfast shipyard (the *Olympic* was completed first).

Among the *Olympic*'s features were three elevators and a huge luxury second class. First-class stewardess Violet Jessop, who was a survivor of the *Titanic* sinking and a stewardess on the *Olympic*, wrote of her experiences on the latter: "I got a fresh thrill every time I went through *Olympic*'s beautiful staterooms. I have always maintained that never before or since have materials of so perfect a quality been used to fit out any ship" (from *Titanic Survivor*, Jessop's recently discovered memoirs, coauthored by John Maxtone-Graham, 1997). The first-class grand dining room is shown here, ca. 1911-20.

A CROWN HE IS ENTITLED TO WEAR.

Panama Canal

Among the vital developments that took place in the early years of the twentieth century was a massive construction project that exponentially expanded the shipping capabilities of Atlantic World nations. The desire for a canal running through the Isthmus of Panama, connecting the Atlantic and Pacific oceans and eliminating the long, difficult route via the Strait of Magellan or the more perilous Drake Passage, dates back as far as 1534, when Spanish king Charles V proposed a canal in Panama that would make it easier for ships to travel back and forth from Ecuador and Peru. In 1881, a French company, Compagnie Universelle du Canal Interocéanique, tried to build such a canal, but after almost eight years of extraordinary difficulty in which some twenty-two thousand workers died from disease, the project was abandoned with only eleven miles dug. In 1914, under the determined leadership of President Theodore Roosevelt, the United States, after ten years of backbreaking construction—in which, despite medical advancements and precautions, 5,609 workmen perished—the canal was finally completed. In 1999, after decades of contentious relations between the two countries—-Panama felt that the waterway should be theirs—the United States turned over control of the canal to Panama.

ABOVE LEFT: This cartoon on the June 4, 1904, cover of *Judge* magazine features Theodore Roosevelt, the driving force behind the building of the Panama Canal. Captioned "a crown he is entitled to wear," Roosevelt wears such a crown labeled "The Greatest Achievement for Trade in Modern Times." Explaining what motivated him in making the canal a reality, the American president wrote in *Theodore Roosevelt: An Autobiography* (1913): "During the nearly four hundred years that had elapsed since Balboa crossed the Isthmus [of Panama], there had been a good deal of talk about building an Isthmus canal...So far it had resulted merely in conversation; and the time had come when unless somebody was prepared to act with decision we would have to resign ourselves to at least half a century of further conversation."

ABOVE CENTER: The concrete construction of the massive Gatun Locks at the Panama Canal, ca. 1910; this lock system comprises three pairs of concrete chambers that lift ships about eight-five feet from sea level to Gatun Lake.

OPPOSITE BOTTOM: This map, from William R. Shepherd's *Historical Atlas* (1923) diagrams the route of the Panama Canal (TOP), connecting the Atlantic and Pacific oceans, and includes a cutaway view (BELOW) that shows the canal's major locks and towns along the canal.

21771—The S. S. Panama in Culebra Cut on Sunday, Feb. 7, 1915—the First Excursion to Go Through the Panama Canal.

TOP RIGHT: The SS *Panama* transverses the human-made valley called the Culebra Cut—an engineering marvel—on the first trip through the canal, February 7, 1914.

RIGHT: More than 850,000 ships have passed through the Panama Canal since its opening; it continues to be a vital artery for international shipping. A typical passage for a cargo ship takes about nine hours. More than 280 million tons of freight is transported through the canal every year. Here, a ship makes its way through the Gatun Locks in 2000.

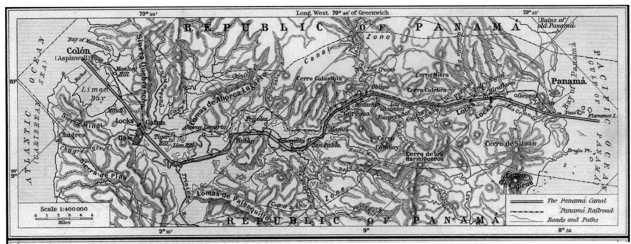

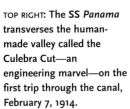

The Titanic

When the RMS *Titanic* left Southampton, England, on April 10, 1912, on its maiden voyage, she was headed for New York with scheduled stops at Cherbourg, France, and Queenstown, Ireland. According to Robert D. Ballard's 2001 book *Adventures in Ocean Exploration*, her passengers were prepared to enjoy days of luxury and pleasure aboard what British newspapers hailed as "the most popular ship ever built." Even the most skittish passengers could take comfort in news reports that confirmed the owners' claim that the ship was not only a technological marvel but was "unsinkable." On the night of April 14, 1912, however, the "impossible" happened. While steaming south of Newfoundland, the *Titanic* struck an iceberg and, within two hours and forty minutes, sank beneath the waves. The sinking, with its enormous loss of life, earned the *Titanic* the unwanted distinction of being the ship involved in the most infamous peacetime maritime disaster in history.

BELOW: Considered the epitome of naval architecture and technological developments, the RMS *Titanic*, more than 882 feet long and almost 93 feet wide, was the largest passenger ship in the world. It was also, according to its White Star Line owners, the most luxurious. The crown jewel among its features was its forward first-class staircase decorated with oak paneling and gilded balustrades, topped by an ornate iron and glass dome that let in natural light. This reproduction of a 1912 painting by German artist Willy Stöwer captures the horrific sinking of the *Titanic* into the sea as viewed by survivors in lifeboats.

OPPOSITE: One of the owners' proudest boasts was that the *Titanic* carried an above standard number of lifeboats. What they failed to mention was that there were still not enough lifeboats to accommodate all the vessel's expected passengers. Once it became clear that the "unsinkable" *Titanic* was indeed in real danger of doing just that, its wireless operators sent out repeated messages of distress. The only ship that was able to come to *Titanic*'s rescue was the RMS *Carpathia*. This blurred photograph shows *Titanic* survivors in a lifeboat on their way to the *Carpathia*. The *Carpathia* received the *Titanic*'s distress call at approximately 12:25 A.M. while over fifty miles away, but did not arrive until 4:00 A.M. and was able to save only 705 passengers—those who had made it to lifeboats. To this day, official figures differ as to how many people died. A U.S. investigator reported 1,517 deaths, while a British investigator listed 1,490 fatalities.

RIGHT: The April 16, 1912, front page of the *New York Times*; the sinking of the *Titanic* made headlines throughout the world, not only because of its status as the largest ship afloat but also because its passenger list included some of the wealthiest and most prominent people in the world. Among its first-class passengers, most of whom died in the sinking, were leading industrialists and railroad magnates from both sides of the Atlantic, French and British royalty, leading journalists, writers, and painters, aviation pioneers, and an American silent motion picture star.

RIGHT: In September 1985 oceanographer Robert Ballard, aboard the Woods Hole Oceanographic Institution's ship the *Knorr*, discovered the elusive, long-sought *Titanic* wreck. This image is from a June 2003 mission to the wreck site aboard the Russian research vessel *Akademik Mstislav Keldysh*, sponsored by the National Oceanic and Atmospheric Administration (NOAA) and their Office of Ocean Exploration. The Russian vessel was equipped with two 3-person submersibles (*Mir I* and *Mir II*) capable of diving to depths of 19,685 feet. (The depth of the sunken *Titanic* is 12,467 feet.) A camera mounted on *Mir I* captured this astonishing photograph of the bow of the Titanic covered in rusticles.

For many of those who traveled on the liners, the greatest joy was on the voyage itself, the opportunity to put work and cares behind and enjoy the luxury of simply relaxing. Here, ladies Sybil and Evelyn Grey, the daughters of Earl Grey, the Governor General of Canada, take a stroll on the Hamburg America Line ship the SS *Vaterland* ca. 1910. (The *Vaterland* was seized by the United States in 1917 to be used as a troop ship and renamed the USS *Leviathan* until after the war, when she became an ocean liner in the United States Lines.)

Passengers line the decks
of the Hamburg America
Line's SS *Imperator* in this
undated photograph.

A German U-36 submarine glides past a German warship in April 1913. The German U-boat was the deadliest naval vessel yet conceived. The entire outcome of World War I's Battle of the Atlantic hinged on overcoming the U-boat menace.

WORLD WAR I

By 1914, the ocean liners had established a golden age of transatlantic travel. But in that year it all came to an abrupt halt with the outbreak of World War I. The Atlantic now became not the premier avenue of ocean travel but a war zone in which the ships and submarines of the German Empire and her allies engaged in deadly naval battle with those of Great Britain and nations allied to her. For the United States, it was a most perplexing time. While most U.S. leaders and the majority of citizens were determined to keep the nation out of the conflict, others felt that both history and sentiment dictated that America should join in the fight on the side of Great Britain. It was during such arguments that one of the strongest cases for the existence of an

Atlantic world was put forth. As Bernard Bailyn notes in *Atlantic History: Concepts and Contours* (2005), America's leading journalist Walter Lippmann urged the United States to enter the war in a 1917 essay in *The New Republic*. Lippmann wrote of the critical need to preserve "the profound web of interest which joins together the western world. Britain, France, Italy, Spain, Belgium, Holland, the Scandinavian nations, and Pan America, are in the main, one community in their deepest needs and their deepest purposes…We cannot betray the Atlantic community… What we must fight for is the common interest of the western world, for the integrity of the Atlantic powers. We must recognize that we are in fact one great community and act as members of it."

> *"We cannot betray the Atlantic community…What we must fight for is the common interest of the western world, for the integrity of the Atlantic powers."*
>
> —Walter Lippmann, an essay in *The New Republic*, 1917

This photograph shows the British battle cruiser HMS *Inflexible* stopping to pick up capsized German sailors from the SMS *Gneisenau* after the Battle of the Falkland Islands, December 8, 1914.

When World War I hostilities began, Germany had cruisers deployed throughout the globe, and immediately it began to attack English merchant shipping. The British Royal Navy, however, was soon able to hunt down the cruisers, most notably on December 8, 1914, where at the Battle of the Falkland Islands, English warships destroyed an entire German fleet. During this same initial period, Britain also initiated a naval blockade of Germany that effectively prevented supplies and munitions from reaching German ports.

But it was neither surface vessels nor blockades that was the determining factor in the critical aspects of World War I in the Atlantic Theater. It was Germany's introduction of a frightening new vessel that, during the first years of the conflict, threatened to assure Germany's victory. The most effective military submarine yet devised, the U-boat (an Anglicization of the German word *Unterseeboot*, "undersea boat") was designed to destroy English merchant shipping, the lifeblood of the British nation. And, for more than two years, it seemed that they would do just that. When the war began, Germany had twenty-nine U-boats; within the first few weeks of the conflict, these vessels sank not only a significant number of British merchant ships but also five British warships, including the HMS *Pathfinder*, which, on September 5, 1914, became the first war vessel ever sunk by a torpedo attack.

Kaiser Wilhelm II, emperor of Germany and Prussia, in his military uniform, ca. 1915.

Throughout this early period of the war, Germany was careful to adhere to those international codes of warfare known as "prize rules," which mandated that civilian ships of neutral countries could not be sunk. However, as Germany's warships continued to be ineffective, Kaiser Wilhelm, on February 4, 1915, suddenly declared all of the waters around the British Isles to be a war zone in which even the merchant ships of neutral nations could be sunk without warning, because, as the declaration explained, "in view of the misuse of neutral flags ordained by the British Government on January 31, and owing to the hazards of naval warfare, it may not always be possible to prevent the attacks meant for hostile ships from being directed against neutral ships."

Just three months later, events took a pivotal turn when the Cunard ocean liner RMS *Lusitania* was sunk by a U-boat. On May 1, the *Lusitania* left New York, bound for Liverpool—not without a certain amount of apprehension on the part of some of its 1,257 passengers. On that morning, newspapers printed a warning from the German Embassy alongside an advertisement for the *Lusitania*'s impending voyage. It read: "NOTICE! TRAVELLERS intending to embark on the Atlantic voyage are reminded that a state of war exists between Germany and her allies and Great Britain and her allies; that the zone of war includes the waters adjacent to the British Isles; that, in accordance with formal notice given by the Imperial German Government, vessels flying the flag of Great Britain or any of her allies, are liable to destruction in those waters and that travellers sailing in the war zone on the ships of Great Britain or her allies do so at their own risk.
—IMPERIAL GERMAN EMBASSY, Washington, D.C., April 22, 1915"

BELOW: A 1918 Berlin poster advises the public that all aluminum, copper, brass, nickel, and tin household items have been appropriated for the war effort, and instructs people where to bring the metal items for collection.

An Irish poster from 1915 depicts the sinking of the RMS *Lusitania* by a German U-boat. When it was sunk, the liner was making its 202nd Atlantic crossing. Along with the warning that the German government had issued to passengers via American newspapers, the *Lusitania*'s captain had received several messages from the British Admiralty when the ship reached waters off the Irish coast that a U-boat attack might be imminent. While the sinking of the popular *Lusitania* and the death of so many civilians did not bring the United States or other neutral nations immediately into the war, it significantly galvanized anti-German opinion among these nations.

THE NAVAL BATTLE: FORCE THE GERMAN FLEET WOULD NOT FACE.

This photograph of a British super-dreadnought battleship firing broadside in the Battle of the Jutland appeared in the *Illustrated London News* of June 10, 1916, a week after the battle.

While the warning worried some of the *Lusitania*'s crew as well as many of the ship's passengers, the liner's captain, William "Bowler Bill" Turner was seemingly unconcerned. As recounted in *The Lusitania Disaster: An Episode in Modern Warfare and Diplomacy*, by Thomas A. Bailey and Paul B. Ryan (1975), when asked by a passenger if there was any cause for alarm, Turner replied that the *Lusitania* was "safer than the trolley cars in New York City." He was wrong. On May 7, the *Lusitania* was struck by a torpedo launched by a U-boat and sank within eighteen minutes. A total of 1,201 people died, including 128 Americans.

In the months following the *Lusitania*'s sinking, German leaders, hopeful of keeping America out of the conflict, actu-

ally rescinded their unrestricted submarine warfare policy and placed increased emphasis on their surface ships, hoping to score a knockout victory. On May 31, 1916, they saw their opportunity when, in the North Sea, a huge German naval force came into contact with the British Grand Fleet. The three-day engagement that followed was known as the Battle of Jutland. Involving some 250 ships, it was the only full-scale clash between battleships; it was the largest naval battle of the war. In the end, although the British lost more ships and many more men than the Germans, both sides declared victory. But there was no knockout blow, and the British Grand Fleet remained in control of the sea.

Now desperate to force England to seek peace before the United States could enter the war, Germany planned to reinstate its unrestricted submarine warfare policy on January 31, 1917. On January 16, 1917, German Foreign Secretary Arthur Zimmermann sent a coded telegram to the German ambassador in Washington, D.C., with instructions to forward it to the German ambassador in Mexico. The so-called Zimmerman telegram authorized the German minister to offer a German-Mexican alliance to the Mexican president, noting that "On the first of February, we intend to begin unrestricted submarine warfare. In spite of this, it is our intention to endeavor to keep the United States of America neutral." If Mexico declared war on the United States, in

" On the first of February, we intend to begin unrestricted submarine warfare. In spite of this, it is our intention to endeavor to keep the United States of America neutral. "

—Zimmerman Telegram, January 16, 1917

OPPOSITE: Throughout World War I's Battle of the Atlantic scenes such as this one, of sailors desperately huddled aboard a lifeboat after their ship has been sunk by the U-boat (seen in the distance), were all too common. The U.S. Navy used this image by Welsh artist Frank Brangwyn on a recruiting poster in 1917.

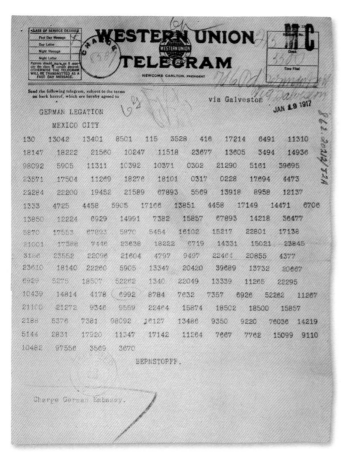

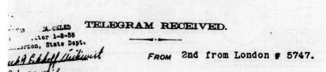

TELEGRAM RECEIVED.

FROM 2nd from London # 5747.

"We intend to begin on the first of February unrestricted submarine warfare. We shall endeavor in spite of this to keep the United States of America neutral. In the event of this not succeeding, we make Mexico a proposal of alliance on the following basis: make war together, make peace together, generous financial support and an understanding on our part that Mexico is to reconquer the lost territory in Texas, New Mexico, and Arizona. The settlement in detail is left to you. You will inform the President of the above most secretly as soon as the outbreak of war with the United States of America is certain and add the suggestion that he should, on his own initiative, invite Japan to immediate adherence and at the same time mediate between Japan and ourselves. Please call the President's attention to the fact that the ruthless employment of our submarines now offers the prospect of compelling England in a few months to make peace." Signed, ZIMMERMANN.

The encrypted Zimmermann telegram (ABOVE), and the decoded version (RIGHT), which instructed the German ambassador of Mexico to "call the President's attention to the fact that the ruthless employment of our submarines offers the prospect of compelling England in a few months to make peace."

return Germany would help support Mexico's repossession of its "lost territory in Texas, New Mexico, and Arizona." Not only did Mexican president Venustiano Carranza reject the proposal, but British cryptographers intercepted the cable transmission in early February 1917, decoded it, and briefed the United States on the twenty-second of the month. The public furor over the plot fueled support for the war. The *New York Times* of March 2, 1917, reported that the scandal caused "hesitating senators and representatives to come out in the open with declarations of support of the President and his method of dealing with the German submarine menace." When, on March 17, 1917, U-boats sank three American merchant vessels, the die was cast. Three weeks later, on April 6, the United States, with its enormous shipbuilding capacity, formally entered the war.

The presence of the United States brought with it a new anti-U-boat strategy that helped the Allies gain the upper hand in the German submarine war. The addition of an increasingly large number of American destroyers to the war effort led to the herding of merchant ships into destroyer-protected convoys with air cover, a strategy that made it much more difficult for the U-boats to reach their targets. A powerful new explosive weapon carried by the destroyers, called a depth charge, also played a major role by providing the most effective means yet developed of sinking a submerged submarine.

The entry of the United States into World War I on the side of Great Britain and its allies brought with it not only more than two million troops but America's industrial might, particularly its enormous shipmaking capacity. Here, the American eagle flies over ships headed across the Atlantic to the war zone characterized as a distant shore in flames, in a 1917 poster for the Emergency Fleet Corporation. The Emergency Fleet Corporation was set up under the U.S. Shipping Board to produce and operate cargo ships that provided what was called a "bridge to France"— the transportation of troops and supplies to France during World War I.

THE SHIPS
ARE COMING
UNITED STATES SHIPPING BOARD   EMERGENCY FLEET CORPORATION

Arrival at Commonwealth Pier, Boston Mass, Troop

"Formerly t

S.C.269

THEY KEPT THE SEA LANES OPEN

INVEST IN THE VICTORY LIBERTY LOAN

LEFT: A poster from 1918 asks Americans to "Invest in the Victory Liberty Loan" to support the ship convoys that "kept the sea lanes open" in the U-boat-infested waters of the Atlantic. The convoys' strategy that turned the tide against the U-boat in World War I was hardly new. Arguably the earliest system of convoys was that employed by the Spanish treasure fleets between the sixteenth and eighteenth centuries as protection against English, French, and Dutch privateers. Convoys were also used in the Napoleonic Wars by both the British and French fleets.

BELOW: The troopship USS *Agamemnon* (the former German liner SS *Kaiser Wilhelm II*) arrives at Commonwealth Pier, in Boston, returning the 26th "Yankee" Division home, April 7, 1919.

Agamemnon with 26th (Yankee) Division boys, April 7th 1919.
an "Liner Kaiser Wilhelm II."

> *"If we could…get people to enjoy the sea, it would be a very good thing, but all we can do, as things are, is to give them gigantic floating hotels."*
>
> —Ship designer Arthur Davis, 1907

The addition of American naval might and the institution of the convoy system spelled the doom of Germany's grand plan of strangling Great Britain before the United States could enter the conflict. On November 11, 1918, with its U-boat menace virtually eliminated and its ground forces faced with defeat, Germany officially surrendered. The world was once again at peace.

THE GOLDEN AGE OF OCEAN TRAVEL

Almost as soon as World War I had erupted, many of the world's great ocean liners had been converted into troopships, carrying hundreds of thousands of soldiers across the Atlantic to the war zones and home again once hostilities ceased. Now, with the seas no longer battlefields, tourists and business-people, forced to remain at home during the more than four and a half years of the war, were free to resume their transat-lantic travel.

Actually, it was more than a resumption. It was the dawn of a whole new Golden Age of Ocean Liners. As luxurious as the pre–World War I liners had been, the new vessels that began to make their appearance within a decade of the con-flict were, in many ways, even more magnificent. It began with the launch of the *Île de France* in 1926. Unlike previous liners, whose designers had striven to endow them with the

OPPOSITE: The Art Deco style influence can be seen in the salon of the MS *Kungsholm* (TOP) and the pool room (BOTTOM) in these photographs from ca. 1928, the year the ship was launched. The *Kungsholm*, built in Hamburg for the Swedish American Line, was one of the first liners to incorporate Art Deco design elements after the success of the *Île de France*.

RIGHT: By the 1920s, travel posters had developed into an art form all their own. Tourism boards used posters such as this Italian one, from about 1920, to entice travelers to cross the Atlantic and visit ancient places and romantic cities such as Venice.

A 1937 poster advertising the post–World War I Compagnie Générale Transatlantique, or French Line. Founded in 1855, the company was anxious to capture both the profits and the national glory that the prewar British liners had attained. To revive flagging profits after the war, the French Line introduced new ships to its fleet such as the *Île de France*, as a new concept in luxury for all. It was not an exaggerated claim.

look of grand European hotels or Renaissance palaces, the *Île de France* was totally different in appearance. The inspiration for its form and decoration had come from the introduction, in Paris, of the Art Deco style of design. And it was the way in which the ship's designers and decorators applied this new stylistic approach that truly gave rise to the immense worldwide popularity that Art Deco would achieve.

No expense had been spared. The *Île de France*'s extraordinary tea salon had been designed by Jacques-Emile Ruhlmann, a renowned Art Deco furniture designer and interior decorator. The ship's magnificent chandeliers, unlike any that had ever graced a liner, had been created by the world's most famous Art Deco glassmaker René Lalique. The vessel's huge, dazzling, dining room was the work of Art Deco's premier architect Pierre Patout.

The *Île de France* soon became the ship of passage for the wealthy on both sides of the Atlantic, and, not surprisingly, served as an inspiration for the construction of similar floating palaces by competing nations. Although Germany had lost many of its liners during World War I, by 1928 it had reentered the competition with the construction of the *Bremen* and the *Europa*. Within a year, the *Bremen* had crossed the Atlantic in a record-breaking four days, seventeen hours, and forty-two minutes, capturing the Blue Riband that had been in the possession of the *Mauritania* for almost twenty-two years. England, anxious to reclaim transatlantic supremacy, in 1934 launched the greatest superliner ever constructed in that country. Stretching a precedent-setting 1,018 feet, the *Queen Mary* combined many of the best Art Deco features with its own modernistic design.

By the latter years of the 1930s, ocean liners had become so opulent, so unlike the ships that had inspired mariners to fall in love with the sea, that complaints about them were actually being heard. As early as 1907, ship designer Arthur Davis had stated that "The one thing that [liner passengers] want to forget when they are on the vessel is that they are on a ship at all…If we could…get people to enjoy the sea, it would be a very good thing, but all we can do, as things are, is to give them gigantic floating hotels" (Alan Villiers, *Men, Ships, and the Sea*, 1962). His was a fruitless frustration, and in 1932 arguably the greatest seagoing marvel of all time made its appearance.

It was the French liner *Normandie*. Designed by Vladimir Yourkevitch, a Russian emigrant to France, the 1,028-foot-long *Normandie* featured a slanting bow like a clipper ship and a streamlined slim hull. But it was her interior that was even more dazzling. The ship's most luxurious suites contained four bedrooms, a private bath, and even a private dining room. Few, however, used the private dining facilities

BELOW: Ocean travel was not only reserved for the wealthy. The American-owned, British-operated Atlantic Transport Line proclaimed itself as "unique in the travel world" on this poster from around 1920. And it was—it's liners were designed to carry only "tourist third class" passengers, making fares far more affordable (forty pounds per round trip) than those of the luxury liners. It was a strategy that attracted legions of low-fare-seeking students who responded to the line's other slogan, "Spend your long vacation in America." Here, a student says good-bye to his professor who has sent him across the Atlantic to broaden his horizons.

since the vessel's first-class dining room was, by far, the largest single room on the seven seas. Three hundred and five feet long, forty-six feet wide, and twenty-eight feet high, its 150 tables sat 700 people at a time and served them meals more luxurious than any that could be found in the world's greatest restaurants. The room was illuminated with twelve enormous glass pillars and two stupendous chandeliers, all created by René Lalique. It was not long before the *Normandie* became widely known as the "Ship of Light." Adding to the vessel's splendor were such features as an indoor and outdoor pool, a chapel, and a theater in which both live productions were staged and motion pictures were shown. The *Normandie's* revolutionary technological features included fuel-efficient turboelectric engines, an early form of radar, and the world's first oceangoing gyroscopic compass system.

All of these technological advancements enabled the 83,423-gross-ton *Normandie* to attain an average speed of thirty knots and to make record transatlantic crossings in its continual Blue Riband competition with Britain's *Queen Mary*. One could only wonder what the next great superliner would be like. But once again world events would intervene, and the world was again plunged into war, this time due greatly to German leader Adolf Hitler's desire for world conquest.

NORMANDIE
C.ⁱᵉ G.ˡᵉ TRANSATLANTIQUE
French Line
LE HAVRE — SOUTHAMPTON — NEW-YORK
SERVICE RÉGULIER
PAR PAQUEBOTS DE LUXE
ET A CLASSE UNIQUE

This 1935 poster of the SS *Normandie* is regarded as one of the most spectacular Art Deco ship images ever created. It was designed by Ukrainian-French graphic artist and typographer Adolph Mouron Cassandre, a pioneer in poster design.

SCHARNHORST
Germany - BB
(GNEISENAU Class)
(1939)

WORLD WAR II

The Treaty of Versailles, signed on June 28, 1919, officially ended World War I. According to the terms of the treaty, restrictions were placed on the tonnage of Germany's surface fleet, and the construction of submarines was absolutely forbidden. Soon after Adolf Hitler came to power in 1933, however, Germany began secretly building new U-boats that were in place when, in 1939, World War II began.

Possessing the largest merchant fleet in the world (some 1,900 oceangoing ships) Great Britain—as an island—required more than one million tons of food and materials to be shipped in each week and depended on its sea trade for its very survival. Thus, as was the case in World War I, German leaders knew that their best hope of winning the war was to strangle England in this new Battle of the Atlantic—a battle that lasted the entire span of the war. The battle began when a German U-47 penetrated the Scottish harbor of Scapa Flow on October 14, 1939, and sank the battleship HMS *Royal Oak*, killing 833 of the 1,234-man crew.

There were other striking similarities between the two world wars, fought only twenty-one years apart. As had occurred in the first global conflict, Britain quickly proved its surface warship superiority at the outset. In the first major naval action, the Battle of River Plate in the Southern Atlantic (December 13, 1939), the HMS *Exeter*, HMS *Ajax*, and HMS *Achilles* severely damaged the infamous German commerce raider the *Admiral Graf Spee*—which was later sunk by its commander to save his crew. The powerful 42,000-ton *Bismarck*, the pride of the German Navy, was silenced by the Royal Navy on May 27, 1941.

Once again, victory for Germany and its allies depended on the effectiveness of its U-boats. With each passing month, new vessels were added to the U-boat fleet. The German cause was

OPPOSITE TOP LEFT: **Adolf Hitler accepts the Nazi salutes of Reichstag members after announcing the Anschluss, or annexation of Austria, March 1938. Bent on world conquest, Hitler ignored the conditions of the Treaty of Versailles that ended World War I and built a massive military force.**

OPPOSITE BOTTOM LEFT: **The submarine *U-37*— responsible for sinking the British battleship HMS *Royal Oak*—is shown here arriving at Kiel, Germany, on October 23, 1939, after its mission in Scapa Flow. The battleship *Scharnhorst* is anchored behind.**

OPPOSITE TOP RIGHT: **On May 21, 1941, an officer from the cruiser *Prinz Eugen* took this picture of the *Bismarck*, anchored in a Norwegian fjord, as she prepared to depart for the Atlantic. Six days later, the *Bismarck* was to be defeated in the Battle of River Plate.**

OPPOSITE BOTTOM RIGHT: **The HMS *Mansfield*, serving with the Royal Canadian Navy, on North Atlantic convoy duty in June 1943.**

BELOW CENTER: **Kriegsmarine commander Karl Dönitz served as a submarine officer in World War I. The mastermind of Germany's U-boat buildup prior to World War II, he was commander of the U-boat fleet from 1936 to 1943, and made Commander in Chief of the German Navy from 1943 to 1945.**

aided also by its early conquest of Norway and France, which gave Germany's navy forward U-boat bases that greatly increased the range of the submarines. In the years between the conflicts, Germans continuously refined U-boat technology, making the boats deadlier than ever. By 1943, German engineers developed an acoustic homing torpedo that could zero in on the loudest noise it heard. At the same time, Admiral Karl Dönitz, commander in chief of the Kriegsmarine (the German Navy), introduced what he named his "wolf pack" tactic, by which a group of U-boats would surface and attack at night—a strategy that, combined with the other new U-boat advantages, resulted in the sinking of three million tons of British shipping in the year 1940 alone.

It was a period so devastating to England that German submariners publicly boasted that this was their "happy time." No wonder that despite the devastating nightly bombings of England and the deadly land battles that took place throughout the conflict, England's prime minister Winston Churchill later wrote in his six-volume masterwork *The Second World War* (1948–54): "The only thing that really frightened me during the war was the U-boat peril" (volume II, *Their Finest Hour*). He expounded on the Battle of the Atlantic in volume V, *Closing the Ring*:

The Battle of the Atlantic was the determining factor all through the war, never for one moment could we forget that everything happening elsewhere, on land, at sea, or in the air, depended ultimately on its outcome... Many gallant actions and incredible feats of endurance are recorded, but the deeds of those who perished will never be known. Our merchant seamen displayed their highest qualities, and the brotherhood of the sea was never more strikingly shown than in their determination to defeat the U-boat.

His fears were well founded, but, as had happened during World War I, a dramatic turnabout took place. Up to 1941, Great Britain had been going it alone, but by the end of that year the Royal Canadian Navy, which had been almost nonexistent when the war broke out, had grown into a considerable force that permitted it to play a significant role in the fighting in the Atlantic.

Even more important was the entry of the United States into the conflict. Almost from the beginning of the war, neutral America had been acting anything but neutral, supplying Great Britain with arms and munitions through the 1940 Destroyers for Bases Agreement (the U.S. government gave England fifty destroyers to use as convoy escorts in return for the right to build military bases on British territory in Canada and the Caribbean)

On August 14, 1941, four months before the United States entered the war, U.S. president Franklin D. Roosevelt met secretly with British prime minister Winston Churchill aboard the USS *Augusta* in Placentia Bay, Newfoundland. This Atlantic Conference resulted in the Atlantic Charter, a joint declaration that enumerated "certain common principles in the national policies of their respective countries on which they base their hopes for a better future for the world." In this photograph taken during the conference, President Roosevelt leans on the arm of his son, Army Air Corps captain Elliot Roosevelt; Prime Minister Churchill is at left.

OPPOSITE: Cargo ships cross the Atlantic in a convoy, carrying guns, tanks, and planes, ca. 1942. Many of them are Liberty ships, built en masse between 1941 and 1945 in American shipyards—many staffed largely by women. Approximately 2,751 Liberty ships were built.

and other legislation that led to the March 1941 Lend-Lease Act, in which the United States was empowered to "sell, transfer title to, exchange, lease, lend, or otherwise dispose of, to any such government [whose defense the President deems vital to the defense of the United States] any defense article." As American aid continued, it became obvious that an undeclared German-American naval war was taking place. And when, on December 7, 1941, Germany's ally Japan attacked Pearl Harbor, the United States, United Kingdom, and other Allies declared war on Japan. On December 11, German Führer Adolf Hitler and Italian dictator Benito Mussolini declared war on the United States.

Ironically, America's entry into the conflict did not immediately turn things around in the Atlantic. Before American ships could reach the war zones in significant numbers, Germany launched its most intensive wave of U-boat attacks. Known as Operation Drumbeat and referred to by German submariners as the second "happy time," the assaults resulted in the sinking of almost five hundred Allied ships. But the impact of the ever-increasing U.S. presence could not be denied. Eventually, American warships became instrumental in the creation of a convoy system far larger and more effective than those that had helped turn the tide in World War I. Critical to this development was the role played by long-range aircraft such as the American Catalina flying boat in attacking German vessels and protecting the convoys.

Many of the other factors that led to the German defeat in the Atlantic were technological in nature. Advancements in radar, for example, played a vital role, particularly once a method for installing it aboard U-boat-seeking aircraft was developed. So too did improvements in both sonar and depth-charge technology. Especially important was the introduction of the Leigh Light, a powerful searchlight that was used along with radar to allow allied aircraft to spot U-boats as they surfaced at night to recharge their batteries. According to several military experts of the day, the drop in allied shipping losses from 600,000 to 200,000 tons per month was due directly to this simple device. Added to all these factors was the invaluable contribution made by British intelligence in breaking what was known as the German naval Enigma codes, ciphers created on a typewriter-like Enigma machine. The codes were broken due to several factors: the stealing of German codebooks, knowledge obtained by the Polish Cipher Bureau, which had constructed a replica of an Enigma machine; and the early use of computers. The breaking of the codes proved vital in directing convoys away from "wolf packs" and in launching attacks against the U-boats themselves.

In the end, just as in World War I, the German plan to deprive England of its needed supplies resulted in failure. By 1945 the great majority of the U-boat fleet had been sunk. The

Sailors work with a Catalina seaplane at the Naval Air Base, Corpus Christi, Texas, in August 1942.

uninterrupted flow of supplies that now flowed into Great Britain led directly to the invasion of German-held France and ultimately Allied victory. On June 6, 1944, D-Day, the Allies launched Operation Overlord on the beaches of Normandy—the largest seaborne invasion in history, with over 156,000 troops facing the Nazi's "Atlantic Wall" of defenses.

The victory came at a staggering price for both sides. Although numbers vary, between 1939 and 1945 some 3,500 Allied ships and more than 780 U-boats were sunk in the Battle of the Atlantic. Approximately 85,000 Allied seamen were killed, while more than 30,000 German submariners (a 75 percent casualty rate) lost their lives.

Aside from the millions of combatants and civilians who were killed or seriously wounded on land, the naval aspect of World War II was the costliest in history. But the greatest threat to democracy ever presented had been overcome. And out of the war came technological innovations that engendered profound transformations. None was greater than the impact of the jet engine, an advancement that led to the fact that, well before the twentieth century was over, and despite the fact that a number of magnificent new ocean liners such as the *United States* and the *Queen Elizabeth II* were built, more travelers would be crossing the Atlantic by flying over it than by sailing its waters.

RIGHT: Torpedo bombers TBF Avengers fly in formation over Norfolk, Virginia, September 1942. In the Battle of the Atlantic, Avengers provided air cover for convoys.

LEFT: Coast Guardsmen on the deck of the U.S. Coast Guard Cutter *Spencer* watch the explosion of a depth charge that sunk the Nazi submarine *U-175*, which had been stalking the center of a large convoy, April 17, 1943.

ABOVE: As in World War I, in World War II America's entry into the war was a major determining factor in the winning of the battle for control of the Atlantic. Again, it was America's ability to quickly muster its shipbuilding resources and capabilities that helped bring about the defeat of Germany and that country's allies on the sea. This painting by famed twentieth-century artist Thomas Hart Benton, called *Cut the Line* (1944), shows a crowd's excitement at the launch of an LST (Landing Ship, Tank), one of the many advanced war vessels developed between the two world wars.

RIGHT: This harrowing photograph was taken on D-Day, June 6, 1944. Under heavy Nazi machine-gun fire, American soldiers exit the ramp of a Coast Guard landing boat that just arrived at "Omaha Beach" on the coast of France.

BELOW: When LaGuardia Airport opened in the New York City borough of Queens in October 1939, it was the biggest and most expensive airport ever built. The Art Deco–inspired Marine Air Terminal was dedicated in March 1940. Used by transatlantic Clipper planes before the war, the terminal was converted to accommodate newer planes after the war. The terminal is still in use today as a base for commuter airlines, air taxis, private aircraft, and a weather service.

ABOVE: Airships—nonrigid, semirigid, and rigid balloons (dirigibles or zeppelins), filled with gas and run by engine—were first developed in the nineteenth century. A German zeppelin was the first aircraft to cross the Atlantic in 1924. Used for commercial travel, and also as bombers in World War I, airships were popular until the famous Hindenburg disaster of 1937, when the Hindenburg burned while landing at the Lakehurst Naval Air Station, New Jersey, killing thirty-six. Here the Hindenburg is shown in Lakehurst about three months before its fatal accident.

OPPOSITE BOTTOM: The *Queen Mary 2 (QM2)*, launched in March 2003, is the largest ocean liner ever built—built at a cost of $800 million, she is 1,132 feet long, 151,400 gross tons, with thirteen passenger decks and a capacity of 3,056. The behemoth is only 118 feet shorter than the 1,250-foot-tall Empire State Building (not including its antennae). In this April 2007 photograph, the *QM2* is shown in the port of Quebec.

RIGHT: Charles Lindbergh's successful solo flight across the Atlantic in 1927 opened the world's eyes to the possibility of commercial flight. That became a reality with the development of the jet engine during World War II. Beginning in 1952, companies from nations around the world began establishing commercial airline companies, steadily drawing passengers away from the oceangoing steamships. In 1976, the Concorde supersonic transport, shown here, a joint venture subsidized by the French and British governments, began commercial service; it quickly became an icon of the aircraft industry and popular culture. Capable of reaching Mach 2.02 speed, the Concorde set many transatlantic records, including a flight from New York to London in 2 hours, 52 minutes, and 59 seconds. For twenty-seven years, the Concorde continued to attract wealthy air travelers. But its only crash in 2000, a drop-off in international travel after the events of September 11, 2001, and the burden of the line's enormous development costs combined to forced the French and British governments to shut it down. Perhaps the Concorde's greatest contribution was the glimpse it provided into what the future of commercial aviation may hold in store.

THE NEW SHIPS

The nature of transatlantic shipping was also dramatically altered by technological advancements begun during World War II. Today, thanks to cutting-edge computers, global positioning and anticollision radar systems, and the most sophisticated sonar equipment yet devised, much of the cargo that crosses the Atlantic is transported aboard enormous vessels hardly imaginable less that a century ago. Arguably the most important of these ships is a type of vessel that has revolutionized the way in which cargo is loaded, unloaded, and moved across the seas. Called a container ship, it is the vital cog in the system for moving cargo known as intermodal freight transport. Under this system, more than one mode of transportation—commonly trucks, trains, and ships—moves freight without handling until it reaches its final destination. The container ship was the brainchild of a North Carolina trucker named Malcolm McLean who, in the late 1940s, came up with the idea of putting truck trailers on cargo ships. By the mid-1950s, ship owners discovered that by placing their freight in metal containers shaped like the beds of truck trailers, they could both maximize the cargo-carrying capacity of their vessels and facilitate the loading and unloading of the freight.

Measuring as long as nine hundred feet, today's container ships can carry ten times as much cargo as the freighters that transported goods in the first four decades of the 1900s. Because all containers are of a standard size, they can lock on to any other container. And, instead of needing twenty men to load twenty tons of goods per hour, the container system makes it possible for a crew of ten, working with giant cranes, to load twice as much cargo in just a few minutes.

RIGHT: A Very Large Crude Carrier (VLCC) unloads crude oil in Antifer Harbor, France, about thirteen miles north of the major port of Le Havre. A separate deepwater oil terminal was built in Antifer in 1972 to receive supertankers. Because of their enormous size, the largest supertankers cannot enter many of the world's harbors. Instead, they drop anchor outside the harbor, and the oil is transported to onshore storage tanks via long pipelines.

As with many advancements, however, the efficient container ship is accompanied by potential serious problems. Because of the size of the enormous ships, ports that receive the vessels are often pressured to expand and deepen their channels. The dredging of these ports presents the very real danger of the destruction of the habitat of bay bottoms and the marine life that depends upon it for its existence.

Even more serious environmental problems have arisen due to the presence of the even larger oceangoing vessels known as Ultra Large Crude Carriers (ULCCs), which have become essential in transporting the world's most important commodity—oil. Over 1,500 feet in length and weighing some one million tons when fully loaded, they are double-hulled to prevent oil spills. But this precaution has not prevented what environmentalists have long believed was an inevitability. The wreck of the *Exxon Valdez* off the coast of Alaska in 1989 is a notorious example. When this supertanker missed the entrance to a channel and crashed upon rocks, it split open and spilled some eleven million gallons of oil into the pristine waters of the Alaskan coastline. The oil polluted more than twelve hundred miles of coast, resulting in the destruction of more than twenty-five thousand seabirds, seals, otters, and other mammals. More than 140 bald eagles, already an endangered species, were killed. Even some twenty years later, scientists and environmentalists are still not certain what the negative long-term effects of the spill will be.

BELOW: The ships of today include vessels that centuries of mariners could never have imagined. The semi-submersible heavy-lift ship is capable of submerging its deck underwater beneath a stricken ship and then raising the deck with its mammoth burden aboard. Here, the Dutch semi-submersible MV *Mighty Servant 2* is shown in a 1988 photograph after it has just extracted the guided missile frigate USS *Samuel B. Roberts*, which was damaged by an Iranian mine in the Persian Gulf.

OPPOSITE BOTTOM: Today, approximately 90 percent of non–bulk cargo (products such as grain, ore, and coal) worldwide is transported on container ships. In the year 2000 alone some nineteen million containers made over two hundred million trips. The Odense Steel Shipyard in Denmark is the builder of the largest container ships in the world, the 11,000 TEU Maersk series (one TEU represents the cargo capacity of a standard shipping container twenty feet long and eight feet wide). Here the *Elly Maersk*—built in 2007 and approximately 1,138 feet long—one of eight in the series, docks at the port in Zeebrugge, Belgium, in September 2007.

ABOVE: The armed galley of ancient times, the man-of-war of the fifteenth and sixteenth centuries, the frigate of the seventeenth and eighteenth centuries, the steam-powered ironclads of the nineteenth century, the U-boats and aircraft carriers of the twentieth century—warships have become increasingly more sophisticated and deadly throughout civilization. During the 1982 Falkland Islands War, fought between Great Britain and Argentina, the Atlantic was the site of the first armed conflict involving nuclear-powered submarines as well as missiles. This image is of a British Trafalgar class submarine of the Royal Navy, the HMS *Turbulent*, docked at Port Canaveral, Florida, in 1993. Originally launched in 1982, *Turbulent* was modernized in 1997.

MS *Freedom of the Seas* is one of three cruise ships in the Freedom Class series owned by Royal Caribbean International. The ships in this series, as of this writing, are the largest passenger ships in the world. Although not the longest (1,112 feet), *Freedom* can hold 4,300 passengers and 1,300 crew members on its fifteen passenger decks. It also boasts the first onboard surf park and a water park with geysers and a cascading waterfall. Her maiden voyage was in June 2006, during which this image was taken.

BELOW: A 2005 photograph of a melting toe of the Athabasca Glacier, part of the Columbia Icefield, the largest icefield in the Canadian Rockies. Because of climate warming, the glacier has been receding for the last 125 years, losing half its volume; the pace has accelerated in the last few decades.

451

THE ATLANTIC WORLD CONFIRMED

OCEAN ECOLOGY

Today's container ships and ULCCs are the result of modern technological innovations. But the twentieth and early twenty-first centuries have also witnessed changes that have profoundly altered age-old Atlantic undertakings. Almost nothing, for example, had a greater lure for the initial settlement of the northeastern regions of the New World than the seemingly endless abundance of life-sustaining and commercially invaluable cod and other fish that dwelled in the Grand Banks in particular. Today, however, centuries of overfishing, and the modern introduction of technologically sophisticated factory-freezer ships, has so depleted the fish supply that international fishing organizations have been forced to impose severe restrictions on fishing in these waters, even closing them altogether for an extended period of time.

The whaling industry has been even more dramatically altered. Beginning in the post–World War II era, the introduction of such cruel and devastating whale-hunting weapons as the explosive harpoon led to impassioned protests from animal rights groups. The most widespread concern, however, centered around the very survival of the whales.

By 1946, it became clear that centuries of unregulated whaling had depleted whale populations so severely that several species were severely endangered. In November of that year, the International Convention for the Regulation of Whaling (ICRW), an agreement designed to make whaling sustainable, was signed by forty-two nations and went into effect. The primary instrument through which the ICRW sought to protect whales from overhunting was the establishment of the International Whaling Commission (IWC). In

1986, the IWC imposed a five-year moratorium on commercial whaling, a mandate that has been extended to the present. It is an edict that, in recent years, has come under attack from pro-whaling nations who argue that certain species have again become sufficiently populous to permit the resumption of commercial whaling, at least on a limited basis. What seems certain is that this issue will remain unresolved for the foreseeable future.

Another urgent topic of debate is the effect of global warming and glacial melting on the world's oceans, which will raise the sea level, change weather patterns, threaten natural habitats, and effect agriculture and commerce in unforeseen ways. One start is the Kyoto Protocol, enacted in 1997 and activated in 2005, which seeks to address the issue by having signatories reduce or monitor carbon dioxide emissions or greenhouse gases.

EARTH'S FINAL FRONTIER

From the heroic voyages of St. Brendan and his fellow Irish monks to the courageous journeys of Christopher Columbus, to the accomplishments of scores of men such as Prince Henry the Navigator, Thomas Newcomen, Isambard Brunel, and Donald McKay, the making of the Atlantic World has been marked not only by national but also by individual achievements in meeting the challenges the Atlantic has presented. It is a tradition that was carried on in a variety of ways in the twentieth and early twenty-first centuries by men and women determined to make their mark in Atlantic history. Among them were British Captain John Alcock and Lieutenant Arthur Whitten Brown who, in 1919, made the first nonstop flight across the great ocean; Charles Lindbergh who, in 1927, became the first to fly across the Atlantic alone;

ABOVE: In 1928, pioneer deep-sea explorer William Beebe, who made record descents in his spherical metal diving vessel that he called a bathysphere, wrote in *Beneath Tropic Seas* (1928): "It was necessary to get used to the strange costume, the complete submergence under water and the excitement of a new world of unknown life... But after all my silly fears have been allayed... I am still almost inarticulate. We need a whole new vocabulary, new adjectives, to describe the design and colors of under sea." Beebe poses with the bathysphere next to his co-inventor Otis Barton, ca. 1930.

TOP AND RIGHT: The breathtaking vistas so eloquently described by William Beebe are displayed in these photographs of reefs at the Florida Keys National Marine Sanctuary.

OPPOSITE TOP: Jacques Cousteau—giant in the field of oceanography, was developer of the aqualung, captain of the famed research vessel the *Calypso*, filmmaker, environmentalist, and much more. The French explorer developed

a successful two-person submersible called a Diving Saucer, which during the period from 1959 to 1970 made over 750 four- to six-hour dives (2,000 dive hours) to depths of about 1,000 feet.

OPPOSITE BOTTOM: *Alvin*, a manned deep-ocean research submersible owned by the U.S. Navy and operated by the Woods Hole Oceanographic Institution, was launched in 1964. Since then, *Alvin* has carried 12,000 people on over 4,000 dives. *Alvin* can stay submerged for ten hours and dive to 14,764

feet. This photograph is from about 1978. "We can only sense," wrote marine biologist Rachel Carson in her seminal book *The Sea Around Us* (1950), "that in the deep and turbulent recesses of the sea are hidden mysteries far greater than any we have solved." Design for an *Alvin* replacement vessel is under way.

Per Lindstrand and Sir Richard Branson who, in 1987, flew 3,075 miles across the Atlantic in the largest hot-air balloon ever built, in the process devastating the previous existing record by 900 miles; Tori Murden, who in 1999, became the first woman to cross the Atlantic alone in a rowboat; and fourteen-year-old British schoolboy Michael Perham who, in January 2007, became the youngest person to sail single-handedly across the Atlantic.

It is this type of exploration of the possible that has characterized the history of the Atlantic world. And today there is yet another type of exploration, not on land, not in space, but deep beneath the Atlantic and the other oceans of the world. It has been called the final frontier and it is an exploration that is already leading to a far greater understanding of the Atlantic itself.

Not that an awareness of the incalculable value of knowledge of the world beneath the Atlantic and other seas is new. "Aside from its importance to many branches of science," J. Harland Paul wrote in his book about the final trip of the first geophysical research vessel, *The Last Cruise of the Carnegie* (1932) "A knowledge of the oceans has a practical value for mankind. The intelligent development of our fishing industries, the laying of oceanic cables, the proper construction of harbor-works, oceanic commerce and navigation, [and an understanding of tides and currents], as well as long-range weather forecasting, are all dependent on an understanding of the ocean."

What is new is that today scientists and oceanographers have the tools to examine the waters of the Atlantic and the world beneath it as never before. As Woods Hole Oceanographic Institution technician Peter Delany has written on the National Oceanic and Atmospheric Administration website, "Our ability to observe the ocean environment has finally caught up with our imaginations."

The technology that makes today's oceanic explorations so effective includes observation tools such as satellites that supply detailed images of the ocean's surface as they orbit the Earth. It also includes sophisticated sonar systems that make it possible to probe and map the deepest regions of the world beneath the sea. As in space exploration, however, the greatest accomplishments undersea have been achieved through personal observation made possible by manned submarinelike vessels called submersibles and remotely operated vehicles known as ROVs (Remotely Operated Vehicles).

Through the use of submersibles capable of diving more than fourteen thousand feet to the ocean floor, remarkable, previously unknown deepwater ecosystems have been discovered. In these ecosystems, and in areas surrounding the hydrothermal vents created by the more than five thousand active underwater volcanoes, oceanographers have discovered

ABOVE: The remotely operated vehicle (ROV) *Kraken*, operated by the National Undersea Research Program (NURP), is lowered for a dive in the Atlantic to further unlock mysteries that lay beneath the great ocean.

RIGHT: Black smoke erupts from a midocean ridge hydrothermal vent in the Atlantic, in a photograph taken for NURP.

As the Australian author, adventurer and master mariner Captain Alan Villiers reminded us in *Men, Ships, and the Sea* (1962), "Man spent centuries planning ways to move ships against wind and tide. But from primitive paddle-wheeler to twin-screw liner took only eighty years." Villier's example is a prime indication of how the advancements made both on and below the Atlantic in modern times have kept pace with the extraordinary changes and achievements that have characterized the long history of the great ocean. Here a mammoth cruise ship passes a replica of Christopher Columbus's flagship *Santa Maria* in 2005, off the Madeira Islands of Portugal.

unique enzymes and other materials that scientists now believe will one day be instrumental in the development of new, highly effective medicines in the battle against cancer, Alzheimer's, and other diseases. Already, a medicine derived from compounds found in a particular species of deep-sea sponge has in a number of cases proved to be effective in reducing the size of brain tumors.

The exploration of deep-sea volcanoes in particular has resulted in a multitude of revelations, including the existence of what may be the world's richest ore deposits produced by hydrothermal vents. Many economic geologists now predict that in the future it will be possible to mine both active and formerly active vents for their massive metallic deposits.

These are but a few of the discoveries that inspire oceanographers from around the world to continue in the same tradition of exploration that has resulted in so many remarkable achievements made on the Atlantic's surface. Among the greatest discoveries of all is the realization that we, as the heirs of the cultures of Europe, Africa, and the Americas, all centering in the Atlantic, are together part of one great community. As Frederick Tolles expressed in his book *Quakers and the Atlantic Culture* (1960): "We first became familiar with the idea of the Atlantic Community as a strategic concept during the Second World War, but the Atlantic Community as a cultural fact was a matter of almost everyday experience…in the seventeenth and eighteenth centuries." Writing in the *American Historical Review* (1946), historian Carleton Hayes summed it up in one sentence: "The Atlantic Community," he concluded, "has been an outstanding fact and a prime factor in modern history."

BIBLIOGRAPHY

Allen, Everett S. *Children of the Light: The Rise and Fall of New Bedford Whaling and the Death of the Arctic Fleet*. Orleans, MA: Parnassus Imprints, 1983.

Allen, Leslie. *Liberty: The Statue and the American Dream*. New York: Statue of Liberty-Ellis Island Foundation with the cooperation of the National Geographic Society, 1985.

Andrews, Kenneth R. *The Spanish Caribbean: Trade and Plunder, 1530–1630*. New Haven: Yale University Press, 1978.

Axelrod, Alan. *Profiles in Audacity: Great Decisions and How They Were Made*. New York: Sterling Publishing Co., Inc. 2006.

Bailey, Thomas A., and Paul B. Ryan. *The Lusitania Disaster: An Episode in Modern Warfare and Diplomacy*. New York: Free Press, 1975.

Bailyn, Bernard. *Atlantic History: Concepts and Contours*. Cambridge, MA: Harvard University Press, 2005.

———. *The Ideological Origins of the American Revolution*. Cambridge, MA: Harvard University Press, 1992.

———. *The Peopling of North America: An Introduction*. New York: Random House, 1986.

Ball, J. N. *Merchants and Merchandise: The Expansion of Trade in Europe, 1500–1630*. New York: St. Martin's Press, 1977.

Ballard, Robert D., and Malcolm McConnell. *Adventures in Ocean Exploration: From the Discovery of the Titanic to the Search for Noah's Flood*. Washington, DC: National Geographic, 2001.

Barker, Felix, Malcolm Ross-Macdonald, and Duncan Castlereagh. *The Glorious Age of Exploration*. Garden City, NY: Doubleday, 1973.

Bartoletti, Susan C. *Black Potatoes: The Story of the Great Irish Famine, 1845–1850*. Boston: Houghton Mifflin, 2001.

Berkhofer, Robert F., Jr. *The White Man's Indian: Images of the American Indian from Columbus to the Present*. New York: Random House, 1978.

Berry, Mary F. M, and John W. Blasingame. *Long Memory: The Black Experience in America*. New York: Oxford University Press, 1982.

Blackburn, Robin. *The Making of New World Slavery: From the Baroque to the Modern, 1492–1800*. London: Verso, 1997.

Boorstin, Daniel J. *The Americans: The Colonial Experience*. New York: Random House, 1958.

———. *The Americans: The National Experience*. New York: Random House, 1965.

———. *The Discoverers: A History of Man's Search to Know His World and Himself*. New York: Random House, 1985.

Butel, Paul. *The Atlantic*. New York: Routledge, 1999.

Carson, Rachel. *The Sea Around Us*. New York: Oxford University Press, 1951.

Casson, Lionel. *The Ancient Mariners: Seafarers and Sea Fighters of the Mediterranean in Ancient Times*. Princeton, NJ: Princeton University Press, 1991.

Churchill, Winston. *The Second World War*. Boston: Houghton Mifflin, 1948–1953.

Chaunu, Pierre, and Hugette Chaunu. "The Atlantic Economy and the World Economy." *Essays in European Economic History, 1500–1800*. Oxford: Clarendon Press, 1974.

Clark, Arthur H. *The Clipper Ship Era: An Epitome of Famous American and British Clipper Ships, Their Owners, Builders, Commanders, and Crews 1843–1869*. New York: G.P. Putnam's Sons, 1910.

Coan, Peter M. *Ellis Island: Interviews in Their Own Words*. New York: Checkmark Books, 1997.

Cooke, Alistair. *Alistair Cooke's America*. New York: Alfred Knopf, 1974.

Craig, Gerald M. *Upper Canada: The Formative Years, 1784–1841*. Toronto: McClelland and Stewart, 1963.

Curtin, Phillip D., et al. *African History*. Boston: Little, Brown and Company, 1978.

Davidson, Marshall B. *Life in America*. Boston: Houghton Mifflin, 1951.

Davies, K. G. *The North Atlantic World in the Seventeenth Century*. Minneapolis: University of Minnesota Press, 1974.

Davis, H. P. *Black Democracy: The Story of Haiti*. New York: Biblo and Tannen, 1967.

Duffy, James. *Portugal in Africa*. London: Penguin, 1962.

Ellis Island Oral History Project. Library at the Ellis Island Immigration Museum. New York, 1973–present.

Ellis, Richard. *Imagining Atlantis*. New York: Alfred Knopf, 1998.

———. *Men and Whales*. New York: Lyons Press, 1999.

Games, Alison. *Migration and the Origins of the English Atlantic World*. Cambridge, MA: Harvard University Press, 1999.

Gillis, John R. *Islands of the Mind: How the Human Imagination Created the Atlantic World*. New York: Palgrave Macmillan, 2004.

Greene, Jack P., and J. R. Pole. *Colonial British America: Essays in the New History of the Early Modern Era*. Baltimore: Johns Hopkins University Press, 1984.

Handlin, Oscar. *The Uprooted: The Epic Story of the Great Migrations that Made the American People*. Boston: Little, Brown and Company, 1951.

Handy, Amy. *The Golden Age of Sail*. New York: Todtri, 1996.

Haring, C. H. *The Spanish Empire in America*. New York: Harcourt, Brace & World, 1947.

Horton, Edward. *The Illustrated History of the Submarine*. Garden City, NY: Doubleday, 1974.

Jacobson, Timothy. *Discovering America: Journeys in Search of a New World*. London: Blandford, 1991.

Jeremy, David J. *Transatlantic Industrial Revolution: The Diffusion of Textile Technologies Between Britain and America, 1790–1830s*. Cambridge, MA: MIT Press, 1981.

Jessop, Violet, and John Maxtone-Graham, eds. *Titanic Survivor: The Newly Discovered Memoirs of Violet Jessop Who Survived Both the Titanic and Britannic Disasters*. Dobbs Ferry, NY: Sheridan House, 1997.

Jones, Gwyn. *The Norse Atlantic Saga: Being the Norse Voyages of Discovery and Settlement to Iceland, Greenland, America*. Oxford: Oxford University Press, 1964.

July, Robert W. *A History of the African People*. New York: Scribner's, 1970.

Klein, Herbert. "The Atlantic Slave Trade to 1650." *Tropical Babylons: Sugar and the Making of the Atlantic World, 1450–1680*. Ed. Stuart B. Schwartz. Chapel Hill: University of North Carolina Press, 2004.

Klooster, Win, and Alfred Padula, eds. *The Atlantic World: Essays on Slavery, Migration, and Imagination*. Upper Saddle River, NJ: Pearson, 2005.

Kupperman, Karen O., ed. *Captain John Smith: A Select Edition of his Writings*. Chapel Hill: University of North Carolina Press, 1988.

Kurlansky, Mark. *Cod: A Biography of the Fish That Changed the World*. New York: Walker, 1997.

———. *Salt: A World History*. New York: Walker, 2002.

Lancaster, Bruce. *The American Heritage History of the American Revolution*. New York: American Heritage/Bonanza Books, 1971.

Lane, Kris E. *Pillaging the Empire: Piracy in the Americas, 1500–1700*. Armonk, NY: M.E. Sharpe, 1998.

Lang, James. *Conquest and Commerce: Spain and England in the Americas*. New York: Academic Press, 1975.

Lovejoy, Paul E. *Transformations in Slavery: A History of Slavery in Africa*. New York: Cambridge University Press, 1983.

Lubbock, Basil. *The Colonial Clippers*. Glasgow: J. Brown & Son, 1921.

Maddocks, Melvin. *The Atlantic Crossing*. Alexandria, VA: Time-Life Books, 1981.

Mangione, Jerre, and Ben Morreale. *La Storia: Five Centuries of the Italian American Experience*. New York: HarperCollins, 1992.

Mann, Charles C. *1491: New Revelations of the Americas Before Columbus*. New York: Alfred Knopf, 2005.

Manning, Patrick. *Slavery and African Life: Occidental, Oriental, and African Slave Trades*. New York: Cambridge University Press, 1990.

Marcus, G. J. *The Conquest of the North Atlantic*. New York: Oxford University Press, 1981.

Meinig, D. W. *The Shaping of America: A Geographical Perspective on 500 Years of History; Volume 1: Atlantic America*. New Haven: Yale University Press, 1986.

———. The *Shaping of America: A Geographical Perspective on 500 Years of History; Volume 2: Continental America, 1800–1867*. New Haven: Yale University Press, 1993.

———. *The Shaping of America: A Geographical Perspective on 500 Years of History; Volume 3: Transcontinental America, 1850–1915*. New Haven: Yale University Press, 1998.

Meir, Golda. *My Life*. New York: G. P. Putnam's Sons, 1975.

Mintz, Sidney. *Sweetness and Power: The Place of Sugar in Modern History*. New York: Viking Penguin, 1985.

Mollat du Jourdin, Michel. *Europe and the Sea*. Oxford: Blackwell, 1993.

Moquin, Wayne, and Charles L. Van Doren. *Great Documents in American Indian History*. New York: Da Capo Press, 1995.

Morison, Samuel Eliot. *Admiral of the Ocean Sea: A Life of Christopher Columbus*. Boston: Little, Brown and Company, 1942.

———. *The European Discovery of America, Volumes 1 and 2*. New York: Oxford University Press, 1971.

———. *The Maritime History of Massachusetts*. Boston: Houghton Mifflin, 1921.

Nicholson, Norman L. *The Boundaries of the Canadian Confederation*. Toronto: Macmillan, 1979.

Outhwaite, Leonard. *The Atlantic: A History of the Ocean*. New York: Coward-McCann, 1957.

Parry, J. H., ed. *The European Reconnaissance: Selected Documents*. New York: Walker, 1968.

Polo, Marco. *The Travels of Marco Polo*. Ronad Latham, trans. London: Penguin, 1958.

Raban, Jonathan. *The Oxford Book of the Sea*. New York: Oxford University Press, 1992.

Rawley, James A. *The Transatlantic Slave Trade: A History*. New York: Norton, 1981.

Reeves, Pamela. *Ellis Island: Gateway to the American Dream*. New York: Crescent Books, 1991.

Rich, E. E. *The Fur Trade and the Northwest to 1857*. Toronto: McClelland and Stewart, 1967.

Sandler, Martin W. *Island of Hope: The Story of Ellis Island and the Journey to America*. New York: Scholastic, 2004.

———. *Resolute: The Epic Search for the Northwest Passage and John Franklin, and the Discovery of the Queen's Ghost Ship*. New York: Sterling Publishing Co., Inc., 2006.

Schama, Simon. *Citizens: A Chronicle of the French Revolution*. New York: Alfred Knopf, 1989.

———. *Rough Crossings: Britain, the Slaves, and the American Revolution*. New York: HarperCollins, 2006.

Schlesinger, Roger. *In the Wake of Columbus: The Impact of the New World on Europe*. Wheeling, IL: Harlan Davidson, 1996.

Schwartz, Stuart B. *Tropical Babylons: Sugar and the Making of the Atlantic World, 1450–1680*. Chapel Hill: University of North Carolina Press, 2004.

Stols, Eddy. "The Expansion of the Sugar Market in Western Europe." *Tropical Babylons: Sugar and the Making of the Atlantic World, 1450–1680*. Stuart B. Schwartz, ed. Chapel Hill: University of North Carolina Press, 2004.

Server, Dean. *The Golden Age of Steam*. New York: Todtri, 1996.

———. *The Golden Age of Ocean Liners*. New York: Todtri, 1996.

Seymour, M. J. *The Transformation of the North Atlantic World, 1492–1763: An Introduction*. Westport, CT: Praeger, 2004.

Solow, Barbara L. *Slavery and the Rise of the Atlantic System*. New York: Cambridge University Press, 1991.

Taylor, George R. *The Transportation Revolution, 1815–1860*. New York: Holt, Rinehart and Winston, 1951.

Time-Life Books. *Immigrants: The New Americans*. Alexandria, VA: Time-Life Books, 1999.

Trudel, Marcel. *Introduction to New France*. Toronto: Holt, Rinehart and Winston, 1968.

Villiers, Alan. *Men, Ships, and the Sea*. Washington, DC: National Geographic Society, 1962.

Wallace, Anthony F. C. *Rockdale: The Growth of an American Village in the Early Industrial Revolution*. New York: Knopf, 1978.

ACKNOWLEDGMENTS

A book of this scope requires the help and support of many people and I have had the good fortune of being aided by a host of incredibly talented and dedicated individuals. First of all, I owe a special debt of gratitude to Carlo DeVito, editorial director of Sterling Innovation, for having suggested this project to me. And I am most appreciative of the support and invaluable suggestions I received from Sterling editorial director Michael Fragnito. I also wish to express my deep gratitude to Dennis Reinhartz for having so thoroughly and expertly checked the accuracy and approach of the entire content of this book and for contributing such a marvelous foreword.

As with my previous Sterling book, I am also indebted to a host of dedicated and accomplished professionals who made this book possible, including, at Sterling, publisher Jason Prince, creative director and book cover designer Karen Nelson, production editor Scott Amerman, senior art designer Rachel Maloney, managing editor Rebecca Maines, pre-press manager Pip Tannenbaum, senior production manager Eli Hausknecht, and manager of contracts and business affairs Brooke Barona. Special thanks to designer Amy Henderson and copyeditor Kalista Johnston.

As always, I am deeply indebted to my wife, Carol Weiss Sandler, who not only contributed her considerable research skills but who once again accommodated to the schedule of a workaholic husband. And I am deeply grateful for the help I received from Katherine Worten, Mark Lewis of the Library of Congress, and Claudia Jew of the Mariners' Museum.

Finally, I have always prided myself for having a facility with words. Yet, I am at a loss to adequately express what Barbara Berger has brought to this book. Her superb editing, her invaluable aid in illustration selection, and her suggestions as to organization and content are at the heart of every page. Barbara: whatever shortcomings the book may contain are due to me. Whatever magic is herein contained is due in great measure to you; truth be told, this book is as much your doing as it is mine.

INDEX

PICTURE CREDITS

Courtesy of the Architect of the Capitol: 120: Discovery of the Mississippi, William H. Powell

Courtesy of Geography & Map Division, Library of Congress

x: g3300 ct000668; xi: LC-USZC2-3365, LC-USZ62-73823; 3t: detail, g3290 ct000342; 21: g9112g ct000136; 29: detail, g3200 mf000070; 54–55: g3200 ct00725; 59: g3290 hl000010; 60–61: g3290m gct00001; 65: detail, g3300 ct000667; 68–69: g3200.ct000270; 80t: detail, g3715 ct000001; 80b: detail, g3300 ct000612; 81: detail, g3300 lh000083; 82–83: g3200 mf000070; 106–7: g492h lh000348; 109: g3290m gct00084, title page; 115: detail, g3300 np000055; 122–23: g3290m gct00084 map 1; 135: g3880 ct00077; 137b: g5751sm grb00001; 138–9: g3934s ct000068; 142–3: g3880 ct000377; 148-49: detail, g3804n ar111100; 160: detail, g3880 ct000370; 174–5: g8200 ct001455; 192–3: g3884y ar301100; 200–201: g3300 ar006200; 206: detail, g3300 ar008700; 206–7: g3300 ar010400; 226–7: g3884y ar146200; 263: g5314y ct000328; 264: g5200 ct000170

Courtesy of Gutenberg.org: 167t: History of Egypt, G. Maspero

Courtesy of Hemispheres Antique Maps & Prints, http://www.betzmaps.com/: 33

Courtesy of the Library and Archives of Canada: 66–67: C-010618; 130t: C-002771; 198: c-001090; 335: c-016105

Courtesy of Prints & Photographs Division, Library of Congress:

i: LC-USZC2-1268; ii–iii: LC-USZC4-12774; vi: LC-DIG-pga-02392; 0–1: LC-DIG-ppmsc-08213; 11: LC-USZ62-50239; 14: LC-USZ62-3032; 18t: LC-USZ62-3028; 22–23: LC-DIG-pga-00710; 25: LC-USZ62-95150; 26: LC-USZC4-2153; 37: LC-USZC4-2919; 38: LC-USZ62-3088; 39: LC-USZC4-4188; 41: LC-USZ62-110343; 44tl: LC-USZ62-39304; 44tr: LC-DIG-ga-00660; 44bl: LC-USZ62-1784; 47: LC-USZ62-103803; 52–53: LC-USZ62-3000; 56: LC-USZ62-26683; 63c: LC-USZC2-2116; 63b: LC-DIG-ppmsc-05876; 64: LC-USZ62-3029; 66: LC-DIG-02616; 72–73: LC-USZC4-5269; 74t–b: LC-USZ62-370, LC-DIG-ppmsca 02937, LC-USZ62-373, LC-USZ62-75947; 75tl: LC-USZ62-4805; 75tr: LC-USZ62-54017; 75br: LC-USZ62-53339; 76l: LC-USZC4-4913; 76r: LC-USZC4-1071 77: LC-USZC4-1397; 78–79: LC-USZC4-4820; 84: LC-USZC4-5352; 85: LC-USZC4-5356; 87: LC-USZ62-52175; 88: LC-DIG-pga-01013; 91l: LC-05ZC4-5350; 91br: LC-USZc4-5367; 94t: LC-USZ62-95197; 95: LC-USZC4-5362; 96: LC-USZ62-68966; 98: LC-USZ62-46082; 101: LC-USZC4-5347; 102–3: LC-DIG-pga-00178; 113: LC-USZ62-3106; 116: LC-USZ62-99516; 118: LC-USZ62-104354; 119: LC-USZ62-104355; 121: LC-USZ62-37993; 126t: LC-USZ62-380; 126b: LC-USZ62-374l 127r: LC-USZ62-3019; 128–9: LC-USZC4-6505; 134: LC-USZ62-53337; 142: LC-USZ62-5254; 144: LC-USZ62-24807; 145: LC-USZ62-3030; 146: LC-USZC4-5132; 148l: LC-USZ62-53584; 150–51: LC-USZC2-1871; 153 inset: LC-USZ62-43066; 154: LC-USZ64-12217; 158: LC-USZC4-4312; 161t: LC-USZC4-628; 161b: LC-USZ62-41172; 162–3: LC-DIG-pga-00199; 164–5: LC-DIG-pga-00675; 167b: LC-USZC4-4043; 169t: LC-USZ62-7841; 169b: LC-USZ62-24232; 170–71: LC-USZ62-66791; 173: LC-USZ62-32008; 178: LC-USZ62-62450; 179: LC-USZ62-15384; 182: LC-DIG-ppmsca-05933; 183: LC-USZ62-15386; 184–5: LC-DIG-pga-02419; 186: LC-USZC4-6204; 187: LC-USZ62-97201; 188: LC-USZ62-125134; 189t: LC-USZ62-41838; 189b: LC-USZ62-103801; 190–91: LC-DIG-pga-01059; 194: LC-USZCN4-627; 195: LC-USZ62-19360; 196: LC-USZ62-10658; 202: LC-USZ62-1473; 203: LC-USZ62-3913; 204: LC-USZ62-47; 209: LC-USZ62-7819; 210c: LC-USZ62-45327; 211lc–r: LC-USZC4-7214, LC-USZ62-10884, LC-USZ62-7340, LC-USZC4-3254; 212t: LC-USZ62-45399; 212b: LC-USZ62-21637; 214: LC-USZC4-1583; 215: LC-USZ62-134241; 216: LC-DIG-ppmsca-01657; 218: LC-USZC4-523; 220t: LC-USZC4-5280; 220b: LC-USZC4-5281; 221l: LC-USZ62-1308; 221r: LC-USZ62-11139; 222–3: LC-DIG-pga-01095; 224t: LC-USZ62-39582; 224b: LC-UDZC4-4970; 225b: LC-USZC2-1855; 232: LC-DIG-ppmsca-02243; 234t: LC-USZ62-59655; 237: LC-USZ62-117942; 238–9: LC-USZC2-3565; 241: LC-DIG-ppmsca-07689; 243: LC-DIG-ppmsca-07502; 245t: LC-DIG-ppmsca-10742; 245b: LC-USZ62-99740; 246: LC-DIG-ppmsca-05417; 249b: LC-USZC2-1969; 250: LC-USZC4-6223; 251: LC-USZC4-6294; 252–3: LC-USZC4-6893; 257: LC-USZ62-74540; 262: LC-USZ62-102147; 265: LC-USZ62-54750; 268: LC-USZC4-5950; 269l: LC-USZC4-5321; 269r: LC-USZ62-59828; 270–1: LC-DIG-ppmsc-08610; 272, 273 detail: LC-USZC4-11219; 274: LC-USZC4-11221; 275: LC-USZC4-11216; 276tr: LC-USZ62-84592; 276bl: LC-USZ62-110387; 282b: LC-USZC4-2860; 283r: LC-USZC4-5155; 284t: LC-USZ62-110446; 285: LC-USZ62-10404; 286: LC-USZ62-110376; 289: LC-USZ62-110377; 290: LC-USZ62-110386; 293tl: LC-USZC4-2564; 296–7: LC-USZ62-116492; 299t: LC-USZC4-2758; 299b: LC-USZ62-110378; 300: LC-USZC4-6492l 301: LC-USZC4-1837; 302–3: LC-DIG-pga-02385; 304: LC-USZ6-1721; 305: LC-DIG-pga-02271; 306–7: LC-USZC4-1006; 308: LC-USZC4-4492; 310tr: LC-DIG-ppmsca-07833; 311tl: LC-USZ62-3394; 311br: LC-USZ62-50967; 312–13: LC-DIG-pga 00821; 315: LC-USZ62-54443; 316: LC-USZ62-73460; 317: LC-USZ62-75170; 318–19: LC-USZC4-6874; 322cr: LC-USZC2-2115; 324: LC-USZC4-4594; 328: LC-USZ62-104557; 329: LC-USZ62-17255; 330–31: LC-DIG-pga-00392; 332: LC-USZC4-10281; 333: LC-USZC2-1759; 338bl: LC-USZ62-70848; 338–9: LC-DIG-pga-00988; 339 inset: LC-DIG-ppmsc-09030; 340tr: LC-USZ62-20997; 342–3: LC-DIG-pga-00809; 345: LC-USZ62-52104; 346–7: LC-DIG-pga-00795; 348: LC-USZC4-3806; 349tr: LC-USZC4-2388; 349br: LC-USZC4-5040; 350–51: LC-DIG-pga-00917; 352: LC-USZC4-7979; 353t: LC-DIG-pga-01840; 353b: LC-USZC2-1987; 354–5: LC-DIG-ggbain-30546; 357t: LC-USZ62-42825; 357b: LC-USZ62-108497; 358–9: LC-USZ62-19550; 360: LC-DIG-ggbain-27081; 361: LC-DIG-ppmsca-05438; 362tr: LC-DIG-ppmsca-07575; 362br: LC-USZC4-954; 363t: LC-USZC4-3659; 363b: CAI – Rogers, no. 73 (B size); 364–5: LC-DIG-pga-02077; 366: LC-DIG-ppmsca-00380; 367: LC-USZ62-118128; 368: LC-USZ62-95431; 369: LC-USZ62-122654; 370: LC-USZ62-62880; 371: LC-USZ62-11202; 372 inset: LC-USZ62-37827; 372–3: LC-DIG-pga-00863; 376tl: LC-USZ62-57385; 376br: LC-USZ62-112162; 377tl: LC-USZ62-19869A; 377b: LC-USZC2-1255; 378–9: LC-DIG-ggbain-50437; 380: LC-USZ62-40104; 381cl: LC-USZC2-7386 381tr: LC-USZC2-37784; 382: LC-DIG-ggbain-08804; 383: LC-USZ62-116223; 385: LC-USZC4-4527; 386: LC-USZ62-24986; 387b: LC-USZ62-23305; 388: LC-DIG-nclc-04148; 389t: LC-USZ62-71201; 389b: LC-DIG-nclc-04208; 390tl: LC-DIG-nclc-04072; 390tr: LC-DIG-nclc-04216; 390bl: LC-DIG-nclc-04303; 390br: LC-DIG-nclc-04104; 391tl: LC-DIG-nclc-04274; 391tr: LC-DIG-nclc-04133; 391bl: LC-DIG-nclc-04305; 391br: LC-DIG-nclc-04252; 392–3: LC-DIG-nclc-01134; 394tr: LC-DIG-nclc-02004; 394cr: LC-DIG-nclc-01205; 395t: LC-DIG-nclc-04898; 395bl: LC-DIG-nclc-01004; 395br: LC-DIG-nclc-01303; 396t: LC-USZ62-13077; 396b: LC-DIG-nclc-04566; 397: LC-DIG-ppmsca-05660; 398tr: LC-USZ62-63967; 398cr: LC-USZ62-41421; 399t: LC-USZ62-37780; 399bl: LC-USZ62-98492; 400–401: LC-D418-9350; 401: LC-USZ62-119031; 402t: LC-DIG-ppmsca-03147; 402b: LC-DIG-ppmsca-08372; 403: LC-USZ62-116354; 404–5: LC-DIG-pga-00601; 406–7: LC-USZ62-38333; 408–9: LC-DIG-ppmsca-02203; 410: LC-USZ62-69219; 411: LC-DIG-ppmsca-02202; 412–13: LC-DIG-ggbain-00082; 414: LC-USZ62-118048; 415t: LC-USZ62-67359; 415b: LC-USZ62-99340; 416tr: LC-USZ62-75561; 416–17t: LC-USZ62-117345; 417tr: LC-USZ62-75717; 417cr: Panama Canal Gatun Locks/Author: S. Shebs; 419t: LC-DIG-ggbain-10348; 420 inset: LC-DIG-ggbain-16135; 420–21: LC-DIG-ggbain-13360; 422: LC-USZ62-59579; 424: LC-USZ62-89797; 425: LC-USZC4-11807; 426: LC-USZC4-10986; 427: LC-USZ62-68015; 429: LC-USZC4-11363; 430t: LC-USZC4-10041; 430–31b: LC-USZ62-52796; 431t: LC-USZC4-2004; 433: LC-USZC4-12504; 434: LC-USZC4-12520; 435: LC-USZ62-107696; 436: LC-USZC4-9976; 437: LC-USZC4-776; 441: LC-USW33-034629-ZC; 442–3: LC-DIG-fsac-1a34914; 446b: HAER NY,41-JAHT,1-1; 452: LOC / San Diego Aerospace Museum

Courtesy of Library of Congress Exhibitions: 117: kc0026s, Jay I. Kislak Collection

Courtesy of the Mariner's Museum: 147: 1975.23.2; 325: 1934.1185.000002

Courtesy the National Archives, Washington, D.C. 231; 266 (www.ourdocuments.gov); 428l: 862.20212/82-A; 428r: 862.20212/69l 438tl: 208-N-39843; 444tr: 80-G-427475; 444br: 26-G-1517; 446t: 72-AF-212965;

Courtesy of the National Oceanic & Atmospheric Administration (NOAA)
2: theb2121; 6: libr0079; 63t: figb0314; 159: figb0002; 337 inset: libr0562; 419br: NOAA and the Russian Academy of Sciences; 453t: reef2559; 453br: reef2557; 453cl: http://oceanexplorer.noaa.gov/explorations/05stepstones/logs/aug15/aug15.html; 454b: nur07551; 456tl: nur06513; 456br: nur04506;

Ogilvy's America, 1671: 97

Collection of Martin W. Sandler: 326; 374tl, br; 384; 387t (Museum of the City of New York); 418; 419bl:

Courtesy of Toronto Public Library
334: Robert Huish, editor. *The last voyage of Capt. John Ross, Knt., R.N., to the Arctic Regions for the discovery of a North West Passage.* London, 1835; 336–7: *The eventful voyage of H.M.S. discovery ship Resolute to the Arctic regions*, London 1857

Courtesy of the U.S. Navy Historical Center
438bl: NH 97503; 438tr: NH 69720; 438br: 80-G-42030; 440: NH 67201; 445: 445t: Thomas Hart Benton, *Cut the Line*; 454t: http://www.spawar.navy.mil/sti/publications/pubs/td/1940/photos/index.html;

Courtesy of University of Texas, Austin, Perry-Castañeda Library Map Collection: 417b: shepherd_1911/shepherd-c-216

Courtesy of Wikimedia Commons
3b: John William Waterhouse - Ulysses and the Sirens (1891); 4–5: Carta Marina-lightened/Upload by Debivort at en.wikipedia; 7: Nemo Aronax Atlantis; 8–9: Claudius Ptolemy- The World/ Upload by S. Ehardt from *Decorative Maps* by Roderick Barron; 12: NorthmenBarques/Upload by A. M. de Neuville; 13t: Överhogdal tapestry detail/Author: Jämtlands läns Museum Jamtli; 13c: Thor and Hymir/Icelandic manuscript SÁM 66, Árni Magnússon Institute, Iceland; 13b: Invasion fleet on Bayeux Tapestry/http://www.dot-domesday.me.uk/; 15: Eric_the_Red.png/Upload by A. Jónsson/http://rmc.library.cornell.edu/exhibits/sagas/eric.html; 17: Vinland Map/Yale University Press; 18b: Soe Orm 1555/Olaus Magnus's Sea Worm, 1555, from *The Search for the Giant Squid*, The Lyons Press, by R. Ellis, 1998; 27t: Marco Polo, Il Milione, Chapter CXXIII and CXXIV/ *Livre des merveilles* fol. 58r. The Khan at war, Faksimile UB Graz Sig.: HB 15 210/P 778; 27b: PoloBrotherAndKubilai/*Le Livre des Merveilles*; 28: Odoryk z Pordenone1; 30: Henry the Navigator/Author: J. A. Gaspar; 31: Namban-11/panels attributed to Kano Naizen, 1570–1616 (detail); 32: Fusta by Jan Huygen van Linschoten/Koninklijke Bibliotheek, Nederland; 34: Bartolomeu Dias, South Africa House/Author: RedCoat; 35: Prester John map/Upload by Cuchullain; 42: 1500 map by Juan de la Cosa/Author: K. Berlin; 44br: Christopher Columbus Face/Author: M. Rosa/Unmaskingcolumbus.com 48: Vascodagama/Library of Congress (Illustration for: *Os Lusíadas by Luís de Camões*, edition of 1880); 49: A chegada de Vasca da Gama a Calicute em 1498/Biblioteca Nacional de

Portugal, http://purl.pt/6941; 50–51: CantinoPlanisphere/Biblioteca Estense, Modena, Italy; 53tr: Amerigo Vespucci; 58: Detail from a map of Ortelius, Magellan's ship, Victoria/www.helmink.com 60: Fernão de Magalhães por Charles Legrand/Biblioteca Nacional de Portugal: http://purl.pt/4674; 62: Henry Seven England/www.marileecody.com/henry7images.html; 70: André-thevet-cashew; 71t: Brazil 16thc map; 71b: Dança dos Tapuias; 86: Illustration Nicotiana tabacum0/Prof. Dr. Otto Wilhelm Thomé, *Flora von Deutschland, Österreich und der Schweiz*, 1885, Germany/Permission granted to use under GFDL by K. Stueber; 89: First Pipe of Tobacco BAH-p24/Montgomery's *The Beginner's American History*, 1904, page 24; 90: Pineapple Ananas_Comosus_Blanco2/*Flora de Filipinas* [Atlas II], 1880-83/ F. M. Blanco; 91tr: Brazilian Fruits; 93: Gerard-Herball-1633; 94b: Samuel de Champlain Carte geographique de la Nouvelle France; 99: Stilleben mit Brot und Zuckerwerk/Städelsches Kunstinstitut; 105: Indigoterie-1667; 108: Moll-A map of the West-Indies; 110: Estatua ecuestre de Pizarro (Trujillo, España) 02/Author: Pikaluk; 111: Dresden Codex p09/ www.famsi.org/mayawriting/codices/dresden.html; 112: AztecSunStoneReplica/Author: A. Wis; 114: Lucas Cranach d Ä. 007.jpg/Gemäldegalerie/°; 124: Catechism 1520 for indigenous by pedro gante; 127l: Serigipe 1560 Forte Coligny/http://serqueira.com.br/mapas/vilega.htm; 130b: Drakt, Adelsman, Nordisk familjebok; 131t: Kardinaal de Richelieu; 131b: Fer - Le Canada, ou Nouvelle France, la Floride, la Virginie, Pensilvanie, Caroline; 132: Elizabeth I (Armada Portrait); 133: Nicholas Hillard 007/National Portrait Gallery, London/°; 136: Sir Francis Drake (post 1580)/National Portrait Gallery, London; 137t: Defense of Cadiz Against the English 1634; 140: Captain John Smith; 141: New England in John Smith's book of 1616; 152–3: Gezicht op Hoorn van Hendrik Cornelisz Vroom 1622 Westfries Museum Hoorn/ www.wfm.nl/; 155: Gezicht Op Nieuw Amsterdam/The Atlantic World: America and the Netherlands—Library of Congress Global Gateway/National Archives, The Hague; 156: Edward Hicks - Peaceable Kingdom/National Gallery of Art, Washington, D.C.; 157: Edward Hicks 001/Abby Aldrich Rockefeller Folk Collection/°; 166: Boulanger Gustave Clarence Rudolphe The Slave Market/ www.artrenewal.org/asp/database/image.asp?id=2978; 168: AfricanSlavesTransport; 172: Loango01/www.brunias.com/africa2.html; 176–77 l to r: Nok sculpture Louvre 70-1998-11-1/70.1998.11.1/Jastrow, Chiwara Chicago sculpture/Author: H. Cook, Mulwalwa helmet mask Berlin-Dahlem/Ethnologisches Museum, Berlin/A. Praefcke, Shoulder mask nimba Louvre/MHNT-ETH-AF127/MHNT-ETH.AF12/Jastrow, Benin bronze Louvre A97-14-1/A 97.14.1/Jastrow, Fang mask Louvre/MH65-104-1/MH 65.104.1/Jastrow; 181: Slave ship diagram/Lilly Library of Rare Books and Manuscripts, Indiana University; 205: Benjamin West 005/National Gallery of Canada/°; 210l: SamuelAdamsLarge/Museum of Fine Arts, Boston; 210r: JS Copley - Paul Revere/Museum of Fine Arts, Boston; 211l: Thomas Paine/National Gallery, London; 218: Gaspee Affair; 225: Washington Crossing the Delaware;

228–9: The Battle of Trafalgar by William Clarkson Stanfield; 234b: Thomas Hobbes (portrait)/National Portrait Gallery, London; 235l–r: Montesquieu 1/Versailles, Musée Nacional du Château, Voltaire dictionary, Allan Ramsay 003/National Gallery of Scotland, David Hume/ Scottish National Portrait Gallery/www.wga.hu; 236: Ludvig XVI av Frankrikr portratterad av AF Callet; 240: Déclaration des droits de l'homme et du citoyen 0613; 242: Duplessis-Bertaux – Arrivee de Louis Seize a Paris/P. G. Berthault; 244: Jean Duplessi-Bertaux 001/Versailles, Musée Nacional du Château; 247: Bouchot – Le general Bonaparte au Conseil des Cinq-Cents/Musée de Versailles et Malmaison; 248t: Jacques-Louis David-007/°; 248c: Nelson door Leonardo Guzzardi rond 1800/National Maritime Museum, Greenwich; 248b: Trafalgar Crespin mg 0578/*L'Empire des Mers*, M. Acerra & J. Meyer; 249t: Napoleon-borodino/Historical Museum, Moscow; 249c: Fireofmoscow/www.sgu.ru/rus_hist/img/x1-0930111.jpg; 254: Bombardment2; 258l: Toussaint L'Ouverture; 258r: Battle of Ravine-à-Couleuvres/www.worldcat.org/oclc/545943; 259: Dessalines; 260t: Jose de San Martin; 260b: San Lorenzo; 261: O'Higgins2; 277: Bas fourneau; 278: Philipp Jakob Loutherbourg d. J. 002/Science Museum, London; 280: Ironbridge003; 282t: John Constable 008/National Gallery, London/°; 282c: Carl Blechen 010/Gemäldegalerie/°; 283l: Jean-François Millet (II) 005/Rijksmuseum Kröller-Müller/°; 284b: Newcomens Dampfmaschine aus Meyers 1890; 291: Adolf Friedrich Erdmann von Menzel 014/Alte Nationalgalerie/°; 292: 1831-View-Whitechapel-Road-steam-carriage-caricature; 293br: ENC 1-NA5 600px; 294: Zeisswerk Jena um 1910; 295: Regent's Canal Limehouse 1823/Museum of London; 309: Pittsburgh 1874 Otto Krebs; 310bl: Crystal Palace Centre transept & north tower from south wing/www.sil.si.edu/silpublications/Worlds-Fairs/WF_object_images.cfm?book_id=191; 314: The Well-Known Packet Ship/Author: Alberto; 320t–b: Vernet-midi-le-calme, Vernet-marseille-1754/Musée National de la Marine/Louvre; 321t–b: Vernet-port-Sette, Vernet-toulon-2/Musée National de la Marine/Louvre; 322tl: Donald McKay; 340bl: Clermont illustration - Robert Fulton - Project Gutenberg e-text 15161; 344: IK Brunel Chains; 356: Irish potato famine Bridget O'Donnel/http://news.siu.edu/news/April02/040302p2036.html; 423: HMS_Infexible_Falkland/ http://www.firstworldwar.com/photos/graphics/cpe_falkland_sailors_01.jpg; 432t–b: MS Kungsholm salong, MS Kungsholm bad/Author: Okänd; 439: Karl Dönitz/Imperial War Museum A 14899; 447tr: Concorde.planview.arp/Author: Arpingstone; 447br: Queen Mary 2 Quebec/Author: Clicgauche; 448tr: Tanker unloading crude oil/Author: H. Cozanet; 448b: Elly Maersk/Author: H. Hillewaert; 449t: HMS Turbulent S87/J. Bouvia, U.S. Navy; 449b: MightyServant Roberts19882turned/K. Elliott, U.S. Navy; 450: Freedom/Author: A. M. Rodriguez; 451: Athabasca Glacier/ 457: AIDAblu-vs-Santa Maria/Author: D. Bartel
° The Yorck Project: 10.000 Meisterwerke der Malerei